From the
BASEBALL LIBRARY
of

KILROY, PITCHER, BALTIMORE

Joseph Giannatelli, Jr.

The Sizzler

Sports and American Culture Series
Bruce Clayton, Editor

The Sizzler

George Sisler, Baseball's Forgotten Great

Rick Huhn

University of Missouri Press
Columbia and London

Library of Congress Cataloging-in-Publication Data

Huhn, Rick, 1944–
    The sizzler : George Sisler, baseball's forgotten great / Rick Huhn.
        p.   cm. , (Sports and American culture series)
    Includes bibliographical references and index.
    ISBN 0-8262-1555-6 (alk. paper)
    1. Sisler, George, 1893–1973.   2. Baseball players—United States—Biography.
I. Title.   II. Series.
    GV865.S525H84   2004
    796.357'092—dc22   2004013514

♾™ This paper meets the requirements of the
American National Standard for Permanence of Paper
for Printed Library Materials, Z39.48, 1984.

Designer: Jennifer Cropp
Typesetter: Phoenix Type, Inc.
Printer and binder: The Maple-Vail Book Manufacturing Group
Typefaces: Palatino, Bernhard

To my family—first and always

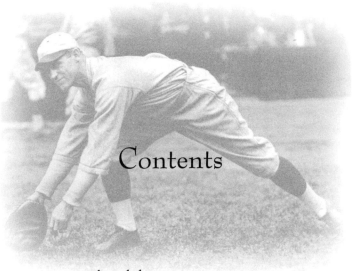

Contents

Acknowledgments   ix

Introduction   1

1. George Who?   4

2. Blue Sweater   15

3. Arm Trouble   27

4. Reunited and Repositioned   45

5. War Clouds   63

6. The Veteran   75

7. Major-League Changes   85

8. Renaissance Man   114

9. Guarded Optimism   125

10. "The Little World Series"   138

11. Missing in Action   155

12. Comeback Kid   186

13. Same Old Same Old   205

14. Brave New World   224

15. Private Enterprise   246

16. Full Circle   253

17. Family Man   273

18. Historically Speaking   283

Appendix   293

Bibliography   301

Index   311

Acknowledgments

I once read that a writer works in a vacuum. Not so—at least for me. In order to complete my work on this book I required quite a bit of assistance from family, as well as friends old and new. That it was given so willingly and competently leaves me with a deep sense of well-being. Hopefully, I thanked each of these individuals along the way. It never hurts, however, to do so one more time. If I leave anyone out, please know it is totally unintended.

This biography germinated from a discussion between friend and colleague Bud Hoffman and his client, George Sisler, Jr. I thank Bud for thinking I was up to the task and George, Jr., in particular and the Sisler family in general for opening their hearts and sharing their late "Pop" with a fledgling writer, allowing me to fulfill a boyhood dream of writing about a sport I love. Everyone I encountered in this family was most gracious and cooperative, but I want to make special mention of the other surviving Sisler offspring, Frances Drochelman and David Sisler, as well as Nancy Schools, daughter of George, Jr., and Peter Drochelman, son of Frances. In addition, I owe a great deal to Helen Mott and Cass Sisler, daughter and son of Sisler's brother, Cassius. I also even received an assist from Jere Sisler, a cousin several times removed.

This nation's public and private libraries are such a treasure trove of information about our national pastime that one needs a good tour guide to navigate their depths. I had the best. My sincere thanks to Russell Wolin-sky and Rachael Kepner, National Baseball Library, Cooperstown, as well as the staffs of the Bentley Historical Library at the University of Michigan, the Boston Public Library, the St. Louis Public Library, the Ohio Historical Society Archives/Library, and the Library of Congress for helping me navigate their collections. Special thanks to Michael Elliott, Akron Public Library, and Jackie Zahler, Manchester Public Schools, who went out of their way to help locate early Sisler material. The same for Iris Oberleitner, Worthington (Ohio) Public Library, and Edie Luce, Ohio University Library, for arranging access to *St. Louis Post-Dispatch* microfilm. Thanks as well to Liz Jones and later Eileen Canepari of the topnotch Society for American Baseball Research (SABR) for providing access to that organization's microfilm resources which preserve the game's rich tradition.

I enjoyed similar expert assistance in locating and securing access to photographs of my subject and his times. In addition to Nancy Schools and Helen Mott of the Sisler family, I thank Bill Burdick, National Baseball Hall of Fame, Steve Gietschier, the *Sporting News*, Beth Swartz Khan, Barberton (Ohio) Public Library, Karen Schnur, Allied Photocolor, and Bill Borst, St. Louis Browns Historical Society for coming to the rescue.

On the technical side I thank Dr. Jeffrey C. Oehler and Dr. Steven E. Katz for helping sort out Sisler's intriguing eye disorder. A similar salute goes to friends and family of friends for various and sundry, but no less important, assistance. They include Jim Blumenstiel, Andy Auld, Jenny Sokoloski, Anthony Severyn, Jennifer Lewis, John Blust, and Don Devore.

A number of other interesting people lent me a considerable helping hand along my way. To Hall of Fame sportswriter Bob Broeg, former *Akron Beacon Journal* sportswriter Phil Dietrich, and Sisler aficionado Jimmy Lindberg for taking their time to talk with me, my sincere thanks. I also owe a debt of gratitude to the esteemed baseball historian and biographer Dr. Charles C. Alexander for meeting with me and so readily providing his knowledge and encouragement.

As to the writing itself, I received a major editing boost from Lee Caryer, an expert on sports and a fine author in his own right. His input was quite simply invaluable. In a similar vein my continuing thanks and appreciation to Marti Blumling, my former secretary and friend. She is one of the few people alive who can read my handwriting—no easy task. She has thankfully been along for the ride from the start of my writing adventures, as has Doris Wagner, who helps cover for my compositional inadequacies.

Of course, no book would come to fruition without a good publisher and its staff. I am most fortunate in that regard. I thank Director and Editor-in-Chief Beverly Jarrett and Series Editor Bruce Clayton for their early interest and unflagging support of this project. I direct thanks also to Managing Editor Jane Lago, Copy Editor John Brenner, Book Designer Jennifer Cropp, and Marketing Manager Karen Renner and her staff for keeping me on course as we headed to the finish line.

Most important, a final personal thanks to my family, beginning with my great son-in law, Rob Bumgarner. Thank you for your valuable efforts at Cooperstown and in the final editing process. To my wonderful daughter, Kimberly Huhn Bumgarner, my thanks first, for just being; second, for just being you; and finally, for your considerable efforts on this book, including your help in word processing and editing, as well as pushing me up and hopefully over the bumpy road of notes and bibliography. Finally to my beloved wife, Marcia, who makes this and all our journeys so very special. For your unconditional love and support, particularly in encouraging and assisting my transition to a new career in midlife, I thank you most of all.

The Sizzler

Introduction

Prior to August 2001 I was not personally acquainted with George Sisler, Jr., the eldest son of old-time baseball player George Sisler. His name was quite familiar, however, frequently appearing in local newspapers during the 1980s when he was the general manager of the Clippers, the New York Yankees Triple-A affiliate in my hometown of Columbus, Ohio. As a lifelong baseball fan, whenever I heard the name I made the connection to his father, but I never seriously thought much about the elder Sisler's baseball career or his place in baseball history. That was about to change.

My purpose in meeting George, Jr., that summer was to determine whether I wanted to write his late father's biography. The idea was generated by Bud Hoffman, a friend and George's family attorney. Bud was aware of my background in writing and interest in baseball. He also knew that his client was somewhat frustrated that his father was not better remembered by chroniclers of the game. We decided to discuss the idea of a book over lunch.

Prior to the luncheon, I did some homework, including a brief search of the Internet. I was quickly able to determine that George's dad was an outstanding performer who was considered by such baseball luminaries as Ty Cobb, Babe Ruth, and Rogers Hornsby to be their equal. Although a number of chapters in baseball books were dedicated to Sisler, there was no single in-depth treatment. I found this surprising. Sisler played and starred in the 1920s. There is no lack of good biographies of any number of base-ball players from that era. I deemed a biography of a player of Sisler's stature necessary to fill the void.

When Bud and I arrived a few days later to pick up George at his home, we were greeted by a tall, impeccably tailored man in a plaid sport jacket who looked nowhere near his stated age of eighty-four. A head of carefully combed gray hair and an erect posture gave him a regal bearing. He was really quite charming, with a warm smile and hearty laugh. We engaged immediately. During our lunch we covered many topics, but our focus remained on the senior Sisler—as a player certainly, but also as a man and father. It was apparent to me that the son felt it was important that if I decided to write about his father, I should at least consider exploring these facets of his character as well. The conclusion, of course, would be my own. Before we parted that day, I told George my interest was piqued. After an evening to discuss the project with my wife, I called him the next day to say I planned to research and write about the life of his father. The following eighteen chapters are the culmination of my efforts.

Given the scandalous nature of so many of Sisler's contemporaries, I fully expected to find much of the same when I finally placed his life under an objective microscope. Despite a thorough examination, I did not. In a society that is obsessed with overturning rocks and exposing the under-bellies of its heroes, this seeming lack of a dark side may explain why less has been written about Sisler than many others. But lack of criminal activity or lewd conduct does not mean Sisler's life played through without controversy and drama. There was plenty of each.

In writing this book, I was fortunate to have the enthusiastic cooperation of the Sisler family. They readily provided me with thirty pages of type-written memoirs from their father to his family, written in his latter days and presumably not intended for publication. While these memoirs are the best available source of Sisler's innermost thoughts, they still leave something to be desired. For despite this recitation, George Sisler was a very private individual and a man of few words. There are several significant forks in his road, recorded in the memoirs with little or no comment. I wish, for example, he would have told us how he felt about leaving his parents at an early age to attend high school in another city, never to return home, or of how the death of his older brother, with whom he lived during those high school days, affected him. The family often could not fill in the blanks, particularly on events during their father's youth. These were subjects he rarely discussed.

Outside the family there are few still alive who knew Sisler personally, let alone saw him play. I was, therefore, dependent in large part on media coverage of the day, which was a far cry from the multifaceted barrage we experience today. In-depth interviews of players were rare. Pre-game and post-game quotes were often limited to owners, managers, or other team management. Reports of the games were at times extracted from poorly imaged microfilm newspaper reports and baseball magazine articles. Every effort was made to be accurate, but that is not a guarantee. For example, I found the limericks and rhymes of L. C. Davis, a columnist with the *St. Louis Post-Dispatch,* particularly amusing and insightful of the language and tenor of the times. They are sprinkled throughout, but I am still trying to figure out the placement of commas, semi-colons, and periods.

Still, I took great joy in writing the story of George Harold Sisler. It is a story of a solid, law-abiding citizen and fine family man. It is also the exciting tale of a young man who was known throughout America in the Roaring Twenties as a baseball superstar, alongside other star players who, unlike him, remain household names. I found the story of Sisler's rapid rise to fame uplifting, and the public's equally rapid loss of interest worth analyzing. I hope you do, too.

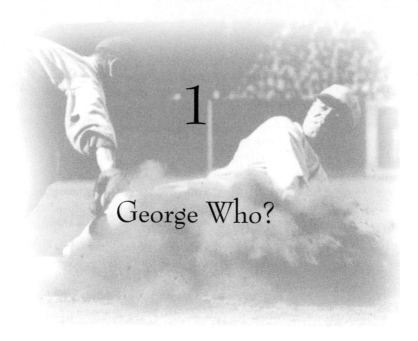

1

George Who?

In St. Louis in the summer, baseball's Cardinals often compete with the humidity to determine which is hotter. Such was the case in 2001. On June 17, Cardinals fans gathered at Busch Stadium for a Sunday afternoon of interleague play with the Chicago White Sox. Their club was embroiled in a tight pennant race. Those who arrived early to enjoy the still balmy weather and check out batting practice were probably puzzled by the sight of a small group of men and women standing together outside the stadium on the walkway at the north end, surrounding a bronze statue of a baseball player. For those few taking the time to stop for a closer look, mere puzzlement quickly turned to disbelief. The player whose statue was about to take its place alongside Cardinals heroes such as Rogers Hornsby, Stan "The Man" Musial, and Bob Gibson never played a single game for the Cardinals, and seldom set foot inside Busch Stadium. In fact, he played the vast majority of his career for a team extinct since 1953. Such is the legacy of George Sisler, longtime first baseman for the St. Louis Browns.

Those in attendance for this strange tribute, appropriately scheduled on Father's Day, included members of the Sisler family, various executives from Cardinals management such as owner Bill DeWitt, the artist Harry Weber, and a handful of members of the St. Louis Browns Historical Society, at whose urging the Cardinals arranged for the honor. Prior to the unveiling itself, Bob Broeg, former writer and sports editor of the *St. Louis Post-Dispatch* and a member of the Baseball Writers Hall of Fame, gave a short speech briefly detailing the honoree's career. Broeg, in his early eighties, has seen a lot of baseball and baseball players pass through the city with the famous arch. He told the small gathering he regards the man he calls "The Sizzler" as "just about the least appreciated player in history and maybe the best."[1]

Earlier that day, in its Sunday edition, Broeg's old newspaper weighed in with a similar opinion, telling readers Sisler "might be the best player most baseball fans don't know about" and admitting he is "largely forgotten even in St. Louis, where he played 12 seasons in his 15-year Hall-of-Fame career."[2] The article mentioned that Sisler is overshadowed by his American League contemporaries Ty Cobb, who once called Sisler "the nearest thing to a perfect ballplayer," Babe Ruth, and even in his own city by the Cardinals' Hornsby.

So how does a Hall of Fame baseball player with a .340 lifetime batting average who twice hit better than .400, ranks among the best defensive first basemen in history, and still holds the major-league record of 257 hits in a single season land in a heap on baseball's back porch? That is not a particularly easy question to answer, but the road to relative obscurity may have all started in 1922 just as George, or Sis to his admirers, reached the pinnacle of his success. However, starting this story in 1922 would not work well, since it is the middle of the tale. And any story that starts in the middle ignores the beginning. In George Sisler's case, the beginning is particularly instructive.

The Sisler saga unfolds in the tiny Ohio town of Manchester, in northeastern Ohio, twelve miles south of Akron and ten miles north of Massillon. In the 1700s this land was Iroquois country. The Indian tribe was firmly entrenched in the area by 1740. The first permanent white settler did not arrive until 1814. The town itself was founded by residents of Manchester, England.

The land around Manchester was blessed with rich, fertile soil. The Tuscarawas River runs through the region, and there are numerous swamps and marshes. The discovery of large pockets of bituminous coal brought mining to the area. Most of the mines were closed by 1940 due to the advent of gas heat.[3]

1. Handwritten Notes, Speech by Bob Broeg, June 17, 2001, at Busch Stadium, St. Louis.
2. *St. Louis Post-Dispatch,* June 17, 2001.
3. Richard A. Gardner, *History of an Ohio Community: Manchester,* 3, 13.

By 1891 local property owners included several with the last name of Sisler, believed to be of Swiss or German extraction. It is uncertain whether the addition of George Harold Sisler on March 24, 1893, raised the population of Manchester to five hundred or sent it over the top.

Trivia buffs will question why birth records list Nimisila, a mere blip on a railroad map, as George's birthplace. The explanation rests with the U.S. Postal Service. At the time there was a second, larger Manchester located in southwestern Ohio. Thus, the tiny farming community was designated Nimisila (Indian for "beautiful water") for mailing purposes.

The Manchester where Cassius Clay Sisler and Mary Whipple Sisler, she of the Scottish McFarland clan, lived with their eldest son Efbert J. and younger son Cassius Carl consisted of four streets aptly named North, South, East, and West. North Street was the north line of the road running between Akron and Massillon, with South Street the south line of said road. West and East Streets respectively were the dissecting roads running between the small towns of Clinton, three miles to the west, and Greensburg, several miles to the east. In its way, Manchester was not unlike much of America in the last years of the nineteenth century. The nation at this time was essentially provincial, the majority of its seventy-six million citizens residing in country towns. It was a nation crisscrossed by dirt roads traversed by horse-drawn carriages where one saw women tightly corseted and men in top hats and bowlers; one in which kerosene lamps lighted homes and an outhouse was a common sight.

Despite its tiny size, Manchester had four churches, each on a different street; the Reformed on North Street, the Evangelical on East Street, the Disciple on South Street, and the Lutheran on West Street. Lest one assume its residents did nothing but build churches and pray, Manchester also sported one saloon, two grocery stores, a barber shop, and a meat market.

George's parents were both graduates of Hiram College, a small private school once led by former president James A. Garfield and located in nearby Portage County. His parents had been college sweethearts. At one time both taught school, and education was a focal point in Sisler family life. No longer a teacher, George's father supervised a coal mine a few miles from town.

Cassius Sisler came from a large family. His father, John, George's paternal grandfather, owned a good deal of land all around the area, but resided in Manchester itself. His brother, Adam, was a practicing physician there. George's Uncle Mace, the brother of Cassius, was also a practicing physician. One sister, George's Aunt Mel, was the wife of Isaac Myers, owner of the I. S. Myers Clothing Store in Akron and former mayor of that city. In addition, there was Aunt Lib and her husband, Thomas Prout, George's favorite aunt and uncle. Aunt Lib and Uncle Tom were half of a singing group that included Frank Rabar and his wife, who was also related to the Sislers. This quartet sang at all local funerals, weddings, and birthday parties. George recalled Frank "singing tenor with a high squeaky voice," but not much else about the group.[4]

Manchester had a two-floor grade school. At noon and after school George and his friends would run home. In later years, George attributed the foot speed that served him well in many sports to these daily sprints. Except for the occasional game of horseshoes and a rainy-day checkers match, Manchester offered little in the way of sports other than baseball. Many would argue fishing and hunting are sport; if so, then Manchester had those, too. Certainly there were plenty of venues. George's favorite was Dakey Reed Lake, where there was an abundance of "very tasty blue gills." During the winter, a favorite steep hill just outside of town was the perfect place for coasting and sledding. However, in the early 1900s, throughout America baseball was king. According to George, Manchester was no different:

[E]very night before dark, most of town, it seemed turned out for the daily game behind the grade school building on North Street. We all had our positions assigned to us and these positions varied but little from day to day. My position was always shortstop even though I was left-handed and I got so I could play pretty well, so I thought. We had no suits for a while but finally we decided to hold a social one Saturday night in order to raise funds to buy suits out of some catalogue we found somewhere. So we sold ice cream, lemonade, soda pop and other little niceties on the grade school property. Well we made enough to buy nine suits and they were the nicest color red that we had ever seen. I suppose they would cost in the neighborhood of four or five dollars a suit and they were certainly worth it. Having suits, we were now ready to schedule games. Our schedule consisted of two home and home games with Clinton, three miles away to the west and our long trip which was with Canal Fulton, four miles away to our south. We would get a wagon and two horses, make seats in the back, and the whole team would get on and we were on our way. We generally won, although I can't remember the scores. We had town support and thought we were pretty good.[5]

Although it is clear George enjoyed playing ball at an early age, there is no indication who, if anyone, instilled the notion or taught him the rudiments of the game. There is some reason to believe his father and one uncle had been fairly decent ballplayers in their day. Having an older brother

4. George H. Sisler, Typewritten Memoirs to His Family, date unknown, 2. Hereafter referred to as Sisler Memoirs.
5. Ibid., 2–3.

such as Cassius, who played the game well, certainly did not hurt either. Still, the root source of what would soon turn into a fountain of baseball talent remains a mystery.

Before long, George was growing up, and the idyllic days of youth ran headlong into reality. Manchester had no high school. In George's case, his family had alternatives. He would move to the city twelve miles away and attend Akron High School. Older brother Bert already lived there with his wife and daughter, working in Uncle Isaac Myers' clothing store. High school bound George moved into Akron to live with Bert. At fourteen, George had left his home, essentially never to return.

When young George arrived in Akron he found himself in an expanding northern Ohio city formed in what previously was known as the Western Reserve. At the end of the Revolutionary War the thirteen states not only secured their independence but also inherited a vast expanse of western land. In time the seaboard states surrendered their claims to most of this territory. Virginia and Connecticut, however, each set aside an allotment for themselves. The Connecticut Reserve, or Western Reserve as it became known, embraced land west of Pennsylvania that fell between the forty-first parallel and Lake Erie. Before 1785 and an intervening treaty this was the land of the Wyandot, Ottawa, Chippewa, and Delaware. The site of the future Akron was immediately north of the forty-first and thus just within the Reserve.

Continued Indian activities in the area were a deterrent to quick settlement. It was not until the War of 1812 and the death of the powerful Indian leader Tecumseh that migration to the area began in earnest. Even then settlers were reluctant to come to the region due to its water-bound nature. Groundbreaking in 1825 for the Erie Canal changed all that. The high point of the canal was the Portage Summit. A town was planned for the area. It was named Akron, a derivation of the Greek word for "high."

The construction of the canal brought streams of workers to the new town. They worked on the thirty-eight-mile stretch that would traverse the Reserve from the Portage Summit to Lake Erie. Still, there was little by the late 1880s to set Akron apart. Its real turning point as a city of influence occurred in the "Gay Nineties," in the midst of an age of invention. It was in this last decade of the nineteenth century that America became fascinated with a new mode of transportation, the bicycle, a contraption that ran on wheels encased in rubber. It just so happened that the material of choice was the main product of an Akron manufacturer, B. F. Goodrich.

In a few short years another invention began filling the nation's streets. By no mean coincidence this new invention, the "horseless carriage," also rode on wheels cushioned in rubber. Before long Goodrich was Akron's largest employer. Others took notice of their success. Soon similar companies such as Goodyear and Firestone, often founded by enterprising locals, called Akron home. At the turn of the century, Akron was a city of approximately seventy thousand inhabitants. From 1910 to 1920 the city's population tripled as one automobile after another rolled off assembly lines and the world turned to the "rubber capital" for the tires needed to give their swift-moving wonders a smooth ride.

Despite the population explosion, there was still only one high school in the growing city when George arrived there. As a fledgling student at Akron High School, he was proud of his academic accomplishments, especially in German class, where he was able to translate an English poem into German without losing its rhyme. This feat clearly pleased his educated parents much more than did his ability with a baseball bat and glove. Still, academics did not get in the way of organized sports. George tried out for the interscholastic squads in each of his school's three sports and made them all. In football, in spite of a slender frame holding but 140 pounds, he was an end. In basketball, at five feet, ten inches, he was a forward. And although he spent a bushel-load of time on the sandlots as a left-hand-hitting and fielding shortstop, in high school he was a left-handed pitcher.

The featherweight receiver recalls that

in football, my crowning achievement was catching a forward pass and scoring the winning touchdown in an important game. In basketball, I can still see our Coach giving signals from the sidelines with various hand in left vest, hand in right vest, hand in coat pocket, and on and on. I even remember my teammates, Joe Thomas at Center, Don Parshall at forward, Glen Killinger at guard and Dave Evans at guard. We had a good representative team. But it was in baseball that I really enjoyed myself. I could, as a kid, throw hard. I had a real good curve ball and I had good control. I don't think we ever lost a game in baseball.[6]

This is not entirely accurate. Akron High School did lose a few games while George Sisler wore its uniform, but not many, and seldom when its budding star took the mound to start the game. In his sophomore year in 1909, George was used mainly in relief, progressing nicely while showing glimpses of coming attractions. Early in his junior year, the local daily, the *Akron Beacon Journal*, took notice in a story with the subhead, "Sisler of Akron, Strikes Out Eleven Men and Gives Only Five Hits—Well Played and Brilliant Game." The report noted that in taming Cleveland's Central High School, the young hurler had "speed to burn and a wonderful curve

6. Ibid., 3.

ball which was a puzzler to the boys of Cleveland."[7] Less than two weeks later, George limited Youngstown Rayen to four hits in a 2–1 victory. He was almost as impressive a week later in striking out twelve Canton High School batters, but errors left Akron on the short end of a 4–2 score.

In late May the rains came, forcing an early end to a game with Oberlin in which George fanned ten and helped his team fashion an 8–2 win with two hits of his own. An article right next to the *Beacon Journal* report of George's game described the batting heroics of the American League's leading hitter, Napoleon "Larry" Lajoie of Cleveland's big-league baseball entry. A decade later George would take that very spot atop the junior circuit's list of hitters, but for now, Akron's star southpaw enjoyed a spotlight of his own by twirling a no-hit shutout against Lakewood in late May. In addition to whiffing seventeen of twenty-seven opponents he faced, he again helped his own cause with his four hits.

Still, George was not the only Sisler playing baseball in Akron. His middle brother, Cassius, was playing the outfield and pitching for Buchtel College. Another all-around athlete, Cassius played basketball in college, as well as baseball. In 1911, as a senior, he captained both squads. Later, Cassius went on to a long career in sales with the Firestone Tire and Rubber Company. In 1910, however, the brothers Sisler were garnering their share of attention from the local press: "The Sislers have been pitching remarkable games recently and in each of the contests they make a record by the number of strikeouts. One pitches for the Akron High School and the other for Buchtel College. Their work is attracting the attention and if they continue to keep up their record, some of the bigger leagues will be looking for their services."[8]

Less than a week later, on June 4, 1910, separate photographs of the brothers appeared in the *Beacon Journal,* accompanying an article that described George's no-hit feat of the week before, as well as the two-hit, sixteen-strikeout performance of his brother against Baldwin-Wallace College. The boys photographed well, each dark-haired, well groomed, and earnestly handsome. If they differed, it was that Cassius had a fuller face and mischievous smirk. Brown-haired George, whose looks would one day earn him the sobriquet "Gorgeous George," was the more chiseled of the two, with steel-blue eyes deep set and penetrating, and a signature cleft chin. The article advised local readers that the brothers "have had offers from semi-professional teams to pitch for them but they have

7. *Akron Beacon Journal,* April 30, 1910.
8. Ibid., May 30, 1910.

decided to finish their college work before entering the base ball field for a living."[9]

The exploits of the Sislers in the spring of 1910 are even more amazing given their family tragedy. Older brother Efbert, at age twenty-seven some ten years George's senior, died of tuberculosis on April 17 after a six-week illness, leaving a widow and a five-year-old daughter. His home had become George's home. As George, now seventeen, entered his senior year of high school, he not only mourned the loss of his older brother but had also, presumably for the sake of propriety, to find a new place to live.

A teammate and friend came to the rescue. Joe Thomas invited George to stay with his family for their last year at Akron High School. Thomas was the center in basketball and played first base in baseball. He went on to a distinguished career as the head of the legal department at Firestone Tire and Rubber Company. In 1910 he and his family were George's saviors.

The end of the high school baseball season in early June did not mean the end of baseball for young George or his brother Cassius. Over summer vacation, George ran errands for his uncle's clothing store, enabling him to play on the company's team. The job offered some spending money; the team provided a chance to hone his skills. "My uncle was the mayor of Akron at the time," George told an interviewer years later. "He owned a store and sponsored a team. I like to believe I made the team because of my ability rather than being the sponsor's nephew, but the fact that I would play anywhere helped to make me an agile fielder."[10]

Although enough major changes took place in George's personal life to make his head spin, his success on the diamond was a constant. In the spring of 1911, baseball was rampant in the Akron area. It seemed there was a team with a crazy name on every corner. It was common for a player with ability, even a high schooler, to play for multiple teams against opponents with a variety of skill levels. It was, therefore, no surprise that on April 18 the *Beacon Journal* reported that George Sisler, "who is properly called the boy wonder," would pitch for the Collegians against the Diamonds.[11] Except for George, the Collegians were a group of college players, including older brother Cassius. George and his brother had played some ball for the Collegians the previous summer and the Diamonds were dutifully respectful, having lost to the younger Sisler then. George's high school

9. Ibid., June 4, 1910.
10. George Sisler quoted in Les Biederman, "Gorgeous George H. Sisler—Michigan Marvel became Game's Man of Distinction," pt. 1, *Sporting News*, February 25, 1953, 13–14.
11. *Akron Beacon Journal*, April 18, 1911.

catcher, Russ Baer, a year older than George, was now the catcher for the Collegians. He received credit from the *Beacon Journal* for much of George's success to date on the mound.

Prior to the game with the Diamonds, however, George's Collegians would tackle the Akron Champs, the city's entry in the Ohio-Pennsylvania League, in an exhibition game. The Class C league, several steps removed from the majors yet professional, included teams from Youngstown and Erie, Pennsylvania. The manager of the Akron team was Lee Fohl, a name to remember. Fohl was missing in action from this early spring outing, having traveled home to Pittsburgh to assure his wife and family that he had not been injured, as was reported, in a gas stove explosion in the Akron area. Had he remained, he would have seen his professional team give the Collegians a 13–0 lesson in the virtues of experience and baseball savvy. Still, the *Beacon Journal* of April 19 waxed eloquently on George's performance, seeking to calm the nerves of anxious Akron High School fans by telling supporters that during the forthcoming high school season, any team that "wins a game off of him [George] must be a peacherino."[12] In fact, George gave up eight hits to the professionals in six innings, quite respectable, but poor fielding support led to his downfall. Also, seven of the Champs' thirteen runs scored after his exit.

The aforementioned game with the Diamonds was a fairer test of George's standing as a high school senior. He pitched four innings with no hits, striking out nine as his team pounded out a 14–2 win. A few days later, George pitched another exhibition game against the Akron Champs. This time he was on the mound for his high school team. The results were similar, with George impressive but shoddy fielding resulting in six runs allowed. After giving up an early run, he held the professionals without another score and with only one hit until the dam broke in the sixth.

In early May, the O-P League made its first reported effort to lure the youthful high school ace into the professional ranks. Although there was still at least a month to go before graduation, the names of George Sisler and his catcher, Russell Baer, appeared on a list of Akron Champs players suspended by league president Moreland for failing to report.[13] Despite the listing, there is no indication that either player asked to be placed on the Champs' roster in the first place, or even considered such a move. More likely, it was an exercise in wishful thinking on the part of the local pay-for-play club.

12. Ibid., April 19, 1911.
13. Ibid., May 2, 1911.

On May 8 George was finally back on an even playing field, making life tough for players his own age as he pitched his team to a 3–2 win over nearby Massillon, striking out fourteen and issuing but five hits. He again showed promise with the stick, getting three hits to support his own cause. A week later he was once again masterful, fanning twenty batters in a 5–2 win over Oberlin Academy.

As the pitching performances mounted in statistical glory, a former big leaguer and O-P umpire named Jim Pastorious weighed in with his opinion of George following a personal view at the Oberlin game. Pastorious was so taken with what he saw that after the Oberlin contest he grabbed a catcher's mitt and caught a few of Sisler's dishes. When they were finished, he offered a few tips and promised continued help. He then told Akron Champs manager Lee Fohl, "Don't let that kid, Sisler, get away from you. He's got better curves than any pitcher you've got. He's the best man around here and if he is handled right, he has the makings of a big league hurler."[14]

A few days after the Oberlin game, the local high school bunch suffered a setback to Youngstown Rayen when Coach Bowman, George's high school mentor, held him out until the end of the game in order to have him ready for the next contest against University School of Cleveland. However, when the going got tough against the squad from Youngstown, Coach Bowman's resistance melted away and George appeared late in the game in relief, striking out the side, even though he did not warm up. Despite the inning in relief, within four days George broke his own strikeout record, fanning twenty-one University hitters in helping his team to a stunning 16–0 win against the highly regarded squad.

Just as George was beginning to peak, the 1911 season was on the wane. On May 27 the *Beacon Journal* reported that the championship of high school baseball in the area would be decided in a two-game dual between Akron and its deadly rival, Canton. Under the heading "Canton High Fears Arm of G. Sisler," the paper claimed the local hero could turn professional and play for the Akron Champs "any time he desired, but parental objections" were keeping him from making the move.[15] Meanwhile, high school rivals, such as Canton, must face the music.

The first Canton game, played in Akron, was easily won by the home team. In between the first and second Canton games, George continued

14. Ibid., May 17, 1911. The article mentions a last name only, but a Jim Pastorious pitched for the 1908 and 1909 Brooklyn Superbas (the forerunner of the Dodgers), posting a career record of 31–55 and a 3.12 earned run average.
15. Ibid., May 27, 1911.

his mastery with a twenty-strikeout one-hitter over Massillon. Then it was time for a final settlement with Canton. This time it was much closer, a real pitcher's battle. Still, in reality, it was no contest. In his final high school performance, George Sisler pitched a no-hit shutout. The game marked another milestone: it was the last baseball game Akron High School ever played. The following school year, the high school system was divided into Akron Central and Akron South.

All in all, the no-hitter against Canton in his final high school appearance put an exclamation mark on the 1911 season and on a spectacular high school career. George, however, was never one to bask in the glory, especially when another game was at hand. The next day he was in right field for the Collegians as they beat the Superbas. Showing he was human, he went hitless in three attempts.

Now that he was a high school graduate, George confined his baseball efforts to the Collegians. The team was sponsored and managed that summer by Joe Thomas Sr., the chairman of the Akron Recreation Commission and father of his high school teammate, friend, and host.[16] On June 26 George struck out sixteen in pitching a two-hit Collegian victory over Babcock and Wilcox, an industrial league team from nearby Barberton that he would come to know well one summer later.

In late June the *Beacon Journal* reported on George's remarkable accomplishments for the season in both high school and sandlot ball, noting he had won all five games started for the high school and all four games he had pitched for the Collegians. In sum, he had pitched eighty-four innings, allowing only twenty-three hits and twelve runs, while striking out 149 batters, an average of sixteen per game.[17] There was now no doubt that the professionals were anticipating his arrival on their stage.

16. Ibid., August 3, 1911. See also Richard McBane, *Glory Days: The Akron Yankees,* 1.
17. *Akron Beacon Journal,* June 29, 1911. In pitching eighty-four innings in nine games the news article has Sisler throwing 9.3 innings per game, indicating either one or more extra-inning games or an error in the author's calculations.

2

Blue Sweater

Despite living within thirty-five miles of Cleveland, George did not see a big-league game until July 24, 1911. His first exposure to the sport on that level was a whopper. The eighteen-year-old traveled to Cleveland with an uncle to see the Naps, the city's American League entry, named after its star player and manager, Napoleon Lajoie. It was one of nephew George's first, if not the very first, visits to the big city on the lake. It would turn out to be one of many.

By now America was moving, some would say "progressing," toward an era of urbanization. The span between 1900 and the country's entry into World War I is often called the Progressive Era. It was a time when progress was measured by reforms in the workplace and battles against corruption in municipal governments and greed in industries such as oil and meat packing; a society where women continued to march for the vote and reformers such as Teddy Roosevelt took center stage.

The game George and his uncle saw that day was a benefit for the late Addie Joss, the star Cleveland pitcher struck down in midcareer by tubercular meningitis, pitting the hometown Naps against an all-star team. A crowd of more than twelve thousand witnessed the special affair, which raised a substantial amount for charity. Stars on display that afternoon read like a Hall of Fame roster: Tris Speaker in center field, Ty Cobb in right, Sam Crawford in left, Hal Chase at first, Eddie Collins at second,

Bobby Wallace at shortstop, and Gabby Street catching. The pitchers included George's boyhood idol, Walter "Big Train" Johnson. Of the bunch, only Chase, who many regard as the best fielding first baseman of all time, and Street, who enjoyed more success as the manager of a Cardinals World Series winner in 1931, failed to make the Hall.

The Naps were not so bad themselves. In addition to the great hitter Lajoie, they had Joe Jackson and Jack Graney in the outfield and the legendary Denton "Cy" Young on the mound. The game was played in League Park. George later recalled, "When I saw those great players, the first big leaguers I ever had seen, I made up my mind I was going to be a big league player and, I might confess, I wanted to be on the Cleveland team."[1]

Knowing he wanted to be a big-league ballplayer, the next logical step for the recent high school grad was the Ohio-Pennsylvania League, wasn't it? After all, everyone agreed he had all the tools. But in George's case it was not to be. His parents had a plan for their youngest son that did not include professional baseball. A college education suited them, and it would suit George as well. Despite his enthusiasm for baseball, George refused to balk his parents, vowing not to disappoint them. "I would play major league ball, if I possibly could, after my college days were over."[2]

Today a player of George's caliber who decided to play college ball instead of turning professional would be the subject of a recruiting frenzy, involving the nation's major colleges and universities. In 1911 it was quite different. "I had played football, basketball and baseball in high school, but baseball was my favorite sport," Sisler told a reporter. "I was offered scholarships at the University of Pennsylvania and Western Reserve, but I passed up both to go to Michigan. I chose Michigan because of Russ Baer, my high school catcher... At that time, he wanted to study law and decided to enroll at Michigan. I thought I would have a better chance in baseball as a pitcher if I had Baer as my catcher, so I followed him."[3] So all Wolverine thanks go to Russ Baer, a fine high school and college catcher who went to Michigan to study law, ended up a banker and, by the way, just happened to bring along a friend.

"I remember when I packed to go away, my first thought was for my somewhat battered baseball glove," George said. "I entered the Engineering Department in the Mechanical Department and my college work be-

1. George Sisler quoted in Henry P. Edwards, "Using a Diploma on the Diamond," George Sisler Clippings File, National Baseball Library, Cooperstown, N.Y., publication and page number unknown.

2. Sisler Memoirs, 4.

3. George Sisler quoted in Biederman, "Gorgeous George H. Sisler," pt. 1, 4.

gan. I studied hard and made good grades. I always liked mathematics and that is why I decided on Engineering."[4]

George's new home away from home owed its unusual name to founder John Allen's wife, Ann, and a grove of scattered trees on the banks of the adjacent Huron River. In 1837, only thirteen years after Ann Arbor's inception, the Michigan state legislature saw fit to locate a university in the growing village. The first class of the University of Michigan graduated in 1841. A law school and medical school were established shortly thereafter. The city was incorporated in 1851. By 1854 there were 244 students in a city of more than 3,300 inhabitants. The city grew to 15,000 by 1910. The university was in a definite growth pattern by that time also; 5,381 students strong, increasing to more than 9,000 by the end of the decade, aided by the completion of dental and engineering buildings, as well as a new library and student union. Needless to say, by the time George arrived on campus, the university and the city were happily joined at the hip.

Although he arrived on campus in the fall of 1911, George was not introduced to Michigan baseball until several months later. Freshmen were not eligible for varsity sports in that era. Furthermore, George had not been recruited by the school for its baseball team and was not on scholarship. So when the new Michigan coach arrived in Ann Arbor, he had no idea who had arrived on campus the previous fall, pining for a chance to display his wares.

Less than a year before, when Phil Bartelme, one of the Wolverine athletic directors, began his search for a baseball coach to succeed the incumbent Lew McAllister, the last thing on his mind was that his top candidate and eventual choice had already been on campus. But a former law student by the name of Branch Rickey was the most suitable candidate. At thirty, Rickey had already played both collegiately and professionally, absorbing a good deal of baseball knowledge and street smarts.

Wesley Branch Rickey was born in 1881 in Duck Run, Ohio, near Portsmouth in the southern part of the state. Early in his career, Rickey was a full-time student and a part-time baseball player. Keeping a promise to his mother, young Branch had the audacity to shun Sunday baseball on religious grounds, a custom that did not sit well with the rough-and-tumble denizens of the dugout. The earnest young man fulfilled his scholarly duties at tiny Ohio Wesleyan University in Delaware, Ohio, and then turned to sports. A catcher by trade, in the beginning he was a member of the Cincinnati Reds, but never played a game for his home state team. In 1906 he caught for the St. Louis Browns of the upstart American League,

4. Sisler Memoirs, 4.

but once again he returned to his alma mater at the end of the season to coach football and act as the school's director of athletics.

During the 1906–1907 off-season, Rickey's contract was acquired by the New York Highlanders, the forerunner of the Yankees. As it turned out, Rickey arrived in New York with a sore throwing arm. On June 28, 1907, the gimpy-armed youngster was behind the plate during what must have been the longest afternoon of his life. Sitting crouched behind the plate during a 16–5 pasting by the Washington Senators, he looked on helplessly as thirteen rivals stole bases on his watch. The forgettable record survived, but Rickey's playing career did not. He caught but one more game and then headed to Ohio State University in Columbus to study law.

A little more than a year into his studies, apparent tragedy struck when Rickey developed tuberculosis. In April 1909, accompanied by his wife, Jane, he traveled to Saranac Lake, New York, for a ten-day internment at the Trudeau Sanitarium. When the fever subsided, Branch headed for Ann Arbor, arriving just in time to enroll for the first day of classes in the University of Michigan's law program. He had only enough money left for a semester of study and planned to complete the law school's three-year program in two years. Then Bartelme stepped in, and Michigan had a baseball coach. Under Coach Rickey the Wolverine varsity did well, and in June of 1911 its coach graduated from law school. Once again baseball took a backseat in Branch Rickey's life. He and two classmates headed for Idaho, where Rickey passed the bar and opted to begin life over in Boise, boosted by its mild climate. But in little time, Rickey realized the money was not in Idaho practicing law. By early 1912 he was back on campus in Ann Arbor to resume coaching varsity baseball and to start an intramural program for the school.[5]

The separate and distinct paths of Wesley Branch Rickey and George Harold Sisler crossed for the first time on a wintry day in Ann Arbor in 1912 when the slender Ohio freshman brazenly reported for varsity try-outs at Waterman Gymnasium. The two versions of that first meeting between Sisler and Rickey are remarkably similar. In *The American Diamond*, Rickey describes the day's events with a coach's unbridled enthusiasm at the discovery of a rare hidden gem:

> . . . I had asked for varsity baseball candidates through notice in the *Michigan Daily*. While registering and interviewing applicants in Waterman Gymnasium, I was confronted by a handsome boy of 18 with serious gray-blue eyes. He was well-built, about 5 feet 9 inches tall and weighing about 160

5. Peter Golenbock, *The Spirit of St. Louis: A History of the St. Louis Cardinals and Browns*, 64–65.

pounds. He wore a blue sweater and a well-used fielder's glove on his right hand. He introduced himself as George Sisler, a pitcher from Akron, Ohio, and an engineering student in the freshman class.

'Oh, a freshman,' I said. 'Too bad. You can't play this year. This inside work is only for the varsity.'

Silent and crestfallen, he reflected deepest disappointment as he turned away. A moment later, the team captain, Norman Hill, came up to ask if I knew about 'that kid in the blue sweater you were just talking to.' Norm then told me about his high-school record and asked that I take another look at the boy before dismissing him. I inquired immediately for a catcher. Lo and behold, young Sisler had his high school catcher right with him, a boy named Baer, and a good catcher, too.

It was a one-minute workout, all that is needed when coaches meet greatly impressive youngsters. This boy was something in grace and delivery on the very first pitch. The freshman battery was made an exception and stayed out with the varsity during the entire practice period. The 'workouts' were unforgettable. George pitched batting practice inside the cage regularly and created no end of varsity embarrassment, although restricted to the use of his fast ball. His left-handed speed and control made him almost unhittable.

He was a major-league pitcher right there!

Sensational as his pitching was, he was truly a sight to see with a bat in his hands. A slender left-hander, unknown to everybody, he was actually a threat to the cage pitchers. Such slashing and driving! Good pitches, bad pitches made no difference. Wham! Boom! Waterman Gymnasium had never known such a drubbing. The whole squad seemed to prefer watching Sisler hit to hitting for themselves with Sisler pitching.[6]

George recalls he

reported to the Coach at the specified time that Monday afternoon. He looked at me and found out I was a freshman. He said that this workout was for upper classmen and that I was not eligible to workout. He noticed the look of disappointment on my face, I suppose, for he said I might work out this one day. So I went in the gym, threw to a catcher for awhile, hit for awhile, and when the work out was over, the Coach appeared pleased with my work and said he would keep in touch with me and recommended that I try out for my Fresh Engineer's team which I later did.[7]

Spurred on by Coach Rickey's encouragement and advice, George joined the Freshman Engineers in the university's intra-campus league, and by season's end his team had earned the right to play for the championship and "inter-class" title by trouncing a team of senior literary students, 9–1. In one game, by George's own account, he struck out twenty of twenty-one batters in a seven-inning game against the "Freshman Lits."[8] In the

6. Branch Rickey, *The American Diamond: A Documentary of the Game of Baseball*, 14.
7. Sisler Memoirs, 4.
8. Ibid.

championship game against the undefeated Junior Law team, George made his first real mark on campus.

"One Sisler, premier twirler of the fresh engineer baseball team, created a great furor in the interclass circles yesterday afternoon when he stood the strong junior law aggregation completely on their heads and clinched the University championship-tag for his team. Sisler not only let the law sluggers down with only four safeties and struck out thirteen men, but himself led the heavy stick work of his team-mates with four healthy clouts, a single, a two-base hit, a three-bagger and a home-run. Only once was he in any danger and then with the second and third bags populated he settled down and struck out three men in succession."[9] The final score was Future Engineers 14 and Future Lawyers 0.

George had not only pitched a gem but also hit for the cycle, baseball's equivalent to basketball's triple-double. His collegiate star was clearly on the horizon, or was it?

Following George's stellar performance for his engineering classmates at the end of his freshman year at Michigan, he returned to Akron for the summer. He was quickly hired by the Babcock and Wilcox Boilerworks, paid a salary for his week's work, and firmly established as the lead pitcher on the B & W's summer industrial league team, which played its ball on Sundays. Its locus, Barberton, was a late-blooming village on the outskirts of Akron. Founded in 1891, it soon became known as the "Magic City," because it grew almost like magic into a city of more than nine thousand by 1910.

The industrial baseball league enterprise was not a money maker for the company, although the free publicity certainly did not hurt. The team was completely made up of locals, with the players equally dividing any money left over after expenses. The company provided no financial support for the team, but did furnish a decent playing field. Somehow, despite payments that smacked of semi-professionalism, the league maintained an amateur status in the eyes of the nation's colleges.

Pending his younger sibling's arrival, older brother Cassius, considered by most the second-best pitcher in the area, was the main man on the B & W mound. According to the *Beacon Journal*, the boys came by their prowess legitimately: "The Sisler brothers are born baseball players and it comes naturally to them as they inherit it from a family of ballplayers. The father, Cad [sic] Sisler, was looked upon in the state at the time when catchers'

---

9. Unidentified news clipping, University of Michigan Microfilm, Reel #1, report undated, 173.

gloves were an unknown thing, and like Cad, Bill Sisler, the boys' uncle, was the premier pitcher in this section and was considered in a class by himself. The Sisler brothers' battery was known all over the country, and their services were always in great demand."[10]

Once back in town from Michigan and out on the diamond, it did not take George long to confirm that his advance billing was, indeed, well earned. His presence paid off not only on the field but also in the stands. The B & W contests that summer of 1912 became a popular Sunday afternoon distraction for local fans. As in the past when he pitched for the local high school and the Collegians, accounts of the games were noteworthy for the number of strikeouts George recorded and the opponents' lack of success in crossing the plate.

The Boilerworkers were winning games behind their nineteen-year-old hurler, and as the summer progressed, fan interest continued to mount. At home the Barberton bunch often drew as many as twelve hundred fans. In early August special rail cars were added to trains leaving both Barberton and Akron to accommodate fans traveling to Elyria, a small city north of Akron, to see George strike out fourteen batters in another victory.

On August 18 George and his teammates received a special treat. The great Cy Young, a fellow Ohioan from neighboring Newcomerstown and winner of a major-league-record 511 games in a career that spanned twenty-two years from 1890 to 1911, traveled to Barberton to umpire a B & W game against the Amherst Grays. If George was in awe of a pitcher who achieved his nickname because of a fastball like a "cyclone," the game results do not reveal it. With the forty-five-year-old Young umpiring the bases—he had failed to bring the proper equipment to work behind the plate—George pitched a no-hitter, striking out eighteen in a 9–0 shutout. After the game, the great major-league hurler with five thirty-win seasons to his credit left no doubt he "was very much pleased with the work of young Sisler, and believes that he will make good in big league ball if he tries to break into faster company."[11]

Then, just as the summer sun was shining its brightest, "a complication arose" from something George had done two years prior. During the summer of 1910, between his junior and senior years of high school, George attended a game between the Akron Champs of the O-P League and one of its rivals. "I got out on the field somehow and started playing catch

10. *Akron Beacon Journal*, May 29, 1912. This information about the inherited prowess of the elder Sisler brothers could neither be verified or refuted.
11. Ibid., August 19, 1912.

with Bend Caffyn, one of their outfielders. I was impressed with him that he would show me this courtesy. I then thought O & P league ball was very good. So, eventually some scout showed me a contract for 100 dollars a month and I signed it. I did not show it to my father, nor did they, nor did they ever get his signature. They tried to get me to accept some cash, but I would not, nor did I ever get any money."[12]

The "scout" George talks about was actually an umpire, Jesse Goehler. The umpire in this case was not an impartial observer. He was, instead, a man on a mission. Despite missing the exhibition game between Sisler's Collegians and his Akron Champs a year or so before, Lee Fohl, the manager of the Champs, had seen George play in a number of high school and sandlot games. Like everyone else, he was impressed with his potential on the mound and at the plate. He telephoned A. Robert "Bob" Quinn, business manager of the professional club in Columbus, Ohio, a member of the American Association, a minor league on a higher scale than the O-P.

"There's a young pitcher on the Akron High School team who looks to me like the greatest prospect I've seen in a long time," Fohl told Quinn. "He can pitch like a professional right now and he hits like a grown man."[13]

No fool, Quinn, who later was a front office fixture for a number of baseball teams, told Fohl to sign the kid for one hundred dollars a month, even if it meant the release of a current player to fit Akron's roster limitations. It wasn't a novel idea in a sport where greed was not a foreign word. The pace to sign young players was magnified at this time by organized

12. Sisler Memoirs, 4–5. Some accounts have Sisler signing his professional contract in the summer of 1911, between his senior year of high school and first year of college. Sisler was eighteen at that time. Since it is clear he was seventeen and, therefore, a minor at the time the contract was signed, it seems more accurate that he signed the contract sometime after the summer of 1910, between his junior and senior years of high school. A statement that accompanied the National Commission's final decision in the matter declares the contract was signed by Sisler on January 2, 1911, more than two months prior to his eighteenth birthday. Sporting News, June 15, 1916. This is further confirmed by a letter Sisler wrote on August 27, 1912, to Garry Herrmann, chairman of baseball's National Commission. In it he stated, "Two years ago this winter, while I was attending high school, I signed the baseball contract given me by an umpire who watched me pitch the summer before. The proposition came very suddenly and unexpectedly, and I suppose I was an easy mark as I now look back on it. At that time, being only 17 years old, I thought it would be a great thing to sign a league contract and supposed that I would be sort of a hero among my fellow students and the people around Akron in general." Letter reprinted in the Sporting News, June 15, 1916. See also Sam Bernstein, "George Sisler and the End of the National Commission," 93.
13. Quoted in J. Roy Stockton in Christy Walsh, comp. and ed., Baseball's Greatest Lineup, 77.

baseball's reliance on the "reserve clause," its particular form of indenture. A fixture in players' contracts until litigation in the 1970s, the reserve clause bound a player to the signing professional club by "reserving" the services of that player for the succeeding year. The player was then barred from signing with any other club until he was no longer wanted by his present one. This placed the owner in control of salaries. It also increased the desire to seek out young prospects and, at minimal cost, tie them up contractually.

In George's case, Fohl didn't really know him well enough to feel comfortable placing a contract on the kid's lap. He apparently knew someone who did. Enter Jesse Goehler, and the game was afoot, with the quarry in sight. It is unclear whether or not umpire Goehler pocketed a finder's fee for his "scouting" that day, but there is no telling how many other young men fell prey to this method of ascertaining talent and tying it to a professional club in the event the prospect turned out to be the real thing. It is, however, highly unlikely that George's education-minded father Cassius would have endorsed his signature on the Akron contract if he had understood the consequences. Still, years later, George breathed a sigh of relief. "After I signed [the contract] I got scared and didn't even tell my dad or anybody 'cause I knew my folks wanted me to go on to college and I figured they'd be sore if they knew I wanted to be a ballplayer."[14] "It was a lucky break that I didn't mention it to my father. He might have okayed the signature and it would have cost me my opportunity to attend Michigan and receive my degree."[15]

It had been almost two years since George inked the contract with the Champs. But in 1912 he could no longer ignore the issue of his alleged obligation. In view of the reserve clause, it was of some significance in the summer of 1912 that Artie Hoffman, a valuable Chicago Cubs utility man in his day, contacted Barney Dreyfuss, the bodacious owner of the Pittsburgh Pirates of the National League, and suggested there was a player he should see playing independent ball in the sandlots around Akron and Barberton, Ohio.[16] Dreyfuss made the trip, liked what he saw, and purchased George's contract for five thousand dollars from Columbus, the club of Bob Quinn, who not by mere coincidence had purchased it from Lee Fohl's Akron Champs just months after their initial telephone conversation. A tenacious sort, Barney Dreyfuss recognized he had a rising star in his pocket and, unlike Fohl or Quinn, was determined to force the issue by insisting George report for duty.

14. As told to Lyall Smith in John P. Carmichael, *My Greatest Day in Baseball,* 158.
15. George Sisler quoted in Biederman, "Gorgeous George H. Sisler," pt. 1, 14.
16. *Sporting News,* March 13, 1919, 9.

Somehow, perhaps from the Pirates owner himself, news of the inter-play between Dreyfuss and Sisler came to the attention of the *Beacon Journal*. A mere two days after Cy Young's visit to Barberton, and well before the luster of his remarks about George had faded, the newspaper went public with George's little secret. In the eyes of professional baseball, he had been their property for two years and now the world would know it. On August 20, after tracing the path of the sale of the Sisler contract from Akron to Columbus to Pittsburgh, the paper spread the news, casting a dour warning. "If he [Sisler] refuses to report to the team which has pur-chased him he will be blacklisted, and will never be allowed to play in organized ball. Sisler has had many friends in this city, who were anxious to see him move to the front, but when he refused to report to Akron, and later to Columbus these same persons lost all interest in him. It is now pointed out that if he is wise he will report to the team which has pur-chased him."[17]

George, now backed by his father, stood his ground and, as predicted by the *Beacon Journal*, the Pirates placed the collegian on their suspended list, essentially barring him from professional baseball. Realizing he was in a jam that jeopardized his undergraduate eligibility, George went to his college coach. A former lawyer, Rickey quickly recognized that a contract signed by a minor and never acknowledged by his parent or guardian was legally nonbinding. He took quick action. First, he obtained an agreement from others in the Michigan athletic department to fight for George's eligi-bility. Then he engaged the assistance of Detroit Judge George B. Codd to handle the Sislers' position in the contractual spat. Rickey, however, re-mained intimately involved.

Rather than enlist the aid of the court system, the Rickey-Codd team took its case straight to baseball's ruling body. The National Commission had ruled baseball since 1903, growing out of the controversy in 1901 be-tween the established National League and the upstart American League. In 1901 the competition between the leagues for players was fierce, espe-cially for star players. The wealthiest owners, the so-called magnates, were already positioning themselves. The American League magnates did so well in luring outstanding players to its rosters that the National League finally capitulated. In Cincinnati in January 1903 a governing body was formed to oversee the administration of the two leagues. It was known as the National Commission and consisted of three members, the National League president, initially Henry Pulliam; the American League president, Ban Johnson; and Cincinnati owner August Garry Hermann. It was the

---

17. *Akron Beacon Journal*, August 20, 1912.

sincerest form of flattery that despite his status as the owner of a National League team, Hermann was considered impartial enough to serve as the third and, therefore, most influential arbiter of baseball's interest.

This, then, was the setup that faced the Sislers' representatives in August of 1912 when they went to the mat for their budding star. Judge Codd initiated the process by advising the commission that the Pirates' persistence in keeping George on their roster jeopardized his college eligibility. At the same time, presumably at the suggestion of their advisers, George and his father wrote separate letters to the commission. For his part, Cassius Sisler described his son as "a bashful, backward boy" who was "very modest" and, therefore, quite easily influenced by Jesse Goehler's flattery. George told the baseball triumvirate he repudiated the agreement with the Akron Champs because he signed it as a minor and did not "in any way understand the nature of the contract."[18]

Coach Rickey and Judge Codd took it from there. A possessor of great oratory skill, Rickey urged the commission to refuse to enforce an illegal contract. Despite his own fling in the major leagues, Rickey understood that most Americans at the turn of the century and beyond still admired amateur sports, while casting a suspicious eye toward the professional game. He predicted doom and gloom for the sport when parents, high schools, and colleges became aware of the seedy maneuvers of one of baseball's member clubs. "For who is going to trust you," Rickey importuned, "if you cajole minors into signing contracts and then declare them suspended—as you have tried to suspend Sisler—when they change their mind?"[19]

The heavy barrage from the Sisler contingent made a dent in the solid brick wall surrounding the sport, although it didn't cause an immediate cave-in. Despite the apparent urgency of the matter, the commission postponed a decision. Ban Johnson, the American League president, accepted George's version of the facts, pointing out that none of the clubs involved

18. Cassius Sisler's account appears in the *Sporting News*, June 15, 1916. George Sisler is quoted in Harold Seymour, *Baseball: The Golden Age*, 259–60. See also discussion in note 12.

19. Quoted in Golenbock, *Spirit of St. Louis*, 71. Although both Sisler and Rickey credit Rickey with successfully postponing the start of Sisler's professional baseball career, one writer attributes at least the initiation of that process to a Professor Thomas of the University of Michigan. Said professor allegedly "showed [Sisler] how that act [signing the document] would prevent his playing baseball or indulging in any other form of amateur athletics." F. C. Lane, "The Dazzling Record of George Sisler," March 1921, 466. Since Sisler does not mention Professor Thomas in his memoirs or other available descriptions of the events, it is uncertain if, or how much, Thomas actually influenced Sisler's decision to fight to protect his amateur status.

had a moral leg to stand on since Sisler signed with Akron "through misrepresentation by an obscure umpire." Still, the ever present business side of the game begged consideration. Owner Dreyfuss had spent good money to purchase Sisler's contract. Therefore, in the opinion of Garry Hermann, the "impartial member of the Commission," when George decided to play professional ball, he should be a free agent, but give Pittsburgh "every opportunity to secure his services."[20]

The wily Judge Codd, however, would not budge. There was no legal contract, therefore no reason to attach strings. And so the controversy raged, then simmered, then raged again as no final decision was reached. In the end a highly dissatisfied Barney Dreyfuss backed off, at least for the time being, and George retained his college baseball eligibility.

While the contract battle waged on, George continued to throw fastballs and "benders," as curveballs were then known. At one point in the summer of 1912, B & W won eighteen of nineteen games. In the ten games George pitched, he struck out 150 batters, allowed but 31 hits and a scant nine runs, and won them all. Five of the ten games ended in shutouts, with the one no-hitter in front of Cy Young. Going into George's last game with the team, B & W had won twenty-eight of twenty-nine and was on a twenty-five-game win streak. But in his last appearance of the summer, before International Harvester from Akron, B & W saw its win streak come to an end, losing 3–2 despite another fifteen-strikeout performance from its ace. The *Beacon Journal* waxed philosophical, however, telling its readers the loss would be forgotten when "it is remembered that he [Sisler] is the pitching sensation of the year" with "a record that will stand in baseball history for some time to come."[21] Noting that George was returning to Ann Arbor to continue his education and collegiate competition, nothing further was mentioned about the professional contract. Once again, George Sisler was Akron's fair-haired boy.

20. Seymour, *Baseball: The Golden Age*, 260.
21. *Akron Beacon Journal*, September 30, 1912.

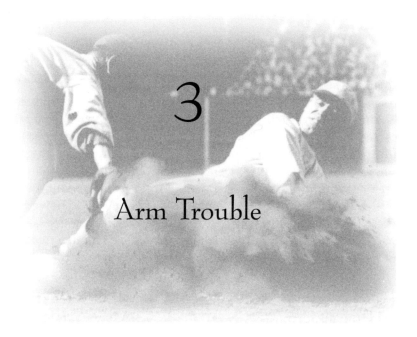

3

Arm Trouble

When George returned to Ann Arbor in the fall of 1912 to begin his sophomore year, it had become clear that baseball was his sport. Still, he had been a star in football at Akron High School, and Wolverine football was already big-time. There was talk by Michigan fans that even at 140 pounds, the athletic kid from Ohio would be an asset on the gridiron. The buzz apparently got around to Coach Rickey. If it bothered him, he need not have worried. Fielding Yost, Michigan's football field general, quickly allayed Rickey's fears.

"He would make a good man for us," Yost was heard to say, "but Michigan needs him more for baseball, and I am not going to run a risk of losing a good pitcher for the sake of getting a fair football player."[1]

With baseball as his obvious catalyst, George still had time to advance his engineering studies, work a job arranged with the aid of the school's athletic department to help defray tuition costs, and even enjoy a spot of fraternity life, joining Delta Tau Delta. Perhaps by design his fraternity brother, albeit as an alumnus, was none other than Branch Rickey.

In the spring of 1913, George joined eight new candidates in tryouts for the baseball varsity. Having made his mark on the coach the previous year, a slot on the team was assured for the slender lefty, who quickened

1. Quoted in Edwards, "Using a Diploma on the Diamond."

even more pulses when he was clocked running from home plate to first base in 3.35 seconds.

As is still the custom in college baseball, northern teams traveled south on spring trips in search of warmer temperatures as they opened their seasons. In 1913 Michigan was no exception. On April 5 George and his teammates trekked south, stopping in Lexington, Kentucky, for a game with the host Wildcats. Heading into the eighth inning with a solid 8–3 lead, Rickey deemed it safe to insert George for his college debut. Pitching the eighth and ninth innings, the southpaw slinger quickly showed his stuff, striking out five and allowing but one hit. It must have impressed because a mere two days later, George made his first start, pitching five innings of shutout, one-hit ball, striking out six in a 10–3 win over the University of Georgia Bulldogs in Athens. The next day the teams played again, and the results were classic. At the end of ten innings, the score was tied 2–2. But then, according to Coach Rickey, more mundane matters intruded.

"Time was to be called by agreement so that Michigan could catch a train. It was the final inning and Georgia filled the bases with the score tied and none out. Sisler was called in from center field to relieve the faltering Michigan pitcher. After a few warm-up pitches, George struck out the side on nine pitches without yielding even a foul."[2] The game ended in a tie, Michigan caught its train, and a legend was hatched.

Overall, the southern trip was a success, ending with Michigan on the long end of a 3–2–1 record. In a 14–2 victory against Vanderbilt, George pitched a solid five innings and excelled at the plate, going four for five and scoring five times. In mid-April under clear weather conditions, the Wolverines returned to Ann Arbor for their opener at Ferry Field. The largest crowd in years for a home opener attended the game, filling the entire grandstand and major portions of the bleachers. Based on his sophomore's strong early showings, Rickey gave the ball to George. Sisler did not disappoint, allowing but one hit and striking out twelve Alma batters in a 4–1 Michigan win. At the plate, he responded to a rousing ovation by slashing a triple in his first at bat, chasing home the first Wolves' run.

While the Wolverines were a force on the diamond, a struggle of a different sort was taking place behind the closed doors of the Michigan Board of Regents. Prior to 1908 the school competed athletically as a member of the Western Conference. In addition to the Wolverines, the league at that time included the University of Chicago, Illinois, Indiana, Iowa, Minnesota, Northwestern, Purdue, and Wisconsin. But in 1908, for a number of reasons, including a reduction in the number of football games, the issue

2. Rickey, *The American Diamond*, 14.

of freshman and graduate student eligibility, and the abolishment of athletic training tables and living quarters, the Ann Arbor school withdrew from the conference. In 1912 the conference added Ohio State. In 1913, reentry into the Western Conference was back on the table where it stayed until June 9, 1917.[3]

While the Board of Regents continued to struggle with the issue of conference membership, George continued to capture the imagination of the school's baseball fans. When Georgia repaid Michigan's early visit with a northern excursion of its own, Rickey found he was shorthanded and placed left-handed George at first base without a left-hander's mitt. Although he went hitless at the plate in a close Michigan victory, Rickey's new first-sacker was flawless in the field. A few days later, George set the college baseball world on its ear when Kentucky paid a visit.

"For the first portion of the game Mr. Sisler occupied the entire center of the stage for the first five innings. This port side deceiver decided that a team was an unnecessary appendage and hence proceeded to make 15 put outs in five innings, not asking his co-laborers for any assistance. Fourteen of the Colonels came to bat, smiled feebly, swung gently three times, and hiked back to the quiet bench, proving their southern breeding. The other victim, a rough person, hit one to Sisler who likewise gently touched him out. About the only bet in these five innings was how many balls would be thrown in one inning, and low calculators won."[4]

Taking mercy on the totally overmatched Kentuckians, Coach Rickey removed George in the sixth, but not before he slugged a home run to aid his own cause in a 13–0 shellacking. In early May, Sisler pitched a one-hitter against Case, striking out sixteen. The sophomore's college statistics were becoming strikingly similar to his high school and sandlot results.

As the season cranked up, the 1913 Michigan squad and its star southpaw began to attract attention nearby. On May 7 Ty Cobb, baseball's biggest star, drove the short distance from Detroit to Ferry Field to see Sisler pitch. The Tiger great missed his chance. George was once again pressed into service as a first baseman as Michigan defeated Washington and Jefferson. He handled eleven putouts without error and went one for four with a stolen base, but probably did not impress Cobb, who sat in the dugout and gave tips to the Michiganders.

Similar Michigan successes followed in short order. George struck out sixteen in seven innings in a contest against Syracuse and followed up by

3. Bill Cromartie, *The Big One*, 62.
4. Unidentified news clipping, University of Michigan Microfilm, Reel #1, April 29, 1913, page unnumbered.

whiffing fourteen more from Cornell. In that victory, he hit another home run. By mid-May the national tabloid *Sporting Life,* in a rare feature on a college baseball player, announced that "the greatest college pitcher" wore Michigan maize and blue. George's first national press coverage heralded his prowess with the bat as much or more than his prowess gripping the horsehide.

"Michigan baseball supporters say that George Sisler, the phenomenal southpaw twirler, is the greatest ball player who ever wore a Michigan uniform. And the figures prove it. In the first place, Sisler is hitting the ball at a .528 clip. Three of his hits have been home runs and three of them triples. In addition, he has scored twenty-two runs, for the best run-getting record of the team, and has stolen eleven bases. In the pitching department, he has pitched thirty-eight innings so far this season, allowing only nine hits, while striking out fifty-three and giving seven walks."[5]

Then, just as everything seemed rosy for George and his mates, he developed a sore arm. In order to continue to use his hot bat, Coach Rickey found a place for him in left field. He responded with a pair of hits in a win over the Michigan Agriculture College, the future Michigan State. A few days later George was patrolling right field, stroking four hits in a win over Cornell.

Now arm-rested, George was slated to pitch against national power Penn, but was again scratched when the pain persisted. With his school down 2–0, he stroked a triple with two teammates aboard to apparently tie the score. However, with two aboard and two out, the Penn pitcher had tried to intentionally walk George, who stepped across the plate to meet the pitch. After some discussion, George was ruled out and Penn survived for a 3–0 win. All in all, it was a bad day for the sophomore and his teammates.

George's frustrations that day were not limited to his action at the plate. In a play more demonstrable of his great desire to win than of his common sense, sore-armed George had been dispatched to the outfield with more than a little fatherly advice from the conservative Coach Rickey. The story was told years later by teammate Ed McQueen, by then a New York businessman. According to McQueen, Coach Rickey had cautioned George, "Now, whatever happens, don't throw! Don't take any chances at all. McQueen will run out and get everything from you and relay it to the infield." But George's competitive spirit prevailed. A runner was on third, ready to score, when the fly ball came. Ignoring McQueen's cry for the

5. Quoted in Ira L. Smith, *Baseball's Famous First Basemen,* 144.

ball and the pain in his arm, George cut loose with a throw hard enough to sail over Russ Baer's head at the plate.

"He was always that way," McQueen said. "When the rest of us slid into a base, the end of the momentum was the end of the chore. But never with Sisler. He came up at the end of his slide to a standing position. He was on his toes, ready to take quick advantage of any error or mental lapse by the opposition."[6]

Probably because of plays like these, as George's sophomore college baseball season wound down, it became apparent that his sore arm was not responding to rest. It was left to George to do what he could to help his team by using his bat. And help he did. In late May in a rematch against M.A.C., he went three for four, contributing to a 7–2 win. He also brought fans to their feet with a diving catch in left.

The M.A.C. contest marked the last game as Michigan's coach for Branch Rickey. Although a handful of games remained on the Michigan schedule, the call of the big leagues was too much for George's favorite coach to ignore. Rickey's jump from college to the majors seemed sudden, but in reality it was not. Over the years, a relationship had blossomed between Rickey and Robert Hedges, the owner of the St. Louis Browns. While a member of the Browns as a catcher in 1906, Rickey had so impressed the Browns' owner with his dedication to his studies that Hedges sent the young student a share of his team's winnings from its postseason series with the crosstown rival Cardinals of the National League. It was an act of kindness that the loyal Rickey never forgot.

As a college coach at Michigan, Rickey was in a position to spot young talent and frequently made recommendations to Hedges and the Browns. They were grateful. In the 1911–1912 off-season, Hedges asked Rickey to administer and manage his new farm club in Kansas City. Rickey, already determined to practice law in Idaho, turned the offer down, but he did agree to scout for the Browns. The man had a keen eye for talent that quickly paid dividends for the Browns, further whetting Hedges' appetite. Prior to the 1913 season, as Rickey prepared to return to Michigan to coach, he and Hedges met and struck a deal. In January, without fanfare or publicity, Rickey was named vice-president and secretary of the Browns. Under the arrangement, he returned to Ann Arbor to continue to coach. But on June 1, shortly before the end of the college season, he left for St. Louis. Initially, he worked his front office job, but on September 6, 1913, he became the team's field manager.

6. Quoted in Arthur Mann, "Baseball's Amazing Sislers," 84.

If the university and its fans were surprised by Rickey's quick departure, the timing of the action made nary a ripple. The popular coach's exit was attributed to "the press of duties in St. Louis." Acknowledging the coach's baseball acumen and ability to pass that knowledge to others, the press found much more to admire in the man than to criticize: "Above all he taught clean ball, gentlemanly tactics, and clean living. A gentleman himself, his ball team followed him, and no greater tribute to him can exist than the conduct of the team. A gentleman, a true sportsman, and a man, he will long be remembered by those who love and help Michigan athletics."[7]

Although their relationship lasted less than a full college baseball season, the attributes that endeared Branch Rickey's players to him, endeared Rickey to his young star George Sisler. Like Rickey, George had chosen a life that placed clean living, gentlemanly tactics, and sportsmanship on the highest plane. In his young, emerging performer, Rickey must surely have seen himself, and vice versa. Whether Branch Rickey created George, or merely molded and buffed an unfinished product, only begs the question. The two men fed off each other and together carved a great deal of baseball history. In time Rickey probably knew George Sisler almost as well as George knew himself. That George is not as well remembered as his mentor says as much about George's retiring personality as anything else, and about that Rickey had this to say:

> The most obvious, initial, and immediate impression on meeting George Sisler is one of modesty almost to a point of shyness, and that impression is lasting. He is modest in the sense that, by nature, he meticulously observes all the proprieties of self-effacement in speech and action. But he has another quality, one sometimes regarded as the antithesis of modesty: ego. Sisler had enough modesty to justify the wide scope of his popularity. Justifiable ego, however, made him a great player. The term, as applied to George, and most great batsmen, simply means an enduring consciousness of one's own rightness, or belief, an inner knowledge that comes out of one's own practice and experience.[8]

Although they would meet again in short order, the man George Sisler would call "Coach" for the rest of his life was gone to grander pastures. And though George and his Michigan teammates would dearly miss him, their 1913 season was still incomplete. Assistant Coach Douglas and cen-

7. Unidentified news clipping, University of Michigan Microfilm, Reel #1, report undated, 218.
8. Rickey, *The American Diamond*, 14.

ter fielder Ball, the team captain, now shouldered Rickey's load for the remaining games, which included a slim victory over the Michigan alumni and a split of two games in Ann Arbor with powerful Penn. At least partially recovered from his arm trouble, George returned to the mound for the 7–2 win over Penn, but lost the season finale, 1–0, to the easterners. In that game, George contributed to his own downfall in the seventh inning by misplaying a ball hit back to him in the box, allowing the lone run to cross the plate.

A final tally of the Wolverines' 1913 season found them on the long end of a 22–4–1 record. For the year George batted a heady team-leading .445. Pitching records, including win-loss figures, were not kept, but George was an overpowering performer before the arm problems. His performance earned him selection to *Vanity Fair*'s 1913 All-American team.

At the end of the season, George was among a number of varsity athletes polled with regard to the school's future in the Western Conference. His "yes" vote was in the majority, but surprisingly the vote was fairly close, even among campus student organizations and alumni groups who were also queried. This lack of consensus would postpone the matter for several more years.

Back in Akron, local baseball fans eagerly anticipated the return of their college hero. In late May, the *Beacon Journal* defended George from comments made by Detroit Tigers manager Hugh Jennings, who stated that talk comparing the Wolverine star to major-league giants Ty Cobb and Ed Walsh, a strong-armed pitcher who won twenty-seven games in both 1911 and 1912 for the Chicago White Sox, would harm George. To the contrary, said the newspaper:

> Sisler is known to almost every baseball fan in Akron. He is not only a ball player, but a gentleman. Publicity in the past has never had a tendency to spoil him. It may even be said that George is too modest. He is a true sport, and would work as hard when losing as when winning.
>
> Those who know Sisler are firm in the belief that Jennings' statement was uncalled for. Publicity will never spoil Sisler. Injuries will alone keep him out of fast company, that is if he desires to follow baseball as a profession after he leaves college.[9]

It was expected that George would spend the summer in the Akron area, once again playing for Barberton's B & W semi-professional team, now known as the "Speed Boys." Yet on June 2 the *Beacon Journal* reported that George was working out with the Pittsburgh Pirates and had been

9. *Akron Beacon Journal*, May 30, 1913.

signed by its manager, Fred Clark. Since the paper attributed the report to "word" emanating from the Great Northern Cigar store in Akron, and George's last game in a Michigan uniform in 1913 was not completed until June 25, the report of the tryout seems both unfounded and not in keeping with attempts by George and his advisers to void the professional contract purchased by the Pirates the year before. What is accurate is that a few days later, Barberton fans made ready to greet George's return in a B & W uniform. During his absence, the club's top pitcher was Cassius, still generally considered the second-best pitcher in the greater Akron area.

One of the biggest crowds of the season was prepared to watch George's reappearance on the B & W mound in early June with a particularly strong opponent scheduled. Alas, George never found the mound. His arm was still giving him problems, forcing him into right field with a bird's eye view as his team suffered a "terrible beating" at the hands of the Girard Independents.[10] As the summer progressed, it became apparent George was suffering from a chronic arm ailment. While Cassius, whose career coincidentally was later ruined by arm trouble, performed admirably on the mound for the Speed Boys, George did his part with the stick and in the field.

A highlight of the 1913 summer for George and his teammates was the appearance of an "all-Filipino" team. Like in many other countries, baseball was introduced to the Philippines by American troops stationed on the island. The game took hold, and the team the Speed Boys was about to face played an excellent brand of ball. But even without George on the mound, B & W was a force. When the dust settled, the Speed Boys were on top 7–2, behind a strong performance by Cassius Sisler.

Interest in this and other B & W games in 1913 was heightened by the loss of Akron's baseball entry in the O-P League. Financial difficulties were the league's Waterloo. Before the season started, the league was renamed the Interstate League and the Champs became the "Giants." In mid-July, the revamped league was reduced from eight to four teams. Poor attendance took care of the rest, and suddenly the B & W Speed Boys were the main game in town.

In mid-August George took a test drive on the mound, but was wild and did not make it out of the third inning. Back in right field, he banged out three hits in the summer's other main attraction, a contest with a Cuban all-star team said to "compare favorably with the American and National leagues." This time, the usually invincible Speed Boys met their match in

10. Ibid., June 30, 1913.

the speed and agility of the men from the Caribbean, suffering a rare defeat. Another loss came at the hands of a Chinese team from Hawaii. In that game, unlike the Cuban contest, George held up his end, going three for four in a one-run loss. But despite success at the plate, as his summer in Akron progressed, George realized something had to be done about the pain in his left arm. By the end of the season he was playing second base in an apparent effort to keep his bat in the lineup while hiding the fact he no longer had the arm strength to hold or throw out base runners from the outfield.

In 1913, however, where did sore-armed baseball players turn for treatment? In George's case, effective medical help was just a few miles away in Youngstown, home to John D. "Bonesetter" Reese, a "baseball specialist" of some national repute.[11] A Welsh immigrant who learned his art from a fellow iron worker, Reese was a master at manipulating muscles and ligaments in a manner more closely akin to the practice of osteopathic medicine than orthopedics. Although his formal medical training was limited to three weeks of study in 1897 at Case University in Cleveland, by 1901 the previously unlicensed healer was awarded a special medical certification, allegedly by the Ohio General Assembly.

Sisler was neither the first nor the last baseball player to make the Youngstown trek. It is estimated that "Bonesetter" treated more than fifty ballplayers during his career, at least twenty-eight of whom reached baseball's Hall of Fame. Before his death in 1931 he also treated Teddy Roosevelt, Will Rogers, British Prime Minister Lloyd George, and baseball-playing evangelist Billy Sunday.

For George the trip to Youngstown to see Reese would be but the first of several such journeys. Diagnosing the problem as a severe strain that had occurred early in the 1913 college season during a workout and persisted as the year advanced, the physician provided George a program for recovery.[12] Only time would tell whether the Bonesetter's reputation was well earned.

George returned to Ann Arbor in the fall of 1913, to live off campus at the Delta Tau Delta fraternity house. While it is uncertain just how much socializing the serious engineering student engaged in during his four-year stay in Ann Arbor—he did not drink, smoke, or swear—it is clear

11. Unidentified news clipping, University of Michigan Microfilm, Reel #1, report undated, page unnumbered.
12. Ibid.

the university provided a special bonus in the presence of one Kathleen Charlotte Holznagle. The exact details of their meeting are unknown, but as the English literature major was a member of Kappa Kappa Gamma sorority, there is a strong likelihood that Greek social life played a part in their initial association.

Kathleen was the daughter of Frank Holznagle, a Detroit wholesale florist of some means. The elder Holznagle owned land where the Ford Motor Company eventually located. A native of Highland Park, a Detroit suburb, Kathleen soon joined George's studies and baseball as constants in his life. On an early visit to the home of Kathleen's family, George took note of the unusual three-car garage and selection of fancy cars, including a Winton, a fancy vehicle sold only in Detroit. Whether or not the Holz- nagles were sports fans is unclear, but Kathleen's mother, English born and bred, made the effort. While conversing about the sport over the meal, she asked her daughter's baseball-playing boyfriend who was "tossing" that day.[13] The story and the daughter made a lasting impression on Sisler.

By spring George and his Wolverine teammates were making a lasting impression of their own on the diamond. The 1914 season is best summed up by the school's student scribes: "Outshining even the remarkable 1913 baseball season, the 1914 record of Michigan's Varsity nine will go down as the most admirable achievement ever accomplished by any Michigan team, either on the diamond, track or gridiron, since, in the light of general opinion and in accordance with the verdict of baseball critics throughout the country, she [sic] was awarded the intercollegiate championship of the United States."[14] This indeed was a surprising result, given that the Wolverines entered the season with its star hurler nursing a sore arm and a novice coach directing the show.

The sore arm was a non-issue by the time spring practice opened. The Bonesetter's regimen was a success. George reported for spring practice with a fit arm, entertaining no thoughts of succumbing to pressures exerted by the Pirates to jump to the big leagues. Michigan had its shining star. He would pay big dividends in this, his junior campaign.

The issue of finding a new coach was only slightly more complicated. Once it was determined that Branch Rickey's position with the St. Louis Browns was full-time and year-round, the Michigan Athletic Association began a search for his replacement. They found him in the person of Carl L. Lundgren, a man of some experience. Born in 1880, Lundgren pitched for

13. George Sisler, Jr., interview by author, August 28, 2001.
14. *Michiganensian* Student Yearbook, 1914, 275.

the University of Illinois before his college coach recommended the Chicago Cubs of the National League take a look at him. They were impressed. From 1902 through 1909, Lundgren performed for the Cubs, ending his major-league career with a 91–55 record and a sparkling earned run average of 2.42. During his tenure with the Cubs, Lundgren played for three successive pennant winners. But despite records of 17–6 in 1906 and 18–7 in 1907, with a 1.17 earned run average, the Cub pitching staff, which included Mordecai "Three-Finger" Brown, Orval Overall, and Jack Pfiester, was so strong that he was never used in the 1907 World Series. In 1909 Lundgren's big-league career came to an end as he was sold to Toronto, then a minor-league franchise. What he did for the five years prior to his appearance at Michigan is not reported, but at Ann Arbor, the train started quickly.

The first item of business for Coach Lundgren was election of a captain, since the initial choice had resigned due to academic problems. Although only a junior, George won the post overwhelmingly. Next, Lundgren changed the setup for the batting cages by partitioning the single cage to allow four pitchers and four batters to work out simultaneously. Since the team faced the difficult logistics entailed by a typical harsh Michigan spring, the maneuver allowed more concentrated practices within the team's limited time frame. The results of the new approach paid quick dividends.

Per past practice, in early April the team headed south for its spring swing, posting a win over Kentucky in the opener. Saving his arm, George worked only the first three innings, allowing one hit. This permitted George to pitch several innings two days later in a win, one of two, over the reigning southern champions, the Alabama Crimson Tide. George was soon at it again, taking the mound the following week as he worked a shutout over Georgia, driving in the only run he needed. One paper following the game noted Georgia had been "Sisslerized."[15] In a second game against the Bulldogs in Athens the next day George had three hits as his team suffered its first defeat, 7–2.

When the extended road trip concluded, however, the final tally was seven Michigan victories and just the one defeat. George led all Wolverines with a .434 average, had eight stolen bases, and was perfect in the field. Despite coming off a significant arm injury with only a short time to practice indoors before the southern swing, George pitched two complete-

15. Unidentified news clipping, University of Michigan Microfilm, Reel #1, report undated, page unnumbered.

game victories on the trip, including a four-hitter against Notre Dame as the team completed its journey. Along the way, he picked up the nickname "Sis," which stuck for the rest of his life.[16]

Back home at Ferry Field, the Wolverines shut out six of their next seven opponents, then traveled to East Lansing to blank the Agricultural College. At one point, the team's string of shutout innings ran to forty-four. In the process, Sis struck out ten successive batters. Unfortunately, against Syracuse he also reinjured his pitching arm.

Battling without their ace on the mound, the Wolverines moved east, winning two from Syracuse and another from Cornell before falling in succession to Princeton, Swarthmore, and Pennsylvania. The Princeton game stopped the Wolverines' win streak at fourteen. Moreover, in his first post-injury appearance on the mound, George was ineffective. His troubles compounded by shoddy fielding, he was pulled in the fourth inning with the Tigers leading 5–0. The final score was a respectable 5–4, but the outing represents one of only three games during George's collegiate career when he was the losing pitcher of record.

Sore-armed, George sat out the loss to Swarthmore, but did play right field in the defeat by Penn, which left the Michigan nine with a 3–3 record from the eastern swing. In Ann Arbor, Sis nursed his arm as his team split with M.A.C. and also with Notre Dame before defeating its own alumni. These last few games served as mere setups for the two-game rematch against Pennsylvania, with the mythical national title on the line. In this era, no tournament existed to determine a national intercollegiate baseball champion. The College World Series was still years away. Teams laid claim to the title of champion by their deeds on the field as they played out their individual regular-season schedules.

In 1914 the University of Pennsylvania was considered the best in the East. The Wolverines had suffered defeat at the hands of Penn during their eastern swing. Princeton was also a power, having already knocked off Michigan, but in head-to-head contests during the season Penn was victorious over the Tigers. Also, Michigan was victorious in all its games against Cornell and Syracuse. During the year, the Wolverines easily disposed of the teams from the South, as well as winning the season series against its "Western" rivals M.A.C. and Notre Dame. Thus, Michigan could claim the crown in the South and West, and likewise in the East, if it won the two remaining games against Penn.

The mythical national championship games were played in Ann Arbor on June 23 and 24. Unfortunately, the home team was again without its

16. Ibid.

star southpaw. Still, the Wolverines prevailed in the first game 4–0, evening the season series on a strong pitching performance by a gangly young six-foot four-inch pitcher named Charles Ferguson. Sisler played a major part in the victory with a double, an infield single, two steals, and three runs scored.

The rubber game and in effect the tilt for the national championship on June 24 was much closer. It took ten innings this time, but once again the Wolverines prevailed 4–3.[17] Sis had a relatively quiet day, but still contributed two hits while playing a flawless left field. Interestingly, Coach Lundgren told George to warm up on the sidelines during each game, but did not use him. It is not clear whether or not this was a bluff, or if George could have physically answered the call if needed.

By winning the two games over Penn, Captain George and his Michigan charges reached the pinnacle. And even though it took a legal brief the size of a New York telephone book to explain it, they had indeed plowed a path to the "national championship." For his troubles, Sis was named to *Vanity Fair*'s college All-American team for a second time. Unlike 1913, his listing on the 1914 team, voted by a panel of seventy-five sportswriters from across the nation, was in bold print, as he was the only "Western" player to make the squad.

Sisler's fans in Akron were proud of their local hero. In his absence, they thirsted for information about him. On May 16 the *Beacon Journal* reprinted an article datelined Ann Arbor. In it Coach Lundgren rated George as good as any college player he had ever seen, stopping short of calling him the best by naming two other pitchers, one already with Philadelphia's National League entry and one with Columbus in the American Association. All three were lefties, but none, the article ventured with a hometown college slant, possessed Sis's all-around ability as a clean-up hitter, fielder, and base runner. If Sis had a weakness, the writer proposed, it was, like most southpaws with a "lot of stuff," his control.[18]

Although no Bonesetter sightings were noted during the summer of 1914, George's arm problems delayed his now annual performance for B & W. It was not until late August that George trotted to the mound in a B & W uniform, but the extended rest must have helped immeasurably. Facing

17. A box score of the June 24 contest lists the umpires as "Bill" Dineen and "Ty" Cobb. A newspaper report of the June 23 game describes Dineen as an umpire from American League President Ban Johnson's staff and indicates Cobb "was in the stands." Unidentified news clippings, University of Michigan Microfilm, Reel #1, reports dated June 23, 1914, and June 24, 1914, pages unnumbered.

18. *Akron Beacon Journal*, May 16, 1914.

Akron's entry in the semi-professional industrial league, Sis's control, speed, and curveball were such that Akron failed to garner a hit and twelve of their batters went down on strikes. One Sunday later George pitched against the same Akron team. In front of fourteen hundred fans, the two teams went at each other for twelve innings. When it was over, B & W was a 1–0 winner and Sisler had compiled seventeen more strikeouts.

On September 13 George took the mound against the Goodlows in front of five thousand partisan fans at Akron's Buchtel Field for a benefit game for the local athletic association. The game was reportedly witnessed by the largest crowd of the season. Once again he lived up to his reputation by pitching a two-hitter in a 2–1 victory in which he struck out twelve. A week later, on September 20, George made his last appearance in the Akron area as an amateur player, this time in front of the largest throng ever to witness a game in Barberton. For the third time that summer the opponent was Akron and B & W was the winner; Sis limited the rivals to three hits while striking out eight.

If George Sisler had an arm problem that summer of 1914, you could not prove it by asking hitters in the Akron area. As the winning pitcher in four games following his late arrival, the local favorite gave up only three runs and eleven hits. He struck out forty-nine, an average of more than twelve per game.

As the summer came to a close, the *Beacon Journal* reported that there were a growing number of college graduates in the major-league ranks. Approximately thirty players from major colleges were on the rosters of the sixteen big-league teams, and there was little doubt George Harold Sisler would soon swell their ranks.

While on campus in the fall of 1914, the Sislers' contract dispute with the Pirates reared its ugly head again. This time the impetus for the uproar was George's own counsel, Judge Codd. In October of this, George's senior year, Judge Codd sought to bring the matter to a close by writing the "neutral" commissioner, Garry Hermann. "(T)he time is at hand when this young man should be allowed to make a profit out of his own ability and every day's delay is adding to the damage which he is sustaining by your deprivation of his legal rights."[19]

The judge threatened that unless the Sislers received a satisfactory decision, they would sue for triple damages. In response, a suggestion was made by one owner that by silent agreement George be deemed a free agent, with a tacit understanding that only Pittsburgh negotiate with him,

19. Quoted in Seymour, *Baseball: The Golden Age,* 260.

thus essentially tying him to that club in the end. Barney Dreyfuss wisely turned down the offer, fearing a conspiracy charge in the offing. Instead, he encouraged Hermann to obtain a legal opinion. The answer was swift in coming: the contract was invalid, and attempts to enforce it in the manner suggested would indeed expose the league to charges of conspiracy. For Hermann, this was enough. After all, he and organized baseball were already embroiled in a contest of wills and bank rolls with the Federal League, an "outlaw" league formed in 1913 by a number of wealthy businessmen with enough money to raid existing teams for star players. In light of these circumstances, the three-member commission unanimously agreed that George Sisler was a free agent, no strings attached.

Thus, as he prepared for a final season of collegiate ball, some degree of order had finally settled upon George's future in professional baseball. Given the glories of the preceding season, optimism was in the air in Ann Arbor, and the drums began to beat as early as January with news that in view of George's past history of arm trouble, Coach Lundgren planned to bring along his star much more slowly than in previous campaigns. Under the plan, George's arm would be well rested. He could then pitch at full strength in the more important games in late spring, when the Wolverines found themselves up against the Penns and the Princetons of the world.

A new season brought a new captain for the Wolverines, with second baseman Edmon McQueen receiving the honor. At least early in the season, the job took on a new twist when in a surprise move, Michigan's Board in Control banned the "varsity coach," in this case Lundgren, from sitting on the team bench or directing the players during the game. In essence, Lundgren was reduced to no more than a very interested spectator. The new policy had nothing to do with Lundgren and everything to do with a reform movement then sweeping the nation's colleges and receiving a more than generous amount of support in Ann Arbor.

The movement for reform stemmed from the proliferation of summer leagues across the country in which college players received pay for their play, which in turn cast doubt on their amateur standing and college eligibility.[20] At least three key Michigan players, George excluded, were charged by the university with voiding their eligibility by such actions. Although George played summer ball under similar circumstances, he was

20. According to local news reports, the Michigan Board in Control favored a proposal by the national magazine the *Saturday Evening Post*, which opined summer baseball should be recognized or college baseball abolished. Nevertheless, the board charged several Michigan players, including Captain Edmon McQueen, who was later cleared and permitted to play.

not under the microscope since he had held a job for the team's sponsor, providing an argument that he was not paid for play but for his work. Also, in George's case, unlike the others charged, he played for a team in his hometown, thus affording an additional degree of legitimacy.

At any rate, like it or not, George's team began its 1915 campaign without the hands-on game supervision of Coach Lundgren. In his absence, Captain McQueen became the on-field general. How much the restrictions on Lundgren's ability to direct his team and the reform furor affected this edition of Michigan baseball is a matter of conjecture. It is a fact, however, that two players were eventually declared ineligible for the season and despite the return of key players at every position but shortstop and catcher, the 1915 Wolverine nine was not the powerhouse of the year before.

Once again, the team started its season in the south with a win over Kentucky, followed by a win over Marshall and two victories over Washington and Lee. Following the preseason plan, George was stationed as far away from the mound as possible, in left field. He responded with multiple-hit games in several of the early outings and capped off a three-for-three day at the plate against Washington and Lee by leaning over the fence to rob a hitter of an apparent four-bagger. The team's quick start and good fortune, however, ended at Virginia, where they fell 6–1. Returning north in mid-April, George made his first appearance on the mound in a relief role against Notre Dame on April 19, helping his cause by tripling in the top of the tenth and scoring the lead run, then striking out the side in the bottom half of the inning to preserve the win.

Ten days after the Notre Dame victory, the Wolverines tangled with cross-state rival Western Michigan, at that time called Western State Normal of Kalamazoo. It was a contest for the record books of both schools. On the mound for Western was Ernie Koob, who would go on to pitch for the St. Louis Browns, and who flashed his promise that spring day by holding Michigan to two Sisler hits. For his contribution, Sis pitched five no-hit innings, striking out twelve. This spectacular performance was almost duplicated by Charles Ferguson, the previous year's pitching star now returned from an early season injury. The tight contest ended in a ten-inning scoreless tie, a feat repeated by Michigan several days later over eleven innings versus the Syracuse Orangemen. These same teams tied again two days later in thirteen innings, this time at 2–2. In this one, George's fine pitching and three hits were not enough to avoid futility.

In mid-May, perhaps out of frustration over the spate of ties, the Board in Control rescinded the rule that banned its team's coach from the bench. In an almost absurd moment of inspiration, or perhaps desperation, the board offered to reinstate the rule for any game in which their opponent agreed to adhere to the coaching restriction they wished to impose. To no one's surprise, there were no takers.

Coach Lundgren's return to the bench did not reap immediate benefits for the Michiganders. The same day the rescission was formally announced, the team fell to M.A.C. 3–1. Then three days later George suffered a rare pitching defeat when his fielders took an inning off, allowing two runs to score in a 2–1 loss. Sisler struck out fourteen, but four walks added to his downfall. Following the loss to M.A.C., the team made a road swing east, splitting a pair of games with Syracuse and with Cornell, then returned home to split a pair with M.A.C. In the main, the squad's inability to put together a winning streak stemmed from weak hitting. At one point midway through the campaign, Sis had one-third of his team's hits, with local reports admitting his work on the mound was "largely wasted with no one else connecting with the ball."[21]

In the eight games after Coach Lundgren's return to the bench, the Wolverines scored only twenty-five runs. Fourteen of those came in two games, eleven in the other six. Five of the six ended in losses. In the one close win, a 2–0 victory over Cornell, George gave up just one hit, a bunt.

Facing Ernie Koob of Western, the Wolves had a return engagement after their scoreless tie. Charles Ferguson was on the mound for the Wolves; Koob prevailed. With five games left in a season that could be viewed as lackluster, the Wolverines responded by winning all five. Following a 4–2 win over Notre Dame, Sisler stepped to the mound and defeated the Golden Domers 4–1 with a fourteen-strikeout performance. Then on June 22, after the varsity easily bested its alums, George faced Penn in his last collegiate mound appearance. Unlike the previous year, due to a rainout in the East, this contest was the first meeting between the two college baseball giants. This time Michigan prevailed 10–0 behind a dominating seven-inning performance by Sis. At the plate, he was equally sparkling, going a perfect four for four.

The next day Ferguson, now nicknamed "Cy" by the local press, was on the mound with George in left as Michigan beat Penn 4–2. In the game, George went three for four, including a home run. He was robbed in his last college at bat when Penn's center fielder made a sensational catch. Until that final at bat, George had hit safely nine times in succession, almost certainly a school record. He added to the glamour of his finale by stealing five bases, including one of baseball's most exciting moments, a dramatic steal of home plate. It was a most impressive exit.

21. Unidentified news clipping, University of Michigan Microfilm, Reel #1, report undated, page unnumbered.

When the results of the 1915 Wolverine baseball season were tabulated, the overall record was 16–7–3. Again, pitching records were not kept, but at the plate George dominated, finishing the year with an awe-inspiring batting average of .451 and adding to his value by playing errorless ball. For the third year in a row, he was named All-American by *Vanity Fair*, once again the only "westerner" on the team.

Despite major talent and persistent interest from professional baseball, George had stayed the course at Michigan for four years. In a matter of days he would graduate with a degree in mechanical engineering. Such dedication to his college did not go unnoticed. Michigan alumni were grateful. Calling George "the wonder of college baseball," Michigan's football leader, Fielding Yost, the same man who turned George away from the gridiron, told reporters he was not just referring to the student's playing ability, but rather to the fact "that such a talented player should pass up numerous opportunities Sisler has had merely for the sake of playing a few games of ball for his alma mater." Yost, for one, wanted to remind all that "(t)he University of Michigan certainly owes Sisler a great debt of gratitude for his self-sacrificing services on the diamond."[22]

Former Michigan baseball captain and Chicago Cubs pitcher Jack Hibbard, a member of the school's athletic board, said much the same as Yost, adding that George's future in baseball, though presently perceived to be based on his ability to pitch, was not nearly so restricted: "The limited experience of college players leaves most of them shy of baseball brains and few collegians can hit well enough for fast company. Sisler, however, is good enough for any team in the country, as the flock of scouts after him testifies. He is not only a sensational pitcher, but a wonderfully fast fielder, a natural hitter and fleet base runner, and has one of the best base ball instincts I ever saw in college ball."[23]

As George prepared to walk across the stage in Ann Arbor to receive his diploma, he was, in every facet of the game, fully prepared for major-league baseball. The only question remaining was whether major-league baseball was ready for him.

22. Ibid.
23. Ibid.

4

Reunited and Repositioned

In June 1915 George Sisler stood on the threshold of a promising professional career as arguably college baseball's top graduate. Thanks in no
small part to Branch Rickey and Judge Codd, he was now free to cut the
best deal he could with any team in baseball. His contract with the Pittsburgh Pirates was null and void according to no less an authority than the
National Commission. Since organized baseball was readily offering contracts to untested players of lesser talent coming straight off the country's
sandlots, bidding for George should have been fierce. Yet the market in
his case was practically nonexistent. According to the national periodical
Baseball Magazine, "everywhere the door of advancement seemed barred
in his face save at Pittsburgh." One club in desperate need of pitching advised Sisler they had all the pitchers they required. The cold shoulder Sis
received was clear "evidence of that gentlemen's agreement between the
owners."[1]

As previously determined by his brain trust, George wrote Garry Hermann, still the neutral panel member of the commission, assuring him he
would give Pittsburgh ample opportunity to sign him. Whether Pittsburgh owner Barney Dreyfuss was aware that the upstart Federal League
was also in the mix with their deep pockets was open to discussion. But

1. John J. Ward, "The Famous Sisler Case," 36–37.

thinking that he was the only bidder, Dreyfuss offered George seven hundred dollars per month for the remainder of 1915, plus a thousand-dollar signing bonus, for a package worth fifty-two hundred dollars. Imagine his surprise upon opening a wire from George in mid-June to read, "Have decided to join the St. Louis American League team."[2]

The St. Louis deal paid three hundred dollars less per month than the Pittsburgh offer, but included a much larger five-thousand-dollar bonus, for a total offer of seventy-four hundred dollars. The Browns also agreed to a substantial salary increase if George remained with the club for 1916. In addition, they agreed to waive the "ten-day clause," a standard contractual term allowing a team to dismiss a "reserved" player on ten days' notice. A player so released could, of course, land elsewhere since he became a free agent, but the clause was seldom used unless the player was disabled or no longer possessed real trade value. Its elimination from the contract of a youngster like Sisler was a definite plus. However, since an average season's pay for a rookie in 1915 was in the twelve-hundred-dollar range, each offer George received was substantial. The clincher in the deal was never the money; it was the Browns' manager, Branch Rickey, Sis's college coach. George signed a contract, this time as an adult. Sisler was now a St. Louis Brown.

According to George, there was a comfort level on his part when it came to Coach Rickey, making it a no-brainer that he would accept an offer from the Browns if it came his way.

> An offer for a small bonus and a rather small salary came from the St. Louis Browns and I accepted willingly and gratefully. The size of the bonus meant little to me at the time because I had definitely made up my mind that I would not play ball in the minors and should any club attempt to farm me out to the minors, I would immediately retire from baseball and go into Engineering somewhere. I felt that with the good education that I had received at the University of Michigan, that it would be foolish to play minor league ball. And besides, I wanted no large bonus to make me think that I owed an allegiance of any kind to the club who paid it, should I want to get out of baseball. The big thing in my mind was whether I could make good in major league baseball or not, and this was what I intended to find out. And so the contract was signed and I was in major league baseball.[3]

As expected, Barney Dreyfuss was not pleased. At once, he filed a formal complaint with the National Commission, claiming Branch Rickey tampered with Sisler and interfered with his Pittsburgh club's ability to sign the Michigan graduate. He called upon American League President

2. Quoted in Seymour, *Baseball: The Golden Age*, 260–61.
3. Sisler Memoirs, 5.

Ban Johnson to suspend George pending a decision by the commission. But Johnson was reluctant to suspend the young player unless the commission, via Hermann, took responsibility. He was "not courting damage suits" and, therefore, "pending further investigation," George Sisler was a St. Louis Brown.[4] Since a team from each league was at loggerheads, it was left up to Dreyfuss's close friend, Garry Hermann, to cast the deciding vote. It would be a year before Hermann finally made up his mind.

Meanwhile, George found himself in the westernmost city in the big leagues. St. Louis, the home of the American League's Browns and the National League's Cardinals, exploited its unique geographical position to draw rooters from both the South and the West. Often Missourians were in the minority at St. Louis baseball games, outnumbered by fans from these outlying regions who yelled just as loud and cried just as hard as they watched their ball-playing heroes battle the dreaded invaders from the East.

In the early twentieth century, St. Louis stood tall as the nation's fourth-largest city. Founded in 1764 when the French arrived to trade fur, the city quickly became the mobilization point for all westward exploration and settlement after Thomas Jefferson's purchase of the Louisiana Territory in 1804. As a thriving inland seaport, St. Louis in the 1850s saw the arrival of passengers and freight by giant steamboat paddlers. These river queens were largely supplanted in a matter of years by the kings of the rail. By the turn of the century more railroads converged on the city than on any other junction in the country. This consolidation of transportation served St. Louis well. Its manufacturers became leading producers and shippers of apparel, cotton, bricks, tobacco, and beer.

In 1904 the entire world turned its attention to the "Gateway to the West" as the city hosted a World's Fair known as the Louisiana Purchase Exposition and also the third modern Olympiad. The country sang "Meet Me in St. Louis" while the city teemed with visitors from anywhere in the world one could imagine. As time would prove, St. Louis, seven hundred thousand inhabitants strong, was at its zenith. In this time of gleeful exuberance locals were often heard telling visitors from near and far that their fine town was "first in shoes, first in booze, and last in the American League." The latter was a reference to George Sisler's new team.[5]

The 1915 edition of the St. Louis Browns was no different: the team was struggling once again. Worse yet, they were contending for the city's summer entertainment dollars with not only the crosstown Cardinals but also

4. Quoted in Seymour, *Baseball: The Golden Age*, 261.
5. Quoted in Elizabeth McNulty, *St. Louis Then and Now*, 64.

the city's entree in the new Federal League. The Terriers, managed by Fielder Jones, stood atop the Federal League standings. To make matters even tougher, the usually hapless Cardinals were enjoying a surprising bit of good fortune themselves, perched in third place in the National League. George's new team, on the other hand, sat sixth in the American League, staggering along eighteen games in back of the first-place Chicago White Sox.

Still in the early stages of earning his spurs as one of baseball's greatest innovators, Branch Rickey was in the process of bolstering the Browns with college players. Players like George who entered the professional ranks straight from college were still a rare sight, but Rickey was trying his best to force a change. In addition to Sisler, he had previously signed Johnny Lavan, the Michigan medical student and future health commissioner of Toledo, Ohio, who was George's teammate at shortstop on earlier Michigan teams. The Browns had also recently signed Western Michigan southpaw hurler Ernie Koob, George's opponent in several legendary battles on the collegiate diamond. Other former collegians would be added to the Browns' roster by Rickey in short order.

What the Browns were getting straight off the Ann Arbor campus in twenty-two-year-old George Sisler was a five foot, ten and one-half inch left-handed batter and thrower who, despite modest size and a slender 160-pound frame, liked to swing a heavy forty-two-ounce hickory bat, using a choked grip. Blessed with blazing speed and extremely agile, the Browns' newest member, despite a great deal of self-confidence, was quite shy and introverted, and thus at times came off as cold and aloof. In reality, he was a most pleasant, modest sort who still did not drink or smoke. Unlike the vast majority of hard-drinking, hard-living professional ballplayers, he was very much a straight arrow. In general, however, despite his passive personality and the fact that he held a college degree in a sport in which such an achievement was rare, he was quickly accepted by all comers and throughout his career was well liked by his teammates. According to Rickey, he "never criticized a team mate or an opponent."[6] In time, however, George's self-effacement, such a strength as an active player, would play a major role in keeping him out of the limelight once his playing days were over.

Fully cognizant of George's personality and playing ability, Rickey early on furnished the *St. Louis Post-Dispatch* with a frank assessment of his newest and most hard-fought acquisition. Aware that George had ex-

6. Quoted in Stockton in Walsh, comp. and ed., *Baseball's Greatest Lineup*, 82.

perienced chronic problems with his pitching arm during his college days, Rickey told the *Post-Dispatch* on June 24, 1915, "My mind regarding Sisler's playing abilities is an open one. I hardly think he is strong enough to last as a pitcher, but I do respect his hitting abilities. I want to see him at work before making up my mind whether to turn him into an outfielder or leave him as a pitcher. Sisler, of course, is not ready for the major leagues. He needs experience and I plan to keep him on the bench for a time."[7]

That time passed quickly, as four days later, on June 28, George Sisler took the mound for the Browns in relief against the first-place White Sox. Like any major leaguer, George's recall of his first big league appearance is vivid:

> I remember that I reported to the Browns at the Chicago Beach Hotel on the south side, a very ritzy and elegant hotel at that time and not too far from Comiskey Park. The White Sox at that time were considered a very good club with excellent pitching and overall balance and were around the top in the American League. My start in major league baseball was to pitch the last three innings against them, and I had the good fortune to shut them out. But the big thing in that game for me was when I went up to bat for the first time. Death Valley Jim Scott was pitching for the White Sox. He was known at that time to have the best curve ball of any pitcher in the league and a tough pitcher to hit. Well, the positive conviction came to me when I first faced him and saw a couple of pitches to me that I could hit him, and if this was a sample of the great American League pitching, then I could most certainly hit any American League pitcher. This confidence from that time on never left me and I never knew the day or the time when I feared or doubted that I could hit any pitcher. It was a comfortable feeling to have, and I was glad I got it so early.[8]

George was absolutely right about Death Valley Jim Scott. He got his first hit off of Scott that day, making his debut a success in all aspects of the game, despite a 4–2 defeat. His play and the loss sparked a rhyme or two from a local sports columnist with a wry sense of humor who often waxed poetic. The reference to George's debut appeared in "Brown Babblings" in L. C. Davis's Sport Salad column in the local *Post-Dispatch:*

> The Brownies lost another game
> (That line perhaps we'd better frame)
>
> The reason why we cannot tell,
> But this we know and know full well—

7. Quoted in *St. Louis Post-Dispatch*, June 24, 1915.
8. Sisler Memoirs, 5–6.

The Brownies lost another game
And have no 'Gloomy Gus' to blame.

Far be it from us to predict
That our old Brownies will be licked;

But it is pretty safe to say
They'll lose another game today.

George Sisler made a glad debut
And made a good impression, too.

We hope the lad from Michigan
Will strengthen Mr. Rickey's clan.[9]

Soon Rickey found new reason to insert George into his immediate plans. The team's first baseman, Jack Leary, was mired in a batting slump. In only his second season in the majors, the twenty-four year old was at least twenty points below his .265 average for 1914. Originally planning to try George in the outfield, Leary's inadequacies at the plate presented Rickey with an opportunity.

"I had been thinking about Sisler for a long time before he arrived. It was obvious to me that he was far too good a ball player to waste his time pitching. He had never played first base at Michigan and though he wasn't as tall as the average first baseman I had a hunch that this might be the spot for him. So the first thing I did when he reported was to hand him a first baseman's mitt and tell him to work out there. Two days later, he started his first game at first and it was easy to see from the start that he was going to be a natural there."[10]

Rickey's memory was a bit cloudy. Sisler's move to first base took a few more days, but it still happened rather quickly. After that brief mound appearance on June 28, George made his first major-league pitching start against the Naps of Cleveland on July 3 in St. Louis. Although he pitched a complete-game 3–1 victory, it was not a work of art. Described by his manager as "nervous and worried" after each inning, Sis walked nine and gave up seven hits.[11] The performance, despite its flaws, was strong

9. *St. Louis Post-Dispatch*, July 2, 1915.
10. Quoted in Thomas Meany, *Baseball's Greatest Hitters*, 181. Rickey was incorrect in stating this was Sisler's first brush with first base. During Rickey's stay at Michigan and after, Sisler was inserted at first base on several occasions due to injuries to key players. Rickey is also inaccurate in stating that Sisler played in a game at first base only two days after his arrival with the Browns. Sisler's initial appearance at first base on July 3, 1915, occurred several days after his first appearance in a game on June 28.
11. Quoted in *St. Louis Post-Dispatch*, July 4, 1915.

enough to garner several more lines of rhyme in "Browns Ballooning" by columnist L. C. Davis:

That Sisler boy from Michigan
Propelled the pill across the pan.

But when they tried to wallop it
That pill was very hard to hit.

And what we had to say is this:
Just keep your weather eye on Sis.[12]

Victory came in the first game of a twin bill. In the second game, a 5–1 loss, George made his initial appearance as a major league first baseman, going hitless in two at bats before giving way to Jack Leary, the man who lent George his mitt and his knowledge of the position. That generosity cost Leary his job and his career; he never played in the majors after 1915. Lou Gehrig, who would one day come to overshadow Sisler among the best first basemen in baseball history, later took Wally Pipp's job in much the same fashion.

One of Jack Leary's lessons stuck. He told George to keep his foot on the bag no matter where the ball was thrown. In George's initial game at first base, his old Michigan mate Doc Lavan threw wide to first on a close play. George lunged for it, but the throw seemed way too wide to allow him to keep his foot on the bag. He fell to the ground, laying there stunned as the runner crossed the bag, rounding for second. The umpire, however, signaled an out, and the rhubarb was under way. Then the umpire stooped to the ground, pointing to George's toe still jammed into the bag. It was only then that anyone thought to help the dazed rookie to his feet.

"Only a player with a mysterious inner glow of greatness could have made that play," Rickey said.[13]

Although at times he was capable of spectacular plays, the move to first base initially affected George's hitting. According to Rickey, after his new first baseman went several games without a hit, he took his young charge for a walk, telling him that he would indeed pitch again. And George did pitch several days later. One day while pitching he got three hits, and it was time for another hike.

"That night Sisler and I walked and talked and I told him he was ready for first base again. I knew he had the confidence once more and during his career it was the last time he left first base because of a slump."[14]

12. Ibid., July 16, 1915.
13. Quoted in Lee Greene, "George Sisler 'Picture Player,'" 77.
14. Quoted in Biederman, "Gorgeous George H. Sisler," pt. 2, *Sporting News*, March 4, 1953, 13.

Although he would pitch and play several games at various other positions in 1915, including the outfield, from that time forward George was essentially a first baseman. But the transition from pitcher/outfielder to first baseman was not as easy as those first outings indicated. During 1916, George's first full season, he led American League first basemen in errors.

Even before that, in early August 1915, with just a little more than six weeks of professional baseball under George's belt and even less time at first base, the manager of the Boston Red Sox offered Dick Hoblitzell, a veteran first sacker with a lifetime .273 average, to the Browns in a straight deal for him. As an alternative, the Red Sox also offered to fork over $10,000 cash, the equivalent of $155,000 in today's economy. Neither proposal interested Rickey in the least.

Meanwhile, with George looking like a find at first, Rickey hit the road to bolster his outfield. Already boasting a .280 hitter in Burt Shotton, who would later manage successfully for Rickey in Brooklyn, and a .270 hitter in Tilly Walker, one of baseball's first power hitters, the team needed a third outfielder. Dee Walsh, struggling in the low .200s, was not getting the job done.

By mid-August the Browns, still needing the outfield help, were resting in seventh place, thirty games behind league-leading Boston. Sisler, who went three for nine in a twin bill at Chicago, and other collegiate heavyweights such as Ernie Koob were not enough. The season was over for the Browns and most of the rest of the league. The only serious contenders left were Detroit, two games behind the Red Sox, and the White Sox, six games off the pace.

If Rickey was beginning to doubt an earlier prediction that he would make the Browns into a contender by 1916, he did not share it. The St. Louis scribes were still patient, trumpeting Koob and Sisler as "undoubted finds." In Sisler they recognized a pitcher, outfielder, and first baseman all in one, though which one he was remained a question: "There never in history was a ballplayer who hurdled from a campus to a major league diamond and demeaned himself as has George Sisler."[15]

On August 18, in an effort to bolster his outfield, Rickey dealt two losing pitchers, Bill James (7–10) and Grover Lowdermilk (9–17) to Detroit for William "Baby Doll" Jacobson. A giant for his time, Jacobson at six feet, three inches tall and 215 pounds, earned his nickname after a tape-measure minor-league home run was greeted in the stands by a chorus of "Oh, You Beautiful Doll." The name was cute, but the trade did not reap

---

15. *St. Louis Post-Dispatch,* August 22, 1915.

instant results: Jacobson was a .209 hitter for the Browns for the remainder of the 1915 season.

Waiting for Jacobson to develop, Rickey continued to juggle his star pitcher around the field. "Rickey would pitch me one day, stick me in the outfield the next and then put me over on first the next three or four."[16] The papers were saying nice things about George, but mostly about his hitting. In his heart, George Sisler was still a pitcher. He was proudest so far of his victory over Cleveland, after which he was awarded a pair of white flannels. In typical fashion, he didn't wear them right away, feeling they were too fancy for his taste.

Then along came a pitching matchup that afforded what George years later described as his greatest thrill in baseball. On Sunday, August 29, 1915, Rickey scheduled Sisler to pitch against his boyhood idol, Walter Johnson. At the time the greatest everyday player in the game was clearly Ty Cobb. There were several legendary hurlers, but Big Train Johnson was by most accounts the best. His fifty-six consecutive scoreless innings in 1912 most certainly caught a Michigan freshman's eye. A fantastic 36–7 pitching mark in 1913 bowled George over, and Johnson's 28–18 record in 1914 was an indication that the Train was still at the top of his game. In 1915, at age twenty-seven, Johnson was on the way to a league-leading twenty-seven victories when the Senators arrived at Sportsman's Park in St. Louis for a game with the Browns.

The owners and managers of the Browns and the fourth-place Senators, often still called the Nationals, sensed a box office bonanza instead of just a so-so late-season game between two also-rans. Clark Griffith, the manager of the Senators, held Johnson back a day so that he would meet Sisler. The two men had faced each other once before, on August 2 in Washington. In that game, George struggled in the first inning, giving up three runs, then settled down too late in a 5–1 loss. A highlight for Sisler in that game was a single off his hero. Now he was about to get another shot at the master, and from the time on Saturday when Rickey poked his head into the locker room and announced he would pitch, George was on edge:

> I went back to my hotel that night but I couldn't eat. I was really nervous. I went to bed but I couldn't sleep. At 4:00 a.m. I was tossing and rolling around and finally got up and just sat there, waiting for daylight and the big game.
> I managed to stick it out, got some breakfast in me and was out at Sportsman's Park before the gates opened. It was one of those typical August days

16. As told to Lyall Smith in Carmichael, *My Greatest Day in Baseball*, 160.

in St. Louis and when game time finally rolled around it was so hot that the sweat ran down your face even when you were standing in the shadows of the stands.

All the time I was warming up I'd steal a look over at Johnson in the Washington bull pen. When he'd stretch way out and throw in a fast ball I'd try to do the same thing. Even when I went over to the dugout just before the game started I was still watching him as he signed autographs and laughed with the photographers and writers.

Well, the game finally started and I tried to be calm. First man to face me was Moeller, Washington's left fielder. I didn't waste any time and stuck three fast ones in there to strike him out. Eddie Foster was up next and he singled to right field. Charley Milan singled to right center and I was really scared. I could see Mr. Rickey leaning out of the dugout watching me real close so I kept them high to Shanks and got him to fly out to Walker in centerfield. He hit it back pretty far though and Foster, a fast man, started out for third base. Walker made a perfect peg into the infield but Johnnie Lavan, our shortstop, fumbled the relay and Foster kept right on going to score. That was all that got in that inning, but I wasn't feeling too sure when I came in to the bench. I figured we weren't going to get many runs off Johnson and I knew I couldn't be giving up many runs myself.

Then Johnson went out to face us and I really got a thrill out of watching him pitch. He struck out the first two Brownies and made Del Pratt fly to short center. Then I had to go out again and I got by all right. In the second inning, Walker led off with a single to center field and Baby Doll Jacobson dumped a bunt in front of the plate. Otto Williams, Washington catcher, scooped it up and threw it 10 feet over the first baseman's head. Walker already was around second and he came in and scored while the Baby Doll reached third.

I think I actually felt sorry for Johnson. I knew just how he felt because after all, the same thing had happened to me in the first inning. Del Howard was next up for us and he singled Jacobson home to give us two runs and give me a 2–1 lead.

Well, that was all the scoring for the day, although I gave up five more hits over the route. Johnson got one in the first of the fifth, a blooper over second. I was up in the last of the same inning and I'll be darned if I didn't get the same kind. So he and I were even up anyway. We each hit one man, too.

There wasn't much more to the game. Only one man reached third on me after the first inning and only two got that far on Johnson.

When I got the last man out in the first of the ninth and went off the field I looked down at the Washington bench hoping to get another look at Johnson. But he already had ducked down to the locker room.

I don't know what I expected to do if I had seen him. For a minute I thought maybe I'd go over and shake his hand and tell him that I was sorry I beat him but I guess that was just the silly idea of a young kid who had just come face to face with his idol and beaten him.[17]

17. Ibid., 161–62. Sisler states Rickey was in the dugout during the game. Since Rickey did not manage on Sunday on religious principle, it is unlikely he was present.

The win over his idol did not go to George's head. Calling Johnson "as fine a gentleman as I have ever known," George stated often and publicly that "he was forever my hero."[18]

George's performance that hot August day had attracted another admirer. *Post-Dispatch* writer W. J. O'Connor labeled the Ohioan "the greatest young player who has entered the major leagues since Ty Cobb's time. And in a matter of all-round efficiency, he stands a fair chance of shoving the Detroit star into total eclipse."[19] The rookie's triumph over the legendary Johnson also got the poetic attention of L. C. Davis, who penned "Some Kid":

> That Sisler is surely a pippen;
> His work, up to date, has been rippin'.
>
> He went into the ring
> With the 'Fireball King'
> And handed Sir Walter a whippin.'"[20]

In September, as his rookie year wound down, George received another special thrill. After a game in Cleveland with the Naps, which the Browns won when he hit a lead-run double and stole home, the entire Brownie team traveled to Akron for an exhibition game with a local squad. In order to display his versatility for the hometown fans, George pitched, played first, and played center field for three innings each. The team was met by a brass band and given a splashy automobile ride around Akron prior to the game. George received a diamond ring and pin as his new team shut out an amateur team that probably consisted of several players George had played with or against just a few years before.

In that same month, the Browns went on a seven-game winning streak, during which Sisler played a lot at first base and had a three-hit game. It was becoming more and more apparent that he was now the Browns' first baseman of the future. Pitching Sis only when he absolutely needed him, the Browns' manager used the last several weeks of the 1915 season as an audition for 1916. The future indeed looked a bit brighter. At one point in September, the Browns posted victories in nineteen of thirty games.

In October the Browns and Cardinals engaged in their annual fall series. A minor figure in this seven-game exercise in futility was a rookie from

18. Quoted in Michael Santa Maria and James Costello, *In the Shadows of the Diamond: Hard Times in the National Pastime*, 210.
19. *St. Louis Post-Dispatch*, August 30, 1915.
20. Ibid.

Texas named Rogers Hornsby. Hornsby's major-league debut was on September 10, 1915, less than three months after George's. More, much more in fact, would be heard from Mr. Hornsby before Sis hung up his spikes.

While the Boston Red Sox were putting the Philadelphia Phillies away in five games in the 1915 World Series, George had time to assess his rookie year. He had appeared in fifteen games as a pitcher, with a 4–4 record and a very respectable 2.83 earned run average. This, of course, was an era of strong pitching, so his batting average of .285 over eighty-one games was quite sufficient for a newcomer. Only second baseman Del Pratt hit a higher average for the team (.291). Ty Cobb, as usual, was another story, leading the league at .369 and stealing 96 bases. George's three home runs were only four behind the league leader, Robert "Braggo" Roth of the White Sox and Indians. In thirty-five games at first base, Sis committed but four errors, remarkable for a novice.

For George Sisler, if not for the St. Louis Browns, 1915 was a year to remember. Playing before 150,358 fans, the Browns finished sixth in the league, with a 63–91 record. The Cardinals, a sixth-place finisher managed by Miller Huggins, outdrew the Browns with 252,666 fans. The St. Louis Terriers finished second in the Federal League. Their attendance figures were unavailable, but each ticket holder represented one less for the established clubs in town. The state of professional baseball in 1915, especially in St. Louis given three teams in a city of just over seven hundred thousand people, was untenable. The system needed a fix. A solution was closer than anyone could have imagined.

In late February 1916, when George reported for spring training in Palestine, Texas, to prepare for his first full professional season, organized baseball in general and the St. Louis Browns in particular had undergone major changes from the previous year. Although St. Louis fans had experienced baseball off and on at Sportsman's Park on the corner of North Grand and Dodier Streets since the mid-1870s, the Browns in their present form had moved to the city from Milwaukee at the urging of American League President Ban Johnson, who persuaded Cincinnati carriage maker Robert Lee Hedges to become sponsor and owner of the club. Adopting the name Brown Stockings, a name used by earlier St. Louis clubs, the team played its first game in a refurbished Sportsman's Park on April 23, 1902. The Browns finished second that first year, but enjoyed little success on the field thereafter. In spite of its lackluster performance, however, the team did surprisingly well at the box office, outdrawing the Cardinals. In fact, Hedges was making enough money that in 1908 he reinvested in his franchise by rebuilding its ballpark and increasing its capacity to almost eighteen thousand. The improved surroundings seemed to help for a season, but after a fourth-place finish, a return to the back of the pack followed. Despite the team's lack of success in the standings, Hedges remained firmly entrenched as team owner.

In 1914 and 1915 the life of the Browns' owner, as well as of most major-league team owners, was muddled by the emergence of the Federal League. To further complicate the situation, Hedges' health declined. His burden was somewhat eased in December of 1915 when the Federal League made peace with its rival leagues. Seeing an opportunity to step aside in a profitable manner, Hedges placed his team on the market and quickly found a suitor.

The sale of the Browns in late 1915 and early 1916 was rather complicated. John Bruce, the secretary of the National Commission, and his partner, Walter Orthwein, held an option on 90 percent of Hedges' shares in the ball club. That option was sold to Phillip DeCatesby Ball for $525,000. Bruce reportedly cleared $90,000 in the deal. Hedges came out with a tidy $400,000 profit from his original investment.

Although in reality the Browns were purchased by a syndicate that included St. Louis brewer Otto Stifel, the team was essentially the property of Phil Ball, formerly the controlling owner of the Terriers, St. Louis's Federal League team. The Browns' new owner was at age fifty-six a rowdy type who had previously worked as a cowhand and construction worker. He once played some baseball in Louisiana, but his path to fame and fortune came through the manufacture of ice machines for large companies such as meat packers and breweries. In sum, he presented a stark contrast to the Browns' incumbent manager, the very orthodox Branch Rickey. A confrontation was imminent.

The friction between Ball and Rickey would involve more than just their personalities. It was a clash of principles. Rickey was an avowed teetotaler, Ball just the opposite. In Ball's opinion, Rickey could not be trusted. According to Arthur Mann, Rickey's biographer, upon Rickey's and Ball's first meeting at Sportsman's Park, Ball, a fellow with a fleshy pear-shaped face and gray brush-cut hair, took one look at Branch and bellowed, "So you're the God-damned prohibitionist!"[21] The relationship deteriorated from there.

Discounting that Rickey was beginning to mold a solid team, Ball's first move was to replace him with Fielder Jones, the former manager of his Terriers. Underlying motives aside, the change was not without a degree of merit. In 1915 Jones had managed the Terriers to a close second-place

21. Quoted in Golenbock, *Spirit of St. Louis*, 75.

Federal League finish. A former player with a .285 lifetime average, Jones's main claim to fame was his managerial effort in 1906 for the Chicago White Sox, when he directed the "hitless wonders" to an unexpected American League flag.

Still under contract with the Browns, Rickey was sent to the front office to work with placement of excess ballplayers. The traditional farm club system he would later create and develop was not in place yet, so he was assigned the tedious and time-consuming task of finding a spot for non-roster players who were under contract to the team. Like a good soldier, Rickey performed his duties, but with one eye open for greener pastures.

For the Browns, 1916 would be a year of transition; for George, it was a year of solidification, coupled with personal change. In addition to a new manager, the team, just like other American and National League clubs, had added Federal Leaguers to the squad. The Browns added eleven. Picked in the preseason for a fifth-place finish, the club met that expectation with a 79–75 record. According to John E. Wray, sports editor of the *Post-Dispatch,* the improvement was due to Federal League "outlaws" such as Ward Miller, who helped solidify the outfield troops with a .266 mark, and Bob Groom, who finished the season at 13–9 with a 2.57 earned run average.[22]

In late July and early August the Browns made a remarkable run, pushing into fourth place, only seven games out of first, by winning twenty-three of twenty-five contests. But they faded quickly. On August 30 Boston's Hub "Dutch" Leonard slammed the door shut 4–0 with a no-hitter. By September 6 the club's pennant chances were purely mathematical. An injury to catcher Hank Severeid was a key ingredient in the late fade, and the club finished thirteen games behind pennant winner Boston.

On the field Sisler solidified his position as the Browns' first baseman, appearing there in 141 games. Although he made a league-leading 24 errors, he handled 1,510 putouts and compiled a respectable .985 fielding percentage. His speed and quickness permitted him to cover a great deal of ground while still scampering back to the bag for numerous spectacular plays. In August a panel of sportswriters in Philadelphia voted George the top first baseman in either league.[23]

At the plate Sis continued to impress, leading his team in batting average (.305), slugging percentage (.400), and hits (177). Spending the bulk of the season batting in the number three slot, a position he essentially held in the batting order throughout his career, he hit four home runs and drove

22. *St. Louis Post-Dispatch,* May 24, 1916.
23. Ibid., August 21, 1916.

in 76 runners, both second on the team behind second baseman Del Pratt, who led the league in runs batted in with 103, a fact that should stump any trivia expert. The league leader in batting average was Tris Speaker, who hit .386 to wrest the title from Ty Cobb. Cobb still led the league in stolen bases with 68. A young pitcher for the Boston Red Sox named Babe Ruth led the league in earned run average with a 1.75 mark while also tucking away 23 wins, only two less than league leader Walter Johnson. The Red Sox made the American League proud by topping Brooklyn in five games to win the World Series.

Despite his significant improvement and frequent brilliance at first base, George's versatility was still a factor in 1916. He played three games in the outfield and even found himself on third base—a rarity for a lefty— for two flawless late season games. He pitched on three occasions, the most pleasing a 1–0 six-hit shutout of Walter Johnson and his Nationals in mid-September. That outing sprouted an effort from L. C. Davis appropriately entitled "George Sisler":

> George Sisler was there forty ways from the ace;
> He walloped the 'Fire Ball King';
> While Jones went around with a smile on his face,
> Suggestive of flowers in spring.
>
> He goes at his work with the grace of a Cobb,
> When playing in any posish;
> Wherever they put him he's onto the job,
> This wonderful marvel from Mich.
>
> Life's always put up a spectacular show,
> No matter which job he may take;
> The boys in the bleachers would now like to know
> What kind of a catcher he'd make.[24]

If George missed the close contact previously afforded by his "coach," manager, and by now good friend Branch Rickey, he did not say so publicly. At least for the present, Rickey was still with the Browns' organization. Seeds the "coach" had sown for his "pupil" came to further fruition in June of 1916 when the National Commission's neutral member, Garry Hermann, finally issued his decision on what was now generally referred to as "the Sisler matter." Feelings about the case still ran high, especially among National League owners. After Commissioner Hermann, giving a strong hint of where he was headed, told Barney Dreyfuss he did not consider George an ineligible player, Charles H. Ebbets of the Brooklyn Club

24. Ibid., September 18, 1916.

told *Sporting Life* that the Browns would never have been permitted to obtain George but for the threat of the Federal League. "[I]f the taking of Sisler, in the same manner was attempted now, the St. Louis Club would never get away with it. That much is certain."[25]

On June 10, 1916, Hermann formalized his thoughts on the case by casting the deciding vote that determined where George Sisler should henceforth ply his trade. The nineteen-page typewritten decision in favor of George and adverse to Hermann's longtime friend and colleague Dreyfuss could be boiled down to three words: "lack of evidence." The contract was null and void, Hermann opined, in that it was signed by a minor who, along with his parents, repudiated it before he came of age.

Now the matter was over. Or was it? For George it was. Other than some public mud slinging in the press with Dreyfuss, he moved on, firmly entrenched as a St. Louis Brown. Dreyfuss, however, was not mollified. He responded by issuing a twelve-thousand-word opinion of his own. At the end, he issued his campaign pledge: "An outsider, some person not affiliated with either league, should be placed at the head of the National Commission. The finding in the Sisler case is a freak of baseball legislation."[26]

Barney Dreyfuss kept that campaign pledge. He never forgave Garry Hermann or Ban Johnson, the man he felt pulled Hermann's strings and influenced his decision in the Sisler case. As the years passed, Dreyfuss's campaign gained support from other owners. After a scandal rocked the game in 1919, a single commissioner for baseball, Judge Kenesaw Mountain Landis, was named. A judge from the federal bench in Illinois, Landis essentially painted his name on the new commissioner's office door by delaying an anti-trust suit brought by the Federal League long enough to force the "mavericks" to capitulate, preserving baseball's two-league status. This made Landis the instant darling of the owners, and a just reward was eventually bestowed on him. On November 12, 1920, he became baseball's ruler. Barney Dreyfuss had lost a battle with the Sisler family and won a war.

Now with the last mantle of uncertainty lifted, George could finally experience the pure joy of playing baseball, a full-fledged Brown at last. The season contained its highs and lows. In May, even prior to the decision, a contingent of more than five hundred Michigan students, professors, and alumni traveled to St. Louis to present Sis with a watch. He failed to return the favor when, in a rare display of nervousness, he wore a "collar" for

25. Quoted in David J. Davies, "Commission Holds Sisler Is Not Ineligible," *Sporting Life*, June 3, 1916.
26. Quoted in Lee Allen, *The American League Story*, 87.

the game: none of his five attempts to hit the ball carried past the infield. His lack of success that day probably stemmed more from his innate shyness than anything else. In August, the *Post-Dispatch* noted he turned down an endorsement opportunity because he "dislikes the spotlight."[27]

As Branch Rickey had noted, however, George's shyness did not equal weakness, but instead shielded a competitive spirit and a self-assuredness that would not allow him to back down from any situation or adversary. In September of 1916, that mettle was tested by teammate Bob Groom, a veteran pitcher brought in from the Federal League. During a game with Groom on the mound in a losing effort, George failed to snag a high throw to first base. By the time he ran the ball down, the runner was on second base. When George reached the dugout at the end of the inning, he felt Groom's wrath.

"Listen, you . . . college boy," he yelled at George, "you run harder for those . . . balls. Where the hell do you think you are, at a . . . tea party?"[28]

The blood drained from George's face. Unaccustomed to such treatment, he was shocked. He did not want his politeness or intelligence to be mistaken for weakness. He realized he needed to make a statement. He stared briefly at Groom and then walked over and hit the startled moundsman in the mouth with a left roundhouse. Sisler never had another problem like that with Groom or any other teammate or opponent throughout his career.

But in reality, attempts at staying out of the limelight were impossible for a player with George's obvious skills. Increasingly, he was compared to the legendary Ty Cobb; closer to home he was co-featured in a *Post-Dispatch* article comparing him to an emerging comet on the Cardinals named Rogers Hornsby. In a report out of Cincinnati, a thirteen-year major-league pitcher who refused to be named listed Sis and Hornsby, along with Dave Robertson of the New York Giants, who ended with a career .287 average, and Benny Kauff, the so-called Ty Cobb of the Federal League, a Giant in 1916 and .311 career hitter, as the four best players to come into organized baseball in the last five years. Calling Sisler the greatest all-around athlete he had ever seen, the pitcher declared that Hornsby surpassed them all with his ability to hit all pitches and his coolness under fire.[29] Already the kettle drums of rivalry were beating. Later in the year the famous sportswriter Grantland Rice, writing for *Collier's*, named George as his utility infielder on his all-star baseball team. In the same

27. *St. Louis Post-Dispatch,* August 27, 1916.
28. Quoted in Bob Broeg, "Gorgeous George . . . Browns' Batting Genius," *Sporting News,* September 13, 1969, 28.
29. *St. Louis Post-Dispatch,* August 13, 1916.

issue George joined Babe Ruth and Rogers Hornsby as one of Rice's "Ty Cobbs" of the future.[30]

The year 1916 was formative for George for other more personal reasons, some happy, some much less so. On October 21 he married his Michigan sweetheart, Kathleen Charlotte Holznagle. A one-thousand-dollar wedding present—a hefty sum at the time, equivalent to more than fifteen thousand dollars today—from Kathleen's florist father sent the couple on a honeymoon to Estes Park, Colorado, with a stay at the Stanley Hotel. When they returned, the newlyweds took an apartment at 821 Belt Avenue on St. Louis's west side.

The year, however, ended on a somber note for George and his new bride. On December 20, less than two months after his marriage, George's father, Cassius, died of a ruptured blood vessel at age sixty-two. Reportedly in good health to the end, in the last year of his life Cassius had moved with Mary from Manchester to Barberton so he could work at the Pittsburgh Valve and Fittings plant in that city. The father who so valued education that he stood with his son against one of baseball's most powerful owners was quietly buried in an unmarked grave in the Glendale Cemetery in Akron, not far from the grave of eldest son, Efbert.

Two weeks later, George's year of solidification and change came to an end. The coming years would see increased maturity for the young ballplayer, as he became a pillar of strength for his struggling team. However, those same years would see sadness and turmoil of a different kind in a world in the midst of a devastating war.

30. Grantland Rice, "The All-Star Baseball Team," 15; Rice, "Ty Cobbs of the Future Chosen by Grantland Rice," 12.

5

War Clouds

Fresh from a winning season and an encouraging fifth-place finish for a team unaccustomed to even that dubious distinction, the Browns of 1917 entered spring training in an optimistic mood. But before the buds were even on the trees, Phil Ball and Branch Rickey were at it again. This time Rickey provoked the dispute. His strong feelings for protégé George Sisler were clearly outweighed by his hatred for the gluttonous Ball. Over the winter, word leaked to Ball that Rickey was leaving his club to assume the presidency of the St. Louis Cardinals, a team in transition between owners. When Ball learned of this in February, he immediately filed and obtained a temporary restraining order, preventing Rickey from making the move. Ball, who was actually happy to see Rickey go, successfully argued that his employee was under contract. It was the principle involved, Ball told close associates. A contract is a contract. A judge agreed, and the case was set in St. Louis in April for a hearing to determine whether a permanent injunction was in order.

On April 5, one day before the hearing on Ball's request for a permanent injunction, the parties reached an agreement in which Ball was able to have his cake and eat it, too. By the terms of the agreement, Rickey was enjoined from jumping to the Cardinals' front office for twenty-four hours, at which time he was released from any further contractual obligations to the Browns. Ball quickly replaced Rickey, naming Bob Quinn as business manager for the Browns. Quinn was familiar with George Sisler, having purchased his contract while running the minor-league franchise in Columbus, Ohio.

If 1917 was a successful year for Ball administratively, it was not a success for his team on the playing field. As the war clouds engulfed the country, culminating with the declaration of war against Germany on April 6, the Browns and all of baseball faced the uncertainties accompanied by such a step. Of most immediate concern to the game was whether or not its players could finish the season in light of the probability of a national military draft. A secondary, but truly more fundamental, business concern was whether or not fans would continue to be interested enough in the sport to attend in sufficient numbers to keep the game profitable to its owners.

As the 1917 season started, these problems were essentially in the background. In his column in the *Post-Dispatch*, Sports Editor John Wray told readers it appeared that most teams could withstand conscription. The only Browns regular in danger of the draft, according to Wray, was George Sisler. Perhaps three other secondary players would join Sis, but that was it. The Cardinals stood to lose more: five regulars, including Rogers Hornsby—the most of any team in either league. In fact, Wray wrote, if conscription took all major-league players nineteen to twenty-five in age, the clubs would still be at 75 percent of their normal strength. Thus President Ban Johnson was not just barking when he said, "War or no war, strike or no strike, the American League will go through with its baseball schedule as planned."[1] It was felt that at the earliest, conscription would not hit baseball until October, after the season was complete. In retrospect, it might have been better for the Browns if it had not taken that long.

The Brownie team that greeted fans in the home opener against Chicago on April 11 was essentially the same as the 1916 edition. One main addition was Allen Sothoron, a pitcher with the Browns in 1914 and 1915, now back for 1917, a year in which he would lead the league in losses with nineteen. In a harsh preview of the team's hitting plight, the Browns were no-hit on April 14 by Chicago's Eddie Cicotte. At least by the end of the month their winning percentage was at .500 and they were in fourth place. George was off to a strong start, hitting .339.

It turned out the highlight of the season occurred for the Browns in early May against the White Sox. On May 5 Ernie Koob, George's college adversary, pitched the best game of his otherwise nondescript career in no-hitting the White Sox 1–0. His feat was followed one day later by Sis's

1. Quoted in *St. Louis Post-Dispatch*, April 13, 1917.

former sparring partner, Bob Groom. Pitching in the second game of a twin bill, Groom, who had already pitched two hitless innings in the first game, threw a no-hit 4–0 shutout. The excitement was short-lived. By the end of the month, the Browns were 15–23, thirteen games behind first-place Boston.

Most of the rest of the excitement for the Browns that year was generated by the bat of George Sisler. Among the league leaders in batting through-out the year, in mid-July he went four for eight in a seventeen-inning loss to the Yankees. That effort, along with several others, had George at .342, trailing only Ty Cobb among American League batters, and he was also leading the circuit in doubles. In mid-August, Sis began a hitting streak that worked itself up to twenty-six games. Perhaps the impetus for the streak was the birth on August 1, 1917, of George and Kathleen's first son, George Harold Sisler, Jr. Moreover, from June 30 to September 4, George Sr. hit in every game he played except for three.

If only George's team had fared as well. By the end of July, the squad was in last place with a six-game losing streak that soon swelled to eight. The *Post-Dispatch* reported that Manager Fielder Jones was dealing with both stomach trouble and Browns trouble. While the stomach disorder was not serious, the problem with the Browns "is in its most acute stage and will become chronic if not relieved soon."[2]

If Jones's stomach ached for the Browns, his frustrations did not carry over to his star attraction. In defending his infield to local writers, Jones told them that in George he had "not only the best hitting first baseman in the game" but also, despite Sisler's again leading the league in first base errors, "the best fielding first sacker living." Why? "Sisler is breaking up sacrifices and making forceouts at second base."[3] A few weeks later, Jones, already looking ahead to 1918, was singing George's praises again, saying that despite his team's miserable performance, he had not abandoned hope because the Browns had George Sisler. Calling him "the greatest young ball player I ever saw," Jones insisted George would keep improv-ing "because he's using his head."[4] Next year, according to Jones, his team would be better. They needed to be. The team finished the 1917 season with a league-low .246 batting average and a record of 57–97, which put them in seventh place.

Of course there was much more than baseball going on as the summer of 1917 wore down. After a rainout in early August, the team stayed at

2. Ibid., July 23, 1917.
3. Quoted in ibid., July 30, 1917.
4. Quoted in ibid., August 17, 1917.

the stadium to practice military drills in anticipation of a contest sponsored by the American League with a five-hundred-dollar prize at stake. On August 25 the Browns showed their fans that bad baseball does not equal bad marching, as with bats on shoulders they bested the Boston Red Sox in a marching contest before twelve hundred soldiers admitted free to Sportsman's Park as guests of the club. The park was decorated in the national colors, and two bands performed. The game itself was less than hoped for, with the Red Sox prevailing 3–2. As the marching tournament continued, the Browns eventually came away with the top prize, winning out over Cleveland.

Any chance of a calm denouement to the disappointing season ended early in September. Brownie players Bert Shotton, Johnny Lavan, and Del Pratt, down fifty runs batted in from 1916, staged a mini-revolt, refusing to play for the Browns because of statements attributed to owner Phil Ball that they were "laying down" on the job.[5] The gossip around the league credited the team's poor season performance to ill feelings on the part of several players about Ball's treatment of Branch Rickey. However, according to John Wray of the *Post-Dispatch*, one look at the play of George Sisler should have dispelled that notion. At any rate, Ball denied the comment, saying he was misquoted, and Pratt and Lavan continued to perform for the Browns, only to turn around and separately sue Ball several days later for defamation, each asking twenty-five thousand dollars in actual damages and another twenty-five thousand in punitive damages.

Despite the lawsuit, the players continued to perform amid speculation they would have been long gone but for anticipated player shortages due to the war. War or no war, Pratt was peddled to the Yankees four months later, and Lavan as well as Shotton, who protested but did not sue, were playing for the Washington Senators by 1918. Fielder Jones, on shaky ground himself, was permitted to return. He repeatedly predicted that with solid pitching the Browns would be a much better club in 1918.

In a personal vein, 1917 was a coming-out party for George. In the field, despite again leading the league in errors, his sparkling play in tracking down balls other first basemen could not reach and in turning double plays was gaining more and more respect. At the plate he trailed only Ty Cobb in the American League batting race, ending the season at .352, in a virtual tie with Tris Speaker of the Cleveland club, now called the Indians. Cobb continued his domination of the game, batting .383 and stealing 55 bases. Comparing statistics with his Browns teammates, George led the team in twelve of twenty hitting categories. He played in 135 of the team's

5. Ibid., September 6, 1917.

154 games, all but two at first base. His two games as a left-handed second baseman surely must have raised some eyebrows. The fact he did not pitch a game during the entire season probably raised a few more.

At the end of the regular season a sore wrist cost him playing time and also limited his action as the Browns and Cardinals waged their annual fall series while catching newspaper accounts of a World Series battle waged by the White Sox and the New York Giants. Despite his injury and the meaninglessness of the series with the Cardinals, George still had enough steam to raise a rare fuss and receive the hook over an umpire's failure to call a balk. Still, when the dust settled, the Cardinals had defeated the Browns four games to two, the same count by which the White Sox outdistanced the Giants.

George and Rogers Hornsby, fresh off his team's fine third-place finish and an excellent .327 season at the plate, joined pitchers Walter Johnson, Grover Cleveland Alexander, and other stars a few weeks later on a tour through the middle of the country. Despite the war, the games drew well and the players pocketed some extra cash. Such teams of traveling professionals, popularly known as "barnstormers," served a valid purpose. They delivered baseball to areas of the country otherwise shut out for any number of reasons, primarily size, location, or both. These logistical shortcomings did not hinder a rabid and growing enthusiasm for the sport. The stopovers were much anticipated in even the most remote areas. Even though the games were always just an exhibition, featuring rosters sprinkled with but a handful of all-stars, a World Series atmosphere prevailed. "Houses were decorated; automobiles carried American flags; shops closed; schools often declared a half-holiday and had the student band lead a player parade from the station through the town, where fans filled the streets and shook hands with the heroes."[6]

As the Browns prepared to face a second war-clouded season, there was cause for concern on the financial front. In 1916 the team drew some 335,000 fans with their fifth-place finish. That figure was sixth out of the eight league teams. The 1917 attendance was significantly down at 210,000 (seventh out of eight).

Perhaps there was more on people's minds in St. Louis that summer than just baseball, or even the war. For some time the growing industrial bases in large northern cities had been attracting black laborers from the South. East St. Louis, immediately across the Mississippi River in Illinois, was no exception. Its large industrial complex served as a magnet for this migration. The city's industrial giants, lured to the area by tax breaks from

6. Seymour, *Baseball: The Golden Age*, 80.

corrupt politicians, took advantage of the abundant labor pool by paying their workforce barely half the prevailing wage in the region.

By midsummer of 1917 workers at the gigantic Aluminum Ore Company had been out on strike for several weeks to protest wage disparities. The plant, however, was able to continue operations by importing black laborers. By late June this city of teeming smokestacks, crammed full of hard-edged laborers of both races, was like a pile of dry leaves waiting for a match. On July 2, for reasons never determined, someone or something lit that match, igniting a series of disturbances that escalated into the bloodiest race riot of the era. Exactly how many actually perished or were injured is unknown. The official estimate is thirty-nine blacks and eight whites killed, hundreds injured, and three hundred homes destroyed by fire. The toll the riot exacted in racial relations in the region will never be fully appreciated, nor will its effect on the interest in baseball in a ballpark where blacks and whites were not permitted to sit together.

Still, while the war and the race riot certainly had some effect on attendance, overall the Browns' main problem was the brand of baseball it played. Attendance throughout the majors, however, was down approximately six hundred thousand from the previous year, and many a team owner wore a furrowed brow.

If 1917 was a tight year financially for organized baseball, the difficulties were a mere preview for 1918. As war raged on across the sea, at home fans stayed away from the ballparks in droves, as the saying goes. Attendance in the American League alone shrank from 2,855,000 to 1,705,000, a figure more than 50 percent lower than in pre-war 1916. Despite fielding a better product, Phil Ball's Browns drew only 122,076 fans in what proved to be a war-shortened season.

As is most often the case in every baseball town, the Browns in early season were an optimistic bunch. The team had added Joe Gedeon, a second baseman formerly with the Yankees; Ken Williams, a twenty-seven-year-old rookie outfielder of great promise; and Urban Shocker, a twenty-five-year-old right-handed spitballer, also from the Yankees, who would bear significant fruit in the future. In addition, 1918 saw the return and emergence of Jack Tobin, an outfielder obtained from the Federal League who had not played for the Browns in 1917. One baseball-related battle was resolved in early April when Phil Ball settled the defamation case brought against him by Pratt and Lavan for fifty-four hundred dollars.

As it turned out, the military draft was enacted during the off-season by passage of the Selective Service Act. Ken Williams played in only two games before being taken. New addition Gedeon, who came to the club along with catcher Les Nunamaker, third baseman Fritz Maisel, pitcher Nick Cullop, and Shocker, would hit only .213. Shocker finished 6–5 with a 1.81 earned run average in spot duty. To get them, the Browns had given up forty-two-year-old veteran pitcher Eddie Plank, who ended up quitting; the lawsuit-toting Del Pratt; plus fifteen thousand dollars. Since Nunamaker and Maisel had mediocre years and Cullop was not heard from again, the trade seemed insignificant. Tobin, however, hit a solid .277 and played well in the outfield.

Williams, Shocker, Nunamaker, and shortstop Walter Gerber were assigned as Class 1, placing them at the top of the draft eligibility list. Sisler, who had been mentioned the previous year as a prime candidate for the draft, and most of the other Browns players were Class 4, seemingly far down the list of potential conscripts.

The 1918 season started on a high note with a 6–1 victory over the defending World Champion White Sox. Sis was two for five, and Grover Lowdermilk had a strong pitching performance. By the end of the month, however, beset by injuries and illness, including catcher Hank Severeid's pneumonia, the club was 3–6 and in sixth place, four games behind the Red Sox.

Although making more and more strong plays in the field, including a spectacular stop and throw for a game-turning double play against Cleveland on May 4, George was off to a slow start at the plate. Then in late April and early May, he hit his stride, including an eleven-game hitting streak. Riding his suddenly hot bat and that of Jack Tobin, the Browns won six straight games and moved into third place by May 25. George was now fourth in the league in batting at .361. Another developing facet of his game was base stealing; he led the league with 13.

Then more uncertainty struck the team. Shocker was called to report to the service, and then placed on hold. On May 23 the government issued a "work or fight" order, giving baseball players until July 1 to find "essential" work in aid of the war machine or become eligible for the draft. Baseball was considered a nonessential employment. Film acting was considered essential, thus making film actors exempt. As it played out, many ballplayers went to work for shipyards or found jobs manufacturing ammunition or steel. These were considered essential endeavors. The players then joined their plants' semi-pro teams and continued playing baseball, albeit in a much different atmosphere. One of the first players to be challenged by the government to "work or fight" was Rogers Hornsby.[7] It turned out, however, that neither Hornsby nor anyone else went the

7. Charles C. Alexander, *Rogers Hornsby: A Biography*, 45–46.

proposed route. The War Department soon granted baseball players a dispensation, postponing their service until after the season, including the World Series.

One of the strangest occurrences in George's career developed during the second week in June. With the Browns holding a sizable lead over the Washington Nationals at Sportsman's Park, the team gave up six runs in the ninth inning, losing 7–6. After the game, Fielder Jones slowly unsuited, showered, dressed in street clothes, and left the ballpark. On his way out Jones, who had been coaxed back to managing and was never a particularly enthusiastic participant, encountered Otto Stifel, the Browns' vice-president. According to Stifel, Jones said "good-bye." Reading more into the remark than a simple good-bye, Stifel asked Jones what he meant. "I'm through. This was too much. I've now seen everything."[8] With that, Jones quit.

Despite their long relationship through the Federal League as well as with the Browns, Phil Ball made no attempt to talk Jones into returning. At the time, the team was 23–24 and in fifth place, seven games behind the first-place Red Sox. Though he was one of baseball's best-paid managers, Jones apparently was working without a contract. At the start of the 1918 season he agreed to a reduction in salary from fifteen thousand to twelve thousand dollars due to the effect of the war on baseball's finances. Perhaps in view of his team's disappointing play, he decided the smaller paycheck was just not worth the aggravation.

The day after confronting Stifel, Jones returned to the locker room at noon, just prior to that afternoon's game, to personally tell team members about his decision. Then he directed shortstop/third baseman Jimmy Austin, the son of a Welsh shipbuilder, to run the team on an interim basis. An inconsistent hitter, Austin, who had a reputation as a comedian and a trickster, was a top notch infielder. He had previously served as the Browns' "Sunday Manager" while Branch Rickey kept his early promise to his mother never to play or manage on Sundays. Austin therefore was a natural choice to step into the void.

The players, however, did not believe what they had just heard. Reality set in when Jones walked from the clubhouse. Several of the players followed, trying to get him to change his mind. Reaching the street, he boarded a streetcar, turning to wave to the players as they rushed down the street after him.[9]

8. Stifel quoting Jones in Bob Burnes, "The St. Louis Browns," April 1951, 61.
9. *St. Louis Post-Dispatch,* June 14, 1918.

Sisler admired Fielder Jones. He and several others publicly expressed their disappointment at his abrupt departure. George's admiration for his manager was returned years later when Jones called him the greatest ball-player of all time at any position.[10]

Although Fielder Jones walked away from a bad situation, the remaining Browns could not. Under Jimmy Austin's auspices they were 8–11 for an overall record of 31–35. They trailed the league-leading Red Sox by just seven games, but had now fallen to sixth place.

Today, changing managers in midseason is a fairly routine tactic. In 1918 it was quite uncommon. Caught off guard, Ball began a search. By the end of June, he and his Browns had a new manager in Jimmy Burke, one of Fielder Jones's coaches. "Sunset Jimmy," as he was sometimes called, took the job under some duress: "[I]f I didn't, he [Ball] would get an outsider."[11] The St. Louis native had played the game for the Cardinals as a light-hitting infielder from 1903 to 1905 and in fact managed that team during his last season with them.

When Burke took over the Browns, Sis was on the bench with a wrenched knee. He was batting .353 at the time. While he was out, the Browns went 7–5. When he returned his bat cooled considerably, as did his team. By the end of July, he had hit only .149 in his previous twelve games and the Browns were 41–52, some fifteen games behind the Red Sox, essentially out of the race. All the war talk may have had something to do with their lackluster play, for in August there was talk of ending the season on September 1. Perhaps an early ending would be best as organized baseball in general and the Browns in particular continued to play before dwindling crowds. Eleven of the sixteen major-league owners in fact favored this move.

As the season progressed, new manager Burke made few changes, merely tinkering here and there. Walter Gerber, the regular shortstop under Fielder Jones, lost his job to Jimmy Austin. Fritz Maisel took Austin's third-base post. George's bat finally did show some spark with a triple and homer in an early August loss to the Red Sox and a five-for-five day in a win against the Yankees in New York on August 3. In addition, he continued to lead the league in stolen bases. Sis's batting spark seemed to awaken the Browns, but just as the picture brightened, the expected was announced. The 1918 season would officially end on Labor Day weekend. As a result, each of the Browns received ten-day release notices on August

10. Harry Grayson, *They Played the Game: The Story of Baseball Greats*, 137.
11. Quoted in *St. Louis Post-Dispatch*, June 28, 1918.

22, advising their salaries would end on September 1. The rest of the season in due course was a shambles. George now found himself pitching several unsuccessful innings on August 27 as the starter in the second game of a doubleheader versus the Yankees; he blew a four-run lead and was yanked after the seventh inning. After the game a number of the players who lived closer to New York than St. Louis left the club, feeling it was senseless to return to finish out the season. The cost of train travel back to the East after the final home stand in St. Louis would be too painful.

The financial hardship sustained by the Browns players was magnified for its owner. Ball's club was paid only $356 total for the three late August games in New York. All told, the carfare for the team during its last eastern swing cost more than the Browns took in for their appearances in Washington, Boston, Philadelphia, and New York. No wonder the early climax to the season was met with more relief than tears by Ball and the other owners.

Hearing they might be witnessing the last baseball played in St. Louis for quite some time, eight thousand fans showed up for a doubleheader with the Tigers on September 1. Late in the second game Sis looked to the mound and saw his hitting rival, Ty Cobb. With the Tigers trailing the Browns in the seventh inning, Detroit manager Hughie Jennings sent in his hitting star Cobb to throw a few. Ironically, Sis was the first batter up. George let the first pitch go by and then swung and missed on the second. On the next pitch, he slapped a double past third base. As he slid into second, Cobb turned toward him and doffed his cap. George later scored, but Cobb was more successful in the eighth inning, shutting the door on further runs. In the ninth, with dramatic flare, Jimmy Burke sent Sisler out to pitch. He shut the Tigers down for a 6–2 win, but some of the drama was lost because Cobb did not get a turn at bat. The Tigers' flash got the last laugh, however, with six hits in nine at bats in the two games.

Adding one more quirk to an already strange year, the Cleveland Indians misunderstood that the season ran through games to be played on Labor Day, September 2. When they found out they were scheduled to end the season with a doubleheader in St. Louis, they refused to make the trip, forfeiting the two games. The "gift" wins aided the Browns to a fifth-place finish at 58–64, just a game and a half behind the fourth-place Yankees.

Financially the season was a wreck for the Browns. Their season attendance of 122,000 stood last in the American League. The *Post-Dispatch* reported that in 1916 the club had made twenty-five thousand dollars, but in 1917 it lost forty-two thousand. In 1918 they would "be lucky to get by as well as that."[12] Unfortunately, the fifth-place finish kept the Browns from sharing in the first World Series "pool," which was divided by the four first-division finishers. The series between the Red Sox and the Cubs was won by the Sox in six games. Little did Red Sox fans realize that their team had won its last world championship of the twentieth century.

Although it was clear baseball club owners such as Phil Ball were suffering serious financial reversals, a number of the players voiced their displeasure at the hit they were taking in their own pocketbooks due to the shortened season. Former Brown Burt Shotton indicated he planned to file a lawsuit against Clark Griffith, the Washington Nationals owner. Of course, the owners' position was based on the government order that players find an "essential occupation" or face induction into the military. Since, the argument went, the players could not offer further services, their contracts were no longer enforceable.

Whatever the feelings about their treatment, be it at the hands of the owners or the government, the players needed to find their place in the war effort. Many left St. Louis in silence about their plans. One Browns player who voiced his plan was catcher Hank Severeid, who told the local press he planned to enlist in the Tank Corps.

While George considered his options, he had an opportunity to review his season. For the year he had batted .341 in 114 games, finishing behind only the ever-present Ty Cobb at .382 and George Burns of Philadelphia at .352. In a category previously dominated by the aging Cobb, George led the league in stolen bases with 45. In all, he led the Browns in nine hitting categories. Defensively, playing at first base in all but two games, he made 13 errors, far fewer than in previous years, and had 95 assists, with a fielding percentage of .990. For the first time Babe Ruth, still with the Boston Red Sox and, in a move mirroring Sisler's, spending more time in the batter's box with each succeeding year, appeared among league leaders in hitting categories, leading the league in slugging percentage and tying former Brown Clarence "Tilly" Walker of the Philadelphia Athletics for the league lead in home runs with 11.

Following the season George began working at the Lebanon steel plant, joining a growing number of ballplayers finding "essential" wartime work. Soon he was headed in an entirely new direction. He joined the army. The Sislers gave up their apartment in St. Louis and stored the furniture. Kathleen and young George returned to Detroit. Through the auspices of Major Branch Rickey, George was commissioned a second lieutenant in Rickey's

12. Ibid., September 2, 1918.

Chemical Warfare Service and assigned to duty at Camp Humphreys in Virginia. While in training he participated in an athletic meet at Camp Kenrick, New Jersey, winning the one-hundred-yard dash as well as contests for punting for distance, drop kicking for accuracy and distance, and, of course, throwing a baseball for distance.

Other baseball figures already in the Chemical Warfare Service, besides Rickey, included Ty Cobb, the great Giants pitcher Christy Mathewson, who was now the Cincinnati Reds manager, and Perry Haughton, the president of the Boston Braves. This group, in fact, had already been sent to France for training and reassigned to various divisions. The training experience proved tragic for Mathewson, who was exposed to the deadly gas the CSW was utilizing. That the exposure had something to do with his death from tuberculosis at age forty-five was seriously considered, but never determined.

George, too, was designated for overseas duty. He was just about to leave when, at 11 a.m. on November 11, 1918, what later became known as World War I ended with an armistice. The steady influx of fresh, well-armed American troops had done the trick. George and the other sports figures were discharged shortly thereafter. The world would try its best to, as Warren Harding would soon put it, "return to normalcy." For Americans, that included the return of baseball.

6

The Veteran

By the spring of 1919, George Sisler was fully prepared to return to baseball a seasoned veteran. If he was at all tired of the yearly grind, the short dose of military activity served as a cure-all shared by many of his major-league compatriots. Thankfully, he and his small family were not among the seven hundred thousand Americans who succumbed to the great influenza epidemic of the winter of 1918–1919.

For a major-league ballplayer, especially a happily married one, time spent on the road going from city to city was a job hazard. In 1918, for example, the Browns' road journeys included several trips requiring absences of longer than twenty days. At one point the grueling schedule found the team playing in unfriendly confines twenty-five days in a row. The notion that theirs was a hard life, however, flew in the face of the public perception of major leaguers as "the most pampered, best cared for and conditioned live stock in the world."[1] The truth actually fell somewhere in the middle.

A typical road trip might involve stops for contests in three or perhaps even four different cities in a week. After a game both teams would shower. This seemingly innocuous task was often accomplished, according to no less an authority than Ty Cobb, in "primitive quarters," where players "waited in line for the single shower to be vacated and dressed next day

---

1. Hugh S. Fullerton, "Between Games," 322.

in damp uniforms" which were "jammed into containers after a game in their natural sweat-soaked state," having seldom seen a laundry.[2]

After their shower, the home team's players headed for their apartment or home, the roadies to their hotel. These were the days of the streetcar and the occasional taxi. In some venues there were subways. In most cities there were no buses to take the players to and from the ballpark, so four or five players would share a taxi. In New York with its fine subway system, Sisler and his teammates took the "E" to the Polo Grounds. On "getaway day," once the series was complete and the visitors ready to move on to their next destination, the equipment would be packed for the players while they showered, and then the team would head to the train station by whatever conveyance was available.

Once aboard the train, the players made the trek to the dining car for a meal, invariably followed by at least one table of poker "with a low limit imposed by the manager, who fears that the loss of any considerable sum of money will cause ill feeling."[3] A few of the more cerebral sought out a game of chess or bridge. Others just relaxed.

On overnight train trips when the players slept in Pullman cars, there was a caste system of sorts. The regulars got the lower berths, with bench types relegated to the uppers. Often train schedules caused teams to arrive in town in the wee hours of the morning. According to Hugh Fullerton, the syndicated Chicago sportswriter, "(A) five-o'clock call in a sleeping car after a hard, hot night ride is a fair test of a man's good nature."[4] There is little question that after a year or so, these masters of the ball diamond were masters of the road as well, packing efficiently and transporting themselves to and from ballparks and train stations like true professionals.

Hotel stays were not all that bad. Upon arrival at the new destination, the traveler's quality of life improved considerably. Even teams at the low end of the financial scale, like the Browns, were able to stay at "good" hotels. Some were on the American plan, with meals included. Sis's favorite hotel was the Aldine Hotel, an American-plan hotel in Philadelphia. The meals there were "simply terrific" with five or six courses and "real good" breakfasts: "It was a delight to stay there."[5] When the team stayed at a hotel under the European plan, the players were provided four dollars per day for meal money. This was an ample stake, providing sufficient funds for two "good" meals plus lunch. A few players abused the system, however, starving themselves in order to save any leftover

2. Ty Cobb, with Al Stump, *My Life in Baseball*, 56.
3. Fullerton, "Between Games," 326.
4. Ibid., 323–24.
5. Sisler Memoirs, 6–7.

meal money for themselves. If caught, they were required to sign checks for their meals.

Sisler never had a weight problem. For those who did, the system was fraught with danger. The hotel food was just too good for these gluttonous types, and way too easy to come by. Once identified, frequently by an expanding waistline, these poor souls would be required to eat in the dining room at one long table under the watchful eye of their manager. After dinner the players, who often were assigned at least one roommate, were on their own, usually subject to a curfew of midnight, if not before. One of the players' favorite pastimes, other than cards, was lobby-sitting. Many a night was filled for a group gathered around a sofa or a pair of comfortable chairs, with baseball as the main, if not only, topic of conversation. Some might prefer more exciting pursuits, such as a venture to one or more of the local "clubs," much to the chagrin of club management.

During daylight hours before games, veteran players such as George passed time by reading, playing more cards, writing letters, or just sleeping or eating. Rookies on their first trip to a city might spend a while sightseeing, but after a few visits to the same towns they too fell into patterns similar to the veterans. By then much of the glamour of the "road" had worn thin. Most, however, would acknowledge there were far worse ways to make a living. In fact, they would be the first to admit they were a "special breed of men following a special way of life."[6]

When the Browns were in town, of course, the players made their own living provisions. During home stands players were required to report to the park for a morning practice. For this reason alone Sis and others often chose living quarters fairly close to the ballpark. As such they were frequently seen in and around the area. Because of their higher visibility, baseball historian Harold Seymour was left with a sense of the deeper emotional attachments and less inhibited loyalties of fans of those times. Parks were smaller and more intimate. Fans felt closer to the teams and the players. Dyed-in-the-wool regulars knew the performers by sight.[7] This was unlike later years when players often commuted to the park from greater distances and only the major stars were immediately recognizable to the average fan.

In contrast to the players' personal abodes, home in the sports sense for a St. Louis Brown meant Sportsman's Park. The park, in northwest St. Louis on the block bounded by Dodier Street, Grand Boulevard, Sullivan Avenue, and Spring Avenue, was expanded in 1909 by Robert Hedges

6. Seymour, *Baseball: The Golden Age*, 75.
7. Ibid., 76.

from a seating capacity of eight thousand to eighteen thousand. This was done by adding a second deck from first base to third. The overall setup created a good spectators' park with many seats close to the action. Not all those good seats were available to everyone, however. St. Louis, the southernmost major-league city at the time, was the last in the major leagues to abolish segregated seating. Until 1944 blacks were restricted to the bleachers and the pavilion, a single-deck structure down the right field line.

Sportsman's Park, which was named by local sportswriter Al Spink, the eventual owner of the St. Louis–based national baseball newspaper the *Sporting News,* was a neighborhood ballpark in the spirit of Chicago's Wrigley Field. Grand Avenue was a busy place in the years between 1910 and 1930, the heyday of the ballpark. Visiting players and managers stayed at nearby hotels, eating and shopping at restaurants sprinkled throughout the area. A visit to Sportsman's Park was an adventure. There was no real parking around the stadium. Neighbors often turned their lawns into parking lots in order to make a little extra cash. Most fans did not even bother to drive to the park, instead spending the nickel it took to ride the Grand Avenue streetcar.

For most of Sis's St. Louis playing days, the park's dimensions were 353 feet down the left field line, 430 to dead center, and 320 feet down the right field line. A punch, push, and slash hitter who could bunt or just leg out hits, such as George, had few complaints. George could also pull the ball in this park with enough power to hit his share of home runs.

An established star in 1919, Sisler was now accorded the accoutrements of that exalted perch by getting an occasional day off during spring training in San Antonio. The extra rest proved a detriment for a player such as George who was accustomed to giving his all every day. Once his team returned to St. Louis to make final preparations for the start of the regular season, George was out-hit in the Cards-Browns series by Rogers Hornsby .409 to .304, though the Browns were victorious in four of the six games. Sisler's batting took a turn for the worse as regular-season play began. By the end of April, he was bottoming out at .222, having hit into a number of double plays. By mid-May the team was responding in kind, resting in last place.

The slow start was especially discouraging given the return from service of the promising power-hitting outfielder Ken Williams and the addition of a slick-fielding, fair-hitting infielder named Herman Bronkie, obtained from Indianapolis of the American Association. As it turned out, the pair played well but in secondary roles. The big surprise was the emergence of Baby Doll Jacobson into a .323 hitter and the solidification of Jack Tobin (.327) as a major outfield contributor.

Despite his uncharacteristic weak start, Sis continued to impress in the field. During an early road trip to Washington, he robbed veteran outfielder Clyde "Deer Foot" Milan of a hit on a play that the American League's top base stealer in 1912 never forgot. The score was knotted at one when the Nationals came to bat in the eighth. There was already one down and one on base when Milan, a lefty, stepped to the plate and proceeded to smack a liner between first and second. It looked like a clean hit because Bronkie, the Browns' second baseman that day, was not at his best moving to his left, and Sis was holding the base runner on first.

"Sisler raced all the way over and was reaching for the ball when it took a bad hop and bounced off his glove and into the air," Milan said. Milan watched in astonishment as Sis raced back to the bag. The ball had caromed to Bronkie, who caught it in midair and flipped it to Sisler in time to nail the swift "Deer Foot" by a short step. George got an unusual assist and a putout on a play in "which he didn't have any right in the world to get his hands on the ball in the first place." When Sisler was on the prowl, "it was like having an extra infielder between first and second."[8]

Then in mid-May, perhaps inspired by great fielding plays like the one described by Milan, Sis caught fire. Strong pitching by Carl Weilman and Urban Shocker, combined with timely hitting by George, ignited a five-game winning streak. Sisler's average finally approached .300. Shocker returned from the military earlier in the month and made his initial appearance of the year on May 11. After a rocky start in which he was knocked out early, Shocker righted himself for a shutout win over Philadelphia on May 15 and another over the Nationals on May 21. George drove home the only run the Browns got in that one. The short winning streak enabled the Browns to climb into fifth place.

On May 26 George stole home in the ninth inning against the Yankees to give his team a 2–1 win, leaving them a mere eight percentage points out of third. In the midst of an eleven-game hitting streak, he had raised his batting average to .330. According to an enthusiastic L. C. Davis in his "Knockout Browns,"

> George Sisler's famous batting eye
> Is working over time,
> And George is just the sort of guy
> Who'll help the boys to climb.[9]

On May 28, the Browns, winners of eleven of their last twelve, were sniffing the rarefied air of third place for the first time in many years. It

8. Smith, *Baseball's Famous First Basemen*, 141.
9. *St. Louis Post-Dispatch*, May 27, 1919.

was to be a relatively short stay, but they did not retreat quietly. On June 3, they split a double bill in Cleveland. George had a big day, even for him, driving in seven runs in the two games with a single, two doubles, and two home runs. The first homer came in the fifth inning of the opener and cleared the right field wall. In an era when many home runs were of the inside-the-park variety, this was the first drive to clear the Indians' right field wall all year. The unusual show of Sisler power continued on June 22, with a home run that cleared the right field wall in a win over Philadelphia. Urban Shocker was the pitching beneficiary.

Then on Friday, June 13, bad luck found Sisler when a batting practice pitch hit him in the right eye. Despite the impact, he insisted on playing. In fact, he contributed a couple of base knocks to a Browns' victory. At the time, the team was in fourth, three behind Cleveland in the loss column. George stood fifth in the league in batting, with a .342 average. The next day George's eye was almost swollen shut. As a result, he was not available when his mates met the Yankees in New York. The Browns lost. The next day he sat again. This time, however, his team got a 1–0 pitching gem from Urban Shocker in front of twenty-four thousand fans.

By the time the team reached Boston, George's eye was much less swollen. On June 19 he played, making a spectacular leaping catch of a line drive that "would have been a double against any other first sacker in either league," as "(w)ithout exaggeration he must have gone up four feet in a straight ascension."[10] The next day the Browns pulled off a rare around-the-horn triple play with Jimmy Austin at third flipping to Joe Gedeon at second, then on to Sis at first.

On July 4 fans in attendance at a Browns doubleheader were treated to a rare sight. George, who usually was "as ferocious as a Belgian hare," whatever that is, and whose strongest language was "Jiminy crickets," was ejected by the umpire for protesting a call. "I never said a word," Sis told the press after the game. "I was just about to add something to what the other fellows had said when Moriarty [the umpire] put me out." The *Post-Dispatch* decided, tongue-in-cheek, that Sis had been removed for "thinking."[11]

In mid-July George added to his growing legend as a remarkable fielding first baseman by ranging far afield to snag a grounder and in the same motion scoop the ball, never taking it out of his gloved hand, to the pitcher in time for the out. That play, along with others, helped the Browns to nineteen wins in their first thirty in Sportsman's Park. On July 10 George

10. Ibid., June 19, 1919.
11. Quoted in ibid., July 5, 1919.

brought ten thousand hometown fans to their feet when he stood at third and noticed a slow windup by pitcher Sam Jones of the Nationals. As soon as he saw it, he tore for home, reaching the plate before the throw for his second steal of home that season. The third steal of home came less than two weeks later, helping the Browns and pitcher Dave Davenport to a win over the White Sox.

More surprising than George's pilfering of home plate was the Browns' increasing win total. By the first week in August, their record stood 47–40, one game behind the Yankees and only seven behind first-place Chicago. George's slow start was now ancient history; the league's leading batter in average and total bases, as well as in stolen bases, was none other than George Sisler. By August 8 he was on a sixteen-game hitting streak. Nonetheless, the bigger news in St. Louis was the continuing emergence of the Baby Doll. When outfielder Johnny Tobin went down with an injury, the longtime "prospect" went on a tear, hitting safely in thirteen games.

By mid-August, however, the Browns had returned to earth, resting in the more accustomed fifth place in a tightly banded group, but still only seven behind first-place Chicago. Then the team suffered a blow. Carl Weilman, the team's star left-hander and one-third of the Browns' "big three" pitching staff along with Shocker and Allen Sothoron, came down with a stomach ailment. A courageous performer playing with only one kidney, Weilman had compiled a 10–6 record with a 2.06 earned run average, at one point winning five in a row. Unfortunately for him and the still contending Browns, he did not pitch another game in 1919. He did return for one more season, but was not nearly as effective.

An August visit from the Red Sox brought to town the American League's new hitting sensation, Babe Ruth. The former pitching ace had finally hit himself into an everyday position in the outfield and was well on his way to a then unheard of twenty-nine home run season. While in St. Louis he proceeded to fortify his emerging bellicose image by engaging in a verbal tennis match with several Browns pitchers, including Urban Shocker and Davey Davenport, as well as most of the Browns fans in the left field pavilion. At one point, "The Babe," as he was now generally known, tapped his nose expressively as the crowd roared its disapproval; they later cheered when Ruth fanned "the air without even a healthy foul."[12]

The series with the Yankees proved a damaging one for the Browns as the two teams sparred for fourth place, with the Yankees exiting Sportsman's Park the victors. In the last game Sis and pitcher Carl Mays, a recent

12. Ibid., August 19, 1919.

controversial late-season acquisition by the Yankees from the Red Sox in a dispute that involved the entire league and the court system, engaged in an open confrontation when George accused Mays of illegally doctoring the ball. The players had to be separated, but the umpire sided with George and three balls were removed. Since the spitter was still allowed, Mays must have been performing some serious alterations. No matter, the Yankees won the contest and the first-division spot.

A week later, it was no coincidence that the *Post-Dispatch*'s John E. Wray revealed the response his paper received from American League President Ban Johnson to a letter asking in part whether the league was contemplating restrictions on pitchers who used the spitball. In a preview of things to come, Johnson indicated he planned to appoint a committee to review the matter. The letter was dated August 22, two days after the Mays/Sisler incident, and gave little hope of controlling the likes of Carl Mays. "I am inclined to believe no great restriction will be placed upon the spit ball pitchers of the present day," Johnson told Wray. Penalties for use of the pitcher's best friend would be reserved for "those who drift into the two major leagues from now on."[13]

The controversy with the Yankees seemed to revitalize the Browns, however. They won their next two outings and regained fourth place when an injured Sisler, gimpy right leg and all, got a pinch-hit single to start a winning rally. The base hit proved cathartic, and less than two weeks later George was in full swing, leading his team to a doubleheader win over the third-place Tigers with five hits, including another home run. In September, after ending the Indians' pennant hopes with still another home run, Sis strained his back while striking out in Detroit and missed several games. He was back by the middle of the month to single, double, and triple off his favorite pitcher, Walter Johnson. It did little good as the Browns lost, further solidifying their hold on fifth place. They ended the season at 67–72, in fifth place in a virtual tie with Boston and twelve games behind fourth-place Detroit, who had in turn fallen behind a Yankee team fortified by its late acquisitions. The Browns trailed pennant-winning Chicago by twenty-nine games in the loss column. The powerhouse White

---

13. Letter from Johnson to Wray, quoted in ibid., August 31, 1919. The letter also addressed the late-season sale of Carl Mays to the Yankees. At issue was the stocking of players for pennant contenders. The Mays trade angered team owners who sought injunctive relief. Several players also threatened not to play. Mays, however, remained with the Yankees. While indicating a need for discussion of the issue, Johnson promised no relief, instead voicing a belief that self-protection would guide teams in the future. His prediction was accurate, although various complicated trading deadlines are currently in place.

Sox, one of the most talented teams of all time, looked like a lock as they got set to take on the rather mediocre Cincinnati Reds in the 1919 World Series.

Attendance for the Browns in 1919 was 349,350, almost triple that of the trimmed-down 1918 season. The numbers placed the Browns sixth out of the eight teams in the league. Overall, league attendance more than doubled, with 3,652,000 fans passing through the gates to see the full return of their favorite sport. Baseball was back in business like never before.

Although frustrated by his team's late-season swan dive, George once again could take great pride in his individual accomplishments. In the field he led the league in assists with 120, fielding a sparkling .991. Once again he committed only 13 errors. At the plate, it was easier to find the one category in which he did not lead his team: Wally Gerber played in more games. That was it. George led in all other hitting categories, although his 31 doubles were matched by the Baby Doll. Sis even led in home runs with 10, by far his best power surge yet, and this a year before the introduction of the so-called live ball. With a batting average of .352, George trailed league-leading Ty Cobb (.385) by a bundle. Babe had his record 29 home runs and a league-leading 114 runs batted in, with George well off that pace at 83.

As it turned out, all predictions aside, the 1919 World Series was won by the underdog Cincinnati Reds. The eyebrows raised by their surprising showing would be raised even higher in the months ahead. Baseball as it was known in 1919 would never be quite the same again, nor would America in general. However, at that moment the multitude of changes on the horizon, if encompassed at all, were mere figments of someone's imagination. The reality was quite different.

For America, the point of embarkation for the third decade of the twentieth century more correctly dated from the end of World War I in November 1918. The war and its aftermath jump-started a period of change, but for a few months after the armistice the country was in a recovery mode. It was a nation where six inches was the "orthodox clearance" of the skirt and short-haired women were regarded as radicals.[14] The high cost of living was a serious topic, with milk at fourteen cents a quart and steak forty-two cents a pound.

This was a time when one drove on lightly traveled roads at the normal twenty-mile-per-hour speed limit, and a Lexington, Maxwell, Briscoe, or Templar was just as likely to be seen as a hand-cranked Model T Ford. On the postwar economic front, business was picking up. Despite an increase

14. Frederick Lewis Allen, *Only Yesterday: An Informal History of the 1920s*, 1.

in strikes, employment was on the increase. A stock market on the up-swing, however, rated little notice in the daily press.

Soldiers were still returning from abroad, and 1919 was a year of parades. The returning warrior could get a drink, since alcohol was legal in most states. Many people favored its demise, however. With the Eighteenth Amendment ratified, Prohibition was mere months away.

In the evening one might watch the magic of Charlie Chaplin or Douglas Fairbanks on film, join others for an evening of lively discussion, or perhaps play auction bridge. The occasional defiant female might even venture a smoke. One did not listen to the radio; broadcasting had not yet come to pass. There were no bathing beauty contests, racketeers, speak-easies, or confession magazines yet, no Al Capone or Charles Lindbergh, no Sacco and Vanzetti, Teapot Dome, or Dayton monkey trial, either. All that and more would wait for the decade to follow: the Roaring Twenties, a decade of sweeping social change.[15] It would be a time also of dramatic change in baseball, as the limelight slowly turned away from an aging Cobb toward the emerging brilliance of Ruth, Hornsby, and for a brief time toward George Sisler too.

15. Ibid., 1–10.

7

Major-League Changes

On the eve of the new decade, an event of major impact to the sport of baseball took place. On December 26, 1919, as George whiled away the winter hours working as a draftsman at the local St. Louis plant of General Motors, the Boston Red Sox, whose owners were desperate for cash, secretly agreed to trade Babe Ruth to the New York Yankees. The deal, when finally announced, involved anywhere from $100,000 to $125,000 in cash and a loan of $300,000, easily outdistancing by more than two times the amount of any previous player deal. The collateral for the loan was Boston's Fenway Park itself.

Coming as it did in such close proximity to several changes in the manufacture of baseballs and rules governing its use that served to tilt the advantage away from the pitcher and toward the batter, the impact of the trade on the game was enormous. The Red Sox, a perennial American League power before the sale of Ruth, did not win another World Series in the twentieth century. In contrast, the Yankees' dominance of the game is known to the most casual observer.

The first change, in the makeup of the baseball itself, was subtle and ripe for controversy. Whether the horsehide sphere was doctored to take advantage of the excitement that could be generated by a man with a big bat, such as the Babe, or whether the modification was purely accidental, with the Babe and his hitting cohorts happy beneficiaries of a mere coincidence, will probably never be known for sure. It is clear, however, that beginning in 1920 American League balls were made with an Australian yarn that could be wound more tightly, resulting in a harder, more elastic product. Causally related or not, baseballs suddenly seemed to travel farther.

The second change affected the condition of the baseball in play. Prior to 1920 foul balls were typically retrieved by stadium personnel and placed back into play. Beginning in 1920, fans were increasingly permitted to keep those foul balls hit into the stands. Thus clean baseballs were used more, and scuffed balls that were harder for batters to see and easier for pitchers to manipulate were used less. In addition, steps were taken to ensure that clean balls would remain in that condition. Previously, as the baseball would travel around the infield, players would doctor it—squirt a little tobacco juice on it here, rub a little dirt and scuff it up there, and so forth. In 1920 such tricks of the trade were outlawed and the offending player subjected to ejection and suspension. The result was a clean, undoctored baseball, which benefited the hitters. And that was only the start.

Finally, the spitball, that hygienically challenged baseball oddity, was banned. So too were all other "doctored" pitches such as the "emery" ball and the "shine" ball. In the past, for reasons known only to physics teachers, a pitcher could put a glob of spit on a ball and get it to do crazy things, giving the hurler a decided advantage. Exactly what it did was always open to question, but the fact it turned fine hitters into mincemeat and gave normally sure-handed infielders fits trying to handle the slippery sphere was not. At any rate, from 1920 on, a pitcher was prohibited from bringing his pitching hand to his mouth, defacing the ball, or applying a foreign substance. If he did, he received fair warning from the umpire. Continued infractions would bring ejection. An exception was made during cold weather, when pitchers could step off the mound and blow on their hands with prior agreement of both managers.

Another concession that evolved was alluded to by Ban Johnson in his letter to the *Post-Dispatch* the previous season. Not intending to ruin the careers of established pitchers who depended on the spitter, and after extensive negotiations that included lobbying by the spitballers themselves, a set number of pitchers in the majors were "grandfathered," allowing them to use the pitch as long as they remained active. Urban Shocker of the Browns was one; others of note included Jack Quinn of the Yankees and Hall of Famers Red Faber of the White Sox and Stan Coveleskie of the Indians. The last legal spitball artist was Burleigh Grimes, another Hall of Famer who retired from baseball as a Yankee in 1934.

So as the decade of the twenties began, batting averages went up, more runs were scored, and many, many more balls traveled outside the friendly confines of major-league baseball yards. This, for some reason—perhaps the presence of Babe Ruth—was particularly true in the American League. And the fans came out in droves on the eve of an enormous baseball scandal. Could a conspiracy theorist have a field day? Absolutely! Could he come up with credible evidence to prove his theory that the ball was altered and rules relaxed to diffuse the effects of a scandal? Absolutely not!

This, then, is the baseball landscape George Sisler faced in 1920. In his book *The Greatest First Basemen of All Time*, Donald Honig wrote that Sisler is "a legendary player without a legend."[1] If this be true, and in terms of how Sis has been remembered, it probably is, then the "legendary" part of the equation began in 1920, for as batters, more and more of whom emulated Ruth and his big swing, took advantage of their new edge and statistics for most players went up, George's statistics skyrocketed even higher. Years later he would look back on 1920, telling others that at twenty-seven he was at his physical peak.[2] On the other hand, the fact that he did not possess the raw power in his slender frame to amass big home run numbers also played no small part in his failure to achieve a lasting fame.

The exhibition season for the Browns in 1920 was a success, although the bulk of the games, as usual, were played against minor-league teams. The Browns, training in the Taylor, Alabama, area, won fourteen of fifteen games against minor-league opposition in Texas, Oklahoma, and Kansas. They entered the spring series with the Cardinals with virtually the same lineup as the year before. The mainstays on the mound for returning manager Jimmy Burke figured again to be Shocker and Sothoron. The Browns beat the Cards four games to two, with Sisler outhitting Hornsby .467 to .250. As the season unfolded, Dixie Davis, a twenty-nine-year-old right-hander, became a major surprise. Davis, who previously spent the majority of a ten-year career in the minors, had last been in the majors with the Philadelphia Phillies in 1918. In 1920 he would compile an 18–12 mark.

Despite the team's penchant for mediocrity, preseason predictions for the Browns were favorable in view of the set lineup and better than average starting pitching. Their shortage of relief pitchers was not nearly as important as it would be today. As the season developed, the team would perform a little better for the year as the league returned to a 154-game schedule.

1. Donald Honig, *The Greatest First Basemen of All Time*, 21.
2. Stockton in Walsh, comp. and ed., *Baseball's Greatest Lineup*, 81.

The season opener, played on April 13 before an overflow crowd of twenty-five thousand at League Park in Cleveland, was not impressive, however. Cleveland's Stan Coveleskie shut out the Browns on five hits. Sis, who had been moved to the cleanup slot, was hitless in four at bats. The losing pitcher for the Browns, Allen Sothoron, a twenty-game winner in 1919, had previously used the spitball as part of his arsenal, but unlike Urban Shocker, he thought he could get by without the pitch. Thus he was not on the original list of spitballers "grandfathered." After his performance sans spitball, Burke sought relief from the restriction, the Browns arguing they thought the list of those permitted to use the pitch was interchangeable. Sothoron was eventually added to the list, raising the number of sanctioned spitballers to seventeen, but in 1920 he fell to 8–15 anyway, although he would bounce back in 1921 to go 12–4.

In April Sis batted .333, but the team started slowly. By May 3 the Browns were in sixth place. Second baseman Joe Gedeon, bucking the team trend, was hitting in the .340s. Close behind was shortstop Wally Gerber. Unfortunately, as Sis got better, this pair cooled down, both ending the season under .300. On May 15, George served notice that this might be a special season. During an 8–4 defeat at Washington he had three hits and stole two bases. Then on May 26 he went four for five in another loss in Boston. For the month he hit .360.

By early June George was batting .350, closely followed by the Baby Doll, who was in the midst of a breakout year himself. Jacobson was on the way to .355, with 122 runs batted in. Still the team was stalled, playing below .500 and ten games behind league-leading Cleveland. On June 4 the *Post-Dispatch* made note of the increase in home runs throughout baseball. Already 152 homers had been smashed, 50 in the National League and 102 in the American. In the American League this was three times the number from the previous campaign. Ban Johnson attributed the increase to the "better material" used in the ball manufacturing process. Whatever it was, Browns' business manager Bob Quinn wanted it to continue, "as it made the game far more interesting."[3] More fodder for the theorist?

In June's first week, Lee Fohl was signed by Jimmy Burke as a pitching coach. Fohl, who managed the Akron club when George still played in the area and later the Cleveland Indians at the major-league level, resigned his Cleveland job in July 1919 when he lost a three-run lead in the ninth inning of a game by pitching to Babe Ruth with the bases loaded. One pitch later, the game was over, and Ruth had added to his legend by hitting his second grand-slam homer of the contest. The resultant criticism

3. Quoted in *St. Louis Post-Dispatch,* June 4, 1920.

caused Fohl to jump ship in favor of Tris Speaker, who became a participant in an emerging trend of great players becoming field generals.

On June 10 George raised his average to .398, managing four hits as the
Browns stopped a three-game skid, beating the Indians 15–1. Speaker went
hitless, dropping his average to .384. As the year progressed, an interesting tug of war began between Rogers Hornsby and George Sisler. At the
heart of the contest was the St. Louis fan. L. C. Davis summed it up in his
Sports Salad column in a poem entitled "Hornsby vs. Sisler":

> Under a spreading chestnut tree
> The rooters congregate.
> Upon a most momentous theme
> They earnestly debate
> And they argue pro and likewise con
> From early morn till late.
>
> The fate of nations seems to hang
> On what they have to say;
> The while they chatter and harangue
> In their emphatic way.
> On what according to the gang
> Is the question of the day.
>
> It's not the price of hats or shoes
> On which they argufy;
> Or if they favor wine and booze,
> Or lean towards the dry.
> Nor do they gather to abuse
> The profiteering guy.
>
> It is the Sisler-Hornsby feud
> That has them in the air;
> For earnestly they have pursued
> The records of the pair.
> And with vehement words and rude
> Their merits they compare.
>
> Some claim that Hornsby isn't fit
> To carry Sisler's bat;
> And every time he makes a hit
> It's mostly luck, at that.
> And anyone denying it
> Is talking through his hat.
>
> While Hornsby rooters loudly claim
> That Sisler makes 'em smile;
> In all departments of the game
> Rog' has him skinned a mile.

And on the outcome of the same
They'll wager quite a pile.

They're for their heroes wrong or right.
At each and every stage;
They carry on with main and might
And let the battles rage.
And for the records every night
They scan the sporting page.[4]

No matter who was really best, by June 19, George was in the midst of a hot streak that took him to .421, tops in both circuits. The Browns were hot as well. On June 20 Carl Weilman, the fourth pitcher in the Browns rotation, won his team's tenth straight game by defeating the Athletics 3–1.

Of course, in 1920 Sis was not alone among the league's hot hitters. In fact, on June 20 the *Post-Dispatch* reported that sixty-one major-league players, forty from the American League, were hitting .300 or better. Sis was the only .400 hitter at the time, but Hornsby was a close second at .394.

Of major interest to local St. Louis baseball fans was a forthcoming series between the Browns and the New York Yankees, complete with their recently acquired "World Champion Home-Run Maker." Calling Ruth and Sisler the "World's Batting Titans," John E. Wray, writing for the *Post-Dispatch,* compared the two men, marveling that either could just as easily make his mark on the pitching mound. Ruth, of course, had certainly done just that, with eighty-nine pitching victories; Sisler had proved his pitching prowess to a much lesser extent.

By comparison, off the mound Wray found Sisler hitting eighty points better than the Babe, while fielding and running rings around the man. However, "Ruth stands out before the world as the more striking figure, because of the spectacular nature of his blows. He is the heavy artillery of the battle—the Paris gun, that blasts the opposition with one mighty wallop." The Babe's accomplishments were out there for all to see; Sis's feats were not nearly so plain. Still, in Wray's somewhat parochial view, "The cumulative effect of his [Sisler's] efforts would probably surpass those of his rival."[5] And this despite having to play for a team that was far inferior to Ruth's.

Then Wray took his readers onto hitherto untraveled ground. Although local fans had been trumpeting one player over the other for years, local sportswriters always kept their distance, making comparisons without definitive statements of any kind. But since he was comparing Sisler to

4. Ibid., June 16, 1920.
5. Ibid., June 20, 1920.

Ruth, why not take it one step further and compare Sisler to Hornsby? Wray did just that; the conclusion was that George's "all around worth probably exceeds that of Hornsby."[6] This from a disinterested observer who for years reported on a daily basis the myriad trials and tribulations of both local teams and both men.

So, how did the Yankees versus the Browns series play out? In the opener, the Yanks' Jack Quinn stopped the Browns' win streak at ten, with a 4–3 victory over Urban Shocker. Sis went three for four, raising his season average to .423, but a rare base-running "boner" in the sixth stopped a rally. After doubling, he took off on a high fly ball by Ken Williams, hustling along halfway to home by the time the ball was caught. He could not return to second base in time and was thrown out to complete a double play. Since Ruth had a hit but no base-running gaffes and played for the winning team, he came out on top in round one. The next game was postponed due to rain. The weather cleared, and Dixie Davis and the Browns bested Carl Mays on June 23, 9–3. The series was finally won by the Yankees the following day when Shocker tried once again, but lost to Bob Shawkey, 6–3. During the remainder of the series, neither George nor the Babe did all that much, Ruth leaving town, at least that week, without resolving anything about baseball immortality.

On June 24 the *Post-Dispatch* dropped a stunner that overshadowed the Browns' series with the Yankees. Beginning July 1, the paper announced, the Cardinals would play their next home stand at Sportsman's Park. While it was announced as a temporary arrangement, in fact when all the dust settled, Sam Breadon, the Cardinals' new president and main shareholder, reached a ten-year lease agreement with Phil Ball. The annual rent was twenty thousand dollars. The new tenants thus included Branch Rickey, still a major functionary with the Cardinals' organization. Sis and his "coach" were in some small way connected again.

On June 30, despite Sis's hot pace and the team's lengthy winning streak, the Browns stood at 30–34, still in sixth place and thirteen long games behind the Indians. Despite a livelier ball, not much had changed in the land of the Browns. On July 10 George banged out three hits, including a triple, to aid a fine outing by Allen Sothoron in a 9–2 win over the Red Sox. At least six Browns, including Gedeon, Jacobson, and Williams, were listed among the league's hitting leaders, with Sis topping the pack in both leagues at .420. Three days later Urban Shocker struck out fourteen Yankees, victimizing the Babe three times to solidify his position as a Babe-killer, in a 6–4 victory. Sis was hitless for the second game in a row, the

6. Ibid.

first time that had happened all season. On July 17, workhorse Shocker was on the mound again in a 3–2 win over the Athletics of Connie Mack. The win boosted the club into fourth, but they still trailed the leaders by a bundle.

Babe Ruth was at it again, already attacking the record books. By June 20, with more than two months remaining to raise the mark, he broke his record of 29 set the previous year. Although nowhere close to matching the Babe's torrid pace, George was hitting some home runs, too. In fact, he would finish the year with 19, a figure he was as proud of as any other during his career. That number at the time represented the most home runs ever hit by an American League player other than the Babe. Coming as it did in the first "year of the hitter" took nothing away from the achievement, at least in George's mind. Even he had succumbed to the intoxication of the long ball.

On July 28, the morning of the initiation of further hostilities between the Yanks and the Browns, the *Post-Dispatch* printed a batting chart, depicting the progress of Ruth and Sisler in linear fashion. What did all the lines prove? Both men were having remarkable seasons at the plate.

On August 1 the *Post-Dispatch* could report that the previous day, despite the Babe's thirty-seventh home run, George had "out-Ruthed the 'Babe.'"[7] Sis had homered, singled twice, scored three, and driven in three to aid a 13–8 rubber-match win for his squad. For one of the few times in Sis's career he was able to bask in the full glare of the spotlight when it came to one of his main batting rivals.

Two weeks later there occurred a baseball tragedy. Raymond Chapman of the league-leading Cleveland Indians was struck in the head on August 16 by a pitch from controversial Yankee pitcher Carl Mays. Chapman never regained consciousness and died in a New York hospital early the next morning. The baseball world, as well as the entire country, was stunned; the incident became front-page news. The twenty-nine-year-old Chapman, a member of the Indians since 1912, was one of baseball's most popular players. In sharp contrast, Mays had a mean streak and a reputation for pitching inside. Mays maintained that the ball he threw to Chapman had a rough cover and sailed on him.

As the players attempted to deal with the loss of Chapman—the only time a major-league player has ever died in this manner—players on several teams, including Detroit and Boston, threatened to petition the league to bar Mays from the game. Ty Cobb was vocal in his support of the effort,

7. Ibid., August 1, 1920.

but after an investigation, Ban Johnson found no cause for action. After a week off Mays returned to the mound, and even faced the Indians with no further trouble as the season proceeded.

If the death of a fellow player from a pitched ball played on the mind of the average ballplayer, it did nothing to stop the heavy hitting barrage of Sis and others. In mid-August Sisler experienced back-to-back four-for-five days in victories over the Washington Nationals. At one point, he went on a thirty-four-game hitting streak, then started a new streak with a four-for-five day against Chicago in a victory that saw him triple twice. In the second game of that twin bill, he had two more hits in a defeat.

On September 5, with the team still hanging around fourth place, the Browns suffered a setback. Their best pitcher, Urban Shocker, injured his knee and appeared finished for the season. Two days later they also found out the hard way that the Indians had recovered with a vengeance from the loss of their teammate. Playing in front of a combined forty-five thousand fans for a doubleheader in Cleveland, the Browns were pounded 7–2 and 6–5.

Since the completion of the World Series the previous October, rumors had been rampant that a number of White Sox players played the post-season games under the influence of gamblers. Although White Sox owner Charles Comiskey and his players continued to deny it, the story did not die. On September 21, 1920, the State Attorneys Office in Illinois announced it planned to convene a grand jury to issue subpoenas for the players, owners, managers, and gamblers it thought were involved in the matter. On September 28 star pitcher Eddie Cicotte confessed to throwing the opening game of the 1919 World Series for ten thousand dollars. Soon others added their names to the list. Even though the players, including the great "Shoeless" Joe Jackson, on advice of counsel denied their culpability and were acquitted the next year by a Chicago jury, the White Sox were now "black" and the sport was tinged a different shade forever. One result was the end of the National Commission. Two months later Barney Dreyfuss finally got his wish. By November 12 Judge Kenesaw Mountain Landis, not Garry Herrmann, ruled the game.

On September 22, with the entire country standing by wide-mouthed while baseball stars made court records, a small article appeared in the *Post-Dispatch* noting that Sis was nearing a significant record of his own. Sisler was only eleven hits shy of Ty Cobb's record of 248 hits in a single season. Since eleven games remained on the regular season schedule, Sis had a legitimate chance. L. C. Davis gave him a send-off in the right direction with the poem "George Sisler":

Who is the present King of Swat?
George Sisler.
Who pounds the pill around the lot?
George Sisler.
Who is it when he's on the job,
Evokes the plaudits of the mob,
As in the palmy days of Cobb?
George Sisler.

Who is the greatest guy on earth?
George Sisler.
Who gives the fans their moneys worth?
George Sisler.
Who is the bird who doesn't pose
As hero in the movie shows,
But busts the pellet on the nose?
George Sisler.[8]

By September 25 Sis was getting support from many quarters in his quest for the record. As he played current record holder Cobb's own Tigers, he was cheered each time he appeared at the plate in a Saturday afternoon contest. Sisler responded with a lone hit in his fifth at bat to come within seven of the record. Two days later, on September 27, he tied Cobb's nine-year-old record by nailing his 248th hit. The joke around town was that the hit made "George Sisler Ty Cobb."[9]

The next day fifteen thousand fans were on hand at Sportsman's Park to celebrate "Sisler Day" as a local group of fifteen hundred admirers presented their hero with a fifteen-hundred-dollar silver service, a check for one thousand dollars, and a bouquet before the game. Then they not only watched the Indians and Browns tangle but also saw Sisler break Cobb's single-season hit record with dramatic emphasis by blasting a home run and following it with a triple. The events were planned long before George approached Cobb's record, but the timing was fitting nonetheless. It was especially satisfying in that George's accomplishment was otherwise completely overshadowed by Eddie Cicotte's confession and the indictments of so many key players on the reigning American League champions.

George's achievements, including his all-around excellence, were again trumpeted by L. C. Davis in his Sports Salad. Describing George's only weakness—"He can't play ball on an open date"—he titled the piece "Our Pennant Nucleus":

8. Ibid., September 22, 1920.
9. Ibid., September 29, 1920.

There is a man in our town,
And he's a wondrous guy;
He is a man of great renown.
And I will tell you why:
He plays that old initial sack
With superhuman skill,
And it's a treat to see him crack
The justly famous pill.

In heading off the ugly bound,
Believe me, he's a bear;
He scoops the pellet from the ground,
And plucks it from the air.
It seems he's everywhere at once,
And all the rooters say
He pulls so many brilliant stunts
It takes their breath away.

Like Walter Johnson, he can pitch,
When Walt was at his best.
He plays the field without a hitch,
Like Speaker and the rest.
You'll always find him on his toes
When he is in the game.
We take it everybody knows
That Sisler is his name.[10]

Poetry aside, for all practical purposes, George's run at Cobb's record provided the only remaining excitement for the Browns as the season drew to a close on October 3 with Sis tallying his 257th hit. The team closed shop on 1920 in fourth place at 76–77, a slight improvement over the previous year. As the team's batting average rose, from .264 to .308, so did attendance. In a year that saw American League attendance increase by almost 1.5 million fans, the club was some seventy thousand ahead of the preceding campaign, finishing fifth out of the eight American League teams. A large percentage of those fans were in attendance that year when the Yankees, a third-place finisher, came to town with Ruth.

The World Series of 1920 featured the Cleveland Indians of Tris Speaker against Brooklyn, then known as the Robins. The Indians won it five games to two, as pitcher Stan Coveleskie, the opening day pitcher against the Browns, pitched three five-hit World Series victories.

In baseball, even the seemingly insurmountable records fall—Babe Ruth's home runs, Ty Cobb's hits, and Lou Gehrig's consecutive games

10. Ibid., September 28, 1930.

played come to mind. But in 1920, when Sis totaled 257 hits, he established a major-league single-season record that has never been topped. It seems safe to say that this accomplishment, coming in a 154-game season in which good fortune permitted him to play every inning of every game, is Sis's living legacy. It is what he is best remembered for to this day. Unlike many of the other fine achievements during his career, the single-season hit record still stands the test of time.

However, in 1920 the single-season hit record was only one facet of a truly remarkable individual season. And it was done with the spotlight pointed for the most part in an eastward direction; toward Gotham, in fact. For as great a hitting year as George put together in 1920, he still finished second in the league to Ruth or others in eight offensive categories, including the following:

Slugging average:	.632	(Ruth, .847)
Home runs:	19	(Ruth, 54)
Runs batted in:	122	(Ruth, 137)
Stolen bases:	42	(Rice, 63)
Home run percentage:	3.0	(Ruth, 11.8)
Runs scored:	137	(Ruth, 158)
Doubles:	49	(Speaker, 50)
Triples:	18	(Joe Jackson, 20)

On the other hand, George led the league in hits, of course, as well as in total bases and batting average. His .407 mark put him in rarified company as one of only eight hitters in the twentieth century to achieve the distinction of reaching the .400 plateau. All told, the Browns star was hitless in a game only twenty-three times all season, striking out a mere 19 times in 631 at bats. He ended the season on a torrid pace, hitting .442 in August and .448 for September. His average in Sportsman's Park for the year was an astounding .473, the second highest home park average of all time, behind only Joe Jackson's .483 in 1912 with Cleveland.

In 1920 there was no question Sisler was at the top of his game and his best was among baseball's all-time best. Billy Evans, an American League umpire with an opportunity to watch George play from close proximity, thought he knew how the Browns star was doing it. "He used his speed to more advantage than any man save Cobb. He used his head every minute of the time, too. He was always watching the rival infield. If they crept in to avoid a bunt, he would poke the ball over their heads. If they dropped back he would lay down a deft bunt and beat the play to first—

sometimes without even drawing a throw."[11] The searing line drives that exploded off George's bat in all directions reminded Evans most of the great early baseball hitter Willie "hit 'em where they ain't" Keeler, despite the fact George's nineteen home runs in 1920 were of some statistical significance at the time.

As great as Sisler's hitting was in 1920, as usual, it was not nearly the whole story. For the season, he fielded his position with aplomb, drawing more and more comparisons to the great-fielding Hal Chase. In 154 games George fielded .990, with only sixteen errors. Even more impressively, he led the league in assists, with 140, a record-breaking mark that stood for twenty-nine years. His speed also enabled him to start more double plays than any other first sacker in either league.

Sis was not the only St. Louis hitter to win a batting title in 1920. Rogers Hornsby led the senior circuit with a .370 average, as well as in hits and runs batted in. Unlike Sis, however, the "Rajah," as he was now known, had a propensity for ruffling feathers. Thus, despite his youth and great success, postseason rumors circulated in St. Louis and elsewhere that the Cardinals star was on the trading block. Most experts scoffed at the idea, and they were right. For the time being, Hornsby had plenty of rope left in St. Louis.

The Rajah was not the only subject of trade rumors in this particular off-season. The Yankees, then as now, were in the habit of buying that which they coveted. When they needed a pitcher, they obtained a Carl Mays. When they needed a hitter, they spent money for a Babe Ruth. Now they were after one George Sisler. For the honor of his company, the Yanks supposedly offered Phil Ball two hundred thousand dollars. Since the Ruth deal the previous year involved a loan, as well as cash, the straight cash offer to the Browns was believed the highest offer for a single player up to that time. The proposal was roundly rejected.[12]

Happiness for the Sislers in 1920 was not limited to the baseball diamond. George, Kathleen, and George, Jr., were now firmly entrenched residents of St. Louis. On November 2, a second son, Richard Allan Sisler, made St. Louis his home, too.

In October and November George tried his hand at managing in a four-team winter league formed in California. George was asked to manage the Maier Brewing Company team slated for Vernon, a suburb of Los Angeles. The other three teams were managed by Harry Heilman, the Tigers'

11. Quoted in Meany, *Baseball's Greatest Hitters*, 183.
12. Greene, "George Sisler 'Picture Player,'" 78; *New York Times*, October 14, 1920.

fine hitter who handled Oakland's entry; Ty Cobb for San Francisco; and Rogers Hornsby for the Los Angeles team. George and the other player/managers received ten thousand dollars for their trouble. At the end of the season, the winning team would divide another ten thousand. George recalled spending his off-the-field time in California in an apartment in Lakeside Park, watching the swans and ducks swimming around.

Although the crowds were rather sparse, "the games were well played," and the sponsors received "advertising value." At the end of the season, George's Vernon team was on top and split the winnings. George refused his share in view of his manager's salary, a move that "seemed to set well with the members of the team."[13] On December 18, Ty Cobb's thirty-first birthday, his Tigers, impressed by player/manager Tris Speaker's success with the world champion Indians, signed him to manage the club in 1921. The era of the player/manager was in full swing. The Browns' Jimmy Burke had yet to field a winner. Perhaps a door was opening for George Sisler, perhaps not.

13. Sisler Memoirs, 23.

Sisler's father, Cassius Clay Sisler, was initially a schoolteacher and later a supervisor at a local coal mine. Sisler family collection.

Sisler's mother, Mary Whipple Sisler, was a schoolteacher and, like her husband, a graduate of Oberlin College. Sisler family collection.

The Sisler clan. Young George is in the front row, second from the right. His uncle, Isaac Myers, a mayor of Akron, is in the second row, second on the left, with George's father, Cassius, to Myers's immediate right. Sisler family collection.

The Sisler brothers, Bert, George, and Cassius. Sisler family collection.

Sisler (third from left) in his early baseball playing days in Barberton, Ohio.
Courtesy of the Barberton Public Library.

Sisler of Michigan, ca. 1914. Courtesy of the
University of Michigan, Bentley Historical
Library.

Sisler stealing home in his last game for the Michigan Wolverines, June 23, 1915. Courtesy of the University of Michigan, Bentley Historical Library.

Sisler in position to field a grounder. He began his professional career as a pitcher, but soon became one of the game's all-time great fielding first basemen. Courtesy of the National Baseball Hall of Fame Library, Cooperstown, New York.

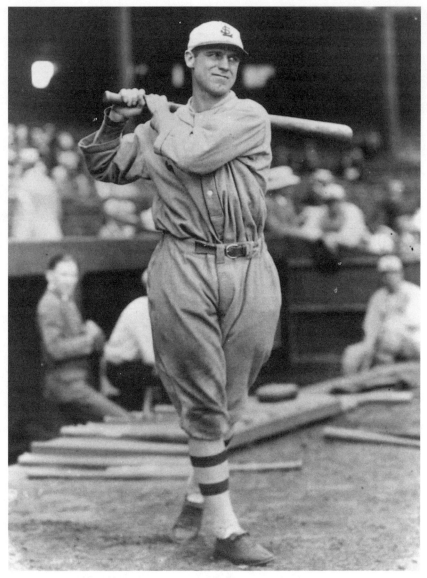

Sisler waiting on deck to bat. Courtesy of Allied Photocolor.

Sisler stirs up a cloud of dust. He led the American League in steals in 1918, 1921, 1922, and 1927. Courtesy of the National Baseball Hall of Fame Library, Cooperstown, New York.

Whether on the mound or at first base, Sisler possessed a strong left arm. Courtesy of Allied Photocolor.

Sisler of St. Louis. An early shot of the man many consider the greatest Brown. Courtesy of the National Baseball Hall of Fame Library, Cooperstown, New York.

Sisler (second row, far right) in 1918 in a much different uniform. Sisler family collection.

Sisler shows the batting style that produced a record-setting 257 hits in 1920.
Courtesy of the National Baseball Hall of Fame, Cooperstown, New York.

Sisler and Babe Ruth greet prior to a game in the early 1920s between Ruth's Yankees and the Browns. Courtesy of the *Sporting News*.

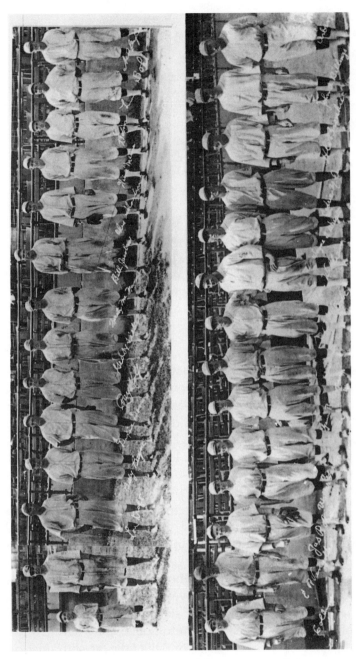

The 1922 St. Louis Browns were runners-up to the Yankees for the American League pennant by one slim game. Notables on the roster on the top row include (left to right): Dixie Davis (fifth), Sisler (seventh), Marty McManus, Bill "Baby Doll" Jacobson, Jack Tobin (twelfth), and Manager Lee Fohl (far right). On the bottom row (left to right): Elam Vangilder (second), Jimmy Austin, Walter Gerber, Ken Williams (ninth), Urban Shocker (far right). Courtesy of Allied Photocolor.

8

Renaissance Man

After the dust settled on George's superlative performance in 1920, the buzz continued. Sports pundits now mentioned George Sisler in the same breath as Ty Cobb, Babe Ruth, and Tris Speaker. All three incumbent stars were outgoing and easy to know, if not downright flamboyant. Fans wanted to know about the new sports god, who unlike the others was quiet and reserved. But Sisler preferred to let his bat, glove, and feet do his talking.

An article by Floyd L. Bell had first appeared in print the previous winter. It told a lot about George the man, even if it did little to change his passive image. Finding his subject "modest, almost to a point of bashfulness, as far from egotism as a blushing debutante," Bell described Sis as one who would rather read a high-brow magazine such as *Atlantic Monthly* than talk baseball. If forced to talk about the sport, his focus was on his teammates, never himself. "[S]hift the conversation to Sisler himself and he becomes a clam." In his home, the shy star preferred "to discuss the current events of the day, tinker with his automobile, play with his two-year old son and prototype George Junior, or talk of the latest dramatic or motion picture success." The writer told readers of George's skill at billiards, swimming, golf, and, of all things, boxing, and of the care he took in leading a clean, healthy life. At the epicenter of that existence was his family, including "a wife whom he adores, the little son whom he worships, the mother whose pride in her son is equaled only by his respect for her." The author found a careful, conservative man who would never be reckless with his finances, but lest one think George a stiff bore, he found him "a good mixer in the better sense of that term. He makes friends readily and holds their friendship without making any special effort to do so."[1]

One of those friends was Paul Simmons. George and Paul became acquainted early in George's St. Louis experience. Simmons and Sis were fraternity brothers, albeit from different schools. Paul's college was just down the road, the University of Missouri. His wife, Anna Mary, was a Kappa from that school; Kathleen Sisler was a Kappa from Michigan. They met through the Presbyterian church both couples attended, and they became fast friends. Initially, Paul Simmons was a salesman for Con P. Curran Printing Company. Unhappy with his situation, he longed to have his own company. In time he spoke with a coworker, Harry Lauder, and talked him into joining in their own venture. There was only one problem—no money. According to George, "I didn't have much money either, but more than they had." He put up the money, "purely on a friendship basis," expecting little in return. Paul was an excellent salesman and Harry "a capable inside man." George said his monetary commitment to the partners "turned out to be the best investment that I ever made."[2]

The printing company, in its initial form, was the River City Press, located at 215 Pine Street in St. Louis. Eventually it relocated farther west on Pine Street just beyond Sarah Street, where it "flourished" as the Simmons-Sisler Printing Company. Although George knew nothing about printing, he sometimes worked at the company during the off-season. Years later the company was purchased by the Universal Match Company, a large national firm, and "large profits emerged."[3]

It might seem strange that a player of Sisler's stature sought off-season employment for supplemental income. Little, however, is known about the salaries of most major-league ballplayers of the era. As historian Harold Seymour wrote, "[T]he baseball industry has traditionally operated behind what might be called a horsehide curtain of secrecy."[4] But the available

---

1. Floyd L. Bell, "The Personal Side of George Harold Sisler," *Sporting News*, December 11, 1919, 2. The author's fascination with the private side of Sisler did not end with the 1919 article. Near the end of the 1920 season, Bell penned a second article on the subject, discussing Sisler's keen intellect, avid interest in worldly matters, and mastery of the game of bridge. See "George Sisler as a .400 Hitter," September 1920, 474, 507.

2. Sisler Memoirs, 14.

3. Ibid.

4. Seymour, *Baseball: The Golden Age*, 172.

information substantiates that the salary of most of these early professionals was not so great. A player was paid for a season's work, nothing more. The term "fringe benefits" was not yet even coined. Nor was there a pension system in place to protect the players after their careers ended. For many years players were not even paid for their work in spring training. No wonder Ty Cobb abhorred it, often arriving well after preseason camp had started.

Many ballplayers in the early twentieth century lived day to day. Some of the more kindly owners took pity on the less astute or frugal, advancing them money during winter months. Robert Hedges, in fact, reportedly advanced thousands of dollars to his players over the years, amounts that remained outstanding and which complicated the sale of the Browns to Phil Ball in 1916. It is said that Giants Manager John McGraw, he of the crusty exterior but warm heart, frequently loaned players money from his own pocket and was less frequently repaid.

That off-season jobs were so plentiful for major-leaguers can be seen as one of the rewards for playing. Those available were quite varied, sometimes even unusual, ranging from farmer to streetcar conductor to policeman to undertaker. A number of the more personable professionals found acting parts. Many of the mainstream jobs involved sales and, as might be expected, played more upon the individual's name recognition than his experience in the field or other qualifications. Still, off-season employment, no matter the prestige or lack thereof, paid the bills until the start of a new season.

During the holiday season in 1920 George fielded a business proposal of a totally different sort. Although Jimmy Burke had his Browns headed in the right direction in 1920, he was a low-key manager whose laid-back disposition was reflected in the type of club he fielded. So what did Phil Ball and Bob Quinn decide to do? They fired Burke and offered the job to low-key, laid-back George Sisler. He declined politely, but firmly, telling his bosses he was reaching the top of his game as a player and wanted nothing to interfere with his play.

"When I tendered the managership to him he did not hem and haw and bristle up over the offer, but straightforwardly voiced his disapproval," Quinn said. "Then I told him of the offer other clubs had made for him [two hundred thousand dollars by the Yankees], and he quietly informed me that he was wholly satisfied in St. Louis and intended to remain here."[5] Although he had a year remaining on his contract, it was torn up and a

5. Quoted in the *Sporting News*, January 6, 1921, 5.

new, extended contract was signed. Like so many things in Sis's career and life, the amount of the new contract remained a private matter.

So George would not join Cobb and Speaker as playing managers. The contrast in styles between the bombastic Cobb, the sensitive Speaker, and the self-effacing Sisler would have been intriguing. For the present, at least, it was not to be. Failing in their attempt to convince George to take over the team's reins, Ball and Quinn turned to Lee Fohl. At first reluctant for fear rumors he had tried to undermine Burke would be viewed as true, Fohl took the job only after much coaxing from Quinn. A players' manager known for giving his troops wide discretion while always keeping the game simple, Fohl at least initially proved a wise second choice. American League umpire and frequent guest sports commentator Billy Evans described Fohl as a manager who would get the most out of his players. Telling readers Fohl was not the "demonstrative" type, Evans predicted the new manager's strength would be that "he works in a quiet way, but always has harmony on his ball club . . . , and that is the big task for any manager."[6]

Over the winter, as George reflected on the previous season, his competitive spirit flared. Despite the fact he had out-hit Ty Cobb and broken his hit record, he fretted that the "Georgia Peach" was injured during the season and not at the top of his game in hitting .334. He wanted to best Cobb in an even contest. In March of 1921, in an interview printed in *Baseball Magazine,* he said, "I have indulged in day dreams, that some time I might match wits with Ty Cobb in a batting dual for the League supremacy, that would not find me second best. This ambition of mine is no secret." He hoped "that next season Ty may have a good year, free from injury, and I can assure every one interested that I shall do my best to outhit him."[7]

Why the increased success? The answer at least to George was simple. First, he was enjoying good health. Second, he was becoming a seasoned ballplayer. Third, the new rules were a batting boost. Still, they helped every batter, did they not? And finally, he had overcome one of his "besetting sins" and "hit at fewer bad balls this season than ever before." He was now a "place hitter," aided considerably as a batter because he was once a pitcher himself.

Despite the almost universal accolades, however, not everyone was quite so willing to switch Cobb's crown to Sisler. Some felt it would come

---

6. Quoted in *St. Louis Post-Dispatch,* April 10, 1921.
7. "My Best Season, So Far" (interview with George Sisler), 461. See also Honig, *The Greatest First Basemen of All Time,* 25.

eventually, but not while Cobb was a continuing force in the game. Others, though at the time there were few, thought it never would be. One of the latter was Hugh Jennings, Cobb's longtime manager at Detroit. In March 1921, shortly before he resigned his Tigers' post, Jennings told readers of *Baseball Magazine* that while Sisler and Cobb were blessed with similar physical talent, Cobb still came out ahead:

> Sisler's personality is at once his strong point and his weakness. He is, I am informed, a very likeable young fellow and his temperament is of the type which never antagonizes or makes enemies. Such a disposition is an admirable one in the business world or in social intercourse. But it has its drawbacks on the diamond.... The domineering, aggressive type of player who rides rough shod over everything between him and his goal is the type which will carry the furtherest [sic] on the diamond. Cobb is distinctly that type.... Sisler is entirely different. He is quiet, almost backward in his way.... I doubt he will ever be Cobb's equal as a personality on the diamond. After all, it is color quite as much as anything else which attracts the public to a player. Cobb has a lot of vivid color. Sisler has little.[8]

All in all, no matter where one stood on the Cobb-Sisler rivalry, 1920 was a headline season for George. Heading into the 1921 season his Browns and their new skipper Fohl had a few things going for themselves, too. In Ken Williams, Johnny Tobin, and Baby Doll Jacobson, they returned a good-fielding outfield of .300 hitters. Williams, with ten home runs in 1920, showed he could stroke the ball with power. The pitching staff looked reasonably dependable, at least at the start, with eighteen-game winner Dixie Davis and twenty-game winner Urban Shocker. Allen Sothoron at 8–15 in 1920 and the six feet, five and a half inch Carl Weilman at 9–13 might be serviceable.

The problem was in the infield, especially at second base. In 1920 the position was ably manned by Joe Gedeon, who arrived in 1918 from the Yankees. Always a fine fielder, Gedeon, a lifetime .244 hitter, took advantage of the "live" ball and in 153 games hit .292 with 63 runs batted in. At the end of the season, however, Commissioner Landis charged Gedeon with "guilty knowledge" of the White Sox scandal. Alleging the Browns' second sacker was aware the World Series was fixed, Landis banned Gedeon from baseball.

In barring Gedeon, Commissioner Landis was using the wide-ranging authority vested in him on January 12, 1921, when every baseball owner except the Browns' Phil Ball ratified the National Agreement, which gave the commissioner enormous power to investigate any act he deemed a

8. "Will George Sisler Equal Ty Cobb?" (interview with Hugh Jennings), 468.

threat to the game and levy fines or blacklist players engaging in such conduct. Ball's vote was not against the vesting of power, but against the commissioner himself, since it was a decision by Commissioner Landis that effectively terminated the Federal League, of which Ball was such a main cog. Certainly, Ball was chafing at that portion of the owners' decision which required that the magnates abide by the commissioner's decisions and refrain from publicly criticizing him.

One of the commissioner's first major demonstrations of his new powers was to permanently ban eight Black Sox players from the game. Judge Landis, like many others, viewed their jury acquittal as the act of a biased body. Those banned were the major participants in the 1919 World Series scandal. Gedeon, at best a fringe player in the scam, allegedly knowing about it but telling no one, shared their fate. Clearly, the Browns shared Gedeon's pain over Landis's decision. Initially, they tried to replace Gedeon with Billy Gleason, twenty-six years old and reportedly the best second sacker in the Southern League. At third base the Browns decided to try converted outfielder Earl Smith, a .306 hitter in 103 games the previous season. The shortstop remained Wally Gerber, an aggressive competitor with quick hands and a good mind for investments who was coming off a .279 season.

The year began in the same way as so many before it, with the Browns taming the Cardinals in an extended city series, four games to three. Sis fielded poorly during the series and hit even worse, chasing bad pitches and ending the seven games at .180. In one game, he escaped further scrutiny for poor base running when he was picked off by the Cardinals' pitcher and sprinted toward second, where he became embroiled in a rundown. The ball eventually ended up in the hands of Jacques Fournier, who chased Sis to second. For some unknown reason, Fournier held onto the ball and lost the race, allowing Sis to reach second base safely and avoid further disgrace.

As the season opener neared, Fohl announced his lineup, alternating lefties and righties as follows: Tobin, Gerber, Sisler, Jacobson, Williams, Gleason, utility infielder Dud Lee, and catcher Hank Severeid. The main beneficiary of Fohl's machinations was Johnny Tobin, who moved from the sixth spot to lead-off.

The new lineup initially helped little. By the end of April, the team was in sixth place at 5–7. The Browns dropped the opener to the defending World Champion Indians. In a victory over Cleveland in the second game, Sis sent a four-bagger over the Sportsman's Park bleacher wall. A few days later he hit another one against the White Sox, this time of the inside-the-park variety. Despite his weak performance against the Cardinals,

George was hitting a robust .440 by April 23. In late April and early May, however, Sis began matching his team's lackluster performance with a slump of his own. At one point, his average dropped to .267. Then he snapped out of it with a pair of four-hit games against the Tigers. He appeared to be hitting his stride on May 14 when a foot injury kept him out for three games, the first games he had missed since the 1919 season.

As the season progressed, it became more and more apparent that the Browns were not achieving anything close to their preseason promise. Business manager Bob Quinn became restless. On May 21 he placed Allen Sothoron on waivers. Sothoron was immediately claimed by the Red Sox. The pitcher had toiled effectively for the Browns for several seasons, but with the restrictions on his spitter and other "freak" pitches, he lost ground. He was 1–2 with a 5.20 earned run average when the club released him. Sothoron's replacement was Emilio Palmero, a Cuban pitcher who started off fast with a 4–2 win over the Nationals but quickly settled into the Browns' doldrums, finishing the season at 4–7.

On May 25 George watched in his home park as Babe Ruth added to his growing legend by smashing a five-hundred-foot home run, the longest hit to date at Sportsman's Park. A few days later George's foot ailment resurfaced, and he remained on the bench in New York as his team overcame Babe's sixteenth slam for a 9–8 win. George was out for three more games, but was soon back among the league leaders in hitting at .404 and in stolen bases with ten.

Once again, the hitters ruled in 1921. The Browns as a team would hit .304, third in the American League. The combination of "Babeitis," the lively ball, and tighter pitching rules had pitchers on the ropes. The average fan, long weary of low-scoring pitching duels, loved it. But all this hitting did not seem to help the Browns much in the early going. By the end of May, Sis was back in action, but the club rested in fifth place, two games behind the Tigers and Washington and nine behind league-leading Cleveland. Taking two of three in Boston helped some, with Sis a perfect three-for-three in a 9–3 win with Elam Vangilder on the mound. The next day Sis participated in an around-the-horn triple play, but the Browns lost anyway, 7–3.

Although George was hitting the ball at a .392 clip, it looked like business as usual as the team headed into July in sixth place at 29–38. By now at least the Browns were feeling good about one position: second base. A question mark going into the year, Fohl struck pay dirt when he penciled in the highly competitive Marty McManus, a move that would pay rich dividends in future seasons. In 1921 McManus, who could play any position in the infield, would play 121 games, hit .260, and drive in 64 runs.

Even more important, he would help solidify the Browns' infield, giving Fohl greater flexibility with his other players.

In July, almost imperceptibly, the Browns' fortunes began to change for the better. The improvement came at an opportune time, because the locals were getting restless. A column by Wray in the July 15 edition of the *Post-Dispatch* wondered how much substance there really was to the oft-quoted statement that St. Louis was a great baseball town. Perhaps, Wray wondered, the fans were getting fed up. Attendance, after all, was not so great. Why didn't a rich man like Phil Ball come up with better ballplayers? Wray asked. Business manager Quinn defended his boss's interest in fielding the best team available: "[Y]ou can't buy what doesn't exist."[9]

Perhaps one reason for the team's progress was the resigning of Lee Fohl for 1922. Ball announced the decision in a letter, stating he wanted to stop any rumors that his manager would be dismissed. He defended his skipper's poor showing to date, explaining it was due to the need to find a second-base replacement for Joe Gedeon as well as a regular third baseman and to a rash of injuries to key players such as Gerber, Austin, and Sisler. News of Fohl's new contract hit the newspapers in the midst of a Browns winning streak, which reached eight by July 24, boosting the club into fifth place. The eighth victory, however, was a costly one. In the fourth inning Sis, "usually one of the quietest players on the field," turned bullish and was ejected from the game for punching the umpire.[10]

It all started out rather routinely. The Browns were playing the Red Sox at home in the fourth inning of a game they would eventually win. Sis grounded one to third and was called out to end the inning in a close play signaled by Umpire George Hildebrand. Sisler screamed, strode over to Hildebrand, and began to shove him around, as ten thousand fans simultaneously screeched their support and booed the ump. When the Browns players took their positions to start the fifth, Hildebrand told Sis he was through for the day. Once again, Sis lost control, this time punching the umpire with his gloved hand. It took both sides to calm the enraged Brownie first sacker.

The next day under the heading "Sisler Thumped Ump Hildebrand on the Jaw, but George Sisler was only one put out about it," the *Post-Dispatch* announced that Sis was indefinitely suspended by the league for his highly uncharacteristic assault on Hildebrand.[11] For George, it was the first and only suspension of his playing career. To add to his frustration, the Browns'

9. *St. Louis Post-Dispatch*, July 15, 1921.
10. Ibid., July 24, 1921.
11. Ibid., July 25, 1921.

streak of eight wins was halted by Boston's fine right-hander Sam Jones while Sisler watched from the bench.

Of course L. C. Davis could not let Sis's rare display go unheralded. Expressing his pleasure at George's fighting spirit and chastening those fans who said that George's lack of feistiness kept him from being "the greatest player in the world," Davis hastened to add that Sis's action was a costly one for the team. He described the incident in "Hitting":

> When Sisler hit G. Hildebrand
> A wallop on the ear,
> He made, according to the fans,
> The hit of his career.
>
> While Sisler may have meant the clout
> To knock him through the ropes,
> It only knocked the Brownies out
> Of first division hopes.
>
> Even though he had been justly roiled,
> We note with quite a pang,
> That wallop on the club recoiled
> Just like a boomerang.[12]

Aided by a couple of rainouts, the suspension lasted but three games and cost George a mere fifty dollars, a small fine even in those days. While George sat, Marty McManus moved to first and helped the Browns to a 7–5 win over the Yankees, pounding out four hits, including a triple and home run. The win helped the club remain in fifth place, just a few percentage points behind the Tigers.

The Browns were finally on the move. By August 3, their upward progression took them into fourth place. Ten days later a three-run tenth inning to defeat the Tigers in Detroit, 7–5, solidified their hold. Sis was on top of his game, hitting for the circuit plus one, with a single, two doubles, a triple, and a home run in his five at bats. The next day on August 14, the hot streak continued with four more hits, including a key double in another win over Detroit. His streak was stopped the next day in the fourth inning by the Tigers' Hooks Dauss. The ten straight hits were a career high, just one hit off the then major-league record of eleven set the year before by Tris Speaker of the Indians. In his next at bat Sis homered with a man on board to aid a 3–2 win.

Back at Sportsman's Park, twelve thousand fans saw the Yankees and a slugging Babe Ruth cool off the Browns, but on August 30, Sis had his

12. Ibid., July 26, 1921.

third five-for-five day and the Browns posted an 11–5 victory over the White Sox as they pushed closer to third-place Washington. And on September 2 Urban Shocker pitched a four-hitter, shutting out the White Sox 3–0. It was his ninth consecutive win on the way to an outstanding 27–12 season. Sis aided the cause with four hits and two runs batted in. The win pushed the Browns to 66–61; they were now in third place. As a result of his hot streak, Sis was tied with Speaker for fourth among American League batters at .373.

Across town another St. Louis ballplayer was having a great year. Rogers Hornsby would end the season with a .397 average—best in the National League—and with 126 runs batted in. In early September Sis joined Phil Ball and others in subscribing to a fund to give the Cards' star a special day. This gesture of friendship, along with others over the years, would one day reap benefits for George.

In mid-September the Browns traveled to New York to take on a Yankee team that had slugged its way into first place. Taking the field fifteen and a half games back, they watched in awe as the Babe slammed a record fifty-fifth home run. The Browns tried to answer with their own slugger, Ken Williams, who hit number 22, but in a losing effort. The next day Sis got into the act with a grand slam as Urban Shocker, adding to a burgeoning reputation as a Yankee "killer," brought his team home a winner. Ruth, however, did touch Shocker for number 56.

Urban Shocker's reputation was founded on more than just the ability to handle the Babe. An intense competitor behind a flat disposition, he was another Brown with above-average skills who was lost in the shuffle because he toiled for a below-average club. A former catcher, he carefully studied his adversaries and was said to possess an excellent book on the hitters in the league. An injury, sustained while catching, left the former Yankee with a crooked finger. The minor deformity aided both his grip and the effectiveness of his pitches, including an accurate fastball, the occasional spitter, and a mixture of curves.

Throughout September the Browns played just well enough to hang on to their first-division spot. On September 27 the team capped off the season by shutting out the Yankees 2–0. Again Shocker was on the mound and Sisler was his top ally, with a home run that knocked in both runs. It was the third time during the season that Shocker held the great Ruth hitless.

The only excitement left was furnished by the Tigers as they played the Browns in the final series of 1921 with the American League batting title on the line between Tiger teammates Ty Cobb and outfielder Harry Heilman. It was touch and go until the end, but Heilman finished first at .394, with Cobb second at .389. Sis was fourth at .371, seven points behind the

Babe, who finished a spectacular year with 59 home runs and 171 runs batted in. Sisler tied for the league lead in triples with 19 and led in stolen bases with 35. His 12 home runs were down from his career high of 19 in 1920, but he had 104 runs batted in, second on the Browns to Ken Williams's team-leading 117. Moreover, he fielded a sparkling .993 in 138 games with only 10 errors.

Although he had not played at quite the same level as in 1920, Sis was still very much at the top of his game. Of more significance to him on the whole, the slight drop in personal statistics was more than made up by the advances the Browns made as a team. For the first time in his career, the Browns were a competitive team. A number of players were contributing to the team's success, including Johnny Tobin and Ken Williams. Tobin was second in the league in hits to Sis's third; fourth in total bases, one ahead of Sis; and tied with his teammate and Howard Shanks of Washington for the league lead in triples. Williams was in the top five in a number of hitting categories, including a tie with Bob Meusel of the Yankees for second in home runs with 24.

Despite the ascendancy of Shocker, the Browns' Achilles heel was still their pitching. They ended the year tied with Philadelphia for next to last in earned run average. Still, the 1921 Browns finally gave real hope that bigger and better results were on the horizon. Now if only the fans would realize it. Despite an 81–73 record and a strong third-place finish behind the Yankees and Indians, the team finished sixth out of eight in league attendance, which dropped by more than sixty thousand from the previous year. Team supporters were so used to poor finishes that even a record of 46–25 after July 15 failed to awaken them from their late summer snooze. In fairness, however, the Browns finished the year seventeen and a half games behind the Yankees, so there was no late-season race to nudge supporters from their nap. In addition, the Cardinals were playing their best ball in years, finishing just out of second place and tugging at the pocketbooks of those Missourians with divided loyalties.

As the Browns watched the Yankees lose the World Series to their hated cross-town rivals the Giants five games to three, they knew if they could just stock their arsenal by adding quality pitching depth to what otherwise was a solid squad, the Yanks could be beaten. What the Browns needed was a good old-fashioned pennant race of their own to swing fans off the fence and into their back yard. Maybe 1922 would be their year.

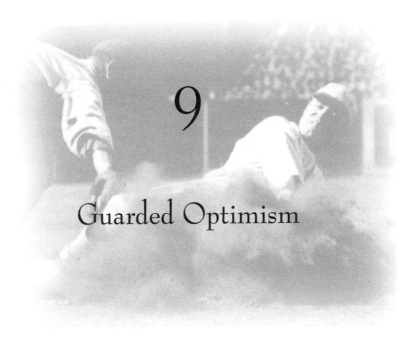

9

Guarded Optimism

Thoughts of previous struggles were far from the minds of the optimistic band of Browns players reporting for spring training in Mobile, Alabama, in early March 1922. Most of the regulars were already in camp when George arrived on March 6 along with Johnny Tobin. Sis had asked to delay his arrival to assure his children's recovery from an illness; Tobin to celebrate an important anniversary.

For one of the first times in the Sisler era, the Browns' everyday lineup was set. The group, which included catcher Hank Severeid, second baseman Marty McManus, third baseman Frank Ellerbe, shortstop Wally Gerber, and the outfield of Williams, Tobin, and Jacobson, had been carefully constructed over a number of years by Bob Quinn. The key reserves Pat Collins, Eddie Foster, Chick Shorten, Jimmy Austin, and Gene Robertson looked rather weak on paper, but actually would perform beyond expectations.

As the team gathered in Mobile, it was the moundsmen, as usual, that brought a frown. The three mainstays, Shocker, Davis, and Elam Vangilder, a twenty-five-year-old Browns' workhorse who pitched in a club-record 323 games from 1919 to 1927, presented little worry, having tallied 54 victories in 1921. Lee Fohl's mission in spring training was to find arms to fill out his dance card. He planned to do this with Ray Kolp, a twenty-seven-year-old rookie pitcher in 1921 who responded with a career best 14–4 and a 3.93 earned run average, and Rasty Wright, another twenty-seven-year-old righty who had played for the Browns from 1917 to 1919. Wright fulfilled Fohl's confidence with a very respectable 9–7 record and 2.92 earned run average with five saves.

The find of spring camp, however, was Hubert "Shucks" Pruett. Commonly known as Hub, the twenty-two-year-old rookie caught the eye of the Browns while he was still a medical student at the University of Missouri. Pruett left the university in June 1921 and pitched well enough the remainder of that season at minor-league Tulsa to garner an invitation to Mobile. Once there, he showed enough speed and control, including the ability to throw a pitch that later became known as the screwball, to catch the eyes of the Browns and solidify a spot as a relief pitcher and occasional starter. His first season with the Browns would prove his best, as he would fashion a 7–7 record with eight saves and a sparkling 2.33 earned run average. His real claim to fame, however, was his pitching performance against Babe Ruth. Pruett and his then unique pitch baffled the big fellow to the point that Ruth struck out ten of the first thirteen times he faced the future medical practitioner.

Completing the staff were relievers Bill Bayne, a reliable hurler with eleven wins and fourteen saves in 1921, and Dave Danforth, recently acquired from Columbus of the American Association, a pitcher with previous success as a reliever for the White Sox. Pitching, which had long been a weakness, was now a potential strength as the Browns headed north with a team that lost just one game all spring.

So-called experts around the country were picking the Yankees to cop the American League flag, despite the fact that on December 5, 1921, Commissioner Landis suspended Babe Ruth, slugger Bob Meusel, and pitcher "Wild Bill" Piercy for playing in an outlawed barnstorming tour. For the first time in recent memory, there were whispers around the circuit that the Browns could surprise everyone and win the pennant. Even the normally pessimistic *Post-Dispatch* was on the Browns' bandwagon early, telling readers that with superior hitting, better pitching, a stronger infield, and an outfield second to none, the team "seem[s] to have a genuine blown-in-the-bottle chance" to win a world title.[1]

As if to acknowledge their glowing preseason review, the Browns took three of four from the Cardinals in the crosstown series, an accomplishment made more meaningful because the Cards themselves were up a tick in the preseason prognostications. The Browns got even hotter once the games were for keeps. In Chicago the team took the first three from

1. *St. Louis Post-Dispatch*, April 12, 1922.

the White Sox, clubbing Sox pitchers for twenty-one hits in the finale. Sisler, who had a four-hit game against the White Sox, had another in Cleveland, as Vangilder three-hit the Tribe, 15–1. On April 20 the Browns stood 4–2 prior to opening their season at home with a 4–2 loss to the White Sox before a crowd of twelve thousand. On the eve of the clash, Ban Johnson, in a surprising statement more than likely for the benefit of local media only, tabbed the Browns as better than the Yankees, telling reporters he planned to "advise Phil Ball to enlarge the seating capacity of his field."[2]

Two days later, the home-standing Brownies and their fans were treated to a little piece of American League history. In a game that saw the Browns outstroke the White Sox 10–7, Ken Williams served notice that his muscle flexing of the previous season was for real by blasting three home runs to break Babe Ruth's mark and set a league record for home runs in a single game. Sis was on base on each occasion. The new mark fell one short of the major-league record held at that time by Ed Delahanty and Bobbie Lowe, each with four.

A week later, Williams hit two more in a 6–5 win over the Indians. His slugging was Ruth-like, but there the comparisons ended. The *Sporting News* once said the pair was so different "that it's almost a crime."[3] Unlike the big-boned Yankee slugger, the Browns' twenty-three-year-old answer was six feet, one inch and weighed 177 pounds. The native son of Grants Pass, a small Oregon town, Ken was one of six sons born to a mother who worked as a clerk in a logging camp and later ran a restaurant that served deadheading railroaders. The smiling, gap-toothed Williams was also a base stealer of some note, having stolen nine in the Browns' first fifteen games. His early exploits had baseball fans everywhere buzzing about the Browns-Yankees series in New York on May 20. By then, with Ruth reinstated, the top two home-run sluggers in the game would be standing face to face.

By May 2 the Browns, powered by the hot hitting of Williams and Sis, were in first place at 12–5, one game ahead of the Ruth-less Yanks. On May 6, with his team still clinging to first, Sis was leading the league in batting at .431, steals with 12, and runs with 23. He carried his hot streak into Philadelphia, where he stroked four hits, including one of four Browns' homers on the day in a 13–4 win for Shocker. Once again Williams hit one out, his eleventh, with George on base. The next day Sis repeated his act with four hits, including another home run. But this time the team

---

2. Quoted in ibid., April 20, 1922.
3. Quote from the *Sporting News* appears in Roger A. Godin, *The 1922 St. Louis Browns: Best of the American League's Worst*, 49.

faltered, 7–4. The following day, a 13–3 battering by the Athletics knocked the Browns out of first. Once again, Sis hit a home run among three hits. His four-day total was an amazing thirteen for nineteen with three home runs, a double, and nine singles.

In Boston on May 16, Urban Shocker stopped the Red Sox 6–5. The next day the Browns lost 4–3 when second baseman Marty McManus booted consecutive grounders in the ninth. The diminutive second sacker had played twenty-six straight errorless games before booting one in the last game in Philadelphia. Showing a kinder, gentler side, Phil Ball telephoned his infielder, telling him to "forget it." According to the owner, "[i]f we did not make mistakes we would all wear crowns."[4] McManus vowed to field better in New York. He would have to, for on May 20, the day of the first meeting of the year between the front-runners, Babe Ruth and Bob Meusel were reinstated.

Heading into the series, Sis was hitting a robust .442. Still, as usual, the eyes of the baseball world were on the Yankee slugger and his team, which held a two-game lead over St. Louis. Fortunately for the Brownies, the only thing the Babe got the day of the first game was a slew of gifts from his fans, including a solid silver bat. He struck out his first time up and went hitless in four at bats against starter Shocker and reliever Bill Bayne. Still, the Yankees were in front 2–1 with two down in the ninth before the Browns made some noise. At that point, Lee Fohl sent Chick Shorten to the plate to bat for McManus. Shorten singled to center. Pat Collins batted for Shocker and also hit safely into center. Then the Browns got a huge break. Jack Tobin cracked one down the first base line that first baseman Wally Pipp knocked down and flipped to the pitcher. The umpire waved Tobin out to end the game, but Sad Sam Jones, the Yankee hurler, dropped the ball. Seeing the umpire wave the runner out, the crowd swarmed onto the field, thinking the game was over. Even some of the players on both sides were already in the clubhouse before order was restored and the umpire clarified his decision that the runner was safe.

The controversial play opened the floodgates. On the play itself, Shorten scored the tying run and Collins took second. When play resumed, Jones was totally ineffective. Wally Gerber singled, scoring Collins with the lead run. Now Sis was at the plate, already with three hits in the game. Jones decided to walk him and then walked Ken Williams to load the bases. The next batter was Baby Doll Jacobson, who swung hard, planting a Jones pitch into the left field bleachers and sending thirty-seven thousand fans home angry and disappointed. The final score was Browns 8, Yankees 2.

4. Quoted in *St. Louis Post-Dispatch*, May 19, 1922.

After that important win, successive losses to the Yanks made game four of the series crucial. In that one, Ken Williams finally came through, notching his twelfth home run of the young season with two aboard to seal an 11–3 win as Urban Shocker pitched his second game of the series. Sis got his licks in, too, hammering a Carl Mays pitch into the right field Polo Grounds bleachers in the fourth inning for his fifth four-bagger of the year. Babe, who had homered for the first time on May 22 in his team's triumph, was again hitless against Shocker. As the Browns left New York with a split of this first series with the co-leaders, they could be certain, at least, of one thing—they had served proper notice to the Yankees and baseball in general that their 1922 edition was the genuine article.

The good feelings accumulated in New York did not last long, however. In late May the Browns went into a hitting slump, losing three straight to the White Sox. Playing a twin bill in Chicago, the team got strong pitching from Shocker and Vangilder, but still lost twice, 2–1 and 3–2. Sisler was in a one-for-nine funk. As the month ended, things began to improve somewhat with the club winning three straight, including two from Detroit.

On May 31 Browns' management celebrated, along with the rest of organized baseball, as the U.S. Supreme Court ruled that baseball was exempt from Federal anti-trust legislation. According to National League President John Heydler, the game "is a sport and not a trade."[5]

As the year wore on, one disturbing pattern emerged for the Browns in close games. Despite the ninth-inning heroics in New York on May 20, on four other occasions the Browns had victory in their grasp in the ninth inning, only to lose the game. The newspapers in St. Louis began calling it the "ninth inning 'jinx.'"[6] The plague struck a fifth time on June 3. As twelve thousand hoarse fans cheered its demise, the jinx pushed the visiting White Sox to victory when with two out and a 4–3 lead in the top of the ninth, Sox hitters banged out three hits to seal a 5–4 win. The painful loss kept the Browns from catching the Yankees, as they remained a full game off the pace.

By June 10 the Yankees carried a two-and-a-half-game lead into St. Louis for their second meeting with the Browns. By now Ruth was rounding into form. He enjoyed a rare home run off Urban Shocker, his sixth of the season, as the Yankees pounded out a 14–5 win. The game was not without controversy, as pitcher Carl Mays, never a St. Louis favorite, accused the Browns of trying to bean him. Quick interaction by the umpire averted a fight. Adding insult to injury, Phil Ball's left cheek was cut and

5. Quoted in ibid., May 31, 1922.
6. Ibid., June 4, 1922.

required stitches when the owner was struck by a foul ball in the seventh off the bat of one of his own players, Gene Robertson. He had only to look around the stadium, however, to see twenty-two thousand loyal Browns fans who could make him feel better. The team was on its way to a Browns record of 712,918 fans, about 400,000 more than the previous year.

The next day, playing before thirty thousand fans sandwiched into a stadium that normally seated nineteen thousand, the Browns lost again, 8–4. Now on the verge of extinction, they battled back in games three and four of the series, winning 7–1 behind the rookie Hub Pruett and 13–4 with Dave Danforth throwing. Sis did his part in the series, going nine for eighteen at the plate with two triples.

Next in town for four games was Washington. The Browns took the first three of four from the middle-of-the-pack Nationals, running their winning streak to five. In the first game George crashed a grand slam in a 7–6 win over the great Walter Johnson. The Browns won the games without their ace Urban Shocker, hospitalized after the second straight day he had pitched against the Yankees and lost. Following that game, Shocker complained of pain in his leg, a condition that had bothered him all season long. Looking at the long haul, business manager Bob Quinn ordered him to the hospital to get the matter under control. In the ace's absence, the remaining Browns pitchers met the challenge. Pruett won two, while Danforth and Davis had one victory each.

For some reason, the Nationals seemed to bring out the best in "the Sizzler," possibly because Joe Judge, the Washington first sacker, was himself a superb fielder. On one occasion in 1922, when the Browns were playing the Nationals in the nation's capital, the home crew had Sam Rice on third with one out and Judge at the plate. The infield was playing in, and George smelled a squeeze play with the batter aiming to just get the ball into play as the runner from third sprinted home. Judge did his job, running down the first base line as Rice sprinted toward the score. Just as the ball reached Judge, however, Sis ran down the first base line toward home, picked up the bunt, tagged Judge before he could get far down the line and threw to catcher Hank Severeid in time for him to tag out the astonished Rice for a spectacular double play.[7]

Plays like this are the stuff of which legends are made, but sometimes in the telling the legend exceeds the deed. One such instance occurred in

7. Sisler Memoirs, 15. Sisler's memoirs confirm the accuracy of the reports of the squeeze play against Washington, although it is described in Santa Maria and Costello, *In the Shadows of the Diamond,* as involving Joe Judge as the runner and Roger Peckinpaugh at the plate (p. 211). According to Sisler's memoirs the errant toss play, also described by Santa Maria and numerous others, is inaccurate.

1921 when Sis fielded a grounder and tossed the ball toward first in the direction of what should have been the pitcher covering the bag. Legend has it that when he realized the pitcher was not there, Sis lunged for his toss and fielded it, landing on the bag in time for the out. Not so, according to the man himself. In reality, when Sis realized the pitcher was not covering first, he ran after his own toss, recovering it in time to keep the runner from taking second on the snafu. It was a terrific play, but not one for the books.

By the final game of the Washington series, Sis was leading both leagues in six categories: batting average (.433), runs, hits, total bases, triples, and stolen bases. On June 22, following a series in Philly in which the Browns took three of four from the Athletics, Sis skipped batting practice in Detroit due to a dislocated thumb, but ripped a first inning double. Still, the Browns lost, 3–2. They lost again the next day. In the third game, won 13–4 by the Browns with Ken Williams slamming his nineteenth home run and Sisler reeling off four hits, a near riot ensued in the sixth inning. A Motor City crowd of twenty-one thousand was on hand to watch the fun. Jimmy Austin, tired of the antics of the Tigers first base coach in trying to distract Browns pitcher Dave Danforth, ran onto the field and swiped first baseman Lu Blue's ball glove, tossing it into the stands just as Ty Cobb whiffed at Danforth's pitch for strike three. At this, the fans and players poured onto the field trying to get to Austin. It took police at least five minutes to restore order and preserve the Browns victory. The win and a 5–0 Dixie Davis shutout the next day came as the Yankees, feeling the effects of Babe's long layoff, were in the midst of losing ten of twelve, including eight straight. Ruth had hit only eight round trippers by the end of June and his average was also down. The Yankees were also getting uncharacteristically weak pitching and missed injured catcher Wally Schang. On June 24, by virtue of this switch in fortunes, the Browns led the mighty Yanks by a full two games.

Then in early July, with Urban Shocker back and the Browns in position to put some light between them and New York, the team hit another batting slump. Between July 7 and 27, George's average dropped from .430 to .407. All statements to the contrary, the dislocated thumb was affecting his grip. Still, the Browns hung in there with great pitching, including Shocker's 1–0 whitewash of the Red Sox in Boston on July 7. A doubleheader scheduled for the next day was postponed due to wet ground conditions. Coming on a day when, according to *Post-Dispatch* writer J. Roy Stockton, "the bright sun . . . had the field in a near dusty condition by 1 o'clock," the cancellation brought charges, heard often before, that the

Red Sox and Yankees were in cahoots.[8] Vice-President Walter Fritsch was certain of Red Sox owner Harry Frazee's purpose. The Browns would now be required to play three doubleheaders in three days, sending the team to the Polo Grounds to meet the Yankees later in the month with an over-worked pitching staff. The games were postponed "deliberately" to aid the Yankees, according to Fritsch, who took photographs of the field to show Ban Johnson.[9] The charges were hard to prove and nothing came of them. The damage was done, however, as the Browns split the six double-header games with the next-to-last Red Sox and headed for New York in a foul mood.

After the Browns' July visit to New York, the westerners held but a half-game lead on the Yankees, who took two of the three games played. Ken Williams's twenty-first home run proved a key in the lone Browns win. That former Yankee-killer Urban Shocker lost his fourth straight Yan-kee encounter, by a 4–0 margin, was a definite factor behind the unease that fell over the team and the city. In addition, a Cobb-Heilman push in late June, which propelled the Tigers to twenty-two wins in twenty-six games, brought Detroit within four and a half games of the top before Heilman injured his back.

A split in Washington and winning three of four games in Philly bright-ened things before the Browns lost the last game of a long road swing that saw them go 9–9. While some of the Browns, such as Marty McManus, were playing good ball, others, including Sis, were not. George's batting woes were carrying over to the field as he bobbled one and threw away another in the 11–6 loss to the Tigers that ended the team's travels on July 23. According to the *Post-Dispatch,* both plays might have been scored hits if fielded by players of lesser stature, but the price of stardom is always high expectations.[10]

As the sputtering team prepared to receive the Yankees at Sportsman's Park, it would seem a call for reserve help might have been in order. Lee Fohl, however, told reporters he was satisfied; his team would stand pat. The sports staff of the *Post-Dispatch* begged to differ. In a column that ap-peared on July 25, the morning of the first game of a four-game set with the Yankees, John E. Wray spoke bluntly about the "unholy alliance" be-tween the Red Sox and Yankees, in particular its taint on American League baseball. Tracing its origins to a loan from the estate of Yankee owner Jack

8. *St. Louis Post-Dispatch,* July 7, 1922.
9. Quoted in ibid.
10. Ibid., July 25, 1922.

Ruppert to Red Sox owner Harry Frazee rubber-stamped by White Sox owner Charles Comiskey, who refrained from opposing the questionable deal due to his long-standing feud with Ban Johnson, Wray felt that whatever would or could be done at this time was too little and too late. After all, the Yankees were led by a group of former Red Sox stars, including Carl Mays and the Babe himself: "[A]ll the red-blood of Boston worth having has already been transferred into the New York organism."[11]

If the purpose of his column was to fire up the local troops, Wray failed. The Browns, who entered the series a game and a half in front of the visitors, could only muster one victory in four, taking the opener 8–0. Sis made up for his recent blunders against the Tigers by racing in to catch a popup bunt and firing to third from the ground to double up Deacon Scott, who had ventured too far off third. Urban Shocker, back to his previous form versus the Yankees, treated the eighteen thousand spectators to a shutout.

In the next game Babe hit two home runs and the Yankees won 11–6. Then New York won again, this time 6–5. The slumping Sis, whose average had fallen to .402, a mark which trailed Cobb for the league lead, got a double. Coming in the midst of another devastating loss, the safety meant little, but as with any record, it all starts somewhere. For George it was on July 27, 1922.

The loss was particularly costly to the Browns for another reason. During the game pitcher Dave Danforth was ejected by the umpire for throwing a "doctored" ball. The infraction brought an automatic ten-day suspension. Coupled with a hand injury to Dixie Davis and Pruett's sore arm, the Browns were facing serious pitching woes. Perhaps they realized it as they finished the series with a 7–3 loss, dropping them from the league lead for the first time since June 16.

The three straight losses at the hands of the Yankees in the face of pitching problems and Sis's long hitting decline added to the team's mounting anxiety. George's problems were particularly galling to the *Post-Dispatch*'s J. Roy Stockton, who called the first baseman "the spark plug, the life, and when he doesn't get on the bases the team just doesn't win, that's all."[12]

The next day the Browns began to prove Stockton wrong. Facing the Red Sox, they won 4–1 behind Urban Shocker. During the contest Sis was spiked just below the left kneecap in the fourth inning while make an "effort" play sliding into first. He was safe, but the single proved costly.

11. Ibid.
12. Ibid., July 29, 1922.

He was knocked from the game and would miss several more games at a crucial point in the season. Catcher Hank Severeid was also injured in the game by a foul tip off the bat of Sox first baseman George Burns. The Browns' everyday lineup, already missing injured third baseman Frank Ellerbe, was now a veritable shambles.

If there was need for an excuse to completely fold, the Browns now had it. Even a slumping George Sisler was better than no George Sisler at all. But the Browns did not quit. Playing with a ragtag lineup that had Jacobson moving to first and Pat Collins catching, the team reeled off three more wins from the Red Sox to sweep the series and regain first place. It was almost too much. Swept up in the excitement, Phil Ball and the Browns announced tentative plans to install temporary bleachers for seven thousand extra seats, raising the capacity at Sportsman's Park to twenty-six thousand, just in case they might need it in October. Since larger crowds than that had already jammed the park for earlier games that season, it seemed that even more seating than proposed was in order.

Now back in first, the team lost one to Philadelphia and then won the next two before Sis returned, recovered and—perhaps more important for the remainder of the season—rested. On August 5, the local press declared his slump over as he recovered from the shock of hitting into a first-inning triple play by tripling and singling in four at bats to aid Ray Kolp in a 4–1 win over the Athletics in game four. The next day Sis proved the scribes right as his three hits helped Urban Shocker prevail over visiting Washington 8–4.

On August 7 the entire Browns team erupted in a 16–1 win over the Nationals. Ken Williams set a modern-day (post-1900) record by hitting two home runs in one inning. In fact, in that inning, the sixth, the Browns belted out nine hits for a total of twenty-four bases. Two days later the team closed a successful 11–5 home stand with an 8–6 win over the Nats. The long road trip to follow, covering twenty-six games, would be the Browns' last for the year.

In preparation for a trip that found the team in its best physical condition of the season, Lee Fohl made a position change in his outfield. "I expect the team to profit greatly through the shift in outfielders, which puts Williams in center and Jacobson in left," he said.[13] The theory was that Williams was a surer fielder with a stronger throwing arm. In addition, he covered more ground than the slower Baby Doll.

Another change, this one more surprising and shrouded in mystery, involved the demotion of Dave Danforth to the minors. Danforth had not

13. Quoted in ibid., August 11, 1922.

pitched since being removed from the game on July 27, which brought his suspension. Apparently a tacit agreement was reached to at least temporarily banish him from the game. Prior to his release on August 11 he was waived by each team in both leagues. Strangely, no one ever learned how he doctored the ball. On numerous occasions, however, since his arrival in the big leagues, examinations had disclosed foreign substances on the ball. The official word from Browns' management was that the pitcher "was of no further use," since "everyone was nagging him and weakening his efforts by criticism."[14] For his part, Danforth never told a soul, even his closest friends on the team, how he doctored the ball, and he denied the allegations to the end. He left with a record of 5–2, having started ten games and earned a save in another, while carrying a 3.28 earned run average in twenty appearances. Perhaps he reformed while in the minors, because he resurfaced with the Browns again in 1923 and pitched for the team until 1925, but not without further controversy.

The final road trip began in Chicago on August 12 and ended in Detroit on September 3. After finishing the trip with a record of 13–11, the Browns trailed the Yankees by two. Sis maintained the hot pace initiated following his return from injury. Managing to garner one hit in each game and multiple hits in most, the Browns' star was in the midst of a major hitting streak. While this was going on, the American League announced its plans to elicit a vote of eight sportswriters, one from each league city, for the year's "greatest all around player." An ill-reasoned rule prohibited player/managers from the ballot, thus eliminating Ty Cobb and Tris Speaker from consideration. Since the Babe was having an off year by Ruthian standards, Sis was the odds-on favorite to capture the award. Now the star attraction on a legitimate pennant contender, he was ten points ahead of Cobb in batting and among the league leaders in a number of other categories, and might well have won the award anyway. In most places in America he was now considered the best in baseball.

In the August 30 issue of the magazine *Outlook*, matchless Giants pitcher Christy Mathewson wrote, "Now there is Sisler of the St. Louis team—he is every bit as valuable as Ruth, some people think more valuable. But he has another temperament. When he makes a great hit or a great play and the crowd is ready to idolize him, he modestly touches his cap and fades out of sight."[15] Even a New York sportswriter got into the act: "If there is anything he [Sisler] cannot do in the national pastime, I would like to see it. Whether it is hitting the ball, playing first base, sliding into a bag or

14. Ibid., August 12, 1922.
15. Quoted in Paul Warburton, "George Sisler," 96.

beating out a throw, it makes no difference. He can do one just as well as the other. I rate him the greatest player we ever had in the baseball sport."[16]

All this praise meant nothing when the road-weary Browns rolled into New York for a twin bill on August 25 in what would be their final appearance at the Polo Grounds. (In 1923 the Yankees would move to a new ballpark, Yankee Stadium, which many still call "The House that Ruth Built.") In game one of the doubleheader, the Browns followed Urban Shocker's lead to a 3–1 win. Sis, Marty McManus, and Bill Jacobson had multi-hit games. It was Shocker's fourth win over the Yankees against five defeats. In game two, the Browns had the winning runs on base in the ninth with Marty McManus, a .312 hitter and the star of game one, at the plate. When Sad Sam Jones got Marty to fly out to end the game, one New York sportswriter wrote that McManus's failure cost the Browns the pennant. Seeing that the teams still had more than a month to play, the comment was more prophetic than based on any sort of logic.

Still, when the Yankees pounded Wayne "Rasty" Wright for a 9–2 win and followed up with a 2–1 victory in the finale, the Browns' pennant hopes clouded considerably. In this last game, it looked like the weather gods paid the Browns a favor when it rained on Sunday, forcing the game to be postponed until Monday. This gave Shocker an extra day of rest and another starting assignment. He and his opponent, Bob Shawkey, thereupon engaged in a truly classic pitching dual that ended in the eleventh when the Yankees loaded the bases and scored the winning run on a deep fly by Bob Meusel. In the tenth, the Browns had failed to score when a liner by Eddie Foster was called foul. Years later Sis could still picture the play, telling a writer, "I can still see in my mind where the ball hit. It was a fair ball."[17] On just such plays are pennants won and lost.

The three straight losses left the Browns a game and a half behind the Yankees. They limped out of New York, but regained some of their form in Cleveland and Detroit, winning two of three from each club. This maintained pace with the Yankees. Since the final twenty-three games would be played at Sportsman's Park, there was still a fever in St. Louis. Heretofore a rare ailment in the city on the long, broad river, it was better known in other big-league towns as "pennant fever."

In anticipation of almost a full month of hometown baseball, John E. Wray reported in his *Post-Dispatch* column on August 30 that in 1922 Phil Ball stood to double the biggest Browns profit: $147,000, earned way back

16. Ibid., quoting from article that appeared in the *Sporting News* by an unnamed New York sportswriter.
17. Quote by George Sisler for Thomas Meany's book *Baseball's Greatest Teams* appears in Godin, *The 1922 St. Louis Browns*, 144.

in 1908. Still, this unexpected bonanza would barely make up for the owner's losses in the Federal League and from past Brown failures.[18]

Wray's prediction of spinning turnstiles was right. On Labor Day, forty thousand St. Louis fans, fifteen thousand in the morning and another twenty-five thousand in the afternoon, watched their beloved team batter the Indians 10–3 and 12–1. Shocker won the first game, his twenty-third, and Vangilder the nightcap. Sisler was on a rampage. In the opener he had a single, two doubles, and a triple; in the second, two singles and a double for a seven-for-nine day. He scored seven of the Browns' twenty-two runs, and of more than passing interest, his hitting streak, which had started amidst a slump shortly before his spiking injury, was now at thirty-four consecutive games. In the thick of his first real pennant race, George was pointed directly at Ty Cobb's American League record of safe hits in forty consecutive games. And to top it all off, he was playing as splendidly in the field as at the plate.

On September 5 the Browns topped the Indians again, this time 10–9 as "Ironman" Shocker won his twenty-fourth game, Ken Williams hit his thirty-fourth home run, and Sis extended his hitting streak to thirty-five games. The triumph lifted the Browns back into first place. As ten thousand fans screamed with pleasure, J. Roy Stockton noted, "[b]aseball in St. Louis has reached a serious stage."[19]

---

18. *St. Louis Post-Dispatch*, August 30, 1922.
19. Ibid., September 6, 1922.

10

"The Little World Series"

The 10–9 win over the Indians on September 5, 1922, was the Browns' third straight. When they followed it with an 11–3 win over the Tribe, riding a strong performance by Dixie Davis, it looked like home cooking was agreeing with Sis and his mates. In the series, the Browns mauled Indian pitching for forty-three runs and fifty-nine hits, pounding each beleaguered pitcher they faced. Such was the grip the Brownies now held on St. Louis that Stockton of the *Post-Dispatch* told readers, "From now until the affair is settled one way or the other everything [else] must be relegated to the classification of non-essential industry."[1]

Next in town for a four-game series were the tenacious third-place Tigers, still playing without former batting champion Harry Heilman. In the first game the Browns lost 8–3, despite a three-run blast by Ken Williams. Having led with their ace, Shocker, and failed, the Browns fell out of first. Sisler extended his hitting streak to thirty-seven games with two hits.

If there was pressure on the Browns due to the loss, they did not show it. The next day they humiliated the Tigers 16–0 on the strength of twenty hits and Vangilder's five-hit shutout. Williams hit his thirty-seventh home run and Sis went three for five, extending the streak to thirty-eight. If all

1. Quoted in Godin, *The 1922 St. Louis Browns*, 153.

138

went well, he could tie Cobb's record playing against the great one himself. The next afternoon, Sunday, September 10, the rains came, postponing the game but giving reporters a chance to talk to the Georgia Peach about the pennant race. Telling reporters the long home stand gave the Browns the edge, Cobb cautioned that the Yankees' experience could play a part in evening things out. Despite their favorable schedule, "[t]he Browns have their backs to the wall today in one of the greatest pennant fights I have ever seen."[2]

The next day Sportsman's Park was the scene of one of the greatest victories in Browns team history. It was also one of the most costly. Early in the contest the Tigers touched starter Dixie Davis for four runs. With his team down in the fifth by a 4–1 count and sensing a potential runaway by the Tigers, Lee Fohl replaced Davis with Hub Pruett, who proceeded to shut down the Tiger hitters. Still, the home team trailed 4–3 with two out in the ninth and two strikes on third baseman Eddie Foster. As seventeen thousand distraught fans made for the exits, Foster worked the count to 3–2, then got ball four on a close call by a rookie umpire. Sis was next up. He had already extended his streak to thirty-nine, one short of Cobb's record, with a blooper in the eighth. As Sis strode to the plate, Cobb made a defensive change in right field, bringing in the speedy Ira Flagstead. It made no difference. George slammed a Howard Ehmke pitch between Flagstead and Cobb, the center fielder, and reached third as Foster scored the tying run. Cobb ordered walks to Williams and Jacobson, to face little Marty McManus with the bases full. McManus was up to the challenge. He lined a single to center, scoring Sis with the winning run and closing doors forever on any idea of a ninth-inning jinx while also winning himself a ride halfway to the dugout by delirious fans.

In retrospect, Sis's triple was monumental. As the tying run scored, it was reported that fans filled the air with straw hats, seat cushions, newspapers, and anything else they could toss. "Men beat each other on the back and women threw their arms around strange men, their men, anybody's man. A woman in the upper grand stand . . . felt her joy so keenly that tears streamed down her cheeks."[3] But those tears of joy would soon turn to tears of sadness. In the seventh frame, shortstop Wally Gerber had made a wide throw toward first on a Cobb grounder. Sis stretched so far to his right to snag the ball that he fell forward onto his shoulder. Nothing much was made of it at the time, and George finished the game, as reported, in spectacular fashion. The next afternoon, however, as the Tigers

2. Quoted in *St. Louis Post-Dispatch,* September 11, 1922.
3. Ibid., September 12, 1922.

and Browns lined up to tangle for the fourth and final game of their series, Sis was missing in action. He did not appear until the second inning, and then as a spectator only as the Browns eked out an 8–6 win behind Ray Kolp.

During the night Sis's right shoulder had caused him so much pain that he was unable to sleep. That morning, unbeknownst to even Bob Quinn and Lee Fohl, George sought medical help from his friend and team physician, Dr. Robert F. Hyland. Later that day Hyland, who doubled as the company surgeon for United Railways, told a stunned city that Sis had severely strained his deltoid muscle. When George moved his arm he was in such misery that Hyland taped it to immobilize the arm and shoulder for at least a week.

Then on the evening of September 12, following the Browns' 8–6 win, Hyland delivered the real blow. "I feel that Sisler will be very fortunate to completely recover before the close of the season," he told the *Post-Dispatch*, "though he doubtless will try to play. For one week it is certain he ought not to attempt anything on the ball field; but I guess he will try to get into the Yankees series [beginning September 16], despite my advice."[4]

As devastating as the injury was to the Browns organization and the city of St. Louis, it came as an even bigger blow to Sis personally. In the thick of his first pennant race, just three days removed from a confrontation with the Yankees in a matchup already dubbed "the little world series" by players, fans, and scribes throughout the land, the availability of the team's star player and the game's current leading light was in serious jeopardy.

Of course, the immediate impact of George's injury was uncertain. Despite his absence, the Browns' most recent victory over the Tigers permitted them to keep pace with the Yanks. However, only three games with Boston stood between the Browns and the big confrontation. They had no other choice. They would have to hang together.

Individually, George's absence, even for a few games, jeopardized a number of potential records. If the injury hampered his ability to hit, as surely it would, his thirty-nine-game hitting streak could end one short of Cobb's 1911 record and five short of Willie Keeler's all-time major-league record of forty-four set in 1897. In addition, Sis was on pace to break his own major-league mark of 257 hits in a season made in 1920.

Then there was the batting average. When he was injured George was hitting .424. This was a mere two points less than the modern-day record of Napoleon Lajoie in 1901 and four points better than Cobb's top mark of .420. Of course, if he failed to play again in 1922 he would be unable to

4. Quoted in ibid., September 13, 1922.

further challenge Lajoie's mark, but he would better Cobb's best effort. On the other hand, if he played with a bad shoulder, the average was likely to drop significantly.

None of that mattered to George. On September 15 it was reported by Hyland that the shoulder was "greatly improved," and that even at the risk of further injury and despite continuing pain when he lifted the arm above a horizontal position, George planned to play in the New York series.[5] He would be needed, as the Browns' series with the Red Sox proved. Moved from the outfield to sub for Sis in the last game against Detroit, Baby Doll Jacobson committed two errors. Not wishing to press his luck against Boston, Lee Fohl shifted McManus to first base, moved Foster from third base to second, and returned Frank Ellerbe to third base, where Ellerbe had not played since a knee injury felled him on July 19.

Against Boston in the first game of the series, Urban Shocker was brilliant. Unfortunately, Rip Collins was even better, and the Red Sox won 3–1 on George Burns's four-bagger with one man aboard. The idle Yankees were now up by a game and a half. One of the runs in the first contest with the Red Sox came on a Marty McManus error. Thus in game two, reserve catcher Pat Collins trotted down to first. Three games, and the Browns had used three different first sackers. This last move paid immediate dividends, however. Collins fielded well and stroked three singles, while Jacobson, back in familiar territory, found his bat for a triple in a 5–3 Browns win. Dixie Davis got the victory. On September 15, one day before the Yankee invasion, the Browns won again 7–1 as Vangilder pitched a complete game, limiting Boston to five hits and issuing no walks. That win and a Yankee loss to Chicago closed the gap to half a game.

Now the "little world series" was at hand. A huge crowd, many from well outside the city, began arriving at eleven for the three o'clock start. The crowd, estimated at a stadium-bursting thirty thousand, took those seats available and then massed on the field itself behind ropes stretched from one end of the bleachers to the other. Hyland's advice to the contrary, when game time rolled around and the Browns took the field, George was at first base. He received a huge ovation before the game when he stepped from the dugout, took two swings at the pitches of batting practice pitcher Jimmy Austin, and connected on both.

In the opener the Yankees pitched tall, slender veteran Bob Shawkey, their answer to workhorse Shocker. The Browns pitched the workhorse himself. Shocker finished what he started, but it was not enough. The Yankees jumped in front early with runs in the second and third innings

5. Ibid., September 15, 1922.

and held on to win 2–1. Despite his shoulder, Sis was able to extend his batting streak in the fourth inning by doubling off the shin of second baseman Aaron Ward. No error was charged. Later Ward made up for his misplay by robbing George of a run-scoring hit that would have scored the go-ahead runs in the sixth.

In the bottom of the ninth inning, an unfortunate incident occurred that may have hurt the Browns' pennant hopes more than their opponent's victory. Eddie Foster, back at third base, led off the inning and sent a lazy fly to right fielder Meusel. Just as Meusel was about to catch it, someone in the stands threw a bottle at Lawton "Whitey" Witt, the Yankee center fielder. The bottle made a direct hit, knocking the team's leadoff hitter out cold. Witt was carried unconscious into the clubhouse, to be diagnosed with a mild concussion and treated by Hyland. He returned bandaged the next day for game two. Phil Ball offered five hundred dollars for the arrest and conviction of the bottle-throwing fan. The fan was never found.

When the incident occurred, a pall fell over the crowd. Many St. Louis fans shouted for the game to be called in New York's favor. When order was restored and George came to the plate, "hundreds in the grandstand crowd set up a cry the like of which was never before heard in St. Louis. They clamored for Bob Shawkey to strike Sisler out."[6] Shawkey did not, but achieved a similar result. Still in shock, presumably as much from the booing as the bottle-throwing incident, Sis bunted poorly for an easy out. Ken Williams then flied meekly to right, and the game was in the books.

Speaking with reporters from the *Post-Dispatch* after the game, George said the vicious act took "the heart out of the Browns."[7] In contrast, the incident, though the act of a single fan and denounced by the fans and the Browns organization, seemed to arouse and solidify a Yankee squad that quite frankly did not get along well all season.

In the locker room after the game Phil Ball inquired about the condition of his own star player. "It's aching terribly, now," Sis told him. "The doctor tells me that the injured muscle is trying to contract." Nonetheless, he assured his boss he would be in the lineup the next afternoon for game two.[8]

In the aftermath, there was some conjecture that but for George's shoulder problem he would have beaten the throw to first after the fine stop by Ward in the sixth inning, thereby allowing the tying run to score. Playing hurt, he ran with his arm hanging at his side, reducing his speed. The

6. *St. Louis Post-Dispatch* article quoted in Godin, *The 1922 St. Louis Browns*, 168.
7. Ibid., 169.
8. Quoted in *St. Louis Post-Dispatch*, September 17, 1922.

Sporting News reported, "His right arm hung almost lifeless at his side."[9] Years later Sis would admit, "Actually I should never have played. The arm was so badly crippled that I had to lift my gloved hand with my left hand in order to catch balls at first base. I told the guys to be sure and throw the ball low and I couldn't possibly catch a ball over my head. At bat, I was practically one-handed. It was ridiculous for me to even try to play but I was young then and you couldn't have kept me out of there with a gun."[10]

While the "little world series" was still in progress, Babe Ruth named his All-America Baseball Team for 1922 in a copyrighted article that appeared in papers across the country. Two St. Louis players made the squad: Rogers Hornsby at second base and George at first base. The Bambino, who unabashedly named himself to the squad, made special mention of the pair, calling them "supreme." About Sis he said there may be a better infielder, "but I don't think very many. And any bird who can bat .422 and steal fifty bases in 130 would play first base on my team if he muffed a million." Describing his adversary as a "university graduate and perfect gentleman," Ruth pointed to Sis as "an object lesson to all ball players."[11]

On September 17 another thirty thousand fans packed Sportsman's Park for a game they felt their team must have to stay alive for a pennant. A loss and they were two and a half games out. On the mound for the Yankees was yet another veteran, the still youthful Waite Hoyt, a future Hall of Famer who had already won nineteen games in 1921 and would win 237 games during his illustrious career. Facing him was Lee Fohl's surprise choice, Hub Pruett, still wet behind the ears, having completed but three games during his first season while nursing a sore arm for a good deal of it. Still, Pruett threw that "fork hand fade away" that had Babe Ruth's number. On paper it looked like the Yankees had a definite edge.

When the umpire signaled the final out, the Browns had their must-have win, 5–1. Sis had hit in his record forty-first straight game and St. Louis had a new hero, the pride of the University of Missouri, Hubert Pruett.

9. Quoted in Warburton, "George Sisler," 97.
10. Quoted in Meany, *Baseball's Greatest Hitters*, 184.
11. Quoted in syndicated article, *St. Louis Post-Dispatch*, September 18, 1922. Although Babe Ruth's byline appears in this article and numerous other syndicated newspaper articles and columns, it is the consensus of baseball historians that Ruth's writing, as well as that of numerous other players of that era whose bylines appeared in newspapers across the country, was the work of ghostwriters. In Ruth's case, the man behind the typewriter was often Ford Frick, who later became the commissioner of the major leagues and protected Ruth's home run record from assault in 1961 by Roger Maris, placing an asterisk by the entry.

The surprise starter covered himself with glory, pitching a five-hitter, striking out eight including Ruth for the tenth time in fourteen chances, walking but one, and throwing an efficient 103 pitches in nine innings. In fairness to the Babe, he did pole a home run in the sixth for the Yankees' only score and finished two for three. Sis broke Cobb's 1911 record in that same sixth inning, hitting a single which figured in the Browns' first score as they broke the game open with three runs.

All was now set for the rubber game on September 18. A win would give the Browns a half-game lead over the Yankees, with only nine games left, all at home, against second-division opponents Washington, Philadelphia, and Chicago. Six of the Yankees' remaining ten games were with third-place Detroit and fourth-place Cleveland, although they would finish with three against lowly Boston and a last game against Washington. All of New York's remaining games were on the road.

So to diminish the importance of the rubber game of the "little world series" would be a mistake. On the other hand, there was still a lot of ball to be played by both contenders. Nevertheless, at noon on the eighteenth you would not want to discuss future possibilities to those fans already crammed into every nook and cranny in Sportsman's Park to witness the Browns secure the pennant, even though a win would in no way ensure their goal. The only question was which pitcher Lee Fohl planned to use to throttle the Yanks. Initially it appeared he would go with another surprise starter, lefty Bill Bayne. The spot starter was penciled into the lineup, but when the game started it was right-hander Dixie Davis on the mound opposing "Bullet Joe" Bush, who had briefly appeared in relief in game two.

Once again, against his doctor's orders, Sis was at first base, but his restrictions were such that he erred in the first inning, dropping a wide throw from shortstop Gerber that he normally would have caught with ease. The miscue did not result in a Yankee score. At the end of seven innings Davis was working on a two-hitter, and the Browns were on top 2–0. In the eighth inning the Yankees cut the lead to one, scoring on a wild throw by McManus playing second base. Bush retired the Browns in order in the bottom of the inning, bringing the Yankees to bat in the top of the ninth. The Browns were three outs away from a huge win, certainly the biggest ever for the franchise.

The way Dixie Davis had pitched through eight innings, a betting man would have wagered on the Browns. He would have lost. Yankees catcher Wally Schang led off the inning by banging one of Davis's pitches off the hurler's glove, reaching first safely without the ball leaving the infield.

Yankees manager Miller Huggins then pinch-hit for Aaron Ward with lefty Elmer Smith. The first pitch got by Browns catcher Hank Severeid for a passed ball, and Schang moved to second.

Now the scene was set for a decade or two of second-guessing. Although Davis still seemed strong and was throwing good stuff—after all the Yankees had only a scratch single so far in the inning—Fohl replaced him with Pruett, the hero of game two. Hub had battled arm problems all season long. Perhaps it was pushing the envelope to send him out again so soon in a pressure-packed situation. Fohl later said his decision to replace Davis was a strategic one only. Since Pruett and pinch hitter Smith were lefties, Huggins then lifted the dangerous Smith for a more benign right-handed hitter, Mike McNally, who in light of his lack of hitting prowess would probably just sacrifice. Fohl felt this would give the Browns a good chance to nail Schang at third.

The Browns manager had a point. McNally sacrificed. Severeid, adept at fielding bunts, pounced on the ball, but threw wide to third. Schang was safe. Now instead of one out with a man on first, there were runners at the corners and still no outs. Here Fohl made his fatal mistake. Instead of replacing the arm-weary Pruett with the fresher, more experienced Urban Shocker, he let Hub pitch to Everett Scott. Pruett was not up to the task. He walked Scott, loading the bases.

With a good deal of the damage already done, Fohl turned to Shocker. The first man up, pitcher Joe Bush, a decent-hitting pitcher, grounded into a forceout at the plate, bringing up the now infamous Whitey Witt. With one swing, the Yankee center fielder dealt his revenge, singling to center to drive in two runs, silencing the crowd and sending the Browns' pennant hopes reeling. Sisler's "heart ached."[12]

Huggins's decision to let Bush bat for himself turned out to be the correct one. In the ninth Bush set the Browns, including Sis, down in order for his twenty-fifth win. The Yankees' 3–2 triumph increased their lead to one and a half games. What might have happened if Davis was permitted to remain on the mound, or if Shocker had been inserted sooner, was now open only to speculation. Babe Ruth later called Fohl's move "the 'break' that decided the game in our favor." In Ruth's opinion, Fohl made two mistakes: replacing Davis, and replacing him with Pruett: "If Fohl had any intention of using Shocker in this game he should have sent him in when Davis was withdrawn."[13]

12. Quoted in Santa Maria and Costello, *In the Shadows of the Diamond*, 212.
13. Syndicated Ruth article, *St. Louis Post-Dispatch*, September 19, 1922.

George's ninth-inning ground-out also brought his forty-one-game hitting streak to an end. It would stand as an American League record until 1941, when a young man named Joe DiMaggio shattered it as well as Keeler's major-league standard of forty-four. DiMaggio's record of fifty-six may stand forever. To this day, no one other than DiMaggio in the American League and Pete Rose in the National have bettered George's forty-one-game hitting streak (Rose had hits in forty-four straight games). It is still the longest streak by a lefthander in American League history. In reflecting on his feat years later, he was most proud that "never once did I bunt to keep the streak alive."[14]

The Browns' loss sent St. Louis into a blue funk. Despite trailing the road-weary Yankees by only a game and a half with nine games to play, the city gave up on its gritty chargers. Phil Ball and Bob Quinn counted gate receipts—approximately sixty-five thousand dollars—and paid attendance of seventy-four thousand customers from their three dates with the Yankees, but only three to four thousand fans showed up for the next game with Washington. The *Post-Dispatch*'s sports staff was little better, the reporters' typewriters fashioning a quick end to the season. John E. Wray told readers, "it will take a calamity to prevent the Yankees from winning" since in the ninth inning of that final contest "the game, the series and the fighting spirit needed to cop the flag were all but made safe."[15]

In this atmosphere of gloom and doom, the Browns moved forward on September 19 against the visiting Nationals. They did so without George Sisler, who was finally reined in and sent to the bench by Hyland. The doctor still felt George should not play again for the remainder of the season, but realizing Sisler would not accept such an edict, he suggested that George at least sit out the Washington series.[16] If nothing else, Sis's injury gave Browns fans an excuse for the ages. In "A Lame Excuse," L. C. Davis penned their lament:

> We don't believe in alibying,
> But there's one fact there's no denying;
> If Sisler hadn't sprained his shoulder
> We might have been the pennant holder.
>
> If Sisler hadn't been a cripple
> And made a homer and a triple,
> We would have made a harder tussle
> If 'Bullet' Joe had strained a muscle.

14. Quoted in Biederman, "Gorgeous George H. Sisler," pt. 2, 13.
15. *St. Louis Post-Dispatch*, September 20, 1922.
16. Quoted in ibid., September 19, 1922.

If Sisler hadn't strained a tendon—
The very man the Browns depend on—
No vain regrets would come to rankle
If 'Bullet' Joe had broke an ankle.[17]

As Sis watched from the bench, the Browns lost the first game of the Washington series 4–3 to Walter Johnson. Pat Collins filled in at first base for the Browns. The next day with Shocker on the mound, the Browns fell 5–0. Now they were really up against the wall. If it was any solace to their fading hopes, their injured star was honored on September 22 as the first "Most Valuable Player" in the American League.[18] The vote by selected sportswriters in each American League city was overwhelming, especially with Cobb and Speaker barred and Ruth in the midst of a shortened season. Sis was the recipient of all but one first-place vote. Pitcher Ed Rommel of the Philadelphia Athletics, the first "knuckleballer" and a 27–13 hurler, received the remaining vote.

The honor, coming as it did on the heels of a series of staggering setbacks, probably seemed quite secondary to Sis at the time. However, on reflection, the first honoree fit the essence of the award to a tee, since achievement on the field was only one of the criteria. In addition to a player's record, deportment on and off the field, regularity of service to the game, cooperation with his manager and teammates, and good morals and habits were given major consideration. According to Wray of the *Post-Dispatch*, "In all these Sisler made his rivals take a back seat." Recognizing George's broader scope, the writer commented that "[o]ff the field there is no finer gentleman than Sisler. There is no swelling up there where his hat fits. And no boy ever trudged to a hotel or railroad station to see Sisler and went away disappointed." According to Wray, Sisler was a $250,000 asset making less than $20,000 a year.[19]

17. Ibid., September 21, 1922.

18. It can be argued that the American League's Most Valuable Player award in 1922 was not the first Most Valuable Player award, although it was the first to actually use the phrase "Most Valuable Player." In 1910 Hugh Chalmers, the president of an automobile company that manufactured the Chalmers "30," offered one of his vehicles as a prize to the top hitter in the majors. Ty Cobb and Napoleon Lajoie ended the season in a closely contested and controversial dead heat. Although the league envisioned Cobb the winner, Chalmers provided vehicles to both men. In order to avoid future embarrassing controversies of this sort, American League President Ban Johnson prohibited prizes awarded solely for winning a batting title. See Charles C. Alexander, *Ty Cobb*, 93, 95–96. Thereafter, through 1914 the Chalmers Award was awarded annually to the best player in each league. In 1913, Sisler's idol Walter Johnson, the only pitcher ever selected, won his luxury sedan with a sterling 36–7 record. See Henry W. Thomas, *Walter Johnson: Baseball's Big Train*, 119–20.

19. *St. Louis Post-Dispatch*, September 22, 1922.

L. C. Davis joined the bandwagon in "The Ace of Clubs":

> The baseball writers took a vote
> Upon the greatest baseball player;
> And though the Yankees got our goat
> St. Louis fans are feeling gayer
> For when it came to who was best
> George Sisler's name led all the rest.
>
> St. Louis fans who had the blues,
> When pennant hopes were disappearing,
> Reacted to the gladsome news
> And overhead the skies are clearing.
> They're now indulging in a smile
> As 'Sis' was winner by a mile.
>
> He led all others with the bat
> As well as in purloining bases.
> His head would always fit his hat,
> Although he was the Ace of Aces.
> A scholar and a gentleman
> He is beloved by every fan.[20]

Perhaps the award, coming as it did in the lowest moment in an otherwise glorious year, lightened the mood in the Browns' clubhouse. Perhaps it was the thought that the league's most valuable player was just one game from a return to the lineup. Whatever the case, the Browns, as so many dying organisms are wont to do, found one more spark of life. Behind the unlikely Bill Bayne, they won 7–6 to salvage the last game of the series with the Nationals. Next in town was Philadelphia, and with both Sis and Frank Ellerbe back in the lineup, an 11–5 win provided further encouragement. Sis was one for five, however, and struggled noticeably with his swing. The next day the Browns took it on the chin from Connie Mack's Athletics. Once again Sis was one for five; he was losing ground to Ty Cobb in the batting race. But on September 24 in the rubber match of the Athletics series, Sis quieted those concerns, scratching out three hits, stealing two bases, and scoring three runs in a 7–4 win behind another clutch performance from Dixie Davis to give the Browns a glimmer of hope in the pennant race.

George's three-hit, three-run performance in the last game against the Athletics once again fanned the poetic flame of L. C. Davis. In "Our Hero," he wrote:

20. Ibid., September 25, 1922.

George Sisler is the King of Swat,
Likewise a noble youth;
He doesn't knock 'em from the lot,
As does the slugging Ruth.
But George is always on his toes
And hits the pellet on the nose.
And makes a lot of safety blows
And that's the solemn truth.

When Georgie ambles up to swing
The hurlers throw a fit.
For that's about the only thing
That Georgie cannot hit.
With eagle eye and steady nerve
He hits the spitter or the curve.
In fact for anything they serve,
He doesn't care a whit.

In stealing the elusive base
He's quicker than a cat
He turns the trick with ease and grace
And lets it go at that.
He's reticent about the way
He soaks the pellet everyday—
When George has anything to say
He says it with his bat.[21]

The Browns' win over Philadelphia set up the final scenario for the season. If they could take all three games in the season-ending series with the White Sox, certainly a distinct possibility, and if the Yankees lost their remaining games with the Red Sox, whom they played twice, and Washington, whom they played once, then the Browns and New York would tie, and a five-game playoff would ensue.

In game one against the White Sox, Johnny Tobin supplied the margin of a 3–2 victory with two home runs. The Yankees cooperated, losing 1–0 to the Red Sox. The next day the Browns did their part and did it well, pounding the White Sox 11–7 as Shocker won his twenty-fifth game. Sis went three for five and Tobin continued his torrid pace. However, as the *Post-Dispatch*'s Wray described it, "[f]or the second time this season the last sad rights were held over the remains of the Browns pennant hopes. Life was pronounced extinct about the fifth inning" when the scoreboard at Sportsman's Park displayed the score from Boston.[22] New York had

21. Ibid., September 28, 1922.
22. Ibid., October 11, 1922.

prevailed 3–1, thus eliminating the Browns. A Browns win and a Yankees loss on the final day of the season left Sis and his teammates one painful game behind the Yankees, with a final record of 93–61.

Perhaps the Yankees were worn out from the tight pennant race, or maybe their lackluster play down the stretch after the "little world series" was the tipoff, but the American League champions lost the World Series in five games to the Giants. Babe Ruth hit a weak .118, with no hits in the last three games.

The World Series that year was significant for more than just the Giants' exploits and the Babe's lack thereof. The annual fall series between the winners of the two major leagues was something akin to a lengthy national holiday. Large crowds of fans gathered in town centers and similar venues throughout the country to watch a re-creation of each game. Reports of the games were disseminated to far-flung corners of the nation via telegraph and then depicted for the eager public gathering in any number of ways, mechanical and later electronic.

In his collection of essays, baseball historian Jules Tygiel describes one such scene, "at once local and national in nature," through the eyes and words of William Thomson, a resident of Chester, Pennsylvania, who "watched" a World Series game unfold on a scoreboard erected adjacent to the offices of the local news journal. "When a ball was pitched they would show a yellow light. For a strike red lights would be turned on. Blue lights would show the number of outs. The bases would have lights to show the positions of runners. Whenever there was a hit they would ring a bell."[23] According to Mr. Thomson, about 150 people gathered each game day to satisfy their baseball appetite. In order to fully appreciate the scope of this annual rite of fall, multiply the crowd in Chester by similar and often larger crowds in the thousands of other small towns and villages across the country. Then add the thousands of "watchers" gathered in New York City, Chicago, and all the other growing metropolises of America.

This had been the national scene for a number of years, and it was also the scene in 1922. But as events unfolded at the Polo Grounds, something else was developing concurrently, privy only to listeners within a three-hundred-mile radius of the stadium. As a promotion by RCA-Westinghouse to boost their new product, the radio, a Newark, New Jersey, station, WJZ, was broadcasting the World Series live. As might be expected, the setup was rather basic, but the result, enabling listeners to actually hear the game at work or in the comfort of their home, was not.

23. Jules Tygiel, *Past Time: Baseball as History*, 64–65.

In fairness, this was not the first broadcast of a baseball or even World Series game, although it was the first "live" broadcast. During the 1921 season, on August 5 to be exact, Pittsburgh's KDKA broadcast the Pirates' game against the Philadelphia Phillies from Forbes Field. It was not a complete success due to a faulty transmitter and excessive crowd noise. Another attempt was made at the 1921 World Series, this time with a reporter watching the games at the Polo Grounds and telegraphing the results to studios in Newark, where an announcer used his imagination to describe the action.

In 1922, however, the indirect and direct approaches were combined with more broad-based success and long-lasting ramification. Sportswriter Grantland Rice sat in a box at the stadium, near one of the dugouts. His voice was amplified by equipment strong enough to send it to the studios in Newark. All other New York area radio stations remained silent to afford the maximum result. While the broadcast did not reach Pittsburgh as hoped, it certainly found a place in New York and the surrounding environs.[24]

The next year's radio broadcast of the World Series would expand to include Washington, D.C. Rice, a better writer than announcer, was replaced by Graham McNamee. McNamee eventually became the voice of the World Series as the new device found a wider and wider audience that quickly discovered baseball was uniquely suited to verbal description. It did not take long for the annual October town gatherings to become merely a fond, fading memory.

Growing audience acceptance of radio broadcasts, however, was not immediately welcomed by the baseball establishment. In April 1922 the *Sporting News*, which often spoke for the sport's ownership group, called the new technology "our latest problem." Radio, warned the newspaper, was only the beginning. Soon there would be extensive filming of games. "When Ruth hits a homer or Sisler slides into the plate, a film will catch him in the act, wireless will carry it a thousand miles broadcast and the family sitting in the darkened living room at home will see the scene reproduced instantaneously on the wall. . . . Then what will become of baseball?"[25]

What, indeed! By 1929, according to Tygiel, one third of the nation's families owned radios. More and more fans were using their radios to bring the world, including their favorite sport, into their home. And in spite of the reluctance of baseball's establishment to accept it, attendance continued

---

24. G. Edward White, *Creating the National Pastime: Baseball Transforms Itself, 1903– 1953*, 207–9.

25. Ibid., 214–15, quoting the *Sporting News*, April 27, 1922, editorial page.

to rise, particularly in cities that began regularly broadcasting games. Many who previously could not attend the games due to finances or logistics now had "a more intimate sense of being at the game." Yet there was a downside, one probably not considered of consequence by baseball's magnates when they resisted the change. The speaking box had replaced "the communal experience with a more isolated one. Radio made baseball, more than ever, a national sport, but in a context far removed from earlier meanings of that term."[26]

It is highly doubtful that the Browns players, by now returned to their respective homes, knew much about the radio and its portent. For all their valiant effort, all that was left for them was to lick their wounds and tally their numbers. They had little to be ashamed of, and many reasons to be proud. They fell one game short of a pennant despite serious injuries to Ellerbe, Shocker, and Sisler. Lacking only pitching depth, which they would try to correct in the off-season, they were a team to be reckoned with, bolstering several stars in their prime, including Shocker, Williams, Tobin, Jacobson, McManus and, of course, Sisler.

For Williams and Sisler, 1922 was a banner year. Williams led the league in home runs (39) and runs batted in (155). He also became the first man to hit more than thirty home runs and steal more than thirty bases in the same season (he had 37 steals). Although Sis repeatedly insisted that 1920 was his best year, his league-leading .420 average tied Cobb for the third highest modern-era batting average ever, behind only Nap Lajoie's .426 in 1901 and Rogers Hornsby's .424 mark in 1924. And close analysis reveals that Sis was hitting at a higher average than either Cobb or Hornsby when he injured his shoulder. His 246 hits, 134 runs, and 51 stolen bases also led the league. Three players, including George, shared the league lead in triples with 18. In addition, he finished second to Tris Speaker in on-base percentage (.474), fifth in slugging percentage (.594), second to Williams in doubles (42) and fourth in runs batted in (105). In 586 at bats, he struck out only 19 times. George's St. Louis counterpart, Rogers Hornsby, also had a great year in 1922 for the fourth-place Cardinals, leading the National League in every important hitting category, including winning the league's triple crown with a .401 average, 42 home runs, and 152 RBIs.

At the close of the World Series, it was announced that the Browns' share of series money was $18,548, meaning Sis and each of his teammates would take home an extra $741. Sis supplemented his share by touring New England with a group of all-stars that included several Red Sox players. He also took advantage of his popularity by appearing in several

26. Tygiel, *Past Time*, 73.

advertisements, becoming one of baseball's first product endorsers. In view of his travails at the end of the baseball season, his endorsement of a liniment, Merrell's Penetrating Oil, was a perfect fit. In so doing he was on the leading edge of an emerging trend in the way American manufacturers went about selling their goods to the masses. As the country prospered under the protective wings of Republican presidents Warren G. Harding, Calvin Coolidge, and Herbert Hoover, who favored big business, advertising itself became big business. As it did so it shifted the emphasis of its message from the special attributes of the product to the popularity of the celebrity messenger who used it. Sisler, with his good looks, clean-cut image, and growing name recognition, fit the prototype perfectly.

To top off the 1922 season, Sis and Kathleen welcomed their third child. On October 26, approximately three weeks after the season ended, they added daughter Frances Eileen to the family.

In retrospect, it is clear that 1922 was the year that George Sisler truly stepped out of the shadow of Ty Cobb, at least for a time. One of many players tabbed as "the next Ty Cobb," George, still in his prime at age twenty-nine and having already eclipsed several of Cobb's records while quietly developing a legend as the best fielding first baseman since Hal Chase, had shed the mantle, becoming a marquis performer in his own right.

The comparisons to Cobb were one thing; the ones to Chase were another. Ironically, George had seen both players on the same field when he attended his very first big-league ball game in Cleveland in 1911 at the Joss all-star benefit. At that time George was still a pitcher, and his attentions were likely riveted to the mound. Nonetheless, a major star such as Chase at first base must have attracted some of his attention.

Following his entry onto the major-league stage in 1905, the admittedly congenial Hal Chase won legions of fans with his grace and style around the first base sack; this despite leading the league in errors seven times during a fourteen-year career. Like many fielders, the true gauge of Chase's ability was in the eyes of his contemporaries. To behold a great fielder is to delight in his ability to perform rare, often unmatched, feats that bald statistics cannot reflect or adequately address. In the eyes of Chase's beholders he was the all-time greatest fielding first baseman. "Prince Hal," as he was often called, was also an above-average batsman. Although not quite on the same page as Sisler, he led National League batters while with Cincinnati in 1916 at .339, hit better than .300 four times, and finished with a career average of .291. There, however, any similarities between Chase and Sisler end. In every other way Hal Chase was the antithesis of George Sisler.

Described by venerable baseball historian Harold Seymour as "the archetype of all crooked ball players," Chase is best known for his active participation in the "fix" that became the Black Sox scandal.[27] That was only his public coming-out party. Long before that he was doing his best to throw ball games in which he or his "friends" had a keen monetary interest. At the same time he was a constant thorn in the side of team management, even succeeding on one occasion in getting his manager fired. That these earlier shenanigans were not better known by the average fan was due in part to the tendency of sportswriters and editors of the era to glorify the subjects of their stories while covering up the blemishes, and in part to baseball owners and administrators fearful of tarnishing their game to the detriment of long ticket lines and crowded stadiums.

Nevertheless, in September 1919 Chase was sent packing by the New York Giants without explanation, never to return to the big leagues. The Giants' manager, the enigmatic John McGraw, later testified that Chase was dropped for throwing games and enticing others to do the same. His indictment for his part in the Black Sox scandal is well documented. Yet baseball's anointed "Prince of Darkness" was never formally banned from baseball and never spent time in jail for his many treacherous acts. In fact, in 1936 this Teflon-coated man received eleven votes and finished in twenty-fifth place in the very first balloting for baseball's Hall of Fame. A much more talented—and more naive—"Shoeless" Joe Jackson, a seeming victim in the Black Sox scandal, garnered but two votes, finishing in a tie for thirty-sixth place.

But in 1922 all comparisons paled. No longer was Sisler the next Ty Cobb or Hal Chase. Now he was the first George Sisler, and in light of a mediocre season by Babe Ruth, who still drew the bigger headlines, he would enter 1923 as the world's greatest living baseball player. In the eyes of one news service, "there is but one Sisler, and the fans of the period will declare he never has had an equal and never will have, when it comes to physical ability, brains and personality."[28] His former college coach and professional manager, Branch Rickey, agreed. "There never was a greater player than George Sisler in 1922," he frequently told listeners. "That year he was the greatest player that ever lived."[29]

---

27. Seymour, *Baseball: The Golden Age,* 288.

28. *Sporting News,* September 17, 1922, 1.

29. Quoted in Santa Maria and Costello, *In the Shadows of the Diamond,* 211. In its September 1922 edition *Current Opinion* agreed, stating, "Who, if not he, is baseball's greatest living player? In St. Louis and elsewhere, George Sisler, the fielding and batting marvel of the Browns is so acclaimed." Quoted in article by Michael Weinreb, *Akron Beacon Journal,* December 24, 1999.

11

Missing in Action

After his banner season in 1922, George's fame was widespread. The story is told that once while the team was in Boston, George attended the stage play *Poppy* at that city's Majestic Theater. This was the show in which the play's star, W. C. Fields, issued his memorable advice, "Never give a sucker an even break." When Fields learned that the famous athlete George Sisler was in the audience, he invited him to his dressing room after the performance.

At the conclusion of the performance Sis paid his respects. "You fascinate me, George," Fields said, his voice and inflection a major part of his shtick. "I've seen you many times and have admired your artistry very much... your consummate skill... Uh, help yourself to the snake-bite cure." It was Prohibition but Fields, famous for his prodigious thirst and resulting bulbous nose, had plenty of whiskey on hand.

He was not alone. By this time the support for Prohibition and the Eighteenth Amendment was significantly eroded. There were far too few law enforcement officers to effectively enforce an act that was frequently the butt of jokes by popular comedians such as Fields, who joined fellow countrymen in introducing the hip flask and speakeasy to the American landscape.

Sis, who did not swear or smoke, declined Field's generous albeit illegal offer, telling his host he didn't drink either. The actor, making a point of showing his disappointment, reached for his glass of rye and replied, "Oh, well, not even the perfect ballplayer can have everything."[1] The offhand comment, made in pure jest, would soon become prophetic.

In March 1923 the Browns began arriving for spring training in Mobile, Alabama, with only a few issues to settle regarding their everyday lineup. One hot spot was the hot corner itself, where Frank Ellerbe had battled injuries much of the previous season. Challengers there included Gene Robertson out of Saint Louis University, rookie Homer Ezzell, and veterans Jimmy Austin and Eddie Foster, who had filled last year's void. The other battle would pit Baby Doll Jacobson against several young candidates for his outfield post.

The previous year's promises and predictions of new faces notwithstanding, the pitching staff that greeted Lee Fohl surprisingly looked like a carbon copy of the staff on hand at the end of 1922. Even Dave Danforth, he of the "dirty ball," was back in harness. Management apparently had tried hard, but no deal could be worked out to bring significant fresh faces and arms to the squad. Still, the statistics revealed that the 1922 staff had the American League's lowest earned run average at 3.33, besting even the heralded Yankee bunch that included Bush, Shawkey, Hoyt, and Mays.

By March 8 all the Browns were in camp. All, that is, except Sis. Reports circulated in Mobile and St. Louis that the star's right shoulder was still on the mend. There was a good deal of grousing about Sis's decision to barnstorm instead of resting his injured shoulder at the end of the year. He had played, they said, and now look at the results. "If Sisler can't play we're ruined," said Ken Williams. "We can fill any other gaps that exist, but there's no other Sisler."[2]

Bob Quinn, the Browns' business manager, added to the consternation of Williams and all Browndom by disclosing that during the off-season the Browns had taken a serious run at Stuffy McInnis, the slick-fielding first baseman of the Philadelphia Athletics and more recently of the Indians. Quinn was responding to criticism from various quarters that the team stood idly by in the face of Sis's shoulder problems. Yet Quinn's response contained yet another surprise. According to him, Sis's shoulder was fine. His absence was due to "weakness resulting from influenza and the injured shoulder is not worrying us."[3] According to the business manager, when the team learned George would be late in arriving, they tried to entice McInnis to join them. His wife balked at leaving the Boston area, so McInnis signed with the Boston Braves. Under the circumstances,

1. Quoted in Bob Broeg, *My Baseball Scrapbook*, 44.
2. Quoted in *St. Louis Post-Dispatch*, March 10, 1923.
3. Quoted in ibid., March 14, 1923.

Quinn told reporters, the Browns would go with minor-league prospect Harry Rice.

Since Sis was merely recovering from a bout with the flu, a quick return was assured. After all, isn't that what Quinn had just said? But it seems Quinn was operating under the same assumption as everyone else, that Sis's main problem was his shoulder. Just a few days later, that theory was exorcised. Joseph F. Holland, writing for the *Post-Dispatch,* reported that Sis was fully recovered from his shoulder ailment. He also was recovered from the influenza he battled early in February. He was now actually suffering severe sinus problems that had bothered him since the influenza and faced a minor nasal operation that threatened to further delay his return. "I have not advised Quinn or Fohl about this condition because I have always believed that I would be ready to play at the opening of the season," George told Holland. "... I am in good physical condition, but it would be useless to go to camp at this time because it would only aggravate this condition and make matters worse."[4]

If Sis's statements were accurate, then Quinn and Phil Ball were acting totally in the dark when they tried to purchase the contract of McInnis. They thought George might still have shoulder problems and wanted McInnis for backup insurance only. Had they known Sis's problem was more serious, perhaps involving a condition of longer duration that included the potential for surgery, would they have upped the ante to McInnis or gone elsewhere? Would McInnis have taken the club's interest more seriously, aware he was more than just an insurance policy? No one will ever know, but in this instance it seems that George's penchant for playing everything close to the vest may have affected his team's outlook for the 1923 season.

No matter the cause, the fuss over George's absence from spring training and the reason for it was drawing huge interest. J. E. Wray of the *Post-Dispatch* compared the interest in Sis to "the Ruhn invasion and [President] Harding's second term," telling readers the average American boy "would rather be George Sisler than Warren G. Harding. . . . Anybody can be president, theoretically, but you have to be born a George Sisler. They make only one Sisler in a generation or two, but potential presidents may be raised in any back yard." Unlike the president, who can hire brains to help him, "the greatest player in the world must stand on his own—and deliver."[5] And now it seemed this rare breed was suddenly on the verge of extinction. No wonder the clamor!

4. Quoted in ibid., March 16, 1923.
5. Ibid., March 19, 1923.

George was still out of commission in mid-March when his team broke camp and started a twenty-two-game exhibition trip ending in St. Louis for the opening game. The experiment with Harry Rice at first base was over even before the team broke camp. On the trip north Cedric Durst, a little-used but good-hitting substitute outfielder in 1922, was inserted at first base.

In late March the Sisler public relations mess continued. On the twentieth Quinn told Wray that George would join the team on April 2, explaining his sinus condition, which had greatly improved, occurred because over the years George had sustained two broken noses and a "heavy cold caused complications in the nasal region." According to Quinn, "[h]e is coming around famously."[6]

One week later the *Post-Dispatch* reported that the local specialist treating Sisler felt his condition was "yielding slowly to treatment," thus postponing his departure to join the team. More ominous, for the first time there was mention of a "slight muscular eye disturbance." It was not, according to the article, "of serious proportions" and would not "cause Sisler any playing inconvenience."[7] This was hardly the case. In reality Sis was suffering from a serious sinus infection that was causing swelling that affected his optic nerve. "I didn't quite realize what was happening," he later reported, "until one day when I was driving I thought I saw two cars in the other lane. There was only one, and I knew something was drastically wrong."[8]

There was some speculation that the considerable waffling back and forth about the seriousness of Sis's condition was a stunt by the Browns to forestall loss of interest in the season and a resulting drop-off in ticket sales if their biggest attraction was out for any length of time. Such was not the case. The fault, if any, was with Sis and not Browns' management. In the early days of the illness he was asked by management to give a detailed statement concerning the nature of his eye problem, to stem the flow of rumors such as the one where he reportedly began sobbing after an unsuccessful attempt at fielding ground balls. In a rare conflict with the bosses he refused, saying "(i)t's my eye and my affair. When I get well I will be ready to play again. If I fail to get well, of course I will never play again."[9]

On the surface George's sour reaction to well-intentioned inquiries concerning his health, and his reluctance to work openly with management on this issue, might seem surprising. It probably should not. His stance

6. Quoted in ibid., March 20, 1923.
7. Quoted in ibid., March 27, 1923.
8. Quoted in Santa Maria and Costello, *In the Shadows of the Diamond*, 213.
9. Quoted in Peter Williams, ed., *The Joe Williams Baseball Reader*, 56.

was totally consistent with the perfectionistic aspects of his nature, his constant attempts to guard his privacy, and a need to be in control of a personally troubling situation. Until this juncture Sisler's entire career had shot onward and upward in steady ascent. In fact, except for the untimely death of his eldest brother years before and the brouhaha with Barney Dreyfuss, his career and the rest of his life had sailed on calm seas. An engineer by trade, as well as a craftsman in his approach to the art of hitting, base running, and fielding, Sis was accustomed to an answer to each question in life. He saw most things as black or white, measuring each step in his life with a micrometer rather than a yardstick. Until now the formula had worked.

Sisler had also been blessed with excellent health. Those injuries he did sustain were incurred within the game of baseball itself, and were easily explainable and quite treatable. He had played through just such a scenario in September 1922. Now just a few months later George was confronted with a problem without a ready solution, an unknown illness with an uncertain etiology or end that was affecting his sight; one that might not be solvable within the scientific framework with which he found so much comfort.

Instead of reporting for spring training to get ready to play as he had done for the past several seasons, Sis was now confronted with his own baseball mortality. Ty Cobb once wrote that "a sick ballplayer was just another liability—unless he got himself well in a hurry, and cheaply."[10] The mere thought that his career might be over, let alone the gravity of the illness itself and its potential aftermath, must have made George fear a loss of control. Only two years before his search for perfection found George publicly questioning the legitimacy of his startling accomplishments and even downgrading them, since they were garnered at a time when his chief rival, Cobb, was not at the top of his game. In the spring of 1923, then, it was not so difficult to understand why Sis, a man who could search out and find fault in his smallest crevice, was not the Sisler the public had come to know and admire to this point in his career. When seen in this light the clipped response to management concerning his illness was, for better or worse, pure Sisler to the end.

But all matter of medical privacy ended on April 11 with the front-page announcement in the *Post-Dispatch* that Sis would undergo surgery to relieve his sinus condition, whereupon further treatment would be in the hands of an eye specialist.[11] The surgery for an inflamed ethmoid sinus

10. Cobb, with Stump, *My Life in Baseball*, 55.
11. *St. Louis Post-Dispatch*, April 11, 1923.

that resulted in "a slight pressure behind one eye and a consequent impairment of vision" was set for April 13 after an earlier postponement due to tonsillitis.[12]

Meanwhile, the club trudged forward toward opening day in the midst of numerous forecasts of impending doom. A copyrighted article by John B. Foster, datelined New York, went so far as to say Sis's absence would alter the American League race. Philadelphia manager Connie Mack planned to change his attack, taking more chances against the Browns with Sis out of the lineup: "(I)t will unquestionably unsettle the team which finished second in 1922 and will change the plans of every manager in our circuit."[13]

At least outwardly, the team refuted predictions of their early demise. Johnny Tobin returned to St. Louis early and vowed the team would remain in the thick of the race until George returned. Sis, too, publicly voiced his support, painting an optimistic picture of a team poised for greatness, with or without him. The enthusiasm had an uplifting effect, at least initially. A pair of victories over the Cardinals in the cross-town series ensued. On the eve of opening day, Sis, at home recuperating from surgery, issued a statement explaining his absence and emphasizing his delight at his team's showing against the Cardinals. "At the earliest possible moment...I will give what assistance I can to [first baseman] Durst if he doesn't mind.... All that I can say is that I am very hopeful."[14]

The previous season it was Babe Ruth on the sidelines. Now it was Sis. This turn in fortune was not lost on the healthy, newly trim Ruth. He graciously telegrammed his rival following the Browns' 9–6 opening-day loss in St. Louis to the Tigers: "Your name missing from yesterday's lineup makes news of season's opening a disappointment. From experience, I know it is a tough job starting the season late. Hope reports of your condition are exaggerated and especially hope you will recover in time to play in first series with New York. Best wishes from Yankees. George Babe Ruth."[15]

Such would not be the case. Following his surgery, Sis did quickly progress to the point where he could attend practices, visit the team in the clubhouse, and even attend a game. On April 23 he was observed seated in the upper deck of the grandstand, wearing dark glasses and telling anyone who would hear it that his team just needed a couple of wins to get them going. By May the Browns were 4–7 and in fifth place.

12. Ibid., April 12, 1923.
13. Quoted in ibid., April 10, 1923.
14. Quoted in ibid., April 17, 1923.
15. Telegram reprinted in ibid., April 21, 1923.

The experiment with Cedric Durst at first base did not last long. He played eight games at the position, making three errors and not hitting much more than his weight. In early May, McManus, who played first at the tail end of 1922 when Sis injured his shoulder, was reinserted at the position. Moving him from second base further disrupted a jumbled infield.

The Browns were missing more than just Sis by May. Hub Pruett, the surprise of 1922, was available, but totally ineffective as a starter or reliever. To make matters worse, Dixie Davis, who was battling neuritis, had yet to make an appearance on the mound. Still, the season was young and the Browns, 11–13, were only two games out of second when Bob Quinn pulled the trigger on a trade that sent minor-league pitcher Frank Henry to the Brooklyn Dodgers of the National League for first baseman Fred "Dutch" Schliebner. The move was further evidence that Sis's eye affliction was long-term and prospects for play in 1923, or even beyond, were most uncertain. A condition that today would pose little threat for long-term disability, according to neuro-ophthalmologist Dr. Steven E. Katz of Ohio State University, if treated with antibiotics by IV in a hospital setting had festered to the point where Sis's career was on the line. One of the earliest memories of Sis's oldest son, George, Jr., then age six, was of his dad sitting alone at home in the evenings during the summer of 1923 with the shades drawn and no lights as he rested his troubled eyes, worrying and wondering what was next in store.[16]

Schliebner's appearance on the scene was a welcome sight. McManus could handle first base, but the move left other gaps that required fixing, in particular a lack of batting punch. In 1922 Schliebner had led the American Association in hitting with a .354 average, and he could field. There was, however, a question whether he could hit major-league pitching. To everyone's delight, the 1923 version of Schliebner was most satisfactory. He hit .275 for his new club with four home runs and 52 runs batted in. Though he disappeared from the major-league baseball scene the next year, for now he fit the bill.

As the summer heat intensified, Sis continued to regularly appear at home games, sitting in what was now his customary seat in the upper tier of the grandstand. Although he continuously claimed to be fit, he underwent a successful tonsillectomy at St. Luke's Hospital in St. Louis on May 25. In mid-June the *Post-Dispatch* reported that Sis had improved to the point that he was able to read "with but slight difficulty" and drive his car. He traveled with Walter Fritsch, a minority owner of the Browns, to a summer camp along the Mississippi, some sixty miles north of St. Louis.

16. George Sisler, Jr., interview by author, Columbus, Ohio, August 17, 2001.

While there they did some fishing, frog hunting, and a good deal of hiking. According to Fritsch, who revealed he had also taken Sis and Frank Ellerbe to the camp for a week's stay back in the spring, Sis was so eager for exercise that they even played "catch."[17] In view of this progress, Fritsch predicted Sis would play ball by August.

It soon became apparent Walter Fritsch's interest in and influence upon George went beyond owner/player. According to Sis, his doctor told him he "would never play again," which certainly was a blow. Fritsch was a believer in Christian Science, a branch of Christianity that in the main eschews science and, in particular, its medical component. He suggested George "look into it." At this point Sis "was willing to try anything." He gave up medical treatment, began reading the writings and teachings of the Christian Science Church, and contacted John Randall Dunn, a nationally known practitioner and lecturer on Christian Science.[18]

As Sis was making this major transition in his personal and spiritual life, the Browns' management was in a transition of its own. Bob Quinn, a longtime baseball executive who had held other administrative jobs prior to his stint as the Browns' business manager and vice-president, longed to run a team of his own. In 1923 he finally got his wish as he and some of his old friends from his minor-league days in Columbus successfully struck a deal for the purchase of the Boston Red Sox. Phil Ball reluctantly let Quinn go, replacing him with William E. Friel, a minor-league manager and executive in the Browns organization who played first base for the team in 1902–1903.

The changes did not stop there. All was not rosy between Ball and his manager, Lee Fohl. Despite relative success with a third-place finish in 1921 and even more success in 1922, Ball was unhappy that the Browns still fell one game short of the brass ring. Like most owners, it was easier to point the finger at the manager than to single out one or more of the players. In Fohl's case, even some of the players joined in the finger point-ing. One game in particular in Detroit raised the players' hackles. In that game Fohl permitted pitcher Hub Pruett to bat in the ninth inning with a runner on third. The whole team pleaded for a pinch hitter, but Fohl ig-nored them. Pruett failed to move the runner and the game was lost. The appearance of Walter Fritsch in the locker room saved a brawl between manager and players, but not Fohl's reputation as a players' manager. Since the Browns finished one game out of the money, memories of lost

17. Quoted in *St. Louis Post-Dispatch,* June 13, 1923.
18. Sisler Memoirs, 12.

opportunities like this one extended beyond the season. The honeymoon for Fohl was over.

Things didn't improve much between Fohl and his players in 1923. In May little-used pitcher Hollis "Sloppy" Thurston was sent home when he refused to pitch batting practice. He was later sold to the White Sox. A few days later, reserve catcher Pat Collins was suspended indefinitely by Fohl for raising a fuss over lack of playing time. Still, despite this internal unrest, the team, with a more solidified lineup including the return of Dixie Davis, was on the upswing. By mid-July they were in third place, only one and a half games behind the second-place Indians as the Yankees held firmly in first place. Shocker already had fourteen wins. Dave Danforth was apparently pitching clean and with a vengeance. He was a strong 7–6, although umpires and players alike were watching his every move.

Even George seemed a little better by mid-July, appearing at a game in Phil Ball's box minus sunglasses. Moreover, he was playing golf, which by his own admission "represents a big improvement in the condition of my eyes." He cautioned, however, "I am not ready to play baseball as yet. There is a very material difference between hitting a little white ball off the tee and following a curve ball thrown with great speed."[19]

That same month, however, the Ball/Fohl freeze turned hot when Ball, his players, and the St. Louis press all blamed the Browns' manager for a move that killed a ninth-inning rally against the Yankees. Held to two hits until that inning by Joe Bush, the Browns had four hits and the tying runs on base in the last frame when Fohl sent Frank Ellerbe in to pinch-hit against reliever Sad Sam Jones. Ellerbe did not get the job done, and the second-guessers scratched their collective heads. Ellerbe had not taken batting practice in three weeks because he was too far down the line for playing time. How, the press wanted to know, could he be expected in a key situation to hit a curveball from a master like Jones? And to make matters worse, the Yankees scored three of their runs on Browns errors. Ball was upset, telling reporters after the game that he did not believe that the Browns' play was well handled. Still, in a vote of little confidence, he said Fohl would remain, stating that Sisler was not yet ready to manage the team in view of his vision impairment. It was an interesting comment in view of Sis's previous reluctance to accept Ball's offer of the managerial reins. As things stood, the Browns would just have to make the best of their situation.[20]

19. Quoted in *St. Louis Post-Dispatch*, July 31, 1923.
20. Ibid., July 9, 1923.

This all changed on August 1 when the Dave Danforth issue resurfaced. At the time, the Browns were 49–44 and in third place, two games behind Cleveland and fourteen behind the Yankees. Fohl was getting great hitting from Williams and strong support from Tobin, Jacobson, McManus, and Severeid. The team was in Washington with Danforth on the mound in the pivotal ninth when suddenly umpire Moriarty charged the mound, examined the ball, and ejected the Browns' pitcher for tampering with the baseball. According to Moriarty, an eighteen-year veteran, he was certain the ball was "doctored." He went on to say he had discovered "slight evidence of tampering" during the game and warned the hurler, but the ball that caused the ejection was "a brand new ball," and that was too much to ignore.[21]

Unlike the previous campaign when the Browns silently acquiesced in Danforth's ejection and eventual demotion to the minor leagues, this time the Browns felt their teammate wronged. The previous year there had been some evidence the ball had "loaded seams." This time the only visible marking was a lone brown spot about an inch square. According to catcher Hank Severeid, "If Danforth were fooling with the ball, surely I would be able to detect it and I declare that I did not see him in any manner illegally handle the ball."[22] Almost to a man Severeid's teammates agreed; all, that is, except their manager, Lee Fohl. The players proposed sending a wire to Ban Johnson supporting Danforth. Fohl declined, telling reporters, "I have no comment to make relevant to Danforth."[23]

For weeks the rumors had been flying around St. Louis that Fohl would follow his good friend Bob Quinn to Boston at the end of the season to take over the direction of the Red Sox. With the Danforth incident challenging members of the Browns organization to stand up and be counted, whatever simmered under the surface now burst into flames. The day following Danforth's ejection, both Urban Shocker and Johnny Tobin were ejected from the first game of a doubleheader with the Senators for arguing calls. Instead of biting their lips, the frustrated players told reporter Dent McSkimming of the *Post-Dispatch* that they would not have to argue calls and risk ejection if Lee Fohl would do his job and argue for them.[24] Add to that Fohl's delivery of a faulty line-up card to the umpire to start the game, resulting in two batter disqualifications in a Browns loss—one of two losses that day—and you had the makings of an insurrection. Phil

21. Quoted in ibid., August 2, 1923.
22. Quoted in ibid.
23. Ibid.
24. Ibid., August 3, 1923.

Ball never let it get that far. Four days later, on August 7, Fohl was fired for the "good of the game and the morale of the players."[25]

Although Lee Fohl's two and a half seasons at the helm of the Browns was anything but calm, it had been relatively successful, especially in comparison with his predecessors. The team was still winning in 1923, but with a record of 51–49 the Browns were in third place. Fohl was proud of his performance and probably deserved better. What he felt he did not deserve was a stab in the back as he left town. As he characterized it, the statement by Ball that he was dismissed "for the good of the game" was just that. Fohl demanded a retraction or he would seek legal sanctions. In addition, he took parting shots at Phil Ball and Vice-President Walter Fritsch, telling the *Post-Dispatch* he had been "fired" in the press by Ball "nearly a month ago" and that "the owner of a ball club should remain out of the clubhouse." He referred specifically to Fritsch, who had accompanied the team on the present road trip, saying "[t]he presence of Mr. Fritsch with the team has done no good, either for the morale of the team or for the winning of ball games."[26]

These remarks accompanied a story in the *Post-Dispatch* announcing that Jimmy Austin, the popular veteran player/coach of the Browns, was their new manager. Further speculation concerning George Sisler as the replacement ended as Sis told the newspaper he was not ready to handle the job due to his continuing eye problems. The statement was notable for what it did not say, in that in a departure from previous pronouncements he did not rule out managing the club in the future. New business manager Bill Friel confirmed, stating that Austin "is manager as long as he can deliver the goods."[27]

Austin, of course, was a popular choice. His loyalty to the Browns was unquestioned. On numerous occasions he had turned down big-league managerial offers, one the past spring from the Senators, in order to remain with the team. There was no doubt the players would perform for Austin, and yet once emotions cooled, some, including Urban Shocker, who called Fohl "the best manager I ever worked for," paid Fohl their respects.[28] After all, he had the Browns in third place despite the loss of Sis and the early season decimation of the pitching staff. According to the *Post-Dispatch*'s Wray, the bottom line was that "Phil Ball doesn't like Fohl." Ball was convinced Fohl frittered away a pennant by allowing the club to

25. Quote from Phil Ball telegram in ibid., August 7, 1923.
26. Quoted in ibid., August 8, 1923.
27. Quoted in ibid.
28. Ibid.

fold after "the little world series" when "any sort of inspiration" could have still secured enough wins for a pennant. Wray, in fairness, thought otherwise. He told readers that the loss of Sisler to injury last year and this year was Fohl's real shortcoming, and his "great failing is his lack of personal magnetism and lack of inspiration. He failed to win his men and he failed to win his employers, even though he won ballgames."[29]

A few days later, on August 11, Danforth was reinstated. Had Fohl still been his manager, it seems unlikely he would have pitched again. Vindicated by his owner, new manager, and teammates, Danforth was ready to take his regular turn under Ban Johnson's watchful eye. Johnson wrote the *Post-Dispatch* that there would be a no-tolerance policy enforced against Danforth, who, in the president's opinion, "has a mania for 'doctoring' the ball and to me it appears that he is incurable."[30]

Two days later, on August 16, the "incurable" Danforth appeared miraculously cured as he beat the Yankees 3–1, tossing a three-hitter in which fifty-eight balls were thrown out after close examination. Lee Fohl watched Danforth's return with more interest than the casual observer since he too had read Ban Johnson's telegram to the *Post-Dispatch*. In his mind, the telegram's tone and wording served as his vindication. Apparently Phil Ball got the message as well. Under pressure from Johnson, he met with Fohl in St. Louis and on August 20 issued a new statement of dismissal rewording the original to read that Fohl was removed "for the good of the game as played by the Browns."[31] In addition, Ball paid Fohl's salary for the entire season, covering the last two months, and the affair, at least publicly, was closed.

For his part, George kept his mouth shut about Lee Fohl or Jimmy Austin, attended games, and somewhat overoptimistically continued to predict he would still be able to play before the end of the season. At the same time, in a more realistic vane he told the *Post-Dispatch*, "I have accepted this condition as it is . . . I have taken the position now that I will just rest until my sight is perfectly normal. That prevents added disappointment."[32]

Years later Sis was much more realistic about his ability to play ball in 1923. "All season long, I suffered," he said. "I felt sorry for the fans, for my teammates, for everyone, except for myself. I planned to get back into uniform for 1924. I just had to meet a ball with a good swing again, and

29. Ibid., 21.
30. Ban Johnson telegram printed in ibid., August 14, 1923.
31. Ball press release printed in ibid., August 20, 1923.
32. Quoted in ibid., August 24, 1923.

then run. The doctors all said I'd never play again, but when you're desperate, when you're fighting for something that actually keeps you alive—well, the human will is all you need."[33]

As Sisler's eyes continued to improve, it must have been painful to watch his team struggle through the last two months of the season. In mid-August Austin's charges lost five in a row. One bright spot was the play of young third base prospect Homer Ezzel. He finished the year at .244 in eighty-eight games, but made up for any batting deficiencies with his solid fielding.

The fans' favorite at this point, however, was Danforth. In St. Louis and everywhere he went, he was an instant celebrity. The timid pitcher of 1922 was now "confident, cocksure and daring."[34] He also was winning games, a surprising sixteen versus fourteen losses for the year. Along with Shocker, who won twenty, and Vangilder, who chipped in with another sixteen, there was some hope for a return to glory, at least the Browns' version, in 1924.

Then in mid-September personnel problems flared again. Urban Shocker was upset about the club's policy barring players' wives from accompanying the team on road trips. When he refused to travel with the team to Philadelphia without his wife, he was fined and threatened with suspension. The rule, which was also adopted by several other teams, appeared to make little sense. At the least, players were less likely to get into trouble when they had the company of their spouses away from home. Apparently management felt the presence of the wives could lead to cliques and cause friction within the squad. Al Demaree, the talented sports cartoonist and a player himself with the Phillies and Giants, told readers of Collier's that more than one team fell apart over groups of wives talking in the grandstand, and one wife asking the other, "Who was that swell-lookin' doll I saw your husband out with last night?" In consideration of this, plus jealousies over salaries and complaints by a pitcher's wife when another's husband boots a ball to lose a game, perhaps the owners had a point in leaving the wives behind.[35] But that is only supposition; no specific reasons, including cost, were ever given.

Shocker soon let the Browns know he meant business by not responding to their initial penalty. The club returned the favor by suspending the star pitcher for the remainder of the season. There were even rumors he

33. Nathan Salant, *Superstars, Stars, and Just Plain Heroes*, 38.
34. *St. Louis Post-Dispatch*, August 26, 1923.
35. Al Demaree, "Grand-Stand Girls," June 2, 1928, p. 22.

might be traded. Shocker retained an attorney who recommended he claim free agency, potentially raising some interesting issues. Commissioner Landis became involved, but the matter was resolved through the auspices of Ban Johnson before he could rule.

Shocker was not the only star in St. Louis battling the "company." Rogers Hornsby and Branch Rickey, now manager of the Cardinals, were squabbling, publicly and privately. In September the fifth-place Cardinals denied Hornsby was on the trading block, but fined him five hundred dollars for refusing to play when cleared by his physicians to do so after an injury.

On September 20 the Yankees clinched the pennant in New York by beating the Browns, rubbing the wound more deeply by sending them below the .500 mark. In the postseason the Yankees faced off with the Giants in a rematch of the 1922 World Series. This time the Yankees were the victors, four games to two. The American League's most valuable player for the year was Babe Ruth, who compiled impressive stats in his comeback year, hitting 41 home runs, driving in 131 runs, and batting .393.

The Browns finished 1923 in fifth place at 74–78. Under Jimmy Austin the team was 23–29, raising speculation that his tenure as manager would be short. It was short, indeed. On October 21, 1923, the Browns announced their new manager would be George Sisler. His agreement with the club was for one season, with pay dependent upon his ability to play as well as manage. Since Sis was no longer under treatment for his eye affliction, there was real hope that he would accomplish both tasks in 1924, but if not, he would just manage. Austin, Sis's friend and former teammate, was named alternate manager. The next day, certainly by no coincidence, Lee Fohl was named to succeed Frank Chance as field boss of the Boston Red Sox.

Sis had now completed an about-face. In 1920 his flat refusal of the Browns' managerial offer led to the hiring of Lee Fohl. Three years later his injuries led indirectly to Fohl's dismissal and the current vacancy, which he now filled, perhaps reluctantly, but without protest in view of the uncertainties in his own future. His playing career in jeopardy, he had a job managing a team that one short year before had knocked on the door of a league championship. Would the shy, retiring Sis be up to the challenge? Would he expect the same performance from others that he delivered himself? At what level would he perform? Would he enjoy his new challenges, or would they hinder his return to form? Only time, with its strong recuperative power, and the promise of a fresh new season would tell.

Sisler and George, Jr., pose for an early family portrait. Sisler family collection.

Rarely photographed, Sisler's wife, Kathleen, is shown with George, Jr.
Sisler family collection.

Sisler and outfield teammate Ken Williams (right). Sisler family collection.

Sisler enjoying the outdoors. Teammate Jimmy Austin is on the right. Sisler family collection.

Sisler and Walter Fritsch, a vice-president and part owner of the Browns during the 1920s. Sisler family collection.

Three of baseball's best: Sisler, Babe Ruth, and Ty Cobb smile and join hands at the 1924 World Series played between the New York Giants and the Washington Senators. Relations between bitter rivals Ruth and Cobb were not always so cordial. National Photo Company Collection, Library of Congress.

FIFTEEN CENTS

TIME

The Weekly News-Magazine

VOL. V. NO. 13

GEORGE H. SISLER
Pittsburgh never forgave him
(See Page 26)

MARCH 30, 1925

Sisler became the first baseball man to appear on the cover of *Time* with the March 30, 1925, issue. Courtesy of Time/Getty Images.

Sisler's baseball home in St. Louis was Sportsman's Park, shown here in a 1926 aerial photo. Courtesy of the National Baseball Hall of Fame Library, Cooperstown, New York.

Sisler hooks up with football great Red Grange in 1926 at Chicago's Comiskey Park. White Sox Hall of Famer Eddie Collins stands to the left. Courtesy of the *Chicago Daily News*/Chicago Historical Society.

Sisler and Rogers Hornsby, the Cardinals' great second baseman, shared the
sports spotlight for many years in St. Louis. In 1927 Sisler and George, Jr., visit
Hornsby (in uniform) at Chicago's Wrigley Field. One year later the pair would
play together for the Boston Braves. Courtesy of the *Chicago Daily News*/
Chicago Historical Society.

Sisler, after a brief stop with the Washington Senators, was traded to the Boston Braves on May 27, 1928. Courtesy of the National Baseball Hall of Fame Library, Cooperstown, New York.

Kathleen Sisler poses with her three eldest Sisler offspring, George, Jr., Frances, and Dick. Sisler family collection.

Sisler played his first minor-league baseball for the Rochester Red Wings in 1931. He poses here with Red Wings Manager Billy Southworth (left) and General Manager Warren Giles. Southworth later led the Cardinals to world championships in the 1940s. Giles eventually served as president of the National League and was elected to the National Baseball Hall of Fame in 1979. Sisler family collection.

Joining Sisler in Cooperstown on June 12, 1939, for a celebration of baseball's one hundredth birthday, as well as the first induction ceremony at the newly constructed National Baseball Hall of Fame, were fellow inductees Eddie Collins, Babe Ruth, Connie Mack, Cy Young (seated) and Honus Wagner, Grover Cleveland Alexander, Tris Speaker, Napoleon Lajoie, Sisler, and boyhood idol Walter Johnson (standing). Ty Cobb was also inducted at this time, but arrived too late for the photograph. Courtesy of the National Baseball Hall of Fame Library, Cooperstown, New York.

Sisler and Branch Rickey, his first college coach and major-league manager, had a special relationship. In 1942 Sisler followed Rickey to the Brooklyn Dodgers. Here Rickey (right) confers at the 1943 All-Star game with Larry McPhail, his predecessor as Dodgers general manager. Courtesy of the National Baseball Hall of Fame Library, Cooperstown, New York.

By Thanksgiving in 1957, Sisler and his wife were reunited in St. Louis with their growing family. Left to right: standing are eldest son George, Jr., son-in-law William Drochelman, Sisler, youngest son Dave, and middle son Dick. Seated in the second row are Nancy and Elizabeth, daughter and wife of George, Jr.; Sisler's daughter Frances Drochelman; Kathleen Sisler; Janet and David, wife and son of Dave; and Dorothy and Patti, wife and daughter of Dick. In the front row are Susan, daughter of George, Jr.; Ann and Bo, children of the Drochelmans; and Kathy and Shari, daughters of Dick. Courtesy of the *Sporting News*.

Sisler not only scouted for the Brooklyn Dodgers and instructed their hitters but also schooled their young first basemen in the art of fielding. He is surrounded in 1947 by prospects (left to right) Howie Schultz, Ed Stevens, future Hall of Famer Jackie Robinson, and Tom Brown. Courtesy of AP/Wide World Photos.

Sisler's last stop on the baseball trail was Pittsburgh. In February 1958 he talked hitting with several Pirate regulars (left to right) shortstop Dick Groat, outfielders Bob Skinner and Bill Virdon, and catcher Hank Foiles. Courtesy of AP/Wide World Photos.

12

Comeback Kid

One can only wonder what thoughts swirled through George Sisler's head on February 2, 1924, as he and Jimmy Austin left St. Louis for Mobile, Alabama. It would be Sisler's first training camp in two seasons. He was not only starting back at the foot of the mountain attempting a comeback from career-threatening illness but also embarking on a new venture as a rookie manager of a team with very high aspirations and possibly unreasonable expectations.

By now a firm believer in the powers of Christian Science thought, Sis invited his spiritual adviser, Dr. John Randall Dunn, to accompany him to Mobile, signifying George's belief that his return to the playing field would require more than just a few turns at bat. As he later told his family, "I realized it was quite an undertaking . . . Playing, managing, and attempting to get myself into my former playing condition was quite a task."[1]

In the latter part of the winter George and his majordomo Jimmy Austin traveled to Laguna Beach on the West Coast for fishing, hunting, and most of all the opportunity to play some ball outdoors. There was still much speculation about whether George would be able to play for the Browns at all, let alone return to first base. There was even an indication from the brass that Sis might pitch if his prospects as an everyday player turned

1. Sisler Memoirs, 13.

sour. This, of course, would lessen the impact of poor vision, although American League pitchers in that day still had to take their regular turns at the plate.

Austin, who worked out with his boss and knew what he could do, was confident that Sis would make it all the way back, telling reporters that in the light workouts "the same old stuff was there."[2] Sis was equally optimistic but refused to make any predictions, having learned a lesson from the previous year. On February 27 the Browns held their first work-out in Mobile. Sisler was the first man in uniform, fielding grounders in a manner indicating no ill effects from his lengthy layoff. The next day he stepped to the plate during an intrasquad match and lashed out a single and a triple, leaving everyone but George certain his star was ready to shine again.

On February 29 Sis took his turn on the mound, throwing for fifteen minutes. Lest someone get the idea the first base experiment was over, he also pounded the ball to all fields in batting practice. On the management side, the press noted a "feeling of good fellowship that exists among the boys," attributing the atmosphere to a manager who "remains in the lobby of the hotel and talks with the players while in past years managers have gone into seclusion after leaving the field."[3]

As the early spring workouts progressed, the "Sisler watch" continued. Not all observers agreed on the extent of the subject's recovery. *Post-Dispatch* staff writer J. Roy Stockton and his photographer were in particu-lar discord. Stockton was with George in October 1923 when the player's right eye was "noticeably crossed." Now, in early March, Sis's eyes were "well coordinated." George agreed, noting that in October, "I couldn't see one baseball. It would have been dangerous for me to try to bat." Still, he admitted, all was not yet perfect, but "the angle at which I do not see accu-rately is very small." He could not, however, "play great baseball right now," he told Stockton, but "[n]either eye has lost efficiency and gradu-ally they are working together better." Still, "[t]here are certain positions from which it is difficult to take throws and that I have to bend my neck around a bit to get a perfect slant on the ball." This, he said "handicaps me in my swing and naturally takes some of the force out of my blows." And yet he was improving daily. Soon even these minor disparities would run their course.

Stockton certainly was encouraged. Not so his photographer, who took a series of photographs of George at work at the plate in 1922 just prior to

2. Quoted in *St. Louis Post-Dispatch*, February 25, 1924.
3. Ibid., February 29, 1924.

his selection as the league's most valuable player. After watching George in Mobile almost two years later, he exclaimed, "My goodness, doesn't George look terrible. He has a terrible time meeting the ball. He glares into the air trying to find it, both at bat and in the field. I noticed it particularly in close-up action photographs. . . . There certainly is a great difference between the Sisler of 1922 and the Sisler of today. You fellows who say he looks great are just spoofing yourselves."[4]

Who was right? It would take time for an answer, but by comparison, the Sisler of the spring of 1924 was most certainly an improved product over the 1923 version. The question, however, was how close he was to the 1922 edition. One mark of his bout with eye problems would never completely disappear. For the remainder of his life Sis would almost constantly squint. Coming off like a frown, the furrowed brow left some people with an initial impression that Sis was an eternally unhappy sort. Nothing could have been further from the truth.

As Sis continued to test his vision at the plate and on the field, he also was taking a close look at his 1924 Browns from the dugout. The high expectation level for the team stemmed in part from his return, which returned the club to essentially the same personnel as the 1922 contender. The regular lineup could certainly hit with the best, but in fairness no longer could be called youthful. The outfield of Jacobson, Tobin, and Williams carried birth certificates that showed their ages to be thirty-three, thirty-two, and thirty-four respectively. Sis was now thirty-one, Severeid thirty-three, and shortstop Wally Gerber thirty-two. Only twenty-four-year-old second baseman Marty McManus was a youngster who played regularly from the start. Gene Robertson, twenty-five, eventually took over at third base. And the pitching, well, that was essentially unchanged, too. Unlike the position players, George and his Brownies could have benefited from a few personnel moves in that all-important department. Still, Shocker was around, and in 1923 he had once again delivered twenty wins, despite the major fracas with management over his wife's presence on the road.

But like every other big-league manager, Sis would play with the cards he was dealt and hope for the best. He would also look for a boost from Ban Johnson's decision to permit "used" balls to remain in play even if discolored. This, it was argued, would weigh in favor of the pitcher, since the use of perfectly clean balls at all times was in part blamed for the soaring batting averages and barrage of long balls. Any edge to the pitcher might benefit a team with a weak staff, such as the Browns.

4. Quoted in ibid., March 4, 1924.

Confidence in the Browns' pennant chances rose dramatically after Sis's first exhibition appearance when he went two for five, garnering predictions from Ken Williams that "George hits .360 or better" and from Johnny Tobin that "he'll be one of the great players of 1924." By mid-March George's ability to hit the ball shelved any further ideas of a return to pitching, although if it were up to George, "I still believe I could go in there and pitch major league ball."[5]

One characteristic of the Sisler managerial regime developed early. After one of the games, Sis called a meeting of older players and a few younger ones. Those present were permitted to voice an opinion. Sis seemed to welcome the advice and carefully weigh it. Then in order to instill a spirit of team fellowship, he and a group of his players went skeet shooting. Sisler broke twenty-one of the twenty-five clay birds when it was his turn to call the shots.

George's faith in his men and his willingness to let them have a say was returned in aces. According to Ken Williams, "(E)very man on the squad will give everything he has to win for Sisler. He is the best man I ever worked for in my life. He's one of the fellows, but he's the leader." Likewise Tobin. "For the first time since I have been on the team, every man . . . has a chance to offer suggestions and discuss the playing policies." As George tells his men, he plans to "make use of the brains on the club."[6] The camaraderie was certainly strong. Whether this mutual admiration society would create a team chemistry producing results was the only question remaining as the team prepared to move north.

After a slow start in exhibition games in Mobile, Sis began to hit his stride, even getting two hits in one inning against hometown Mobile and hitting well overall. The pitching, however, was minor-league level. Sis would not issue a definitive statement as to where he would be on opening day. But one thing had not been seriously affected by his long absence from the field: his popularity. As he trained for the 1924 season, he fielded at least fifty letters a day from admirers. Many were sent by kids asking for baseball equipment after hearing their champion supplied one group with the bats, balls, and gloves they needed to keep playing the game.

When the Browns returned to St. Louis on April 4 to prepare to play the Cardinals, then open the regular season, the spring scorecards showed George batting .324 in sixteen games. In seventy-one at bats he put wood to ball in all but four, strong numbers indeed for a guy still working out a

5. Quoted in ibid., March 7 and 11, 1924.
6. Quoted in ibid., March 15 and 18, 1924.

problem with his eyes. His performance was enough to give pause to Ban Johnson as the league chief cast about for challengers to the defending Yankees. Johnson decided a Browns squad with a fully recuperated Sisler in the regular lineup would be "dangerous."[7]

Whether that was really the case or not, the season's new drama received its dress rehearsal on April 12 at Sportsman's Park, where a "friendly... but critical" crowd of twenty-two thousand stopped in to see the state of George Sisler for themselves. When he came to bat the first time, "the applause was thunderous." When he struck out, the crowd was "still friendly, but... reserved." When he batted again in the fourth, the stands were silent, "as profoundly silent as the audience at a thrilling drama."

The lead actor in the drama fouled off two offerings from Cardinals pitcher Wee Willie Sherdle, a crafty left-hander who won 165 games in his career. Working the count to 3–2, Sis met the next ball solidly, sending it on a rope to right-center and into the overflow crowd stacked around the fence. He streaked into third, and the crowd let out "a tumultuous roar that would have done credit to a home run winning a world's championship.... At last the crowd was satisfied." And so was Sis, later telling family members that this was a "very important hit for me, making me believe in myself once more." Ban Johnson, who had stayed over from a speech the previous Friday just to see how Sisler would play, "was most agreeably surprised. He certainly looked as great as ever."[8] Great enough to elicit some lines from L. C. Davis in his poem, "Today's the Day":

> George Sisler, who has been upon the shelf,
> Is on the job and full of pep and scrappy;
> He seems to be his former brilliant self
> And all the fans accordingly are happy.[9]

Alas, Ban Johnson and all those happy Browns fans were wrong. As the long 1924 season would prove, George was not "as great as ever." But as the team traveled to Chicago for the season opener versus the White Sox, he was back in the regular lineup, managing and playing first base.

There was an air of anticipation in the Windy City as twenty-four thousand fans greeted the new-edition White Sox and also stopped by to catch a glimpse of the new-edition George Sisler. Even a Browns' victory did not dampen their spirits as the Chicago fans cheered wildly when Sis made

7. Quoted in ibid., April 11, 1924.
8. Ibid., April 13, 1924; Sisler Memoirs, 13.
9. *St. Louis Post-Dispatch*, April 15, 1924.

a graceful catch of an infield popup while dancing away from a collision with Frank Ellerbe, and when he singled twice. In the excitement, the fact he was frequently hitting to left, a sign of a late swing for a left-handed batter, was overlooked by the Chicago press. The *Tribune* called Sis's return "[t]he one bright spot in the day's proceedings." The *Daily News* noted he was "gun-shy," but "proved there is little or nothing to his eyes to bother him." The *American* marveled that Sis "was the most popular player on the ball field," and the *Herald-Examiner* remarked that sadly for the White Sox, "he performed brilliantly." Only the *Journal* was cautionary, saying "he did not seem to get over his usual swing."[10]

The conclusion of hostilities on April 15 was significant for more than just Sis's return to the field. At game's end, the league's newest player/manager had his first managerial win. The excitement quickly disappeared when the White Sox won the next three. When the Tigers took the next three in Detroit, the Browns were 1–6. More personally troubling, Sis struck out three times in the White Sox series. For a man who rarely struck out during his career, 327 times in fifteen seasons, the frequency and the timing set tongues wagging. Then in Detroit he went hitless in his first eight at bats before getting a single in the final loss.

The home opener, played before fourteen thousand loyal fans on April 23, provided some relief. Looking more like his old self, Sis banged out three hits in a 9–5 win over the White Sox behind Dave Danforth, who bested future Hall of Famer Ted Lyons to break the Browns' six-game skid.

Late in the month Urban Shocker was lost to the team for several starts with tonsillitis. When Shocker returned to the team, he was fourteen pounds lighter. His loss was softened by the emergence of Ernie Wingard, a twenty-three-year-old lefty from the University of Alabama whose previous experience was in semi-pro ball. Starting as a reliever, Wingard soon became a starter. By season's end, his record was 13–12 with a 3.51 earned run average.

Despite the pleasant addition of Wingard, the Browns' main problem was still pitching. The change in rules regarding the condition of the baseball was not impacting the game, and hitters continued their domination. One beneficiary of the change, however, was Danforth. It was now harder to criticize the hurler and, in fact, there were no further allegations of ball doctoring as he finished the season at 15–12. His unimpressive earned run average of 4.51, however, was typical of a staff that averaged 4.57 for the season, a lowly seventh in the league.

10. Newspaper composite, ibid., April 16, 1924.

While the pitchers frittered away leads on a regular basis, Browns hitters were more than solid. For the most part, after his shaky start, George was holding up his end in the early going, including a four-hit game on April 26 in a win over Cleveland and his first home run on May 8 against the Tribe, in a win that pushed the team above .500 (11–10) for the first time since the opening game. At that point, the Browns led the league in hitting at .315. They would finish the season at a .295 clip, good for third among league rivals. By early May, Sis was hitting a robust .352.

One former associate of Sis's who took note of the team's improving performance was his old manager, Lee Fohl. Seldom effusive, the Red Sox skipper praised his former star for showing "lots of nerve in shouldering the double burden of managing while under the strain of his attempt to come back." Wistfully, Fohl pointed out that George "had the advantage of holding the good grace of his players when he took over the work."[11]

In an ironic twist, Sisler made his first appearance in New York on May 14. He watched with his mates and twenty-five thousand others as Babe Ruth was presented with his certificate as the league's Most Valuable Player for 1923. George, who had not yet received his own award for 1922, must have had a twinkle in his eyes when in the next hours he and his Brownies pummeled the Yanks 11–1 with Shocker, now recovered from illness, besting Waite Hoyt. The next day Sis's home run in the sixth gave his team a 2–1 win over the Yanks.

On May 22 the Browns were at 16–11 and in second place after a 3–1 win over the Senators. Credit for the victory went to Ernie Wingard, who outpitched Tom Zachary. The team's hold on second lasted but one day. They never reached that level again. On May 24, in another rarity, Sis removed himself for a pinch hitter in a 2–1 loss to the Phillies at Shibe Park. After the game, Sis insisted there was no significance to the move. Despite a left-hander on the mound and darkness caused by inclement weather, he could see the ball sufficiently to hit it. "I was just hitting poorly, in a slump and thought perhaps Pat [Collins] might win a ball game for us."[12]

Sis was right on point about his slump. In the three-game series with the Athletics that preceded his removal, he failed to reach first base in ten at bats. Perhaps he was distracted by the actions of his star hurler Shocker, who reported to the ballpark late, apparently not his first rule violation. Sis fined and reprimanded the pitcher, then hinted to the press there was more here than a single tardiness. "Shocker is a great pitcher, the greatest in the game when he takes care of himself . . . However, infractions of the

11. Quoted in ibid., May 12, 1924.
12. Quoted in ibid., May 25, 1924.

unwritten rules of baseball cannot be overlooked. A man must keep in condition, fit to play, and if he doesn't, something must be done."[13]

Shocker's actions had forced a "players' manager" to take action that he certainly must have detested. Sisler had drawn a line in the sand. Even if it was the correct action, he was now clearly management in the eyes of his players. Just as with Lee Fohl, the "honeymoon" was over. How Shocker's attitude would affect the marriage was still unclear. What was clear was that Sis and his Browns were slumping. By June 22, just one month after their climb to second, the team rested in fifth place at 28–28. Early that month, Fohl and his Red Sox came into town. With Fohl now the manager of a second-place team, local scribes revisited his managerial prowess. Perhaps, the *Post-Dispatch*'s Wray posited, he and others of the local press were too quick to decide that Fohl's clubs in Cleveland and St. Louis succeeded in spite of him. After all, the resurgence of Boston, a team that had pitching woes similar to the Browns, was further proof that the man could manage.[14]

Lest George feel left out in all the newfound love thrown Lee Fohl's way, the Browns scheduled a special day, with the Yankees in attendance, to present George his long-delayed MVP certificate. In the first game of the Yankees series, Urban Shocker showed Sis and the team he had not lost his stuff with a 6–3 victory over Yankee ace Bob Shawkey in front of a crowd of twenty thousand. Two more wins over the Yanks before huge crowds followed. Then on "George Sisler Day" the team faced an old "friend," Waite Hoyt, and folded, 5–0. A classic photo of the awards presentation shows the grinning 1922 MVP taking his award from Rear Admiral W. F. Fullem, with Babe Ruth standing next to the pair with his arms folded and a pleased expression.

In mid-June Sis was batting .315 and actually hitting better against southpaws (.327) than righties (.310). Under the circumstances, perhaps Sis could be excused if he was more disappointed with his team's performance than his own. After all, even though he was more than one hundred points under his 1922 mark, he was still hitting above .300 just months after being written off the baseball scene entirely. No one will ever know for sure if it was personal or managerial frustration, or both, that led Sis to blow his cork on June 21. The result was his ejection from the first game of a doubleheader the Browns eventually split with Chicago.

It all started off innocently enough, with Browns catcher Pat Collins protesting a couple of pitch calls by the home plate umpire, "Ducky"

13. Quoted in ibid., May 27, 1924.
14. Ibid., June 4, 1924.

Holmes. Sis stood up for his player, but Holmes was not impressed and sent both Collins and Sis to the showers. When the fans learned of the decision, someone threw a pop bottle that landed at Holmes's feet. Phil Ball tried to get onto the field to confer with Sisler and police officers, but the rotund Browns owner became wedged in between the iron railing separating the field and the stands and had to be helped through. The situation settled down when Sis refused to heed the fans' call for further action and the Browns won the first game. They lost the second 7–6 without Sis or Collins. Neither was permitted to play because of a league rule prohibiting an ejected player from any further play on the date of his banishment. The incident did not end with the Browns' loss. After the game an irate fan found Holmes as he departed the stadium and punched the ump in the eye.

Interestingly enough, even though the Browns were in fourth place at 31–31 by the end of June, the American League teams were so bunched at the top that only five games separated them and first-place Washington. The team was very much alive in the pennant race. In July the Browns stayed afloat with eighteen wins and sixteen losses, remaining in fourth, six games out of first. Considering an injury to Marty McManus, problems with Urban Shocker, the noticeable aging of speedster Tobin, continued failures by Hub Pruett (3–4 for the year with a 4.57 earned run average) and Dixie Davis (11–13 and 4.10), the "miracle," according to John E. Wray, "is that Sisler has the Browns moving as well as they are" with a "mirage of hope left."[15]

In early August the team caught fire, winning six in a row and raising the hopes of the most skeptical Browns fan by climbing to within three and a half games of the top. But the Browns remained in fourth place. By September 5 they stood at 68–66, a full ten games from the top. One interesting characteristic of the 1924 Browns was their success against the league's top teams. They did not fare nearly as well against the medium-weights and lowlights. What really hurt was a twin bill loss to the Athletics on August 7, the second game a 2–1 misfire in which Vangilder pitched well but Stan Baumgartner pitched even better.

August saw the last Ladies Day game for at least that era in Sportsman's Park. The popular events, in which the distaff side were admitted for free, supposedly were terminated due to the danger of foul balls headed toward women who made no effort to catch them, thus exposing themselves to serious injury. Of course, if the ladies paid to get in they incurred the same risk.

15. Ibid., July 19, 1924.

The public learned in August that in an overall effort to strengthen the club, the Browns planned to abandon Mobile for Tarpon Springs, Florida, the following spring, so they could schedule games with the numerous major-league clubs that already held spring training in that state. This was a move heartily endorsed, if not instigated, by Sis in an effort to toughen his ball club's training experience.

On September 2 Browns fans were given a bitter sample of why the 1924 team was floundering: bad pitching. On Labor Day, in the midst of a doubleheader, six Browns pitchers were touched for twenty-three hits. Still, the team gained a split. What a difference a few days later and one great pitcher would make. On September 6 the Browns trimmed the White Sox twice by identical 6–2 scores, behind complete-game performances by its iron man Urban Shocker. Sis helped the cause with five hits in eight trips to the plate.

As the season wound down, the Yankees and the Senators staged an exciting race for the pennant. The Browns made a contribution to each team in mid-September, losing three straight to the Yankees and two of three to the Senators. At season's end, the Senators stood at the top of the American League, and they eventually won the World Series over the Giants in seven games. The Browns lost nine of their last ten, finishing fourth at 74–78, seventeen and a half games from the lead.

At the World Series George joined baseball notables Babe Ruth, Ty Cobb, Walter Johnson, John McGraw, and beloved White Sox and Senators pitcher and coaching clown Nick Altrock to describe the action for the Christy Walsh Syndicate. The articles appeared in newspapers throughout the country. It is anyone's guess how much George, or for that matter any of the others, actually wrote under their bylines. The grouping is probably more noteworthy for bringing Cobb and Ruth together after years of jealous carping. They appear with Sisler in one published photo, hands joined, beaming broadly.[16]

For the year Sis hit .305 with nine home runs and 74 runs batted in. The Browns' perennial leader in most batting categories, Sis led his team only in hits with 194. His average, 115 points lower than in 1922, was next to last among regulars, beating only Jack Tobin, who hit .299. His 19 stolen bases in 36 attempts were a far cry from his 51 in 70 in 1922. Although still smooth on the diamond, his 23 errors represented another step back. He led the league's first basemen in that category. But George Sisler in 1924 was not the same player that struck fear in opposing pitchers in the late teens and early twenties, a point perhaps best summarized by the Yankees'

16. Thomas, *Walter Johnson,* 221–22. See also photo on page 173.

Bob Shawkey, one of the better pitchers ever to stare him down: "When he came back, we soon learned something. And this shows you how mean it was in those days. When he was up at the plate, he could watch you for only so long, and then he'd have to look down to get his eyes focused again. So we'd keep him waiting up there until he'd have to look down, and then pitch. He was never the same hitter again after that."[17]

If Sis heard comments like this he never said so, but comments or not, he was not pleased with his season in 1924 as either player or manager. He had, however, proven he could still play the game. Under his tutelage the team had shown slight improvement in the standings, going from fifth place in 1923 to fourth, and in the stands, where an additional one hundred thousand spectators paid to see his club play. As an eternal optimist, he could only keep working hard. And work hard he would, using the season as a springboard for the next.

In February 1925 the Browns gathered for spring training in their new quarters at Tarpon Springs. By now professional baseball in general and the club in particular was becoming big business. A report in John E. Wray's column in the *Post-Dispatch* on March 19 indicated the Browns organization, worth $80,000 in 1905, was now valued at $750,000. Perhaps this was why George was earning the tidy sum of $25,000 to manage and play for the team. This was his highest salary during his career, and in baseball circles it was a very good one at that, although not even close to the money Babe Ruth or Ty Cobb were making. As early as 1922 it was widely reported that Ruth's salary was $52,000 per year, a veritable fortune at the time.

In one important aspect, the squad that greeted Sis in Tarpon Springs was different than the Browns teams of seasons past. On December 17, 1924, the Browns and Yankees engineered a blockbuster trade, exchanging star hurlers Urban Shocker and Joe Bush. The Browns were willing to part with the thirty-four-year-old Shocker, their one ace, partly because of his attitude and partly because after a run of twenty-win seasons his 16–13 record and 4.17 earned run average in 1924 made the parting a bit less painful. In Bush, they received a front-line pitcher who was a perennial thorn in their side, although a bit of a swizzle stick himself when it came to attitude. In 1917, when he was with the Athletics, he was suspended for two weeks by Connie Mack. His 17–16 record and 3.57 earned run average in 1924 showed that at age thirty-two he could still get the job done,

17. Quoted in Honig, *The Greatest First Basemen of All Time*, 26.

although not at his 1922 pace of 26–7. His lifetime batting average was .253—a bonus for any pitcher. What set the trade over the top for the Browns was the inclusion of right-handed pitcher Milt Gaston, 5–3 the year before for the Yankees, and left-hander Joe Giard, a minor leaguer. The new additions gave Browns' followers hope the team's pitching woes were finally solved.

Upon his arrival at Tarpon Springs, Sis told local reporters he was feeling great, acknowledging he was still "convalescing" the previous season. "I have been playing squash tennis all winter and you know how fast the squash tennis ball travels and how good your eyes must be to follow the ball."[18] At the same time, Sis denied rumors he had wagered a suit of clothes that he would hit .340 during the upcoming season.

Continued interest in the extent of Sis's recovery was not limited to the local scene. The nation still looked on as well. On March 30, 1925, he graced the cover of *Time*, the first major-leaguer so featured. The accompanying article reviewed Sis's illness: "Will he, fans wonder, regain his former prowess?"[19]

Of course, now Sis's career was not judged solely by his performance on the field. He was on the management grill as well. Had the fourth-place finish of a year ago turned up the heat? Not so, it would seem. St. Louis fans were willing to be patient, sensing that George's concentration in 1924 was on hitting and fielding the little round ball rather than directing players. In 1924 Jimmy Austin was seen as shouldering some of that burden. In 1925, however, since George knew he could play, "the business of striving to develop the Browns into a pennant winning machine will be the big business."[20] Sisler's year of grace was up—it was now show time. George need look no farther than the morning paper if he needed a reminder. In "The Passing Show," L. C. Davis of the *Post-Dispatch* wrote:

> George Sisler says his batting lamps
> Are showing rapid improvement.
> Which indicates the coming champs
> Will start their upward movement.
> If George can land upon the pill
> With his old time precision
> The thriving town of Pennantville
> Will burst upon our vision.[21]

18. Quoted in *St. Louis Post-Dispatch*, February 20, 1925.
19. *Time* (March 30, 1925), 28.
20. *St. Louis Post-Dispatch*, February 24, 1925.
21. Ibid., February 27, 1925.

If the Browns were to scale the walls in 1925, it was clear one of Sisler's most important projects, as usual, was himself. In early spring he gave abundant evidence he was back to pre-1923 status, slamming one line drive after another into the fence at Tarpon Springs.

If Sis was indeed back all the way, he and his Brownies might well be chasing pennants and doing so before more and more Sportsman's Park spectators. In early March Phil Ball confirmed plans to extend the park's grandstand on both wings by framing the pavilions. The additions had been proposed previously, then abandoned when the Cardinals balked at the increased rent. This time nothing was said about whether or not the Cardinals would have to ante up. Adding ten thousand seats by redesign meant the city's entries into Organized Baseball could play before up to thirty thousand seated fans. Construction of the pavilion in right field also meant more difficulty in hitting home runs in that direction since the fence would sit farther back from home plate.

At almost the same time as the Browns were announcing ballpark plans back home, the people of Tarpon Springs were dedicating a park of their own. Sisler Ball Field was dedicated on March 11, 1925, amid a sea of politicians, a local band, and a rousing cheer for George as he stood at home plate thanking the city and its fans for the honor.

On the field Sis was continuing to raise eyebrows. An eastern baseball writer touring training camps noted that he was "taking his full clean swing at the ball, where in 1924 he was chopping and pushing." In fact, Sis told him, "[T]aking everything into consideration, I feel just as good as I ever did in my life." This was good for the Browns, the writer surmised, since "[t]here is a baseball axiom to the effect that as Sisler goes, so go the Browns."[22]

As the spring wore on, Sis spoke confidently about his team, particularly its increased speed and the addition of Joe Bush. He was pleased with the move to Tarpon Springs, where better weather afforded more time on the field. He also agreed with the glowing assessments of his hitting stroke, admitting that in 1924, "it was only on rare occasions that I hit the ball with snap and force." In a rare display of tooting his own horn, he predicted that his average would be better in 1925.[23]

Despite the promise of spring, however, including a preseason split with the Cardinals, the reality of the regular season set in quickly for this second edition of Sis's Brownies. In the opener at home with the Cleveland

22. Ibid., March 11, 1925.
23. Quoted in ibid., March 30, 1925.

Indians the Browns sent Bush to the mound, eager to see their new savior in action. The opening-day batting order was Tobin in right, Gene Robertson at third, Sis at first, Williams in left, McManus at second, practicing physician Dr. Joe Evans in center in place of holdout Jacobson, an aging Hank Severeid behind the plate, and Gerber at short. It was a veteran lineup, with sufficient experience to be very embarrassed at the end of the day. The final score was 21–14, Indians. In the eighth inning alone the Tribe scored twelve times. Sis aided the visitors from Lake Erie by committing a career-high four errors, two on one surefire double play grounder. If that wasn't enough, the Browns lost three more, all at home, before Dixie Davis stopped the bleeding when the Browns bested the White Sox, 11–4.

Already shorthanded by the absence of Baby Doll, Sis's problems increased when Joe Evans came down with the flu. Asked if he would consult with his manager about increasing the team's offer to Jacobson, Phil Ball replied in the negative, "No, sir. I'm running this ball club. And from now on it will be run on a business-like basis."[24]

All was not lost, however. By the end of the month, the ship was back on course to some degree. Sis, with the aid of a two-out single in the ninth on May 2, was in the midst of a hitting streak that had reached seventeen games. The streak was marked by low line drives to all fields, characteristic of his MVP season. After nineteen games, the team was a disappointing 9–10, but the fault was not with the play of its manager. He was hitting .422 and since the opening-day disaster had fielded his position with his usual aplomb.

On May 5 the Browns showed some of their expected promise by edging the Tigers in St. Louis by a 5–4 count. Sis continued his streak with a home run and a pair of singles. The real excitement occurred in the ninth when Ty Cobb, who represented the tying run, was caught off second by a great throw from Severeid. The next day, the Georgia Peach, who probably spent the previous evening in a rage, enacted his revenge with a six-for-six day that included three home runs and an American League record sixteen total bases in a 14–8 win over Joe Bush. The following day the Tigers won again. Cobb stayed red hot with two more home runs to tie Cap Anson's 1884 record of five home runs in two games. The Tigers' manager also drove in six runs in the 11–4 win over Dave Danforth.

Through all the ups and downs of a lumpy start, the one constant for the Browns was the hitting of George Sisler. By May 10 his streak was at twenty-four games and his average stood at .419. This was twenty-four

24. Quoted in ibid., April 15, 1925.

points better than his 1922 average at the same point. Thus far he had hit safely at least once in every game of the season. When asked to account for his comeback, Sis shrugged it off. "I don't try to account for it," he told J. Roy Stockton of the *Post-Dispatch*. "During the summer of 1923 I decided that medicine and surgery were not doing me any good. Since then I have let nature take care of itself."[25]

One player who was mightily impressed was Babe Ruth, who had spent the first two weeks of the 1925 season in a hospital. He wrote that George was "staging the greatest come-back ever known to baseball . . . (T)he league ought to strike a medal for iron nerve and give it to George. He has whipped the worst odds any ball player ever played against. I know what it is to be helpless, but I am thankful there isn't anything wrong with my eyes. I got discouraged after I was in the hospital two weeks. Sisler might as well have been in the hospital two years."[26]

Indeed, Sis was making a strong statement, while playing and managing for a team with an almost nonexistent pitching staff. During one early season eight-game streak the Browns scored forty-four runs, an average of 5.5 runs per game, and won only three times. Only twice in those games did the pitching staff hold the opposing batters to fewer than ten hits. On May 20 when Joe Bush finally gave the team a strong pitching performance in an 8–2 win over the Red Sox, Sis's streak was at thirty-five, including the last game of the 1924 season. The string was only six shy of his own record and the second longest of his career. His triple and single aided the win, but he gladly would have traded the streak and his .399 average for a few more wins. At 15–18 the Browns rested in fifth place and were already eight games out of first. The next day they lost again as the Athletics' Lefty Grove and Slim Harris overcame a Ken Williams grand slam for an 8–6 victory. The A's at 21–7 were looking very good. Sis had just three official at bats in the game and his long streak ended. Thirty-four consecutive games remains the longest American League hitting streak to start a season. Willie Keeler's forty-four in 1897 represents the all-time record.

While all this was going on, major management changes were under way across town. On May 30 the Cardinals reassigned Branch Rickey and replaced him with a player/manager of their own, Rogers Hornsby. Although not immediately apparent, the move set in motion a shift in fan allegiance that did not end until the Browns left St. Louis following the 1953 season. All this Cardinals/Browns fuss, however, was for another day. For the present, now that the pressure of the streak was over, Sis could

25. Quoted in ibid., May 10, 1925.
26. Quoted by Babe Ruth in his syndicated column, ibid., May 10, 1925.

concentrate on getting his team started. Winning a doubleheader against the Tribe on May 26 helped, and by June 5 the club reached fourth place at 24–24.

As the season progressed, Sis's hitting tailed off to some extent, but he maintained a pace well above his efforts of the previous campaign. Although his red hot bat was now only lukewarm, he was happy with what he saw on June 23 in Philly against the front-running Athletics. A 9–2 win behind Joe Bush brought the smile. "That's all we need . . . ," George told reporters following the game. "There is nothing the matter with the rest of the team. We can hit; . . . but weak flinging has kept us down in the race."[27]

But one well-pitched game does not a season make. While the team batting average for 1925 was .298, placing them fourth in the league in that category, the pitching staff's earned run average was a miserable 4.92, next to last in the league. Bush, the hero of the encouraging triumph over the Athletics, would finish the season at 14–14 with an embarrassing 5.09 earned run average. In addition, as time went on it became apparent Bullet Joe, as he was still called, was about as disruptive in the clubhouse as the man he had replaced. The starter with the most wins for the club was his trade mate, Milt Gaston, who finished 15–14 with a 4.41 earned run average. Dixie Davis at 12–7 and the surprising throw-in in the Shocker deal, Joe Giard, at 10–5 fared better in the win-loss column.

Still, this group of Browns was spunky. For once they were also much better than their nemesis, the Yankees. Ruth's team was struggling through a rare bad season, lodged uncomfortably in seventh place. In a five-game July series at Sportsman's Park, the Browns won four, including a July 10 doubleheader win in which they battered eight Yankees hurlers, among them Urban Shocker. Shocker, following the blockbuster trade, was not performing much better than Bush. He finished the year with a subpar 12–12 record, but a more respectable earned run average of 3.65. He also pitched better in his last two full years in baseball, going 19–11 in 1926 and 18–6 for the legendary 1927 Yankee powerhouse. Bush, on the other hand, was gone from St. Louis by 1926 and was never a winner again in a career that ended in the shadows in 1928.

In mid-July Sis was still hitting well at .362. The skipper was in the midst of a twenty-two-game hitting streak, his second long string of the season. On July 11 he tripled with the bases full in the fourth inning and followed with a grand slam the next inning to account for seven runs in a 10–7 Browns' win over the Senators. "It's the timing of the swing," he told

27. Quoted in ibid., June 23, 1925.

reporters. "Perfect timing is what enables a little man, even, to get long hits."[28] The victory was not inconsequential. The Senators were resting in first place.

The wins were beginning to mount up. The July home stand was successful, with the Browns going 17–10 during the stay. Three of four from the Senators was particularly impressive, and started a streak of six in a row: the last two Senators games, three from the Red Sox, and one from the Athletics. The streak lifted the team into third at 47–42. Then, as so often seemed the case during the Sisler years, the wheels came off as the team lost eight of the next nine. On July 30 the club was back under .500 at 48–50. They were in fifth place, a full sixteen games out of first, and very frustrated.

Successes, failures, streaks, and slumps all fell by the wayside in late July when news reached Sis of the death of his mother. Mary Sisler, who had spent a number of her last years residing in St. Louis with George and his family before returning to Ohio, died on July 27, 1925, at age seventy-three, of cerebral hemorrhage. Two days later George left New York to attend his mother's funeral in Ohio and be with his brother Cassius and the surviving Sisler family members. He left town with a heavy heart, as well as a swollen right ankle sustained when a ball took a nasty hop, clipping his leg. The injury would have kept him out of the lineup for several games even without his personal loss. Marty McManus moved to first base in his field boss's absence.

Sis's injury and return to Ohio came during the midst of the disastrous nine-game stretch. He was back in the lineup on August 3 to help his squad to a 12–4 win over the Red Sox and Howard Ehmke. The team continued to flirt with .500 the remainder of August, the highlight being a three-game sweep of the Athletics at Sportsman's Park. In one of those victories Sisler had a game-winning triple and some sensational plays in the field, proving there was still life in the old ball glove, as well as the bat. On one play he saved teammate Bobby LaMott, now the Browns' regular shortstop, from an error by going low to scoop an errant throw and preserve the out. On another he successfully stretched far into the stands to glove a foul ball.

In late August a six-game winning streak, including three over the first-place Senators, left the team at 66–59, their best record in some time. Still, they were in fourth and a distant thirteen and a half games behind the front-runners. Joe Bush's one-hit 5–0 shutout over the Senators and the still-effective Walter Johnson silenced a few critics of the Urban Shocker trade. While the on-again, off-again Bush and Shocker were canceling each

28. Quoted in ibid., July 14, 1925.

other out, the Browns could gloat over the performances of the throw-ins, Gaston and Giard, with each win by the pair a bonus for the locals.

In 1925 it was apparent the "rabbit" ball was still very much in play. The Browns were not the only team shy of pitching depth—lack of stoppers was an American League epidemic. On August 28 there were fifty-eight American League batters hitting better than .300, and at least half of those hitters carried averages above .330. The increase in home run production was even more glaring. In 1918 American League players hit an all-time league low of ninety-six round-trippers. The figure climbed to 240 in 1919—interesting, since that was one year prior to the "modification" in manufacture of the baseball. The number reached 369 in 1920 with the modification and the rules changes, then see-sawed back and forth between the mid-400s and mid-500s over the next few years. In 1925 the league's home run total would complement the increase in batting averages by reaching 533.

On September 5, even though the season would not play out for another month, Babe Ruth named his annual All-American team. Despite Sis's healthy .362 average, 11 home runs, 10 stolen bases, and 198 hits, Ruth chose another St. Louis ballplayer, Jim Bottomley, as his first baseman, "in the hardest of all positions to decide." The National League star was hitting .378 at the time with eight more home runs, but "the big point in his favor" according to Ruth is that "Bottomley is younger and perhaps has more pep."[29] At thirty-two, for the first time in his career, a new evaluator had crept into the mix for Sis. Now there were youthful footsteps behind him. In 1925, however, age was still a minor matter for the Sizzler. The Babe's snub, if it even was one, was softened a few days later when John McGraw, the wily manager of the New York Giants, came out with an all-star team of his own, naming Sis over Bottomley and telling readers his selection has "that poise of experience, that polish that goes with an artist."[30]

As satisfying as all this fuss must have been for a player who had drifted from the limelight the past few seasons, it must have seemed small potatoes when compared with the surge of pride Sis was feeling in his team. In September the team won sixteen and lost eleven, enough to complete an 82–71 season in third place, fifteen games behind Washington. Now referred to consistently as the Senators, the American League champs lost the World Series to Pittsburgh in seven games.

In St. Louis the drums were beating. Both its Browns and its Cards finished their seasons on the upbeat. The Cardinals finished fourth in the

29. Syndicated story by Babe Ruth, ibid., September 5, 1925.
30. Syndicated story by John S. McGraw, ibid., September 13, 1925.

National League as player/manager Hornsby won the batting Triple Crown for a second time. The Browns had clinched third place from the Tigers on October 1 by besting them 4–3 at Sportsman's Park. The win assured team members a healthy share of the 1925 World Series receipts. Despite a season attendance figure of 462,898, which placed the Browns seventh in the league in attendance, owner Phil Ball had another profitable season. On September 9, 1925, the *Post-Dispatch* reported that the club cleared $174,000 in 1924. It marked the eighth time in eleven seasons the team earned money for the present ownership.[31]

The third-place clincher also assured George Sisler a place on the Browns' bench and field once again in 1926. Such was the release of tension that in the second game of the October 4 season-ending double bill, Sis and Ty Cobb faced off on the pitching mound in relief for the clubs they managed. Cobb was perfect in his one inning, while Sis held the Tigers scoreless in two. George, however, was the victim of such a barrage of line drives up the middle that third baseman Gene Robertson offered his frowning skipper a pair of shin guards. It would be Sisler's last American League appearance on the mound.

For the year, Sis hit .345 with 224 hits, 100 runs, 12 home runs, and 105 runs batted in. By any standard, "rabbit" ball or not, he had completed a robust comeback that would satisfy all but the most demanding of athletes or critics. Sis, however, was just such an animal, always seeking perfection and disturbed by anything less. Like an Oscar winner who now seeks only gold, he was dissatisfied with his performance. Years later, he would say, "Oh, I know I hit .345 and got 228 [*sic*] hits in 1925 but that never gave me much satisfaction. That isn't what I call real good hitting."[32] Over the years many members of the Hall of Fame posted less impressive numbers, but then few were playing against the backdrop of record-breaking hit totals and two .400-plus seasons.

31. Ibid., September 10, 1925.
32. Quoted in Meany, *Baseball's Greatest Hitters*, 187.

13

Same Old Same Old

George Sisler had set a very high standard for himself and for his team in 1925. Would 1926 be the year it finally all came together? Could they finally make the World Series, or would they slide backward? Talk around the hot stove league centered on the Browns' need for additional catching strength, reinforcements in the outfield, and of course, pitching. The team's strengths were hitting and fielding. One local scribe, while giving the Browns their due, boldly predicted the end of the city's thirty-seven-year pennant drought would more likely come from the success of the Cardinals than the Browns.[1]

George spent the winter of 1925–1926 honing his managerial skills as a skipper of a team in the Florida Winter League. It was a boom time for real estate in Florida, with great rivalries between the various real estate companies. By the time he arrived in the state it was said Miami alone had two thousand real estate offices and twenty-five thousand agents.[2] The competitors sponsored baseball teams and formed them into a league. Sis was asked to manage the Miami Shores team. Bucky Harris, the player/manager of the Washington Senators, managed the Coral Gables team.

For his time and trouble, Sis was given room and board, plus a bonus at

---

1. *St. Louis Post-Dispatch*, October 5, 1925.
2. Allen, *Only Yesterday*, 205–18.

the end of the season to include real estate. At season's end, his Miami Shores team faced off with Harris's Coral Gables team in a final show-down. Miami Shores won, and Sis was a local hero. He came back from Florida with rights to a number of prime lots.

If Sis was excited about his newfound largesse, he was not alone. In an era when almost everything, including skirt lengths, stock prices, and batting statistics, was going up and up, acquisition of land, even hereto-fore untouched swampland, was quickly becoming part of the equation. Florida was a natural, with its inviting climate and accessibility to large, automobile-filled northeastern cities. Couple this with a pervasive sense that everything anyone, even the average workaday American, touched was turning to gold and you had the perfect recipe for a buying frenzy.

Soon, however, in a precursor to a much more serious tumble, the Florida boom became a swoon. People who purchased the land, paying only a fraction of the total cost to bind it in their name, gave little thought to making the remaining payments covering most of the total cost. The main idea was to resell the land at a profit in a rising market. Few stood back from the buying blitz to think about the consequences if the ardor for this land cooled. When the market stalled by the end of 1926, overex-tended buyers were defaulting on their purchases right and left. Unlike Sis, who earned his land through skillful managing with no outlay of money, most investors were left holding a very expensive bag, with little or noth-ing in it. In the end, however, George's land was equally worthless.[3]

After a brief stay in St. Louis, Sis returned to Florida on February 21, 1926, for a second season of spring training Tarpon Springs' style. His club had made waves in the trading circles earlier in the month, peddling the troublesome Joe Bush and veteran outfielder Jack Tobin, only a part-time player in 1925, to Washington for lefty pitchers Tom Zachary and Win Ballou. Zachary was the son of a minister. In World War I he went over-seas with a Quaker Red Cross unit and paid his dues. At age thirty he was a solid citizen and a solid performer with an 85–82 record for the Senators from 1920 through 1925. Along with the twenty-eight-year-old Ballou, he would be one of the few bright spots in what turned out to be another dismal season for Browns pitchers. His 14–15 record and 3.60 earned run average led the team.

In addition to pitching, the club attempted to shore up their inadequa-cies behind the plate by acquiring thirty-seven-year-old Wally Schang from the underperforming Yankees in exchange for seldom-used pitcher George

3. Sisler Memoirs, 24.

Mogridge. A .284 lifetime hitter and strong defender, Schang's .330 average in 1926 exceeded expectations, turning catching from a Browns' weakness into a strength. Another key acquisition was infielder Oscar Mellilo, purchased from minor-league Milwaukee for sixty thousand dollars. The twenty-six year old, known for his smooth infield play, quickly made a place for himself on the squad. His .255 average was not exciting, but Mellilo remained the Browns' second baseman until 1935.

Upon his arrival in camp, George once again proclaimed his vision problems old news. "I have trained with my team down in Miami although I did not play. my practice has shown me that my eyes are O.K. in fact there was practically nothing the matter with them last year. . . . My worries are not about myself. . . . If there is a criticism I could make of my own club it is that we have no pitcher of supreme merit."[4]

Unlike some managers, Sis did not insist on early to bed, early to rise. He left his team's conditioning up to the players themselves, a policy that would come back to haunt him. Sometimes it takes a team through training camp and well into the regular season to find its identity and establish its place in the race for the prize. Early inadequacies and failures can be corrected in plenty of time to salvage a season. Sadly, this was not true for the 1926 Browns. They were just plain awful from the beginning.

The main advantage to training in Tarpon Springs versus Mobile was the close proximity of other major-league clubs. One such club was the Brooklyn Dodgers. In an early spring series between the teams the Browns lost four of five, setting the tone for the entire season. The storm warnings were clear, but the forecast had not yet reached St. Louis. On February 25, a heading in the sports page enthused that "Harmony and Enthusiasm Give Browns Advantage Over Team of Last Season."[5]

One item of more than passing interest to the press and Browns fans was the appearance in camp of former Stanford football star Ernie Nevers. A right-handed pitcher with some promise, the twenty-three year old would stick with the club, but he would cause considerable controversy over his lack of playing time and his Shocker-like insistence on his wife's company on road trips. He did, however, pitch a complete-game victory in August on his way to a 2–4 year and 6–12 career mark before returning to pro football and eventual enshrinement in Canton.

Unlike previous seasons, 1926 would see a more focused Phil Ball. The Browns' owner, recently divested of all remaining ice plants due to ill

4. Quoted in *St. Louis Post-Dispatch*, February 22, 1926.
5. Ibid., February 25, 1926.

health, was now fully devoted to baseball. Having spent six hundred thousand dollars on a new, improved Sportsman's Park, his expectations were rising at the same time his patience was thinning. Telling the press, "I want a winner," he ventured that "[w]ith reasonable luck I hope the club will do in 1926 what it narrowly missed doing in 1922."[6]

One problem in achieving Ball's expected level of success was the club's reliance on Joe Giard as a pitching mainstay. The youngster had pitched admirably in 1925, making him fair game for optimism in 1926, but the emphasis and optimism were ill-founded. In fifteen starts he could only muster a bleak 3–10 record and dreadful 7.00 earned run average. The staff itself almost matched its 4.92 earned run average of the previous year, doling out a hefty 4.66 runs per game. Meanwhile, team batting fell from .298 to .276, sixth in the league, not nearly enough to overcome the lack of quality pitching. In order to move up from third, the club needed at least as much hitting as in previous years and much better pitching. It got neither. The result was not pretty. Even before the horses were out of the gate, critics were sharpening their fangs just in case the play of the Browns turned sour. In a copyrighted article appearing in the *Post-Dispatch*, Sis was called "the least demonstrative of any major league manager, though he is a charming fellow to meet."[7] This was followed closely by a report that as the Browns prepared to return to St. Louis to begin the season, they were behind in their training schedule with Sis scheduling twelve-inning practice games for the last three days at Tarpon Springs to make up for lost ground.

Whatever their condition, when the Browns returned to town they must have been thrilled to see their renovated ballpark. Now seating 34,023 fans, an increase of more than 15,000, it featured an extended fence in right field. Once 300 feet from home plate, the new fence sat twenty feet back at 320, an imposing distance for left-sided hitters such as Sisler and Williams, but a shot in the arm for a team with weak pitching.

In the annual cross-town spring series, the Browns surprised a loaded Cardinal squad by winning both games. When Oscar Mellilo stole home in the second game to seal a 3–2 Browns win, it marked the last laugh the longtime hometown favorites would have over their National League cousins for a long, long while. In seemingly good spirits, the Browns left St. Louis for the season opener in Chicago with a lineup that included Harry Rice, a .359 hitter in 103 games in 1925 in right field, Mellilo at third base,

6. Quoted in ibid., March 8, 1926.
7. Ibid., March 28, 1926.

Sis at first base, an aging Williams in left field, McManus at second base, Jacobson in center field, Leo Dixon catching, and Gerber at shortstop.

In Chicago, a crowd of thirty-three thousand fans watched their heroes whip the Browns, 5–1, behind pitcher Ted Lyons. Sis hit safely three times, including his team's first hit of the season. But much like the previous season's start, the Browns as a team were not up to the task. They lost five straight, and any remaining goodwill, before posting their first win in Detroit on April 19 by a 4–1 count.

In the home opener Tom Zachary came alive to preserve a 5–1 win and some team dignity, but by the end of April the Browns were at 5–11, looking up in the standings at all seven American League rivals. "I don't know what's wrong with my team," George cried. "They're not hitting and they're not fielding. I don't know what's wrong. I must make some changes."[8]

In the midst of a league controversy concerning the use of rosin bags by pitchers, John E. Wray told *Post-Dispatch* readers tongue-in-cheek that the Browns needed a "sand-box" more than the rosin.[9] In fairness, the team was beset by injuries, which required Sis to constantly juggle his everyday lineup. At one point, he even had outfielder Rice at third base, with McManus, Gerber, and semi-regular Herschel Bennett shelved with injuries. A bright spot was the play of catcher Bill "Pinky" Hargrave, a thirty-year-old redhead who had played sparingly in previous years with the Senators and in 1925 with the Browns. He handled backstop duties with aplomb and showed some pop in his bat in the early going with a two-home-run game.

In early May league figures showed Sis off to a relatively slow start at .301 with eight runs batted in and but one stolen base. His team mired in eighth, it was only a matter of time before he would feel an early dose of warm temperatures in his adopted hometown. On May 1, the first crack in the dam appeared during an 11–2 pasting by the Tigers at Sportsman's Park. The play of the Browns was so listless that it was met with "loud, raucous hoots and jeers" as the Browns were charged with five errors and "performed like cast-offs from a municipal league." It appeared the team had stopped caring less than a month into the season. According to one close observer, Sis "denies that he is going to quit the Browns. But there seems to be no denying the Browns have quit George."[10]

8. Quoted in ibid., April 29, 1926.
9. Ibid.
10. Ibid., May 2 and 25, 1926.

Phil Ball, however, had not come this far with his star player/manager to abandon him so quickly. Speaking through the team's traveling secretary, Willis E. Johnston, he quieted talk of Sis's demise. "Mr. Ball is not satisfied with the team's showing," Johnston told the *Associated Press*. "But it is not the fault of Sisler or any one else. We have had a string of accidents and the end apparently is not in sight. No manager can be held responsible for injuries that rob him of his best players."[11]

At the time, pitcher Charlie Robertson had joined outfielder Bennett on the injured list, along with infielders Gerber and McManus. These were hardly the team's heart-and-soul players, but they were solid contributors who might have made a difference. In finding the right combination to produce wins, Sisler's hands were tied by his roster's injuries. No lineup had played together more than three or four days since the season started. Their absence, however, provided a reason to keep Sis off the firing block, at least for now. But as local scribes were quick to point out, it still seemed strange that despite the horrible start, the club made no personnel changes, willing to stand pat on a rapidly sinking ship.

The vote of confidence from Browns ownership may have served to set the record straight for the time being, but it did nothing to jump-start the team. On May 26 the Browns returned to St. Louis from a horrific road tour in which they lost sixteen of nineteen. They remained in eighth place, now twenty games behind the resurgent New York Yankees. Then, seemingly out of nowhere, the club reeled off four wins in a row over the Indians, a decent middle-of-the-pack team. In each of the contests, the locals showed a bit of spark. In one, Pinky Hargrave saved the win by blocking the plate, tagging the potential tying run three feet short of a score. Suddenly the scribes were looking for a reason to be supportive.

At this same time across town, a steamroller was shifting into high gear. On May 23 the Cardinals reached .500 behind the stellar play of another Branch Rickey "find," Jim Bottomley, the man who had challenged Sis's first base supremacy the year before. Around town the Cardinals were certainly catching everyone's fancy. The Browns, however, were playing better, too. Perhaps some of it was the improved play of their cross-town rivals, more probably it was just a good dose of home cooking. Relying on a home stand that began on May 27 and ended twenty-four days later on June 20, the Browns won sixteen and lost only eight, rising into sixth place at 25–37. A highlight of the home stand was Sis's daring exploits on the base paths. Admittedly a step or two slower at thirty-three, the skipper

11. Quoted in ibid., May 9, 1926.

still had a head for the art of legal theft, rallying his team to a 9–7 victory over the Tigers on June 1 with a steal of home.

The base-stealing heroics came on the heels of stinging criticism of Sis and his club in the *Post-Dispatch*. On June 1, J. Roy Stockton wrote that the Browns' problem was lack of pitching "[a]nd someone who knows a pitcher when he sees one and who knows how to coach pitchers and how to pick them for duty."[12] A few days later, Stockton wrote that the Browns "have taken advantage of his [Sisler's] kindness. They have loafed and retrograded. Men have lost their speed and their punch because they have not worked and the result . . . , a terrible disappointing slump and howls for a remedy. Sisler has suffered already for his kindness. There have been howls for his scalp. . . . [H]e must be a tough manager, if he is to keep that fat salary and his job."[13] Stockton's words were biting. His reference to Sis's kindness, a backhanded compliment at best, was probably the truest assessment of the failure of George Sisler as a manager.

That all this criticism came during the club's one significant surge of the season was of little matter. The cards were on the table. Something had to be done on the field and in the clubhouse to salvage the season. Cries for personnel changes, however, were met with a blank stare. On June 11 business manager Bill Friel announced that the only change contemplated was an additional scout. The announcement was merely a camouflage. On June 15 the Browns revealed that the answer to their woeful pitching problems was a trade of outfielders: longtime fan favorite Baby Doll Jacobson was sent to the Athletics for Edmund John "Bing" Miller. In the deal, the Browns received the younger player. Bing was thirty-two to Jacobson's thirty-six, and a batter of comparable ability. Miller had hit .318 in 124 games in 1925. Jacobson, on the other hand, was by far the better outfielder. In most circles, the trade was rated a standoff. There was from the outset, however, one big problem with the new Browns' outfielder. He was not a pitcher.

Management might have been excused had no pitcher been available, but someone was available at the time in the person of Howard Ehmke, a thirty-two-year-old Red Sox pitcher who won twenty games in 1923 and nineteen in 1924. In 1925 he fell off, but only days after the Browns traded Jacobson to the A's, Baby Doll was traded again, this time to the Red Sox for none other than Mr. Ehmke and an outfielder named Tom Jenkins. Ehmke proceeded to win twelve games for his new club. The Browns

12. Ibid., June 1, 1926.
13. Ibid., June 7, 1926.

claimed he was too expensive, but it is hard to believe outfielder Jenkins was a deal breaker. A better answer is that Jacobson was traded from the Browns because he was old and a holdout the year before, not because his replacements would help the team. Sis was left to sink or swim with the present set of hurlers.

On June 21 when the Browns again hit the road, their recent good fortune did not make the bus. Despite another Sisler steal of home to give his club a split of a doubleheader in Chicago on June 26, the club went back to its losing ways. They were 13–16 in July, finishing the month on a seven-game losing streak, including five straight upon their return home.

Outside St. Louis, Sis still had his supporters. In mid-July Connie Mack came to his defense, claiming that all the first sacker's ball club needed was the right combination, which according to columnist John E. Wray "is what the burglar said as he looked at the bank safe's time lock."[14]

Although still desperate for pitching help, Phil Ball spent fifty thousand dollars and peddled three ballplayers to Milwaukee for Fred Schulte, a minor-league outfielder. The "can't-miss" prospect did miss over the next several weeks. He made nary a dent in the major-league records book in 1926. His purchase and Ball's failure to spend one red cent on improving his club's pitching staff makes one wonder just how much he wanted Sis at this point to remain his manager. The string of losses at the end of July had the town buzzing about the Browns' next manager and the sale of the club. Phil Ball quickly denied the latter while delicately stepping over the former. Betting odds were on Washington's Roger Peckinpaugh, the 1925 American League Most Valuable Player, as Sis's replacement.

Hidden among the shambles of this last season were George's own struggles at the plate. During his team's first seven games in August he had but one hit in twenty-six trips to the plate for an .038 average, including a hitless streak of seventeen at bats. The team's struggle on the field was finally taking its toll on its manager's trump card, his hitting. On August 10 columnist Wray wrote:

> Manager George Sisler seems to have subsided with the remainder of his club. The man who once led the League and set a record and who last year swatted the old pill at around .350, for the last 14 games at home has batted .179 and has driven in only five runs!
> That's showing the way!
> It's like setting a snail to pace a greyhound race.[15]

14. Ibid., July 19, 1926.
15. Ibid., August 10, 1926.

Wray and the rest of the critics had a point. George's run production was way down. In 110 games he had driven in but 54 teammates. On August 19 the *Boston Herald* noted that the Browns "are merely playing out the string" and despite Sis's denials, "the report grows apace that it is settled he will not be holding the reins next season."[16]

As he watched his team flounder and defended his position, George must have wondered aloud at the good fortune of Rogers Hornsby. The Cards were beginning to dominate the news in St. Louis. Hornsby now had a daily column in the *Post-Dispatch,* and the Cardinals were the daily lead story. On August 23 they took over first place in the National League, playing to banner headlines. In a small corner of the sports page a story announced the Browns would open a home series with the Senators. Fans at future Brownie games would not be forced to miss reports on the games that mattered most. Radios were installed throughout the grandstand to allow fans to get play-by-plays of Cardinal road games.

A doubleheader win at Sportsman's Park by the Yankees on September 25 clinched the American League pennant for the New Yorkers. One day earlier the Cardinals had clinched the National League pennant, ending the city's long drought. By the end of the weekend, the Browns' misery was over. At 62–92 they were twenty-nine games behind the Yankees, in seventh place only because Boston was even worse.

At season's close, George was batting .290 for 150 games, his lowest average since his rookie year in 1915. His seven home runs and 71 runs batted in were also revealing. He did not lead the team in any category except stolen bases and triples, with twelve each. His fielding average had improved somewhat from a career low .983 with twenty-six errors in 1925 to .987 with twenty-one errors in 1926.

If George was worried about how he stood with the boss, he needed to look no further than the local sports page. "It is a fine celebration for me," Phil Ball told the *Post-Dispatch.* "Here I go to work and build a fine, big, modern plant for my team, and the other guys come along, win a pennant, and get all the gravy of what promises to be the biggest series ever played."[17]

Ball had reason to be envious: As he prepared to watch the Cardinals fill Sportsman's Park to the brim in the October Classic, he could look at his team's league-low attendance figure, 283,986, and shake his head. But if Phil Ball or the Browns in general were looking for any sympathy,

16. Reprint of *Boston Herald* article, ibid., August 19, 1926.
17. Quoted in ibid., October 5, 1926.

October of 1926 was not the right time. The city of St. Louis was on fire with Cardinal fever. And when the objects of their affection topped the Yankees 3–2 in game seven of the World Series in New York on October 10, the town's kettle boiled over. Fans spilled out into the streets of St. Louis. Front-page banners large enough for a presidential election or assassination blared the news. The Cardinals were World Champs.

In a smaller story, on the lower right-hand side of page one, those readers still interested in non-Cardinal news read that Browns Manager George Sisler had been notified "a few days ago" by President Ball "that his showing with the club was not sufficient to justify retaining him except in the capacity of first baseman. The complete failure of the team this year is all the explanation that is necessary to make, I think." Sis, whose contract had expired, declined to comment, other than to say that he had no "special plans for next season. If Mr. Ball says I will not be manager next year, I guess I'm out. He ought to know."[18] According to reports, George was visibly upset that the news of his dismissal was out. Reports claimed that Sis's lenient nature led to his downfall and, for the first time, alleged Sis had resisted pressure to resign in midseason.

The termination, coming as it did in the face of the Cardinals' triumph, was certainly a bitter pill to swallow for Sisler and his supporters. In typical fashion, as allegations concerning his managerial deficiencies continued to swirl around him, George maintained his silence. "Nothing I could say would help the situation," he said. Ball, meanwhile, held back little, telling reporters that "the next manager of the team will be a rigid disciplinarian and a man able to command the enthusiasm of the players and their best efforts."[19] Making sure everyone knew he still considered Sis a value to the club and a good player, Ball refused to discuss his star's future.

Years later George would look back at his three-year stint as a big-league manager and tell his family he felt he "had done a respectable job" and "had no apologies to make."[20] About that, few could really argue. He had done no better, but really no worse than the many that came before and after him as manager of the hapless Browns franchise. When his team "really came apart at the seams," he had, however, "let the way the club was going affect my hitting."[21]

In 1923 when Phil Ball convinced his one major star to both play and manage the Browns for 1924 and beyond, the new venture, like most, com-

18. Quoted in ibid., October 11, 1926.
19. Quoted in ibid., October 12, 1926.
20. Sisler Memoirs, 13.
21. Quoted in Meany, *Baseball's Greatest Hitters*, 187.

menced with resounding platitudes and an aura of goodwill. It also ended, like most, with a thud. No one was happy, least of all the player-manager in question. A perfectionist who knew his limitations, George turned down the job initially because he was afraid it might affect his game. To his deep and eternal frustration it probably did, but since his return to the field coincided with his start on the bench, the degree can never be accurately ascertained. Nor can one calculate the toll it took on a player of superior talent who liked to be in total control to place his baseball legacy in the hands of lesser lights. One thing is certain, however. The slow, inevitable erosion in George's skills began, perhaps prematurely, while he shouldered the burden of juggling two demanding jobs, attempting to please owners, players, fans, and the media alike. A few player-managers of the era, such as Tris Speaker, Bucky Harris, and Rogers Hornsby, were successful in the short run. Most, including George Sisler, were not. It is interesting to note that in the mid-1920s eight of the sixteen big-league teams were at least for a time managed by active players. Today the player-manager is an extinct species.

As George's managing odyssey concluded, Phil Ball did not want to discuss his fading star's future. Still, the question persisted. Now that he no longer had the job he never wanted nor sought in the first place, had the burden of performing that job diminished George Sisler's skills to the point that his career was at an end, or, with the burden lifted, could the playing career revive? In October of 1926, no one was talking and perhaps no one, not even the man himself, knew the answer.

On November 3, 1926, about a month after Sis's dismissal, the Browns hired Dan Howley as their new manager. At forty-four, Howley's major-league career contrasted markedly from that of his predecessor. A former catcher, he appeared in a total of twenty-six games for the Philadelphia Phillies in 1913, and then made his mark as a minor-league manager. After a four-year stint in Montreal, he won the International League pennant in 1918 while managing in Toronto, then spent three years coaching for the Tigers before returning to Toronto, where he won another pennant in 1926. That, plus a reputation as a former catcher who could develop young pitchers, caught Phil Ball's eye. Ball brought Howley to St. Louis with but one problem—the Browns had practically no young pitchers to develop.

While St. Louis baseball fans were combing through the daily sports pages for news about a Sisler trade, the unexpected happened. On December 20, 1926, after demands for a three-year contract fell on deaf ears, Rogers Hornsby, still perched on his pedestal as the managing genius of the Cardinals' 1926 run for glory, was traded to the New York Giants for star second baseman Frankie Frisch and a pitcher named Jimmy Ring. The trade stunned the baseball world, nowhere more so than in St. Louis.

On the Sisler front, all remained surprisingly calm. If management intended to unload their quiet star, they kept the negotiations to themselves. On March 2, 1927, Sis reported to Tarpon Springs, "glad to get rid of the managing burden" so "I could concentrate more on my playing."[22] He could have been excused if his mouth dropped open when he read the papers in early March and saw that Babe Ruth's salary was now up to $70,000, making him the second highest paid athlete in sports. Boxer Gene Tunney had reached the magical one million dollar plateau. Other baseball luminaries at the upper end of the pay scales included Ty Cobb, who was now with the Athletics and reportedly earning $75,000, but more likely was in the $60,000 range; Tris Speaker, pulling in $40,000; and the recently departed Hornsby at $40,000. If the disparity between those salaries and George's $25,000 (believed reduced to $18,000 when he lost the manager's position) rankled, the Browns' star never said a word. Perhaps he was mollified by a gentlemen's agreement that reportedly provided a bonus if his play in the upcoming season met certain unspecified high standards.[23]

During the 1927 exhibition season, Sis hit the ball with authority. On March 11 he was three for six against Cincinnati, hitting in his customary number three slot in the lineup. In the early going, he alternated at first base with Guy Sturdy, a twenty-seven year old who would end up playing only five games for the year. Sturdy had hit 49 home runs for Browns' affiliate Tulsa in 1926 and in March, at least, the headline read, "Only a Brilliant Sisler Can Keep Tulsa Slugger Away From First Base Job." Sturdy, it seemed, "is stymied by the greater glory of a rejuvenated Sisler."[24]

In March all was tranquil in Tarpon Springs. Manager Howley liked what he saw from his first baseman, predicting a great year for George. Phil Ball liked what he saw from his new manager. He told reporters the club had an entirely different morale than the previous year. "It has the spirit . . . Manager Howley has shown real progress."[25]

If indeed the Browns under Dan Howley were going to make "real progress," they were going to have to do it with essentially the same team makeup that George had juggled and struggled with in 1926. There were, however, a few differences. Fred Schulte, the youngster obtained from

22. Sisler Memoirs, 13.
23. *St. Louis Post-Dispatch,* March 3 and 15, 1927.
24. Ibid., March 10, 1927.
25. Quoted in ibid., March 23, 1927.

Milwaukee near the end of 1926, was now with the big club and would provide a .317 average off the bench in sixty games. He would post a solid .292 career average in six seasons with the Browns and five with the Senators and Pirates. Marty McManus was now with the Tigers. Frank O'Rourke, obtained from the Tigers when he came down with the measles and was permanently replaced by future Hall of Famer Charlie Gehringer, took over as the regular third baseman and hit a respectable .268. On the mound, Dixie Davis was released in February, while well-respected thirty-four-year-old Sad Sam Jones was obtained the same month from the Yankees for Joe Giard and outfielder Cedric Durst. A consistently successful pitcher in New York, Jones's one-year stay in St. Louis with the Browns changed all that. He would end the season 8–14 with a 4.32 earned run average.

Unless your name was Ball or Howley, it is hard to believe any serious student of the game could have looked at the 1927 version of the St. Louis Browns and found reason to be optimistic. Still, Wray of the *Post-Dispatch* felt the team had improved, with stronger catching, a stronger outfield, better pitching, "100 percent better spirit," and "a better manager."[26] If true, an upward move was surely in the works for this club, was it not?

Lest anyone forget, the 1927 Browns were a team whose star player had been its manager less than six months before. As opening day approached, to show there were no hard feelings, a testimonial dinner was planned in George's honor. Proposed by his friends Roland Hoerr, Walter Fritsch, and C. D. Hicks and supported by a committee that included Phil Ball and Missouri Governor Sam A. Baker, the affair was scheduled for April 11 at the Chase Hotel. About 250 people, including the entire Browns team, attended the dinner, watching and listening as Sis received an engraved silver platter, then attempted to deflect pressure from his successor by telling the audience, "Don't expect the Browns to finish any higher than fifth this year. It is not fair to Dan Howley to expect more."[27] The celebration was broadcast by local radio station KFVE. A number of listeners may have viewed George's attempt to downplay his team's prospects as a strong case of sour grapes.

The cross-town series between the Browns and Cardinals ended in a draw, with Sis going two for four in the victory after wearing an oh-for-three horse collar in the opener. The Browns finally opened their regular season on April 15 after three weather postponements. Howley's opening-

26. Ibid., April 3, 1927.
27. Quoted in ibid., April 12, 1927.

day lineup showed Harry Rice in right field, O'Rourke at second, Sis at first, Bing Miller in left field, Schulte in center field, Otto Miller at third, Gerber at shortstop, and Schang catching. The opening-day pitcher was Tom Zachary. Accustomed to losing opening games, the Browns were tied 2–2 in this one before inclement weather again sent everyone packing. They followed with a 3–1 win over Chicago with Sam Jones on the mound and looking sharp, then left town on April 19 at 3–1. Hopes were riding high.

By the end of April, the club was 6–6 and heading toward more familiar territory. Sisler was hitting over .400 early on, including a four-hit showing in a 15–10 win over the Tigers on April 23. There were, however, some lapses. For example, on April 28 he was caught napping off first base in the eleventh inning in a game his mates eventually lost 2–1.

In May Sisler continued to hit well and began to run the bases better, with three hits and a steal of home in a 13–3 Sportsman's Park win over the Indians on May 3. On May 10 the Yankees hit town to begin a season series that would be nightmarish for Dan Howley's club. In fairness to the new skipper and his team, this was the 1927 edition of the Yankees, considered by many to be the greatest ball club of all time. The Bronx Bombers with Ruth, Gehrig, Meusel, Tony Lazzeri, Dugan, Earle Combs, and more, ended the year at 110–44, besting the Browns a major-league-record twenty-one straight times before a 6–2 win on September 11 prevented a complete season sweep. Only the 1909 Cubs equaled the Yankees' success against an opponent in one season; Chicago went 21–1 against the Boston Braves.

The Yankees' Gehrig was a special case. In May 1925 the handsome native New Yorker out of Columbia University, then twenty-two, replaced Wally Pipp at first base. Following two promising seasons, he emerged in 1927 as a hitting machine and key component in a batting order dubbed "Murderer's Row." In short order he replaced Sisler in the eyes of most as the game's greatest first baseman. George's reign at the top had been brief.

On May 11 Gehrig's batting mate, Babe Ruth, served notice that this would be another long season for the Browns, specifically against his Yanks, when he belted one off the center field pole in Sportsman's Park. It was the longest home run ever hit in the park, and was described locally as "a sky-scraping bulls eye."[28] Surprisingly, the shot by Ruth and the home-stand drubbing at the hands of the Yankees did not have an imme-

28. Quoted by *St. Louis Post-Dispatch* staff writer Martin Haley in review of 1927 Yankees season on www.baseballlibrary.com.

diate effect on the Browns. They rebounded and actually won five in a row in mid-May. By May 26 their record stood at 17–17. That would be the last time the scale would balance out, though. By the end of June, the team had lost five straight, was eleven games under .500, and had already fallen twenty games from first place. More important, after much careful research, the cause of the Browns' demise under their new manager had been discovered—it was, believe it or not, lack of pitching. According to the *Post-Dispatch*, Howley "has a fighting, slugging ball club that is going nowhere. . . . Lack of pitching has cramped Daniel Phillip Howley's hopes and his style."[29] If that sounds like a broken phonograph record, it is because in St. Louis, on the Browns' side of town, the record was definitely broken.

To be sure, pitching was not the Browns' only woe. Second baseman Mellilo was ill coming into the season and never really got up to snuff, hitting a team-low .225. Schulte, the promising outfielder, went down with a fracture and a concussion, and was ruled out by midseason. But all in all, it was their old nemesis, pitching, that kept the Browns at the bottom of the ladder. The club's hitters, Sis in particular, continued to do their part. In one stretch of games in mid-July, the team hit .321 collectively, but still lost thirteen of twenty-one as the pitching staff was brutalized for an average of more than seven runs per game. As so often happens with shoddy pitching, the Browns' fielding suffered as well.

Sis had his good days and his bad. At least, there were more of the former than in 1926. In back-to-back wins over the Red Sox, George went eight for eight, including a home run, a triple, and two doubles. The performance was a double-edged sword. While it proved he was still a valuable, productive force on his team, it also meant he would be coveted by others. He was one of the few Browns who could bring significant value in a trade.

On July 26, with his team in seventh place, fifteen games below .500, Phil Ball announced plans to scrap his team during the off-season in order to undergo a major rebuilding project. After reporting that his club had lost seventy-six thousand dollars in 1926 and was already one hundred thousand in the red for the present campaign, he admitted he was "completely disillusioned." After a meeting with the brass, "we could agree on only four men who were unanimously voted as necessary to the club's future." He refused to name names, but did admit George was not one of the four. "Sisler is about the best trading material we have, but I will not

29. *St. Louis Post-Dispatch,* June 12, 1927.

say at this time that we will dispose of any particular player. But you can depend upon it that there is nothing sacred about Sisler or any other player's connection with this team, if we can strengthen the club by sale or trade. . . . Sisler has been something of a disappointment to me, although he has not done badly this year. He is still a great player, but if trading him will help our team, he will go."[30]

It was not exactly endearing commentary from his boss, especially when Sis was hitting .340, but nevertheless, from July 26 forward, George and his teammates pretty much knew where they stood. The ground beneath was shaky indeed. A few short years before, Sis was untouchable in the face of a two-hundred-thousand-dollar offer from the Yankees. Now he was on the trading block. Rumors were flying. It was said Connie Mack was interested in a cash purchase, but Ball wanted players. The deal was put on ice.

Once Ball so brazenly revealed his hand, the situation for Dan Howley, for the present season, turned hopeless. Howley was on the first leg of a three-year contract, which allowed him to survive for two more years. He finished the three-year run at 220–239, remarkably close to Sisler's 218–241.

At one point when the Browns went on a five-game winning streak, there was some question about Ball's decision to scrap the team. Sis remained solid during the streak, scoring frequently and driving in runs, including a triple in one game that broke a tie and sent his team to a 4–2 win.

"Sisler has proved a real asset to the club," wrote John E. Wray. "In fact, were it not for the surprising flash of Lou Gehrig, Sisler would have the first base championship of the American League wrapped up and tucked away. He is hitting around .340, leads his league in stolen bases and only two men—Gehrig and Combs—have made more hits than George." What, Wray asked, can the Browns expect to get for their lone star? They should get "one or two first class" pitchers at the least. But just try to "[f]ind the manager with two to let go."[31]

One manager who appreciated George was his own. "Sisler has been a great power," Howley said. "He has given me every assistance, has played lately with an injured ankle with never a complaint. I think he is a greater player than he has ever been given credit for being."[32] On September 22, in one of his last hurrahs as a Brown, Sis went four for five against the

30. Quoted in ibid., July 26, 1927.
31. Ibid., August 22, 1927.
32. Quoted in ibid., August 23, 1927.

Senators in a 10–7 loss in Washington. Perhaps, like Howley, Washington's manager Bucky Harris and his boys liked what they saw, too.

Most of the excitement involving the Browns during the remainder of the 1927 season came when they played the Yankees as fans rushed to the ballpark to marvel at the home run race between Gehrig and Ruth, which ended on September 30 in New York against the Senators when the Bambino stroked his record-breaking sixtieth off former Brown Tom Zachary in a 4–2 Yankee win. The home run propelled the Yankees to a dominating World Series performance as they punished the Pirates in a four-game sweep. On the same day that Ruth struck his historic blast, the Browns played a doubleheader against the Indians at Sportsman's Park. Guy Sturdy, up from Tulsa, played first base, where he would finish the season. Although he did not know it at the time, George Sisler had played his last ball game as a St. Louis Brown.

In this, his last season with the Browns, George's club was a hapless 59–94, finishing in seventh place and a jaw-numbing fifty and a half games behind the Yankees. A league worst 247,879 fans found their way to Sportsman's Park to support their hapless warriors. Phil Ball could be excused for wanting to shake things up a bit. His pitching staff ranked last in earned run average, giving up 4.95 runs per game.

On a team that batted .276 in the aggregate, George hit a much healthier .327 with 201 hits, five of them home runs, and drove in 97 runs. Moreover, his 27 stolen bases led the league for the fourth time. At first base, he committed a league-leading 24 errors, the third time in four years he held that dubious distinction, but he also led the league in assists. At thirty-four he led his team in batting average, hits, total bases, doubles (tied with Bing Miller), runs batted in, stolen bases, and times on base. He was anything but a washed-up infielder. Now all he could do was return home and await his fate.

In career terms, it did not take all that long, although his high salary was a stumbling block. On December 14, 1927, after considerable effort to deal Sis to Philadelphia or Chicago for players, and even some consideration of handing him his unconditional release when those efforts failed, Phil Ball sold him to the Washington Senators. Reports concerning the sale price varied, depending on who was talking. In Washington one heard that the deal cost the locals fifteen thousand dollars. In St. Louis the word on the street was twenty-five thousand. In either event, it was not even close to the two hundred thousand Ball reportedly rejected seven years before from the Yankees.

One wonders what the effect on baseball history might have been had Ball made the trade the Yankees sought in 1920. What kind of numbers would George have compiled hitting in front of the Babe? Would the Yankees have even bothered to sign Lou Gehrig four years later? No one will ever know.

The Sisler deal came in the midst of a trading frenzy for the Browns that saw them also peddle pitcher Elam Vangilder and outfielder Harry Rice to the Tigers for future Hall of Famer Heinie Manush and Sis's first-base replacement, Lu Blue. That trade on December 13, Sis's sale the next day, the sale of aging slugger Ken Williams on December 15, and the trade of Bing Miller for Phillies pitcher Sam Gray on December 16 completely changed the makeup of the Browns, but did little to improve the club's performance in future years.

Sis's departure from St. Louis was not only expected but even anticipated. Coming as it did during baseball's winter meetings, sandwiched in among trades that brought new talent rather than mere cash to the St. Louis baseball scene, the sale was accomplished with little fanfare. Only L. C. Davis paused for a moment to contemplate the departure of the Brown's star. In his poem "The Trade Wind," he wrote:

> A Baseball blizzard's blowing,
> A trade-wind struck our town;
> George Sisler will be going
> For Blue is now a Brown.
>
> Unless the trade wind fails 'em
> The Brownie fans agree
> It ought to cure what ails 'em—
> Whatever that may be.[33]

A day later as part of his poem "House Cleaning," he wrote:

> The trade winds are blowing,
> George Sisler is going,
> To play with the Griffith brigade.
> When Ball gets his hand in
> He'll throw the grandstand in
> Along with himself in a trade.[34]

And then on December 16, in "The Passing Show," one last time Davis rhymed:

> The Brownie fans received a shock
> That made their timbers shiver;

33. Ibid., December 14, 1927.
34. Ibid., December 15, 1927.

George Sisler from the auction block
Was peddled down the river.
So long, old boy, take care yourself
You made the owners richer
They sold you for a bunch of pelf
And didn't land a pitcher.[35]

It was as close to criticism of the sale as anyone would get. The town of St. Louis was excited about the new prospects. Sis was yesterday's news. It would take the city and its fans a number of years to realize what they had just lost.

35. Ibid., December 16, 1927.

14

Brave New World

George's new club was certainly one he was familiar with from years of struggle. The Senators, or Nationals if you prefer, were owned, at least in part, by their president, Clark Griffith. Known widely as "The Old Fox," Griffith had pitched professionally from 1891 to 1914 and managed from 1901 to 1920, the last nine seasons in Washington as he went about purchasing the club. They were presently managed by Stanley Raymond "Bucky" Harris, a friend of Sis's who had managed against him in the Florida Winter League and who also played a pretty fair second base. In 1924, at age twenty-seven, he took the previously hapless Senators to a world championship. Of course in 1924 the ball club still had Sis's idol, the great Walter Johnson, and American League MVP shortstop Roger Peckinpaugh, as well as Mr. Consistency, Sam Rice. Only Rice was still with the club; Johnson and Peckinpaugh were no longer active. After their great triumph in 1924, the Senators repeated as American League champs in 1925 and then flopped against the Pirates in the World Series. In 1926 they finished fourth, and they came in third in 1927.

The acquisition of George Sisler in 1928 had many baseball experts scratching their heads. The Senators already had a first baseman by the name of Joe Judge. A year and a half younger than George, Judge had hit .308 in 1927 with two home runs and 71 runs batted in. He was a career .298 hitter and a fine fielder to boot. The only knock on Joe Judge was his susceptibility to injury and perhaps a lack of speed on the bases. As one of the leftovers from the championship year, Judge was "one of the most popular players on the roster," having "gained many friends during his tenure of office here."[1]

Initially, it appeared the Senators would trade Judge and the first base job would be Sis's for the asking, but a suitable deal for a player of Judge's ability could not be found. As the Senators gathered for their spring fling in Tampa, Florida, for the first time in more than a decade Sis was in a serious fight for a regular job. But the Senators had not invested cold cash in George just for the fun of it. He was afforded the first crack at the job, with manager Harris "giving Sisler the call on all occasions" in the early going.[2] And Sis responded with three doubles in a Grapefruit League win over the Dodgers in mid-March and with another three-hit game that produced five runs for his new club three days later against Buffalo's minor-league entry.

The local press, however, was not mollified. They still thought highly of Judge. Pressed about how he planned to utilize his two first-class first sackers, Harris told the *Washington Post*, "I simply am giving Sisler a thorough tryout."[3] Harris insisted that he was giving the early nod to Sis because he already knew what Judge could do on the field and at the plate. He seemed to be speaking the truth. In late March, as the opener neared, the manager announced that Judge would get his first start in a contest against the New York Giants. It was about time Sis sat down, according to reporter Frank Young of the *Post*, who told readers that from his vantage point, it appeared "the former Brownie either has slowed up considerably or is having trouble getting his legs functioning properly. Compared to Judge, who has been working hard and appears to be in tip-top shape, Sisler looks slow, both as a base runner and in starting for balls hit in his direction."[4]

It was a fair observation. Sis was struggling with tired legs. He admitted it had a negative effect on his play. "The big thing at Washington was that I found my speed had vanished over night. I'd spent the winter out at Laguna Beach in California and I'd done a lot of mountain-climbing, hunting mountain quail. I think now that was the craziest stunt I ever pulled because when I reported to the Senators I found that my legs just weren't what they used to be."[5]

1. *Washington Post*, December 14, 1927.
2. Ibid, March 16, 1928.
3. Quoted in ibid., March 28, 1928.
4. Ibid., April 1, 1928.
5. Quoted in Meany, *Baseball's Greatest Hitters*, 188.

Two days later, in a complete reversal, Bucky Harris announced that Sis would be his first baseman. "Sisler right now is wielding his bat more effectively than is Joe."[6] Then in what was becoming an almost comical situation for all but the pair of players involved, Sis was absent from the opening-day lineup announced by Harris. As the Senators prepared to watch President Calvin Coolidge toss out the first pitch at Griffith Stadium prior to their April 10 season opener versus the Red Sox, the "former great first baseman of the Browns" would give way at first base to "[t]he familiar figure of Joseph Ignatius Judge."[7] Sis's preseason average of .363 was not enough to overcome his heavy legs, even though Judge had batted just .205.

In the opener, a 7–5 loss, the competition fared mighty well. Judge was four for four, a showing that solidified his hold on a regular job. Sis did not get a hit in his one at bat as a pinch hitter. He did not appear again until game five at Shibe Park, this time as an outfielder substituting for an injured player. How playing left field jibed with his slowness afoot is a mystery, but Harris defended the move, saying "he didn't look bad in left yesterday,... is perfectly willing to play there...and, if he shows any ability, he not only will be used in utility roles but may replace one of the regulars who gets in a slump."[8] Perhaps it was the layoff or the new position, but Sis went hitless in five attempts in the game, a 5–4 win over the Athletics. His performance at the plate did nothing to help his cause at first base.

Over the next several games, as the team struggled to reach .500, Sis was relegated to the bench again, appearing only occasionally and then as a pinch hitter. Judge, despite strong play around the bag, was not hitting the ball all that well himself, and on May 8 an article appeared in the *Post* indicating that Sisler would be back on first base soon. As if to signal the event, on the day before the announcement, when his new team met his old team, Sis replaced Judge at first base in the late innings and went one for two in a 15–2 loss to the Browns.

In retrospect, the announcement that Sis would become the Senators' regular at first was much like a new coat of paint on an old house, no more than an attempt to make George more attractive to prospective buyers. Sisler did replace Judge over the next several days, and also continued to appear intermittently in a pinch hitter's role. Then on May 16, in response to a "leak," the club denied plans to release Sis after admitting

6. Quoted in the *Washington Post*, April 6, 1928.
7. Ibid., April 10, 1928.
8. Quoted in ibid., April 18, 1928.

when pressed that waivers were asked and received for the veteran from all American League clubs. According to President Griffith, the maneuver was used to see if there was any interest in Sis. The answer was: not much. Only the White Sox wanted to trade for him, but they also wanted Senators catcher "Muddy" Ruel, the clutch-hitting star of the 1924 World Series, and according to Griffith, the Chicago club had nothing to offer for the pair.

"I had no particular trade in mind when I made the request, but simply did it to clear the decks for action in case I saw an opportunity to strengthen myself. As far as I know now Sisler will be with us all season," Griffith told the press.[9] What Griffith didn't say was of more import. Once a player cleared waivers, he remained in that status for thirty days. If during that period of time Griffith saw an opportunity to trade George to the National League, he would not be required to run him through an obstacle course again.

On May 18, two days later, Manager Harris announced that George would be inserted into the regular lineup. The change followed a 9–7 loss to the Tribe the day before that left his club in sixth place at 11–16. George went one for four in his first game back at the position where he had starred for so many years. Then he went zero for four the next day. Both contests were lost to the Indians. Sis's insertion into the lineup for the popular Judge was met with disapproval from the fans.

Over the next few days Sis played both at first base and in the outfield against the Athletics in Philadelphia, going three for seven in an extra-inning contest, then zero for four and finally two for five while in left field. If Griffith and Harris thought Sis's sudden emergence as a regular was fooling anyone, they were wrong. An unnamed Philadelphia club official told the *Post* that the Senators were "using Sisler in the hope that he will make good, and thus create a demand for him."[10]

On May 24 newspapers around the country reported that Rogers Hornsby was the new manager of the Boston Braves. The former Cardinals' star had only stayed a brief and controversial time in New York as a Giant. Over the winter he had landed with the bottom-dwelling Braves and now replaced Jack Slattery as field boss. Three days later on May 27, the Braves' new manager made his first move. At his specific request, Boston purchased the contract of George Sisler from the Senators for a mere seventy-five hundred dollars.

In his brief time with the Senators, George appeared in but twenty games of the thirty-five played to that point. "I hit .245 in those 20 games for

9. Quoted in ibid., May 17, 1928.
10. Quoted in ibid., May 22, 1928.

Washington," Sis said years later, "and what hurt most was the fact that I couldn't steal a base. I couldn't blame them for getting rid of me as fast as they could."[11]

By virtue of Hornsby's ascendancy to the managerial helm of the Boston Braves and Sis's failures in the capital city, the two greatest stars in St. Louis baseball history up to that time were now reunited, in Boston of all cities. And for the first time, George Sisler was about to perform his magic in the National League. If Hornsby was just doing an old friend a favor, you would not have known it. Before his new acquisition even arrived in town, he announced Sisler as the Braves' regular first baseman. In Washington George never really had a chance. If Sis was really all washed up, at least now everyone would find out once and for all.

When the Braves' new first sacker caught up with his club in Philadelphia, he found himself in familiar territory, although afloat in a new league. The Braves, like most of Sis's Browns teams, were firmly entrenched in seventh place, slogging along at 12–23 and already eleven games out of first place. The Braves had not always been such a wretched bunch. In business since 1871, the club had won eight pennants before 1900. To the chagrin of New England fans, the turn of the century brought a downturn of fortune for their National League entry. Still, the team won a championship in 1914 when the "Miracle Braves" went from last place to first in less than two months, then defeated the Athletics in the World Series. That was basically it, however. Financially strapped most of the time, the team continually struggled on the field. On February 20, 1923, Hall-of-Fame pitcher Christy Mathewson became the team's new president. Mathewson and two partners, Judge Emil Fuchs, a New York attorney who earned his title by serving briefly on the Magistrate's Court, and Bostonian James McDonaugh, purchased the club for three hundred thousand dollars. Mathewson died in October 1925. Judge Fuchs became the club's president and held the position in 1928 when Sis was acquired.

Under the Mathewson-Fuchs ownership, the club, which played at Braves Field, one of baseball's newest venues (1915), finished in seventh or eighth place every year except 1925, when they reached fifth. That depressing situation would not change anytime soon. Unlike Phil Ball, a hard-nosed businessman short on pleasantries, the fifty-year-old Fuchs was a large, likeable sort. While Ball's financial resources were sound, Fuchs worked on a much more restricted budget, in part due to poor at-

11. Meany, *Baseball's Greatest Hitters*, 188.

tendance complicated by a Massachusetts law that prohibited the club from playing home games on Sundays. One trait the pair shared in common, however, was a limited amount of baseball acumen.

In 1928, despite limited funds, the Judge was in a spending mode. The outlay of cash actually had started in January with the acquisition of Hornsby, baseball's second-highest-paid player, behind Ruth. In order to obtain the former Cardinals star from the New York Giants, Fuchs gave up two .288 hitters in catcher James "Shanty" Hogan and outfielder Jimmy Welsh. In his one year as a Giant, Hornsby had done little to sully his reputation as a great batter, hitting .361 with 26 home runs and 126 runs batted in. He also did little to dispel his sandpaper-personality image, as he caused hard feelings in the Giants' clubhouse and during the off-season became involved as the defendant in a highly publicized lawsuit in which the plaintiff claimed the ballplayer failed to pay off gambling debts. Hornsby won the lawsuit, but lost the support of Giants ownership and was promptly sent to the Braves in what must certainly have been a major blow to his large ego.

In the fall of 1927 Judge Fuchs replaced his manager, Dave Bancroft, with Jack Slattery, a former major leaguer of limited ability and playing experience who was coaching the Boston College team at the time. A few months later when Hornsby was obtained from the Giants, Slattery received more than he bargained for in a highly successful former manager and star performer who had little use for "collegiate-types." To make matters worse, the Braves' new star would make $40,600, about four times what Slattery was making.[12] Perhaps Hornsby's very presence made Slattery uncomfortable, or perhaps the temptation of inserting a proven winner into the managerial slot was too much for Fuchs, but on May 23 Slattery "resigned" after only thirty-one games at the Braves' helm. Immediately Fuchs "asked" Hornsby to take over. Hornsby accepted the offer, but according to his biographer Charles C. Alexander, it is doubtful he really wanted it.[13] Given the Braves' poor track record, including a pitiful pitching staff, who could really blame him?

What Hornsby did want, however, was George Sisler. It seemed strange that would be the case given Hornsby's open hostility toward ballplayers with a college education, but Sis and his new manager got along quite well, having developed a friendship during their steak-and-potato years in St. Louis. "I always liked Rog," Sisler said. "We respected each other's

12. Alexander, *Rogers Hornsby*, 144.
13. Ibid., 147.

ability and I liked the fact that you always knew where you stood with him."[14]

Sis and Hornsby were friendly off the field as well. Once the shift to Boston appeared to be long-term, Sis moved his family to the city for the summer, where they encamped at Brandon Hall, a "very nice" private residential hotel located on Beacon Street. The facility ran on the American plan, which included steaks for breakfast, a nice lunch, and a full-course meal in the evening. Hornsby stayed there also, and according to Sis, "seemed to have a fondness for children, and in particular, my Dick [second eldest son], and they would very often be going down to the drug store for ice cream or a soft drink."[15]

According to reports in the Boston papers, Sisler and Hornsby spoke before the trade, and George assured his prospective boss there was still fuel in the tank and nothing physically wrong to prevent the purchase. The Boston press in general greeted the acquisition with enthusiasm. Unlike Washington, where Joe Judge was a popular fixture in the infield, the Braves' incumbent, Dick Burrus, was adequate but not deemed irreplaceable. In seventy-two games in 1927 Burrus batted a fine .318, but his fielding average of .973 was less than noteworthy and "[h]is work, so far this [1928] season, has not been anywhere near the standard indicated by those figures, and, on the whole, has been a disappointment and has cost some ball games."[16]

Sis wasted no time in introducing himself to his team and to National League fans. On May 29 he started at first base for the Braves in Philadelphia and beat out an infield hit in the ninth inning of a 9–3 win. In addition, "he played his customary brilliant game at first base, and received a big ovation from the fans."[17] The trade had apparently put new life in tired legs. The next day against those same Phillies, Sis went three for ten in a rare Brave doubleheader win. On May 31 in the Braves' fourth straight win, he lashed out a homer, double, and single. The home run hit the street and bounced through the open window of a passenger bus, for a time raising concerns that the driver was injured. In no time Sis was drawing kudos, with his "work" a "great surprise, making fans wonder more and more how he happened to be waived out of the American League."[18]

14. Quoted in Bob Broeg, *Superstars of Baseball: Their Lives, Their Loves, Their Laughs, Their Laments,* 423.

15. Sisler Memoirs, 13–14.

16. *Boston Globe,* May 28, 1928.

17. Ibid., May 30, 1928.

18. Ibid., June 4, 1928.

After seventeen games he was hitting a robust .342, much more representative than his weak showing in the nation's capital.

When the Braves returned home for the debuts of Hornsby the manager and Sisler the player, the team was greeted with news of changes at Braves Field. Judge Fuchs decided to move the left field bleachers and fence back another thirty-two feet. When that didn't help, a few weeks later a thirty-foot screen was erected. The Judge made the change in an effort to decrease the number of home runs hit in the ballpark. Since the change affected Braves right-handed batters just as much as the opponents, the fence and screen were not a panacea. The main problem with the Braves was the same problem that plagued the Browns—lack of pitching. The 1928 Braves hit .275, sixth best in the National League. Hornsby finished the year with a league-leading .387, graceful outfielder Lance Richbourg batted .337, and Sis hit .340, so these three could provide enough support to make a half-decent pitching staff into a winner. The Braves did not have such a staff. There was no such thing as an ace. Bob Smith (13–17 with a 3.87 earned run average) and Art Delaney (9–17, 3.79), both age thirty-three, came the closest. Twenty-three-year-old Ed Brand, at 9–21 and 5.07, offered scant promise for the future. From there it only got worse. It was at best a sorry brigade.

The ban on Sunday baseball did more than just cost the Braves money in attendance. It created a scheduling nightmare that forced the Braves to play more than their share of twin bills. This played havoc with the pitching rotation, overworking an already tired staff and rendering it practically useless. From mid-June to July 1, at Braves Field the team split doubleheaders with the Cubs and Giants and then followed that by losing a pair of duos with the Dodgers and one with the Giants. A twin whipping of the Phillies on July 2 was quickly rectified by a twin loss to the same team the next day. And on and on it went.

On July 7 Sis returned to Sportsman's Park in a different uniform and against a different St. Louis team, the Cardinals, but it made little difference to his fans. A "day" was held for the former Brown, and seventeen thousand looked on as Sis picked up yet another silver tea service, a basket of flowers, and a framed proclamation from Mayor Victor Miller. The honoree responded with a pair of singles and three runs batted in during an 11–3 win for the Braves. The fans gave Sis a large ovation when he appeared at the plate, and the applause continued even after he responded with a hit. "No matter how it hurt the Cards, whatever Sisler did was applauded." Hornsby received a floral arrangement, too. Still, the *Boston Globe* wondered "[w]hy the fans booh [sic] Hornsby, the only manager in the history of St. Louis National League baseball who produced a pennant and a World Championship."[19]

In August the Braves made an off-day stop in Akron for another George Sisler "day" as the major leaguers played the Akron General Tires. Sis played, and by way of thanking the fans for their many gifts, pitched a perfect ninth inning.

Although Sis continued to do his part, the remainder of the 1928 season was quite forgettable. Losses came in bunches, and wins were few and far between. Sis did play a key role in several of the victories, including a six-hit day in a twin bill sweep over the Reds during which he had two doubles in one inning. The club was making some strides in late August when Hornsby pulled a tendon and the team went into another tailspin, losing six in a row.

In mid-September the baseball world was stunned when Urban Shocker, Sis's longtime teammate and a major American League pitching force for more than a decade, died of heart disease and pneumonia. The Braves could have used a workhorse like Shocker. In September the pitching staff, already on its last legs, played one doubleheader after another. From September 10 to 14 they played four straight doubleheaders with the Giants and lost all eight games.

In late September the Cardinals visited Braves Field with their pennant hopes very much alive. In what was a difficult moment for Hornsby, he watched as his replacement, Frankie Frisch, stole home to ignite a record seven-run fifteenth inning that decided the game and enabled the Cardinals to clinch a tie for the league title. Later, when the Giants fell to the Cubs, the Cardinals were National League champs. Their excitement was short-lived, however, as they lost four straight World Series games to the Yankees. Game four featured a power show by Babe Ruth, who was earning his ninth World Series check. Despite his individual brilliance, Sisler had never played in a World Series.

The 1928 Braves finished their season in seventh place at 50–103. Only the pathetic Philadelphia Phillies stood between them and the cellar. Under Hornsby, the team was 39–83, tarnishing his image a bit. In 118 games after his arrival in mid-May, Sis hit .340, good for a fourth-place tie in his new league, with four home runs and 68 runs batted in. While Hornsby and Richbourg led the team in most hitting categories, Sis did tie Richbourg in stolen bases with 11. His .988 fielding percentage with 15 errors was respectable, and an improvement over his predecessor. In a nutshell,

19. Ibid., July 8, 1928.

he had proven that rumors of his demise were exaggerated. He looked forward to 1929 with eager anticipation. It would be interesting to see what he and Hornsby could do given a full year together.

But the two Hall of Famers would never play on the same team again. Reeling financially from yet another year of weak attendance (227,000, seventh out of eight National League teams) and sporting a hefty payroll with the likes of Hornsby and Sisler, among others, Judge Fuchs needed some relief. On November 7, just weeks after signing him to a new three-year contract to manage the Braves, he sent Hornsby to the Chicago Cubs for two hundred thousand dollars and several players, including second baseman Freddie Maguire and catcher Lou Legett, as well as pitchers Percy Jones, Bruce Cunningham, and "Socks" Siebold. All would contribute, but none would star. The cash, however, permitted the Braves to play another day.

One day after the blockbuster deal, the Braves got relief of another kind. Massachusetts voters approved a referendum permitting the team to schedule Sunday baseball games in Boston. Perhaps, despite the departure of Hornsby, things were looking up. The Red Sox took advantage of the new ruling also, but since Fenway Park was quite close to a church, they arranged to play their Sunday games at Braves Field.

Shortly after the trade, Judge Fuchs made another decision. Why pay for a new manager for his club when he could manage them just as well, and much more cheaply? One possible drawback—the Judge's total lack of managerial experience—was cast aside as inconsequential: "The time has gone when a manager has to chew tobacco and talk from the side of his mouth. I don't think our club can do any worse with me as manager than it has done the last few years."[20] Fuchs was partially right and partially wrong; the Braves won more games in 1929—six more to be exact—but they fell from seventh to eighth place in the process. Baseball learned its lesson. Except for a one-game stunt in the 1970s by Atlanta Braves owner Ted Turner, Judge Fuchs is distinguished as the last man without professional baseball experience to manage a major-league team.

Of course, even the Judge was wise enough not to try to go it alone. He surrounded himself with seasoned coaches and players, including future Hall of Famer Johnny Evers of Tinker to Evers to Chance fame and a major-league manager of the 1913 and 1921 Cubs, as well as the 1924 White Sox. Evers had also played second base for the Miracle Braves in 1914. Now forty-six, he became the Judge's right-hand man and, in the opinion

20. Quoted in Burt Solomon, *The Baseball Timeline*, 290.

of many observers, its real manager. Former big-league catcher Hank Gowdy, another member of the Miracle Braves, also extended a helping hand from the coaching box. Gowdy, who was infamous for costing the Giants a World Series win by tripping over his catcher's mask in the 1924 World Series, was also now in his fourth decade.

On December 8, 1928, in an effort to strengthen his infield as well as add even more whiskers to his team, Fuchs purchased Walter James Vincent "Rabbit" Maranville from the Cardinals. At five feet, five inches, the Rabbit was one of baseball's legendary practical jokers and a close buddy of Babe Ruth. He was also one of the game's finest fielding shortstops, and from 1912 to 1920 had been a fixture in the Braves infield. He, too, was a Miracle Brave and a future Hall of Fame inductee. Perhaps the Judge was trying to re-create the magic and produce another miracle for 1929.

What did Sis, himself a thirty-six-year-old veteran with three years as a manager on his résumé, think about the Judge and his "brain trust"? In the first instance he thought Fuchs "a nice man."[21] The Judge as a manager—well, that was something else again:

> The Judge himself knew very little about baseball, but he figured the two coaches did and that would take care of things satisfactorily. So he signed Johnny Evers and Hank Gowdy...Both were popular in Boston and were former great players and both were fine baseball men. Where the Judge made the mistake was that he insisted on giving the signals to Evers at third base and Gowdy at first base. The Judge was a great storyteller and quite often he would be telling stories on the bench when he should have been giving signals. I remember one time when Evers at third during a critical time in the game, looked in to the bench for a sign from the Judge. At the time he was telling a story. When he was told Evers needed a sign, the Judge said with a very straight face, 'Tell him to hit a home run.'[22]

By 1929, with a productive National League season in the books, it seemed appropriate for the baseball world to get some perspective on Sis's move to the senior circuit. After all, at one time he had been mentioned in the same breath as Cobb, Ruth, Speaker, Johnson, and Eddie Collins, the best of baseball's recent past. In the heading of a magazine piece that appeared in the June 1929 issue of *Baseball Magazine*, Publications Editor F. C. Lane, who described himself as a "life-long admirer and intimate friend," asked of Sisler's passing waivers, "Did the American League blunder?" Branding the chain of circumstances that brought Sis to the Braves "one of

21. Quoted in Broeg, "Gorgeous George," 28.
22. Sisler Memoirs, 13.

the most extraordinary episodes of the season of 1928," Lane concluded that "the records would belie" the "theory" that Sis was so near the end of his career. At the end of 1928 he interviewed a "very guarded" Sisler, "fearful as ever of giving possible cause of offense," finding a player whose "pride had been touched a bit by this humiliating transfer."

Asked about the role his eye problems played in his release by the Senators, Sis replied that he was doing fine now. "The injury to my vision which occurred some years ago, was real and serious. But it seems to me unnecessary, as well as unjust, that the memory of that injury should overshadow the remainder of my career." As to any more .400 seasons, that was probably asking too much, but "[i]f I had not been incapacitated when I was, in my player prime, lost an entire season and been obliged to begin all over again the next season, I, myself, might have crossed the .400 mark at least three times. This late in the game I can hardly expect to do so. . . . Must I apologize for an average of .350?"

As for St. Louis, he found it "rather easy to understand why the Browns" let him go: "They had resolved to make a sweeping change in the club personnel. They went the limit."

What then about Washington? "Joe [Judge] had been a fixture in the Washington infield for many years. I was an interloper. Joe had staunch friends among the Washington newspaper men. They backed him vigorously, which was all right. . . . But they talked overmuch about my impaired eyesight, and the impression gained headway all over the circuit that I was on my last legs. . . . Possibly the salary I was getting may have deterred some of them who might otherwise have taken a chance."

Maybe too, Lane surmised, Sisler's situation "was complicated by his avowed acceptance of Christian Science doctrines. Sisler has little use for doctors. Nor does he discuss ailments with the terms of the man in the street. He is particularly prone to ignore even painful injuries. When one of his ankles was swollen to double its normal size, he did not seem to spare it, even when sliding bases.

"But whatever Sisler's religious beliefs, and he does not discuss them publicly, he patronizes medical experts, under certain circumstances. . . . Though game and inclined to minimize ordinary injuries, there is nothing bigoted in Sisler's attitude toward such things. Quite possibly, however, these beliefs of Sisler reacted against him."

What then about the future? If there was a problem, Sis insisted it was not with the eyes. However, "I am no longer a rookie and not so fast in the field as I used to be. No one needs to remind me of that. But certainly my eyes haven't slowed me. It's my legs."

Perhaps, Lane concluded, in the "strange case of George Sisler" baseball people were a little "too shrewd" for their own good. In 1928 as a new member of the Boston Braves, Sisler had certainly answered the doubts.[23]

It was now almost time for another season. When faced with the Braves' prospects for 1929, a fair question throughout the baseball world was to ask how a seventh-place team fresh off trading the league's leading batter and sole source of legitimate home run power could expect to improve upon its performance. The answer was simple: it could not. At second base in place of Hornsby, the Judge inserted Freddie Maguire, one of the players obtained in the deal. In 1929 Maguire would hit .252 with no home runs and 41 runs batted in—a difference of 135 points in average, 21 home runs, and 53 runs batted in. At shortstop, Maranville was an improvement over Doc Farrell, but that was about it. The pitching remained horrible, giving up an average of more than five runs per game. There was nothing Sis or his teammates could do to make up the difference.

On their way north after a lackluster spring training in Florida, the team suffered an embarrassing loss to one minor-league squad, then almost blew a lead to another. In the spring preview with the Red Sox, they won 4–0 in front of humorist Will Rogers. Even that victory did little to perk up the team, since the Red Sox were picked to finish last also. One can only wonder what great punch lines floated through Rogers's head as he watched two clubs that were seemingly going nowhere.

In the home opener with Brooklyn on April 18, only four thousand spectators saw a 13–12 Braves win. Braves' center fielder Earl Clark crashed into the fence chasing a fly ball and was carried from the field on a stretcher. Sis was three for five with two singles and a double. Winning the slugfest injected new life into the club, lifting them to a surprisingly strong start as they won their first three games. On May 4, with his team riding the crest of what would be a five-game winning streak, Judge Fuchs told eager reporters he was pleased but not surprised by his team's quick rush from the gates. He predicted in lawyerly fashion that his team would "finish" in the National League.[24] He neglected to say where they would finish—a wise decision, indeed. As late as May 7, however, they sat in first place at 9–4.

23. F. C. Lane, "Did the American League Blunder?" 305–6. Sisler's eyes remained a sensitive subject throughout his time with the Braves. Third base teammate and bridge partner Les Bell is quoted as saying the eyes were "the forbidden subject with George—you weren't allowed to ask him about his eyes." Quoted in James O. Lindberg, "At First Base for the Boston Braves...George Sisler," 28.

24. Quoted in the *Boston Globe*, May 4, 1929.

Unlike his team, Sis was off to one of the slowest starts of his career. On May 5 he was hitting only .222. Soon the Braves joined him, returning to form as they began losing more games than they were winning. On May 22, however, they were still 14–14 and only five and a half games from the lead. A doubleheader loss to the weak Phillies that day spelled doom; the losing streak grew to eleven. Even though Sis finally picked up the pace with a .400 month, lifting his average to .312 by June 3, things only got worse for his Braves. But in a season of few highlights, all was not lost for George. In one contest during the eleven-game losing streak, he completed an unassisted double play when the Phillies' Fresco Thompson, later an executive with the Dodgers, walked and Lefty O'Doul singled. Chuck Klein then lined to Sis, who tagged O'Doul to complete the play.

In early June with his team really beginning to flounder, Judge Fuchs reportedly offered full managerial reins to Johnny Evers. Evers declined, agreeing only to manage the club when Fuchs was away on club business. This had been the arrangement all along. And even if Evers had accepted the Judge's offer, it is unlikely much would have changed. By June 10 the Braves were 17–29 and in the basement. They would remain there briefly, then climb to seventh and even back to sixth for a brief time. They would climb no higher.

In early July Sis raised his average to .322. Although frustrated with the managing of Judge Fuchs and the trade of Hornsby, the *Boston Globe* could find nothing wrong with the work ethic and play of George Sisler, telling its readers, "[t]hat boy is hitting the ball, and working hard all the time."[25] At one point in August, Sis reached .341, coming off three-hit games against both the Pirates and Cubs.

On August 18, as a treat for loyal fans, the Braves inserted the forty-year-old Hank Gowdy into the lineup. He responded by going four for four in a 10–9 win over the Reds. The next day the Reds knocked the Braves back into the cellar, where they remained, finishing the season at 56–98. On the last day, even Johnny Evers got a special salute, playing an inning with Gowdy.

For the year, Sis played in all 154 games, hitting .326 with 205 hits in 629 at bats. This was the sixth time he had reached 200 or more hits in a season. He led his club in average, games played, at bats, hits, total bases, doubles, extra base hits, runs batted in, and times on base. His slugging average of .424 was second among regulars on the team. If he was slowing

25. Ibid., July 10, 1929.

down, it was, as he said to F. C. Lane, in his legs. He committed 28 errors at first base and, a sure sign, stole but six bases.

On October 6, only days after season's end, Judge Fuchs threw in the towel, hiring a man with a fine track record, "Deacon" Bill McKechnie, as his manager. A future Hall of Fame honoree with a keen baseball mind, McKechnie had already delivered pennants for the Pirates and the Cardinals. During an eight-year run with the Braves, he never finished higher than fourth, but later he proved he still could manage, winning pennants in Cincinnati in 1939 and 1940. His 1940 Redlegs won the World Series over the Tigers. No other manager has directed three different pennant-winning teams.

The 1929 World Series was won in five games by Connie Mack and his Philadelphia Athletics over a Chicago Cubs team powered by Rogers Hornsby and Hack Wilson. However, in October 1929 there were more important events than the World Series and the simmering managerial situations that were about to come to a boil. For a number of years an overly optimistic business community had diverted attention away from a weak American economy. Despite years of declining business activity and rising unemployment, more and more Americans representing a wider range of social strata purchased common stocks sold on the New York Stock Exchange. In a manner hauntingly similar to the way speculators had purchased swampland in Florida short years before, much of this stock was purchased on the margin at a fraction of the cost, with the remainder floated through loans. As in Florida the system flourished as long as there were others interested in purchasing the stock. The problem arose when others were no longer interested and stock prices thus declined. Then your markers were called in, and if you did not have cash to cover, you were in big trouble.

As early as 1928 a series of selling sprees began that quickly dropped stock prices. These fits and starts should have given investors reason to pause, but each time the market sputtered, powerful speculators saw the lower prices as a buying opportunity, and the market recovered. This was fine in the short term, but it continued to mask the serious economic problems the country was facing.

In October, just days after the World Series, the market declined again. Once more ignoring strong economic warning signs, speculators bought low. When the decline continued, however, the margin calls went out. In order to meet those calls, people sold more stock to raise cash, turning a downward spiral into an avalanche. On October 24 so many people sold their holdings that the ticker could not keep up. It was indeed a "Black

Tuesday." Although it would take another couple of weeks to bottom out, the boiling point was reached. The result was a stock market crash in full swing. In the words of historian Frederick Lewis Allen, "Prosperity is more than an economic condition; it is a state of mind."[26] In the midst of a celebration lasting a decade, the nation had unknowingly wandered to the precipice of the Great Depression. At the end of 1929 it went over the brink.

Just how much the market crash hurt George Sisler and his family is unknown. Sisler never publicly commented, but he was still earning a sizable baseball salary, and if he also was the conservative investor characterized years earlier by writer Floyd Bell then it is doubtful George and his growing family suffered immediately or greatly. For George the effects of the crash would be felt down the road, in more subtle ways.

Now entering his third season as a Brave in 1930, Sis and his family rented from a friend of Kathleen's a house in Newton Center, a Boston suburb. In spring training, despite Sis's strong 1929 campaign, there was some question about who would be the Braves' regular first baseman in 1930. At least for a time it appeared twenty-nine-year-old speedster Johnny Neun, best known for completing an unassisted triple play with the Tigers in 1927, might wrest the job away. It was not until game four at Ebbets Field in New York that Sisler made his first appearance of the regular season. In a pinch hitter's role against the Dodgers' Dolf Luque, he hit the ball so hard it injured the Cuban pitching prospect and brought Sis his first base hit.

By May 1 it looked like Sis might be relegated to the bench for the entire year when Neun went three for three with his first major-league home run. Neun's heroics helped the Braves defeat the Pirates 4–3 to secure their hold on third place with a 6–5 record. Then the Braves went into a tailspin, losing seven in a row. Sis entered the lineup on May 11 and contributed timely hitting to a four-game Braves winning streak. By the end of the month, he was once again, at age thirty-seven, the Braves' regular first sacker.

The Braves were still only a lackluster 18–18 on June 1, but they were catching on with starved baseball fans in Boston. The futility of the Braves was measured against the futility of the Red Sox, so that even mediocrity was met with enthusiasm in Beantown in the late twenties and thirties. A record crowd of 43,120 showed up for the June 1 doubleheader with the Giants, almost 10 percent of the 464,835 fans who saw the Braves during the entire season. The attendance figure was a vast improvement over

26. Allen, *Only Yesterday*, 256.

previous years, particularly since it was accomplished in the midst of a growing economic crisis that would soon envelop baseball. Twin losses sent the team into a six-game tailspin, however, with Braves pitchers giving up sixty runs in one five-game stretch.

Actually, 1930 was a season of all-around improvement for the Braves. Perhaps it was the managing of McKechnie or the experience of the veteran coaches and players. Sis for one "devotedly spent hour after hour in graciously volunteering his vast knowledge to the younger players and no player on the team gained such genuine affection and respect."[27] The beneficiaries included such teammates as twenty-four-year-old rookie outfielder Wally Berger, who hit a National League rookie record 38 home runs with 119 runs batted in; twenty-seven year olds Jimmy Welsh (.275) and Earl Clark (.296); and Sis's understudy, Johnny Neun (.325). And a somewhat improved pitching staff led by Socks Siebold (15–16, 4.12 earned run average) and old ally Tom Zachary (11–5, 4.58) did not hurt either. An early season trade that brought Hall of Famer Burleigh Grimes, one of the last legal spitballers, to the club from the Cardinals did not pan out. Grimes was gone by mid-June, but at least the Judge and his boys were trying.

At the plate, Sis struggled a bit. In late July he went four for five against lefties, dispelling any lingering notions he could no longer hit the portsiders, but in late August his average was at .308. He found himself sitting out the second games of several of the many Braves doubleheaders, giving way to Neun, who was having a fine season at the plate and was versatile enough to lead off for his team. On one occasion at Wrigley Field after George was thrown out trying to tag up and score on a routine fly ball, he told teammate Wally Berger, "I must be through if [I] couldn't score on that play."[28]

Sisler's last start at first base was on September 3 at home in the first game of a doubleheader with the New York Giants. On September 8 Sis watched from the sidelines during an all-star game between Braves old-timers and a group of all-time all-stars, including Ty Cobb and many of Sisler's contemporaries. In his mind, could he be far behind?

As the last full month of the season wound down, Sis played only sporadically, due in part to a leg injury but perhaps also to give Neun more playing time. His unsuccessful pinch-hit appearance on September 22 would be his last game of the season and of his major-league career. At

27. Robert S. Fuchs, son of Judge Emil Fuchs, Letter to author, June 11, 2002.
28. Quoted in Lindberg, "At First Base for the Boston Braves ... George Sisler," 28.

the end, his club stood in sixth place at 70–84, a fourteen-game improvement over the previous year.

On December 13, 1930, the Braves gave Sis his unconditional release. The decision to release George was not an enjoyable one for Judge Fuchs. It was undoubtedly made more difficult because despite his earlier remark to Berger, Sis apparently was not contemplating retirement. In an article that appeared in the *Sporting News* in November he denied telling his boss he would retire if sent to the minors. In fact, when asked, he was noncommittal, leaving the impression he would consider the demotion rather than quit the sport. But at least in November such a move was not on his mind. "When I left Boston at the close of the season, I was under the impression that I was to return to the Braves next year and I have no reason to believe otherwise.... Of course I did not play in every game, because I was out part of the time with a leg injury, but I had a pretty good year."[29]

Indeed, Sis did have a "pretty good year" in 1930, especially for a thirty-seven year old. In 116 games he batted .309 with 133 hits, three home runs, and 67 runs batted in. One cautionary sign, though, was that 1930 was the year the National League caught up and even surpassed the American League in "live ball" statistics. Giants manager John McGraw didn't care what the ball manufacturers said; he believed the ball was "lively, and every sensible baseball man knows it."[30] Certainly the statistics did not lie. The league's hitters averaged a whopping .303, with forty-five players, approximately one quarter of the league's batters, hitting better than .300. The senior circuit's Wild West show took a good deal of the luster off Sisler's showing.

For one of the few times in his career, The Sizzler had not led his team in any hitting category. With seven stolen bases, his base running was no longer a plus, and his fielding percentage was lower than Neun's. At the same time, he was still drawing a healthy salary. During the off-season, the Braves drafted first baseman Earl Shelly, the leading hitter from the Pacific Coast League, and added him to their roster. Thus on December 13, when Sis's string ran out, he may have been the only one truly surprised. Under the league's rules, as a ten-year man, Sis could not be sold or traded to the minors. It is doubtful Judge Fuchs, who greatly admired Sis, would have degraded the veteran star with such a move even if it was permitted. Instead, Fuchs, who had a full cadre of coaches in Boston with Gowdy and

29. Quoted in the *Sporting News*, November 6, 1930.
30. Quoted in Charles C. Alexander, *Breaking the Slump: Baseball in the Depression Era*, 30.

Evers already in place, tried his best to land a coaching assignment for Sis with another team, or even a manager's post, major-league or minor. When he was unable to do so, he granted George his unconditional release. Sisler was now a reluctant free agent.

For a free agent not yet ready to quit playing ball and unable to garner interest from other major-league clubs, there is only one choice—the minors. Would a player of George Sisler's stature accept such a demotion? Yes, he would. Unable to catch on with a major-league team, the next step for George Sisler was Rochester, New York, and the International League.

In his fifteen-year major-league career, George Sisler amassed an impressive array of statistics. In 2,055 games he officially batted 8,267 times and scored 1,284 runs with 2,812 hits, which included 425 doubles, 164 triples, and 102 home runs. He drove in 1,175 runners, walked 472 times, and struck out only 327 times. He batted .340 with a slugging percentage of .468 and an on-base percentage of .379. He stole 375 bases and was caught stealing 127 times. His career fielding percentage was .987. Now for the first time in his career, after all these years and all these games, George Sisler was a minor-league performer.

Once, many years before, when he was a young player chasing Ty Cobb, Sis shared his views on playing minor-league ball. A college graduate, he commented, should only play professional baseball if he is fortunate and skillful enough to jump directly to the major leagues, bypassing the minors. "There is no money in being a minor league ball player," he said, "and the college man who wastes five or ten years in the bush leagues finds himself without either money or the ability to follow what he prepared for in college." Heading directly from college to the big leagues was in Sis's opinion different; that was easy enough for him to say, since he made the transition so seamlessly.

His next statement was even more rigid: "I will never play in the minor leagues and I think it would be a mistake for any player who has shown the capability to stick in the big leagues for a few years to gravitate into the minors when he feels himself slipping. Better, by far, that he should take up the career for which he was fitted before he went into baseball."[31]

Now here he was in 1931 in Rochester eating his words—big time. Why the minor leagues, and why Rochester? Why not engineering? Why not

31. Quoted in Henry P. Edwards, "Using a Diploma on the Diamond," publication and page number unknown (George Sisler Clippings File, National Baseball Library, Cooperstown, N.Y.).

his printing business? The answer to the first question is twofold. In Sisler's mind he was not slipping—well, not all that much. Despite his age and diminishing skills, he believed he could still play the game, and he loved doing it. In this regard he was no different than countless others, both in and out of sports. It is a rare individual who is not the last to recognize when it is time to step down. It is particularly difficult for the athlete to imagine a life outside their sport and call it quits, even more so an athlete such as Sisler who has accomplished so much for so long with a rare combination of natural ability and fierce competitive determination. It was no real surprise, then, that Sis was willing to succumb to a case of convenient memory lapse when it came to playing in the minors.

Then there was the matter of money. The depression was deepening, and good jobs were hard to come by. After a brief rebound in April 1930, the country realized its "economic disease was more than a temporary case of nervous prostration."[32] For almost a decade U.S. corporations had overproduced capital and goods. Now, when it was most urgent for someone to buy those goods, the increasing unemployment of the American worker was decreasing buying power. The deck of cards was tumbling. Ebbing sales led to less corporate income, which forced companies to cut wages and then lay off more workers, which increased unemployment further, reducing sales, and on and on toward rock bottom. The positive impact of many years of prosperity was now counterbalanced by an equally negative force and a resulting lack of confidence. In 1931 the "mob psychology" that had fueled a bull market was now fueling a depression, too.[33] Sis was no fool. He earned a very comfortable living for more than a decade playing baseball. He knew he could make more money continuing to play ball than he could by jumping into something new. In that assumption he was correct.

In Rochester, New York, professional baseball was king—the minor-league brand, that is. The Rochester Red Wings, three-time defending International League champions, were a key link in Branch Rickey's innovative minor-league chain in which the major-league team, in this case the Cardinals, owned its minor-league affiliates and thereby the bulk of its players. Managed by Billy Southworth, a successful outfielder with a number of big-league clubs and a more than successful manager for the Cardinals for part of 1929 and later from 1940 to 1951, the Red Wings played before 328,000 fans in 1930—better attendance than Sisler's Browns and Braves teams had attracted in several of his seasons with them.

32. Allen, *Only Yesterday*, 258.
33. Ibid., 262.

The savior of Sis's floundering professional career in 1931 was a familiar figure, Branch Rickey. Under fire for pillaging his perennial-champion Red Wing squads after the 1930 season (the defections included promotion to the Cardinals of future stars such as Rip Collins, Paul Derringer, and Pepper Martin), Rickey mollified the Rochester faithful by signing Sis to a contract with a five-thousand-dollar bonus. The revamped Red Wing team, under Southworth and general manager Warren Giles, who later became president of the National League, continued its winning ways. In 1931 the club was 101–67 and played before 293,091 spectators. On opening day a crowd of 19,006, a minor-league record, saw Sis play his first minor-league game at age thirty-eight, a 4–1 loss to the Newark Bears.

When Sis first donned his Red Wings uniform, "[m]ost of the Wings players were in awe, . . . but he quickly put them at ease. He would be a calming influence. . . . And despite his declining skills, he would play a crucial role during the pennant drive."[34]

It was a tight race for the pennant. The Wings did not clinch the title until September 10 when they swept a doubleheader from the Montreal Royals. The clincher came in the nightcap and provided the club with a lasting memory of George and the season. It was the bottom of the ninth inning. Neither team had scored. George, who had enjoyed a fine season, batting .303 in 159 games and striking out only 17 times in 613 at bats, hit a short fly ball to left field. Jocko Conlan, the Royals' left fielder who later would enter Cooperstown as an umpire, was playing in shallow left, but lost the ball in the sun. "The ball grazed his ear, struck him on the shoulder and bounced away. As Jocko lunged toward the left field foul line, he fell and skidded into the wire fence that fronted the bleachers. His spikes locked in the wire and before he could extricate himself, Sisler had circled the bases," wearing a big grin.[35] The pennant belonged to the Red Wings. For the first time in his career, George, already an uncrowned champion in many a fan's eye, was a member of a championship team. But unfortunately, days before the start of the Junior World Series, Sis pulled a muscle. Except for a sentimental start in game one and a single in his only at bat, he watched from the bench as his team bested St. Paul five games to three.

The Rochester days were good ones for George, even though he was away from his family. "I stayed at the home of a German family along with the left fielder of our club, who was a University of Alabama alum-

34. Jim Mandelaro and Scott Pitoniak, *Silver Seasons: The Story of the Rochester Red Wings*, 47.
35. Ibid., 50, quoting A. C. Weber of the *Rochester Times-Union*.

nus.... The one thing about this arrangement was that a cucumber dish was always on the table.... They would add cucumbers, onions, and sour cream daily and it was always... truly appreciated."[36]

Although Sis's term in Rochester was an artistic success, he was once again made a free agent at the end of the season. In 1932 he accepted a position as playing manager for the owners of the Shreveport entry in the Texas League. As usual, the hand of Sisler's mentor was in the mix. "The persuasive powers of Branch Rickey, vice-president of the St. Louis Cardinals, and L. C. McEvoy, vice-president of the Browns, are said to have in no small measure induced Sisler to accept overtures of the new owners, after a Coast League club had tendered him, for his playing services alone, almost the same salary which he will receive here in his dual capacity of player-manager."[37]

If Sisler hoped to return to managing in the majors, the move proved a bad idea. His new team played miserably in the early going. When their record reached 9–21 it seemed things could get no worse, but they did— much worse. Following another home loss, this time to Galveston on May 4, Shreveport's ballpark caught fire. The grandstand as well as the team's equipment and uniforms were destroyed. The owners decided the next several games would be played in East Texas, in Tyler, a baseball hotbed before the depression forced the East Texas League to fold. The games were well attended, so the team was transferred there and renamed the Sports.[38]

During his tenure in Texas, Sis played first base in seventy games, hitting .287 but committing 15 errors. A highlight was a string of thirty-eight games without a strikeout. This was small consolation, however, for an athlete who set his sights on the top in every category, refusing to accept anything less. "I could no longer play very well, although I could still hit pretty well. But my speed was not good and I was ready to give up baseball. One day I muffed an easy pop fly, was advised to give up playing, whereupon I resigned my managership and came home, never to play again."[39]

36. Sisler Memoirs, 15.
37. *Sporting News*, March 10, 1932.
38. Bill O'Neal, *The Texas League, 1888–1987: A Century of Baseball*, 304.
39. Sisler Memoirs, 15–16.

15

Private Enterprise

On a sunny afternoon in early 1933, a slender, tanned gentleman with a trim athletic build walked through the turnstiles at the Spring Avenue entrance to Sportsman's Park. His arrival was noted by a columnist who saw the man nod to one or two friends, then sit down in one of a sea of empty seats, essentially unrecognized by those baseball fans in attendance. The columnist knew the man's identity. It was George Harold Sisler. Only ten years before, the sight of this same man under similar circumstances would have made quite a stir—a buzz followed by a smattering of applause, then a thunderous ovation. But not today. George was merely a spectator, and like most retired sports figures, he was not entirely comfortable with his present plight in life.

"It's a great game," he told the columnist. "The trouble with many of us is that we don't appreciate the profession while we are in it.... [T]hen the first thing we know why we are through. We don't admit that we have reached the end of our string, but suddenly it dawns upon us—it did with me, I know—that we have slowed up to such an extent that we must get out for younger players."

On that day Sis talked philosophically about his decision to keep playing after his trade from Washington to Boston, saying he was "determined to show American Leaguers I wasn't a has-been." But now, after two years

246

in the minors, he was "willing to admit the owners are right and I'm wrong. I'm through as a player."[1]

After describing Sisler's exploits, columnist Sid Keener went on to tell readers that it was not George's intent to become divorced entirely from baseball, but in essence that is what happened for the next eleven or so years. Perhaps Sis was forthright when he told Keener he intended to maintain his ties to the game. After all, baseball is loaded with former players who become managers, coaches, scouts, and even umpires. Under normal circumstances, despite a spotty record as a manager, these avenues would be open in the baseball world to a man of Sisler's stature. But the circumstances were not normal. In 1933, the first full year of Sis's retirement from the game, the American economy bottomed out. Baseball attendance, which did not immediately suffer from the downturn, was now some four million below the total for the 1930 season. The sport, like any other good business, tried to hold the status quo, cutting costs where necessary, but baseball staffs, if anything, were contracting rather than expanding.

There is no indication George ever inquired about a job in baseball upon his retirement. If he had, though, he might well have run up against a stone wall. One retiree who was finding that out was Bill Wambsganss, a fine major-league infielder for many years who drifted to the minors and, like Sis, retired in 1932. "I was thirty-eight years old," Wambsganss recalled, "it was the middle of the depression, opportunities for scouting and managing just ceased to exist, and other jobs were even scarcer.... Having to leave the game is a very difficult adjustment to make, and that goes for every single ballplayer. Don't let any one of them tell you different."[2]

When he left baseball, unlike Bill Wambsganss and many other players in his heyday, George was not without the tools for a successful career outside the sport. He held a degree in engineering from Michigan and was a part owner of a successful printing business. However, he was forty years old by then. Whatever interest he once held in engineering seemed to have passed. And the printing business was a means, not an end, despite an occasional foray into the office in the baseball off-season.

Twice before, once in high school at seventeen and then again at college graduation, the intoxication of sports had lured George away from more

1. Quoted in unidentified news column by Sid Keener, ca. 1933, source and page number unknown (George Sisler Clippings File, National Baseball Library, Cooperstown, N.Y.).

2. Lawrence S. Ritter, *The Glory of Their Times: The Story of the Early Days of Baseball Told by the Men Who Played It*, 239.

conventional pursuits. It would do so again. Since boyhood, sports, and in particular baseball, had forged an identity for George, setting him apart from others. But unlike for most people, it also earned him fame. So it was only natural that even in retirement, he found a business connection through sports. He arranged to go into the sporting goods business with Charles Nelson, who was then managing the Leacock Sporting Goods Company in St. Louis. Each man put up a portion of the required capital, and drawing upon George's name, the Sisler-Nelson Sporting Goods Company opened for business in 1933 at 1102 Locust Street in the Lieberman Building.

In later years, George would look back and question the decision as "a little hasty because I had no love for that type of business and saw no great future in it."[3] In 1933, however, it seemed to fit the bill. Yet in the midst of an epic economic swoon, something more than simple hard work would be required to lift the new business venture off the ground. In an effort to stimulate business and provide a form of recreation for the city's youth, Sis and Nelson formed the American Softball Association, with Sis as president. The plan was to construct softball parks, put in lights, play scheduled games every night, and charge admission. Since organized baseball was still a daytime only game, the softball leagues would not compete with the sport George loved. If anything, this creative new scheme would increase interest in baseball.

Each team in the softball league would have a sponsor who would outfit the squad in exchange for the advertising. Of course, the Sisler-Nelson Sporting Goods Company was perfectly suited and well situated to sell equipment to the teams, along with softballs, bats, and gloves. According to George, the steady income from these sales "was a boon to our business."[4]

The first park was constructed on leased premises at Grand and Natural Bridge Road in St. Louis. Under Sis's directions, a lighted park and concession stand was constructed, teams formed, and schedules prepared. Meeting the projected start date was a chore but the schedule was met and the opening game, as well as those that followed, were played before an average nightly attendance of one thousand fans at what became known as Northside Park. Success at the first park soon led to construction of a second, known fittingly enough as the Southside Park. Located at Kingshighway and Chippewa, this park had a seating capacity of twelve hundred to fifteen hundred. The city's softball leagues soon became so popular that one night when the champions of the Northside and Southside Parks

3. Sisler Memoirs, 16.
4. Ibid.

met, the game drew thirty-five hundred spectators, with scores of additional fans turned away. The Browns and Braves should have been so lucky.

Before long, several other parks were up and running, in other cities as well as in St. Louis. Eventually, however, the owners of the leased land became greedy. Rental at Southside Park went from one hundred to three hundred dollars per month, forcing the association to close it down. Nonetheless, Sis had his first real taste of baseball as a retired player.

Shortly after his retirement in the 1932 off-season, George joined the staff of the All-Star Baseball School in Hot Springs, Arkansas. The school was run by Ray Doan, a sports promoter. Other instructors at the school included Rogers Hornsby, Grover Cleveland Alexander, and Les Mann, the veteran Braves and Cubs outfielder who later formed the National Amateur Baseball Association. St. Louis Cardinals scout Jack Ryan was also on the staff. Sis and Hornsby returned to the camp again in the off-season of 1933–1934 and at least once more in 1935–1936.

During 1936 and 1937 the shy Sis tried his hand at another facet of the game. In May of 1936, he was hired by St. Louis radio station KWK to be what is now known as the color analyst on the radio broadcasts of all home Browns and Cardinals games. In this capacity, he assisted regular announcer Ray Schmidt by giving a between-inning review of each game as it was played and a summary of baseball happenings each night at 9:30 p.m. The broadcasts were sponsored by General Mills, the maker of Wheaties.

In the early years of his baseball retirement, Sis found more time for his growing family. He also enjoyed time with friends outside of baseball. One such friend was Roland Hoerr, who along with Sis belonged to the University Club in St. Louis. Hoerr was a former tennis star, and for exercise, the pair met at the club to play squash. As an accomplished racket player, Hoerr held the upper hand, but the games were "close enough to be interesting."[5] George fared better at three-cushioned billiards.

The Hoerrs and Sislers and their families vacationed together. Kathleen's parents owned cottages at Morpeth, Ontario, and the two families spent two weeks together there one summer. Rollie and Sis also enjoyed hunting together, especially on Rollie's land at Winfield, twenty to thirty miles outside of St. Louis. Sisler became an accomplished hunter, bagging several white wild geese during one excursion to Hoerr's place.

As with many outdoorsmen, hunting soon became a primary source of pleasure for George. His printing partner, Paul Simmons, and Paul's

5. Ibid., 11.

friend Herman Radke went on one unforgettable quail hunting adventure. Radke lived in Leeper, Missouri, a small town in the southern part of the state. A small railroad line eighty miles long was based in the town for farmers to get their produce to the larger Missouri Pacific Railroad network. Radke owned an old Ford that he fitted with railroad wheels to run on the tracks. He and his friends, including George, would run the Ford up the tracks several miles until the group found a good spot for quail, get out to hunt, and then move along the tracks to the next favorable spot. It was a hunter's delight. In addition to quail, the hunters might bag a woodcock and even a pheasant or two. When they were finished, they might be forty to fifty miles from Leeper, whereupon they would return to town and await the midnight train to St. Louis. On one particular occasion, the group arrived back in Leeper with time on their hands. Before long, Dr. Owens, one of the hunters who lived in Leeper, found a deck of cards. The men began playing small-stakes poker inside the station. All at once, three masked men charged into the station. Two of the men were armed. The robbers began searching the card-playing hunters for money and jewelry. Paul Simmons was wearing a wedding ring and asked the men not to take it. Surprisingly, they agreed. Sis turned his wedding ring around to make it look like a plain band and was able to save it also. The robbers departed without causing anyone physical harm, but Sis and Simmons now had nothing to pay for a ticket home, and so they spent the night in Leeper.

The story does not end there, however. Dr. Owens noticed that one of the robbers wore a distinctive Mackinaw coat that he had seen around town before. He described the coat in detail for the local sheriff. Using this slim lead, law enforcement officials captured all three men. George and the other hunters later returned to Leeper twice in connection with the case, once to try to identify the robbers and once for the trial. Nevertheless, in the end, the charges against the crooks were dismissed. The old white-haired judge ruled Sis and his friends were gambling at the time of the robbery. In rural Missouri in the 1930s gambling of any sort was illegal, even though the stakes were low. The seemingly innocuous actions of the card players were enough to let the bad guys stroll.[6]

In 1938 Charles Nelson sold his interest in the sporting goods business to Walter Hummel, a young man who trained and then worked with the company as a salesman. Nelson moved to California. Sis was tired of the sporting goods business himself by that time and looking for a way out. About this same time, he became involved with Ray "Hap" Dumont and the National Baseball Congress, an organization that administered semi-

6. Ibid., 12.

pro baseball throughout the country. The organization, started on a shoe-string budget, somehow thrived in the midst of the depression. Head-quartered in Wichita, Kansas, it conducted state tournaments throughout the country, including a World Series event each year in Wichita. Quite a number of future major-league stars honed their skills in Dumont's semi-pro league, including Tom Seaver, Satchel Paige, Allie Reynolds, Ralph Houk, Billy Martin, Pete Reiser, Willie Horton, Jackie Jensen, Dave Win-field, and Roger Clemens.

In 1938 Dumont needed a new commissioner to replace Pittsburgh Pi-rate legend Honus Wagner. Heeding a suggestion by J. G. Taylor Spink, the publisher of the St. Louis–based national baseball weekly the *Sporting News,* Dumont approached Sis. George quickly accepted, becoming a good-will ambassador for the semi-pro game, a position he held and enjoyed for many years by attending the tournament in Wichita in the fall, certify-ing the participants, and settling issues that arose. Dumont, of course, ran the league top to bottom, making use of Sisler's name recognition to lend prestige to the annual tournament and to act as a buffer "to cover up de-cisions that might be difficult to make as the goodwill organizer of the games."[7] Sis, with his handsome features, sparkling reputation, and calm demeanor, fit the bill to perfection. It meant little to him that he was a figurehead—for him it was just another tie to baseball.

One day in early 1939, Sis was at his sporting goods store checking on an order for ice skates when he learned of his election by the Baseball Writers Association of America to baseball's Hall of Fame. He was the top vote getter and initial first baseman so honored. The class of 1939 also included star second baseman Eddie Collins of the Athletics and White Sox and Willie Keeler of New York baseball fame.

Sis was now in lofty company. Counting the newly elected, the Hall consisted of but seventeen members. The first class elected in January 1936 included Ty Cobb, Walter Johnson, Christy Mathewson, Babe Ruth, and Honus Wagner. Since that time, the other players actually elected included Napoleon Lajoie, Cy Young, Tris Speaker, and Grover Cleveland Alexan-der. A special committee had previously named several baseball pioneers, including George Wright, John J. McGraw, Ban Johnson, Connie Mack, and Morgan G. Bulkeley. Since the official opening of the Hall of Fame Mu-seum at Cooperstown, New York, was scheduled for June 1939, George and his fellow inductees would be the first class to actually enter with an induction ceremony at the Hall itself.

    7. Bob Broeg, *Baseball's Barnum: Ray "Hap" Dumont, Founder of the National Baseball Congress,* 59.

In the early years of the Hall of Fame, some ballplayers did not put much stock in the honor. Sis disagreed and was not embarrassed to say so. "I've heard that some former players are rather cynical about this Hall of Fame business pointing out that 'it doesn't buy any groceries.' I don't feel that way. I think it's the greatest honor the game can offer a retired player and it's a satisfaction to know that your career is still remembered, years after you have hung up your glove." The honor was particularly gratifying to George because it could well "prove an inspiration to the boys"—a group that now included seven-year-old David Michael, born in 1931.[8]

In June, Kathleen and George took a plane from St. Louis and several connections later arrived in Utica, New York, where a limousine took them to the Otesaga Hotel on Otsego Lake. Sportswriter Ken Smith, who later became the Hall of Fame's director, was present at the induction proceedings on June 12, as "through the Hall of Fame portal, one by one as they were presented, walked the mightiest stars of the Twentieth Century—heroes whose deeds on the diamond were still fresh in the memory of the audience."[9] George marveled at the beauty of Cooperstown and the "rather simple, but dignified" ceremony. He was awed to be a member of a "very exclusive organization" and "knew it was a great honor." He returned home with a "grateful attitude."[10]

Following his induction into the Hall, George returned to St. Louis and sporting goods, but perhaps his renewed connection with baseball, this time with organized baseball itself by virtue of the Hall of Fame induction, fanned a flame. A year or so later, his new sporting goods partner Hummel bought Sis out at "a nice profit for me."[11] For one of the first times in his life, George Sisler was in a state of limbo. However, it would not stay that way for long.

8. *Sporting News*, January 26, 1939, 3.
9. Ken Smith, *Baseball's Hall of Fame*, 15.
10. Sisler Memoirs, 26.
11. Ibid., 17.

16

Full Circle

In the dozen or so years after George had performed his magic for the St. Louis Browns, the team remained grounded in despair. In the meantime the fortunes of their National League cousins, the Cardinals, were in full flight. Under the studied executive tutelage of Branch Rickey, the team prospered, winning six pennants and four World Series. They were clearly now "the team" in St. Louis. But despite their success on the field and in the profit column, there was unrest in the Cardinals' front office. On October 29, 1942, just twenty-four days after an exciting World Series victory over the Yankees, Rickey tendered his resignation as the club's vice-president, leaving behind a roster of star players he had developed, including future Hall of Famers Enos "Country" Slaughter and a youthful Stan Musial. Two days later, on November 2, Branch took a new job, president of the Brooklyn Dodgers, the team his Cardinals had replaced as pennant winners, but a club with a dismal outlook for the future due to an aging roster.

Rickey was the perfect antidote for an organization on Geritol. The strength of his organization in St. Louis was just that, organization. Rickey was the architect of the major-league farm club system. Prior to Rickey, minor-league clubs did their own scouting and training, and then sold their players to the highest-bidding major-league club. This meant the richest clubs just got richer. Under the Rickey system, soon copied by other clubs who marveled at his success, the major-league club developed a farm system of its own, by either owning the minor-league clubs itself or entering exclusive working agreements with them. The success of this system depended on a strong bevy of scouts, highly skilled coaches and trainers, and state-of-the-art training facilities. Rickey's ultimate success rested on his ability to find and develop talent. At the core of the plan were his scouts and coaches.

Before he left for Brooklyn, Branch's friends and associates in St. Louis gave him a going away party at the old Jefferson Hotel on Twelfth Street. George attended the luncheon affair. At some point in the festivities, he strode to the head table to greet his old coach and friend. Much to his surprise, Rickey asked his former pupil on the spot to consider coming back to baseball to scout for his Brooklyn organization. According to Sis, the timing was just right. He quickly said yes. He "couldn't have been happier."[1] On December 20, 1942, just days after the banquet, he wrote to Rickey, confirming the offer made at their "chance meeting" and assuring his new boss that "I will be of value to you."[2] In addition, he reminded Rickey of his work in semi-pro ball and the potential for the discovery of baseball talent during his yearly sojourns to Wichita.

Perhaps it goes too far to say that Sis, estranged from organized baseball for the past ten years during the midst of the Great Depression, had been going through a bit of a depression himself. Or perhaps not. If that was the case, then it is fair to say that in 1942 America was coming out of its deep trough, and Sisler was too.

At any rate it was official: at forty-nine, George Sisler was back in the game. Perhaps to signal the rekindled flame, he agreed to play first base for the all-time all-star team that appeared at the Polo Grounds on August 26, 1943. His infield mates were Eddie Collins at second, Honus Wagner at short, and Frankie Frisch at third. Walter Johnson pitched, and the outfield included Ruth and Speaker. The all-star treatment was repeated in Philadelphia for a Shibe Park crowd a year later.

The initial plan with the Dodgers, as outlined by Rickey, called for George to attend their training camp in the spring and then scout as many semi-pro, college, and high school games as Sis could see in the Missouri area and surrounding states. Then there was the occasional special assignment. One time, for instance, he was sent to Chicago to sign a highly publicized high school pitcher. Upon his arrival, he found a number of scouts

1. Sisler Memoirs, 17.
2. George Sisler Letter to Branch Rickey, December 20, 1942, Branch Rickey Papers, Manuscript Division, Library of Congress, Washington, D.C., Box 26, Folder 13.

had beaten him to the punch and made offers. Sis made his offer on behalf of the Dodgers and much to his delight, the youngster signed. Then came the bad news—the kid had not graduated from high school. As such, the contract was void. Sis knew all about such things from his own youthful dealings with the Pirates. He immediately reported the problem to Albert B. "Happy" Chandler, the man who had replaced Judge Landis as baseball's commissioner. He did not have to report the signing, since the commissioner's office had not known of the deal, and neither Sis nor any of the other scouts were aware of the situation when they made the prospect an offer. "I did this because I thought it was the right and honorable thing to do. . . . Well, all I got for my attempt to do what was right was to have the contract voided and a fine against the Brooklyn club of $500.00."[3]

Sis had better luck of much more historic proportion with another prospect. The groundwork for this assignment was plowed by Branch Rickey shortly after his arrival in Brooklyn, but took several years to come to fruition. The Cardinals, Rickey's previous employer, were one of the last teams in baseball to prohibit blacks from sitting in the main grandstand area at their park. Rickey did not agree with the owner's stance. In the 1930s, as a top Cardinals executive, he tried to change it, but to no avail, finding "effective opposition on the part of ownership and on the part of the public—press—everybody."[4] Perhaps this stemmed, in no small part, from the undercurrent of distrust and resentment that lingered following the East St. Louis riots more than two decades ago.

In New York City, home to three major-league teams, baseball dominated the landscape of sports like nowhere else. The Yankees, playing in the Bronx, ruled the roost in the American League. They played in Yankee Stadium, one of baseball's largest stadiums. In the National League, the Giants played at the Polo Grounds, while Brooklyn's Dodgers played their ball at Ebbets Field, one of the smallest major-league stadiums. Located on Bedford Avenue fairly close to downtown Brooklyn, just one famous bridge away from the southern tip of Manhattan, the aging edifice accommodated only thirty-two thousand fans. But size in this particular case meant little. Although they often called their heroes "dem bums," the Dodgers' fans were baseball's most loyal. Faced with the prospect of yet another bad season, they always cried out, "Wait til next year!" In some cities baseball was merely a game. In Brooklyn, where young boys played stickball in the middle of the street and could only dream of outfield grass, baseball was a religion.

3. Sisler Memoirs, 17.
4. Quoted in Murray Polner, *Branch Rickey: A Biography*, 146.

Rickey found the climate in New York different from St. Louis in more ways than just the humidity. When he arrived on the scene he found that blacks were already allowed to sit where they wanted at Ebbets Field. That was commendable, but to Rickey it was still not enough. He wanted to take the issue of race in sports several steps further. Shortly after taking over the club as president, he approached a major shareholder of the team and secured his agreement in exploring the possibility of bringing a black player into the Dodgers' organization, and if warranted, onto the Dodgers' roster itself.

Rickey saw the breaking of the color line from the moral perspective, but ever the sharp businessman, he also saw the introduction of the first black player into organized baseball as a good business decision. After all, many black players performing in the Negro leagues were equal to and in many cases better than their white counterparts. This was proven every year when groups of the better major leaguers and Negro leaguers played barnstorming games on an equal footing against each other in October. Brooklyn had a large black population to boot. The introduction of the first black ballplayer, with others sure to follow, would increase the team's skill level, as well as its gate count.

Having secured the approval of at least one major owner and with the feeling that the remaining owners would fall in line, all Branch needed was a plan—something he was never without for any length of time. In this case, Rickey's plan needed to be a solid one since the Dodgers would be like an island lashed by a stormy sea in trying to remove a barrier so ingrained in the American fabric.

Rickey's plan was simple in design, if not in execution. It centered on finding a man capable of facing all associated pressures on the field and off. It was to be aided by obtaining a good reaction from the press and the public, an appropriate understanding and acceptance of the plan by the black community to "avoid misrepresentation and abuse of the project," and in the final analysis, the acceptance of the chosen one by his white teammates.[5] Rickey succinctly summed it all up: "I had to get a man who would carry the burden on the field. I needed a man to carry the badge of martyrdom. The press had to accept him. He had to stimulate a good reaction of the Negro race itself, for an unfortunate one might have solidified the antagonism of other colors. And, I had to consider the attitude of the man's teammates."[6]

5. Quoted in Arthur Mann, *Branch Rickey: American in Action,* 214–15.
6. Polner, *Branch Rickey: A Biography,* 160.

In order to fulfill the core requirement—the perfect black ballplayer—
Rickey turned to his scouts. On the pretext that he planned to form a new
Negro league and field a team at Ebetts Field called the Brooklyn Brown
Dodgers, he called in his main scouts, Tom Greenwade, Clyde Sukeforth,
Wid Mathews, and Sis, telling them he wanted them to travel the country
looking for black ballplayers to stock his new team. At the time, major-
league clubs did not bother to scout black ballplayers. If George was at all
bothered by this prospect he never voiced it publicly or privately, entering the project with typical enthusiasm and energy, with the chief consideration being to find Mr. Rickey good players. Given his sense of fair play,
had he known his boss's true purpose in sending him and the others out
to beat the bushes, it is doubtful it would have made any difference.

A number of black ballplayers were under consideration. Rickey got
one tip from Wendell Smith, a sports reporter for the *Pittsburgh Courier*, a
black newspaper with a wide circulation. Smith's candidate, Jackie Robinson, a twenty-six-year-old four-sport star from UCLA, was playing shortstop for the Kansas City Monarchs, a top Negro League team. After checking further into Smith's suggestion, Rickey moved into action, sending
Mathews, Greenwade, and Sis on separate assignments to watch the Monarchs and Robinson, who was totally unaware of their interest.

During the summer of 1945, Sis went to Chicago, where the Monarchs
were playing, and liked much of what he saw. The only problem was
Robinson's throwing arm. In George's opinion it was inadequate for a regular shortstop in the majors. Still, he sent his boss "a glowing report."[7] So
did Greenwade, who was impressed with Jackie's prowess as a bunter,
and Mathews, who liked the way the prospect protected the strike zone.
The reports were enough to convince Rickey to take the next step. He sent
Sukeforth to view the player and, if convinced, to bring him to Brooklyn
for a meeting. Sukeforth liked what he saw.

The meeting between Rickey and Robinson took place on August 28,
1945. It was lengthy and exhaustive, witnessed only by Sukeforth. In a
classic use of reverse psychology, Rickey first told Robinson he had decided
he was not the man for the job, and then gave him a sample of the cruel
treatment baseball's first black could expect as he made his rounds of the
major-league cities. When he was through showering Robinson with in-
vectives and Robinson was still interested, as well as anxious to give it a
try, Rickey was satisfied. He made Jackie an offer. Robinson was signed to
a minor-league contract on October 23, spent the 1946 season with the

7. Sisler Memoirs, 17.

Montreal Royals, and did not actually break the major-league color barrier until April 15, 1947, in a game played before 25,623 at Ebbets Field. The crowd included an estimated 14,000 blacks.

It is arguable just how much effect World War II had on the acceptance of Branch Rickey's efforts to end baseball's segregation. That blacks and whites fighting together in a bloody war for a common cause had some effect is much less uncertain. Sisler was too old to participate in the war itself, but he did go to Europe with several other baseball notables to visit the troops. The group flew to Germany, where they met American troops on a daily basis, lecturing on various baseball topics and talking baseball with them. As busy as he was, Sis still had time to stop in Austria to purchase a double-barreled shotgun at a bargain price as a gift for his friend, Branch Rickey.

During Rickey's early years in Brooklyn, the team was erratic. In 1943 they finished third, but fell to seventh in 1944, then climbed back to third in 1945. In 1946 the club started profiting from the infusion of young players through the improved farm system engineered by Rickey. They took second that season. Prior to 1947, Sis's activities for the Dodgers remained confined to scouting and assisting with spring training. In the spring of 1947, in an effort to avoid unnecessary controversy with the presence of barrier-crasher Robinson, the Dodgers trained in Cuba. Kathleen Sisler accompanied her husband on the trip, as did Jane Rickey. The couples were friends outside of baseball with much in common, including the desire for a quiet, conservative lifestyle. The Cuban government was determined to provide a first-class experience for their important American guests. One night after the Sislers and Rickeys retired for the evening, the telephone rang in Sis's room. It was Branch, telling him that the Cuban government had contacted him by phone moments before, telling him they were awaiting his arrival at the world-famous Tropicana nightclub for that evening's performance. Rickey had previously accepted the invitation and then promptly forgotten about it. In order to pacify the Cubans, he needed Sis and Kathleen to accompany him and his wife to the show. Ever obedient, Sis and Kathleen dressed. The two couples arrived at the nightclub close to midnight, where they tried to down a large meal and then sit through what turned out to be a lavish but lewd show that ran into the wee hours of the morning. Later, the government apologized for the x-rated affair, which had undoubtedly shocked their teetotalling guests to no end, and closed the Tropicana until the Dodger family was off the island.

Incidents like the one at the Tropicana where Sis came through for his boss in a moment of need convinced Rickey that he needed even more of

George than he was getting. That same year he called to ask if his friend would consider moving to Brooklyn. Rickey's many obligations were keeping him from Ebbets Field and the essential task of monitoring the progress of younger players, including the many "bonus babies"—promising young players given bonuses to sign with the club. Sis could be of valuable assistance with those tasks. In addition, Rickey wanted Sis to meet with the manager and coaches before and after each game, and also to sit in the stands to chart each pitch, assisting Dodger catchers with information on opposing batter traits. Would he consider taking the job?

Unlike the last offer from Rickey, which Sis jumped to take, this one required more thought. Aware that Kathleen would be reluctant to leave their lovely family home on Pershing Avenue in Parkview, he still felt extreme loyalty to Branch for bringing him into baseball, and then bringing him back to it after his playing days were over. That loyalty eventually won out. Sis packed and pushed off for Brooklyn while Kathleen stayed behind to sell the house. It eventually sold for twenty-two thousand dollars, less than George was asking but still a tidy sum for the times. Some furniture was stored in St. Louis for an eventual return. Also "stored" for the time being was his youngest son, David, then a promising baseball and basketball player at the John Burroughs School in St. Louis. Arrangements, not unlike those made by George's parents when he was a youth, were made for David to remain in St. Louis and live with a school chum for the rest of the school year before joining his parents in the East. The other children were already in college or beyond.

While awaiting Kathleen's arrival, George rented an apartment for the couple in Kew Gardens in Queens. In order to get to Brooklyn, he took the subway an hour each way. Soon tired of the crowded conveyances, he rented a Brooklyn apartment next to the Rickeys.

George's first full-time year with the Dodgers in 1947 proved very much worth his while. This was Robinson's first year with the big-league club, for whom he played first base, an affirmation of Sis's concerns about the young player's arm strength. The addition of Robinson turned a second-place team into a pennant winner. The success was particularly remarkable considering that the team's manager, Leo Durocher, was forced to sit out the year on suspension for contact with gamblers. Under the direction of manager Burt Shotton, the old Brownie outfielder, the team went 94–60 before losing the World Series to the Yankees and Joe DiMaggio in seven games.

While George never grew to admire life in the big city, he thrived on his increased involvement with the Dodgers. In 1948 the team fell off a bit, finishing third with a number of young players such as Gil Hodges and

Carl Furillo earning their spurs as full-time players. In 1949 George was placed in full charge of hitting, beginning with spring training. The results were palpably discernable in short order. His most notable project was Jackie Robinson. In 1947 and 1948 Robinson hit .297 and .296 respectively; respectable figures, but nothing spectacular. In the spring of 1949 Jackie turned to George for help. At Sis's suggestion, the game's most recognizable figure, now a second baseman due to the trade of second baseman Eddie Stanky and the development of Hodges, spent hours with a batting tee at the Dodgers' Vero Beach, Florida, training complex, learning to hit the ball to right field.

Robinson's average showing at the plate was really not so difficult to understand. For years organized baseball in general and Commissioner Landis in particular had publicly proclaimed there was no policy in the major leagues excluding blacks. It was maintained, rather, that players in the Negro leagues were incapable of playing major-league-caliber baseball. This, of course, was total hogwash, quickly disproved by Robinson in the National League and Larry Doby upon his arrival in the American League, as well as many others. Blacks were more than capable of playing major-league baseball. What they often lacked were fundamental skills. The great catcher Roy Campanella, a player in the Negro leagues before his days with the Dodgers, acknowledges this in his autobiography, as does longtime Negro League star Buck Leonard, who admitted there was no one in his league to "tell me how to hit."[8] In 1949 with Sisler at Vero Beach, Jackie Robinson found someone to give him just such a boost.

George began by teaching his subject to prepare for the pitch, always looking for the fastball, not a curve. It was George's theory that if you expect a fastball, it will be easier to adjust to a slower curve than vice versa. "Sisler showed me how to stop lunging, how to check my swing until the last fraction of a second," Robinson said. "He showed me how to shift my feet and hit to right. I'll never stop being grateful to him."[9]

Sis's instruction and Robinson's hard work paid major dividends. In 1949, Jackie raised his average to .342 and was second in the league in doubles and triples as he was elected the National League Most Valuable Player. He followed with years of .328, .338, and .308, ending his career with a .311 lifetime batting average.

There were other players Sis helped considerably while he instructed hitting for the Dodgers. In 1946 Carl Furillo was a twenty-four-year-old

8. Quoted in White, *Creating the National Pastime,* 150. See also Jules Tygiel, *Baseball's Great Experiment: Jackie Robinson and His Legacy,* 20–21.
9. Quoted in Arnold Rampersad, *Jackie Robinson: A Biography,* 208.

center fielder for the team. In his first three years he hit .284, .295, and .297 with little power. Like Jackie Robinson's, these were respectable numbers, but not eyebrow-raising. Then George got a hold of him. According to Sis, Furillo "had a slight hitch. I helped him correct it."[10] And correct it Furillo did. In 1949 under Sis's watch, he raised his average to .322, with 18 home runs and 106 runs batted in; the following season he had identical power numbers and a .305 average. By 1953 he was a .344 hitter, ending a long career at .299 as a two-time All-Star.

In 1948 Gil Hodges was a twenty-four-year-old, weak-hitting (.249) first sacker. Sis "taught him how to hit curves."[11] In eighteen seasons, eight as an All-Star, Hodges hit .273 with a high season of .304. Under Sis's direct tutelage in 1949, he raised his average thirty-six points. Moreover, Sis used his knowledge of fielding the first base position to turn Hodges, originally a catcher, into an outstanding first baseman.

Edwin Donald Snider was another case in point. In 1948 Snider was a twenty-one-year-old outfielder with—for a baseball player—a major problem. According to Branch Rickey, he had "an appalling unfamiliarity with the strike zone." "Duke," as he came to be known, soon became George's obsession, and ultimately his greatest accomplishment as a hitting coach. One of the earlier recipients of batting cage workouts with a mechanical pitching machine, Snider was instructed by George to stand for twenty minutes at a time without swinging. He was merely to judge each mechanical pitch, identifying whether it was a ball or a strike. Sis would be the final arbiter of Snider's judgment. During the next twenty minutes Snider was to swing—which he often did—at low-inside pitches, his major weakness. Slowly, Sis taught his student to lay off that particular pitch. At the time, unlike Rickey, Sis believed Snider's "fault was not so much in poor judgment of the strike zone as in starting his full swing before the curve broke. He could pulverize the fast ball . . . There never was, and still isn't, any doubt in my mind as to Snider's ultimate place among the truly great hitters of the game."[12]

And as was so often the case when it came to hitting, Sis was right on target. In 1948 when he first took control of Snider's batting technique, the pupil hit .244 in only 160 at bats. By 1949 he was at .292, with 23 home runs and 93 runs batted in. The next year Snider's figures climbed to .321 with 31 home runs and 107 runs batted in. In eighteen seasons the Dodgers' main slugger hit .295 with 407 home runs. One season he batted .341. Over

10. Quoted in the *Sporting News*, March 10, 1954, 7.
11. Quoted in ibid.
12. Quoted in Arthur Mann, "The Dodgers' Problem Child," 112.

his career, he compiled four forty-plus home run seasons, was an eight-time All-Star, and entered the Hall of Fame in 1980.

Three days after Duke Snider's election to Cooperstown he reflected on his mentors, Rickey and Sisler, assuring fans it was their fatherly hand that had guided him to baseball's august body. "Mr. Rickey oversaw the project," he said, "and Sisler, was my batting instructor. Between the two of them, in Florida, I learned the strike zone, learned how to hit the change up, learned how to go to the opposite field."[13]

In the midst of all of his instructing, George still had time for a bit of scouting. Sometimes his experience as a pitcher stood him in good stead as a scout, and sometimes it did not. One time he was sent to look at a black pitcher named Dan Bankhead, who lived in the South. When George saw the young man pitch, his heart pounded. The youngster had "as much natural stuff as any pitcher I had seen in a long time." He immediately called Rickey, who came over to try to sign the married man to a contract. The pair were invited by Bankhead and his wife to stay for dinner, "a rather dry chicken," according to Sis. But the home cooking worked and the kid signed the contract, much to the delight of the scout and his boss, neither of whom apparently gave the first thought about the social impact of two northern white men dining in a black family's home in the American South in the 1940s. The end result was that Bankhead pitched for three years in the majors, winning nine games and losing five. Years later, Sis recalled the player. "I still do not understand why he did not become one of the great pitchers in baseball. He had more natural stuff than [Don] Newcomb [sic]."[14] Perhaps things like that happened much to George's amazement because unlike engineering, baseball is not an exact science.

George had better luck with Johnny Podres, another young pitcher he tracked for the Dodgers. The first time he saw Podres was when the young man's father brought him to Ebbets Field for a workout. After a twenty-minute stint, Sis told the proud dad, "He'll be in the majors in four years."[15] According to Sis, Podres had great "aptitude" for pitching. Since Rickey based his decisions about young pitchers on their aptitude, George immediately knew Podres was someone the Dodgers would want to sign. He followed the pitcher to New England, where Podres was playing summer ball, and offered him a six-thousand-dollar bonus—the most then allowed, unless the player was kept on the team's major-league roster—

---

13. Quoted in the *Sporting News,* January 26, 1980, 48.
14. Sisler Memoirs, 19.
15. Quoted in Bill Libby, "The Ten Years of Johnny Podres," 41.

to sign. When Podres accepted, it was a proud day for him and his family and for the Dodgers as well.

Sis was wrong about one thing, though, when it came to Podres: he was pitching in the major leagues in two years, not four. In a career that spanned fifteen years, Podres won 148 games. Moreover, his World Series record in six games pitched was 3–1, with a sparkling 2.11 earned run average. In 1955 he was the World Series Most Valuable Player, beating the Yankees in Games Three and Seven, the latter a 2–0 shutout that gave the Dodgers their first world championship and broke a run of five consecutive World Series defeats at the hands of their bitter neighborhood rivals. The youth Sis fawned over is today a Dodger legend.

Sis's hard work with the Dodgers' young hitters paid off as well. Behind Robinson's MVP season in 1949 the team won the pennant before losing one of those five consecutive World Series to the Yankees. In 1950 the team, by then stocked with several additional All-Stars such as Newcombe and Hall of Fame catcher Roy Campanella, finished second, losing out to the Phillies on the last day of the regular season.

Despite the Dodgers' obvious success on the field, however, all was not biscuits and honey in the front office. By 1950 Rickey was a part owner of the team as well as its president and, for all intents and purposes, its general manager. On October 26, whether by design to clear debts, a version Rickey preferred, or, more likely, under pressure from the other Dodgers owners, in particular Walter O'Malley, Rickey resigned as president, selling his stock for a tidy profit by any account. He was succeeded by O'Malley, at one time a lawyer for the club.

Rickey told everyone within range that he was fired by the Dodgers for finishing second. All of baseball, even Rickey's detractors, and there were some, mourned the loss of one of baseball's greatest innovators. But eleven days later, before the body was even cold, Branch Rickey signed a five-year contract with the lowly Pittsburgh Pirates, becoming that team's executive vice-president and general manager. Baseball's "most successful resuscitator of decrepit baseball teams" was on the move again.[16] Would Sisler be far behind?

Branch Rickey was in charge of the Pittsburgh Pirates for only a few days before he started filling his staff. His first choice was a natural, his son, Branch, Jr., assigned to assist his father in the front office. His next choice was almost as easy: George Sisler, Chief Scout. On November 15,

16. J. B. Griswold, "Rickey Starts in the Cellar Again," 111.

1950, the *Sporting News* announced that George's territory would include players within a one-hundred-mile radius of Pittsburgh, the region previously handled by Pie Traynor, the former Pirate star who also broadcast the team's games over the radio. The paper did not overlook the irony that George's career was now full circle, employed as he now was by the team he had battled to avoid in his teenage years.[17]

As with the move from St. Louis to Brooklyn, the decision to accept Rickey's Pirates offer was not so easy. Sis had invested a lot of his heart and soul in the young Dodger talent. "I really did not want to go at the time," he later said. The new Dodger boss, O'Malley, did not want Sisler to leave either. He tried to entice him by throwing a separate office and secretary into the mix. "I explained that I owed allegiance to Mr. Rickey... He understood, and dictated a letter right in front of me that if I ever needed a job, to come back to him; a very generous offer from a really big man."[18]

So despite some misgivings, loyalty reigned, and the Sislers were off to Pittsburgh. George's official title was Scouting Supervisor. To make him feel a little better, he got his own office and a secretary anyway. Before long, former Dodgers scout Clyde Sukeforth joined Sis's crew. Branch, Jr. took over a minor-league system that needed first aid, much like the Dodgers network had eight years before.

After an initial orientation period, the Sislers settled in the Amberson Gardens Apartments, a new development close to Forbes Field, home of the Pirates. Branch, Jr. and his wife, Mary, became their good friends. The couples quickly learned the lay of the land. As one writer put it, "Pittsburgh is smoke and dirt. Pittsburgh is raw and alive. Pittsburgh is poverty and railroad tracks. It's also the home of extreme wealth—big, brick houses in residential districts, far away from the game and the smog. Pittsburgh is crowded, noisy, scrappy. But most of all Pittsburgh is a working man's town. The working man built it. His speech is heard everywhere, rough and honest. And baseball is his game."[19]

As the new management of the Pirates, Rickey and his intrepid staff had their work cut out for them. From 1945 through 1950 their new organization had produced two fourth-place finishes, one sixth, two seventh, and one eighth. Unfortunately the eighth-place finish was in 1950, immediately prior to their arrival. Under Rickey and company, the club fared little better. Managed by Billy Meyer the first two years, the team finished

17. *Sporting News,* November 15, 1950, 6.
18. Sisler Memoirs, 19.
19. Unnamed journalist quoted in Andrew O'Toole, *Branch Rickey in Pittsburgh: Baseball's Trailblazing General Manager for the Pirates, 1950–1955,* 7–8.

seventh in 1951 and eighth in 1952. Fred Haney took over the reins in 1953, but they still finished last. The same results followed in 1954 and 1955.

On paper the five "Rickey years" must have seemed more like fifteen to beleaguered Pirates fans. But behind the scenes, deep underneath the surface, where Sis and his compatriots worked, the embryo of a winning organization was developing. One early change was in the Pirates' spring training sites. When Rickey arrived, the club trained at San Bernardino, California. In 1954, after one season in Havana, they shifted the site to Fort Pierce, Florida, which proved too small for the type of operation the new group planned to run. Finally, the organization moved its training base to Fort Myers, which provided an ideal gulf setting with two practice fields, plenty of locker space, and an overall uplifting experience.

Slow, steady progress was made in increasing the quality of the Pirates' pool of players as well. One product of Rickey's master plan was a minor-league school that he opened in October 1951 on an old army base in De-land, Florida. Telegrams were sent out to seventy of the organization's top prospects, whose development Rickey hoped to speed by at least a year through the individualized schooling. Rickey promised to supervise on site, assisted by Sisler and additional members of the staff, none of whom were paid a dime for this extra assignment. The development process was continued the next spring with a rookie camp at San Bernardino. Once again Rickey attended in person to offer instruction, assisted by George and others with extensive minor-league experience.

Prior to the mid-1950s the Pirates were pretty much a one-player team. Ralph Kiner was a true star. Still, he needed help, and before long it became apparent that as the team's sole financial asset, he would have to be traded for the assets needed to build a winning team. When Rickey pulled that trigger in June of 1953 and sent the wildly popular Kiner packing, he set in motion his own eventual demise. However, in the meantime the Pirates continued to move forward under Rickey's command.

With a team languishing in the National League basement, Rickey and Sis felt they must try just that much harder than the other teams. Regular tryouts were held on almost a daily basis, along with a number of special tryouts in an effort to find quality players in high quantity. The results were often mixed. Bill Mazeroski was one player of note from the general Pittsburgh area who was added through this process. When he arrived as a shortstop, Sis immediately noted his quickness and accurate arm, attributes that served him well as an eventual All-Star second baseman, legendary for turning the double play. Needless to say, the Pirates were thrilled to add a player of Mazeroski's caliber to an organization "on the build." Their faith in Maz was justified when years later he joined other Pirate greats in Cooperstown.

On the other hand, one of the prospects who got away was a big one. One day Ed McCarrick, a scout Sis assigned to the New York area, called to say he had a young pitching prospect by the name of Sandy Koufax who deserved a closer look. Since Koufax was an unknown quantity, the Pirates sent Branch, Jr. and Clyde Sukeforth to take a look. They reported Koufax "not only was very wild, but that he was ungainly and perhaps would never get control."[20] McCarrick persisted, however, and Koufax came to Pittsburgh, where Sis got a look that greatly impressed him. At his insistence, Sandy's parents were invited to town. After some discussion, it appeared certain the Koufaxs would place their boy in the Pirates' hands for a most reasonable sum of $12,500. Nevertheless, Branch, Sr., who would not be trumped when it came to having the final say on talent, particularly pitching talent, would not bite. In a major lapse in judgment the Pirates turned their back on a player who would become one of baseball's all-time greatest stars, when they could have signed him for a song.

Still, the baseball gods smiled on the Pirates in another case. In 1954 Rickey sent Clyde Sukeforth to minor-league Montreal to check out pitcher Joe Black, a Dodger prospect Rickey was tracking for a potential trade. While watching fielding practice before the game, Sukeforth noticed a young Montreal outfielder with a rifle arm. In the seventh inning of the game, the same kid came to the plate to pinch-hit, grounded to short, and flashed down the line so fast he almost beat a good throw. Deciding nobody could run or throw any better, Sukeforth wrote down the kid's last name: Clemente.

When Sukeforth returned to Pittsburgh, it was clear to him that he must have the Clemente kid for his Pirates. There was only one hang-up: Clemente was the property of the Brooklyn Dodgers and was not for sale. The Dodgers were aware of Clemente's potential, but Sisler pupil Carl Furillo was already a Dodger fixture in right field. They tried to hide Clemente in Montreal and hoped to get away with it. Sukeforth was not ready to give up so easily. He did some homework, finding that the Dodgers had signed the youngster for ten thousand dollars. At the time, there was a rule in effect that any bonus player who signed a minor-league contract for more than four thousand dollars was subject to the draft. As the last-place club, the Pirates drafted first. Sukeforth got word to Rickey, who sent Sis and another scout to Montreal to check out Clemente. They

20. Sisler Memoirs, 20.

liked what they saw, and for four thousand dollars Roberto Clemente, a future perennial All-Star and Hall of Famer whose career could be marred only by a tragic fatal airplane crash, was the property of the Pittsburgh Pirates.[21]

As with the Dodgers, Sis's duties with the Pirates were not limited to the evaluation of prospects. Once again, Rickey made use of George's teaching talents to improve Pirates hitting, an acute illness not easily cured. "He's an even more remarkable teacher of hitters than he was a hitter himself," Rickey once said. "He has the greatest eye for detail and he's the most meticulous person in correcting mistakes I've ever seen. He has a wonderful knack of making his pupils do what he wants them to do and conning them into thinking it was their idea all along."[22]

Sis didn't find the art of hitting all that complicated. "It's easy to spot a man's batting flaws," he told a reporter, "but it's something else entirely to find ways to overcome them. All that I do is offer suggestions on batting."[23]

Quite often the suggestions worked. One grateful convert to the "Sisler method" was Frank Thomas, a Pittsburgh outfielder and first baseman of the 1950s. A big fellow at six feet, three inches and two hundred pounds, the native of Pittsburgh had "big swing, low average" written all over him. Since at twenty-four he was tabbed as the Pirates' successor to Ralph Kiner, his development was not to be taken lightly. In 1953 the slugger-to-be hit .255 with 30 home runs and 102 runs batted in, not too bad for a neophyte. But in 1954 he was struggling mightily at the plate, hitting .204 with much lower run production and 39 strikeouts in 74 at bats. He was, in fact, targeted for a return to the minors when he looked to George for help and found it. By season's end, he was at .298 with 23 home runs and 102 runs batted in. More important, his major-league career was still on track.

"Sisler made me what I am today," Thomas told the *Sporting News*. "He watched me for two weeks and then told me I was taking my eye off the ball. He moved me back in the box so I could watch the ball better. He told me to hit the ball where it was pitched. Warned me not to pull it."[24] It was simple advice, yet according to the record books, it was effective.

Another star pupil was Dick Groat, the former All-American basketball player from Duke. Under Sis's tutelage, the slick-fielding shortstop became a dangerous stick man, too. In 1960, in fact, Groat was the National

21. Clyde Sukeforth interview in Donald Honig, ed., *Baseball When the Grass Was Real: Baseball from the Twenties to the Forties Told by the Men Who Played It*, 182–84.

22. Quoted in Meany, *Baseball's Greatest Hitters*, 189.

23. *Sporting News*, June 29, 1960, 7.

24. Ibid., March 10, 1954, 7.

League's Most Valuable Player with a .325 average, fifty points higher than he had batted the previous year. "Sisler teaches us to be ready for the fast ball and adjust our swing for the curve," Groat said. "If you're looking for a curve and get a fast ball, you never hit it. But you can cut down on the speed of your swing to hit the curve."[25]

Even Clemente, a natural all the way, benefited from Sis's touch. In the spring of 1956, George instructed the young man from the Dominican Republic who had hit a disappointing .255 in his rookie campaign. At the end of the spring, the normally reserved Sis surprised reporters by predicting that the kid would hit thirty-five points higher in 1956. He was wrong, as usual understating the results. Clemente batted .311, some fifty-six points higher than the previous year. In 1960, Clemente, still under Sis's eye, would hit .351.

For Sis, the Dominican Republic was more than just memories of Clemente.

> While with Pittsburgh, I was called upon to make three trips [there], generally to look at some of our players who were playing winter ball there, but specifically to work with Dick Stuart, our first baseman who needed not only work on instruction with his fielding, but also with certain phases of his hitting. He was a power hitter who had great power, but who also struck out a lot and was weak on certain pitches. I went one year to Santiago in the northern part of the island, and twice to Santa Domingo.... Of my stay at Santiago, I stayed at the hotel there where the coaches and managers stayed. We left for the ballpark in an old type bus.... The main thing I remember about Santiago was the attitude of the people concerning their team. When we won, we were acclaimed all the way from the ballpark to the hotel, but when we lost, it was a different story. They had a way of wrapping flour in a throwable package and when we would pass after losing a game, they would certainly pelt us, and although the weather was warm, we had to close all windows for protection.[26]

Such was George's success as a teacher of baseball that eventually he decided to set his theories down on paper. He had already set forth some of his ideas on hitting way back in 1934 in a pamphlet called "The Knack of Batting." Distributed by Hillerich and Bradsby Co., the manufacturer of the popular Louisville Slugger bats, the book was directed at the player with average skills. In it George listed his six fundamental qualifications for great hitting: correct balance, proper timing, a level swing, a good follow through, average strength, and a good eye. Each could be acquired, in George's opinion, except the last two. "It is self-evident also that a good

25. Quoted in Tex Maule, "The Thinking Hitter," 59.
26. Sisler Memoirs, 9.

eye is important," he wrote, "for a boy must be able to see the ball every inch of the way from the time it leaves the pitcher's hand until it strikes the bat."[27] Of all people, George would know the importance of a good eye. He had learned that lesson the hard way.

Another lesson Sis hoped to pass on to future sluggers was his view on place hitting—the act of moving base runners along by intentionally hitting the ball to one side of the diamond or the other as the situation warranted. He and Ty Cobb were considered by many as the best place hitters ever. By the 1930s, however, place hitting was a lost art among major-league batters, having yielded to the big swing. Sisler, unlike many other fine place hitters who shifted their feet to place the ball, felt successful place hitting was a matter of timing, meeting the ball early or late by design. Ever the pragmatist, he cautioned, "The art of batting does not consist merely in swinging at the ball to see how far you can send it."[28]

In 1954 his second effort, *Sisler on Baseball: A Manual for Players and Coaches* was published by David McKay Company, Inc. of New York City. Although George's ideas on the art of hitting were featured in the book, the work touched on all aspects of the sport, even including a chapter on baseball signals. The forward of the book was written, unsurprisingly, by Branch Rickey, who told readers that in writing about the techniques and skills of the game, Sisler, in characteristic fashion, does not come off as an inventor or originator of ideas, but "as nothing more than a player who did it all naturally, and then learned the specific reasons for his greatness toward perfectionism. . . . (F)or he is an intensely modest man—exceptionally so for one so gifted in the field of physical achievement."[29]

The book was well received. In fact, fifteen years later Red Barber, the legendary radio broadcaster for the Dodgers and Yankees, wrote that Sisler's manual "is still the definitive book on hitting."[30] In developing an effective approach to hitting, Sisler had discovered another effective outlet for his relentless pursuit of perfection.

Given the book's excellent reception and his success in improving the hitting techniques and, thereby, the legends of star players such as Robinson, Clemente, and Snider, it is curious that unlike Ted Williams and others, George did not achieve a lasting reputation as one of the game's greatest hitting teachers. As one of the first hitting specialists, perhaps he was ahead of his time. Of course, as usual he did little to boost his image, pre-

27. George Sisler, *The Knack of Batting and How to Select and Care for Your Bat*, 6–7.
28. Ibid., 16.
29. Rickey writing in George Sisler, *Sisler on Baseball: A Manual for Players and Coaches*, vii.
30. Red Barber, *Walk in the Spirit*, 73.

ferring to let his students' bats do the talking. As with so many of his attributes his legacy as an instructor is left to the eyes of the beholder, in this case the recipients of the fruits of a lifetime spent in pursuit of hitting excellence.

Sis's abilities as a scout and even more as a hitting instructor par excellence stood him in good stead in Pittsburgh when the road got bumpy for Branch Rickey. When he took the job, Rickey had a five-year contract. In 1955, after five years of basement baseball, the Pirates owners felt the aging baseball magnate's run was over. The Kiner trade had soured those few fans remaining, and attendance in 1955 was alarmingly low. In October of that year, Rickey resigned as general manager, utilizing a clause in his contract to remain with the team in an advisory capacity. His successor was Joe L. Brown, the thirty-seven-year-old son of star comedian Joe E. Brown. Rickey, who had trained Joe L., now was in the untenable position of working for the man.

Brown quickly made changes, many of them to Rickey's chagrin. One of the first was to replace Sisler, now sixty-two, as scouting director. According to Rickey biographer Murray Polner, Brown "privately, deprecated Sisler's administrative skills." If Sis saw the move as a demotion, he never spoke about it, at least publicly.[31]

In 1956 Brown replaced manager Fred Haney with Bobby Bragan, a former player with the Phillies and Dodgers. It was Bragan's first shot as a manager. The move boosted the Pirates but one spot, into seventh. This was followed by another seventh-place finish in 1957, but in that year Bragan named Sis his "special batting coach," a position that brought him onto the Pirate bench.

On February 16, 1957, Sis underwent a serious abdominal surgery at Presbyterian Hospital in Pittsburgh. Although the operation was a success, at his age convalescence was slow. He remained hospitalized into March. By May, when a reporter caught up to Sis, he found "his once marvelously coordinated physique has been ravaged by time and illness. He walks slowly now, eats carefully and tries not to get overly excited. He sits quietly in the Pirate clubhouse before the game and answers questions put to him by the Pirate players."[32]

In the fall of 1957, George and Kathleen moved their home base back to St. Louis. Perhaps the illness had forced some serious thinking about living closer to family and old and dear friends. In November Sis's return was celebrated at a banquet hosted by the Traffic Club of St. Louis, where

31. Polner, *Branch Rickey: A Biography,* 245.
32. Robert Creamer, "The Sad Song of Bobby," 56.

he appeared with a host of local sports notables including basketball's Bob Pettit and broadcaster Jack Buck. Speaking briefly, Sis told diners, "I've lived in many cities, but I've never felt at home any place but here."[33]

As far as baseball was concerned, George planned "to stay in the game as long as I can be of any help."[34] In 1958 and 1959 the Pirates, under new manager Danny Murtaugh, a former Pittsburgh player who had replaced Bragan in midseason 1957, began to benefit from the minor-league setup installed by Branch Rickey with Sis's assistance. The team finished in second place in 1958, and in fourth the following year. In 1960 the Pirates hit the jackpot, winning the National League pennant with a 95–59 record sparked by the strong hitting of Clemente, Groat, Mazeroski, Smoky Burgess, and Bob Skinner and the solid pitching of Vern Law, Bob Friend, relief ace Roy Face, and others.

In the 1960 World Series, the Pirates met the Yankees and their usual boatload of stars, including the spectacular pitcher Whitey Ford. In the ninth inning of the deciding seventh game, with the score at 9–9, Mazeroski blasted what many believe is the most dramatic World Series home run of all time to give Pittsburgh the title. As the team's traveling batting coach, Sis joined in the club's post-victory celebration, relishing for the first time, albeit not as a player, the sweet taste of ultimate team success.

The championship year was impossible to duplicate in the ensuing years, with the Pirates finishing sixth in 1961 and fourth in 1962. In February of 1963, a year that would see the club resume its position as the National League bottom-dweller, Sis, now almost seventy, was reassigned by General Manager Brown to teach hitting to minor-leaguers during spring training, now held by the Pirates in Daytona Beach. Under this new assignment, he would also remain in St. Louis during the regular season, scouting National League clubs as they came through town to play the Cardinals. In addition, he was asked to supervise the organization's team in Chandler, Arizona. The team was the Pirates' entry in the Arizona Instructional League, which was held in that state in October and November of each year to hone young talent. George was permitted to bring Kathleen; the couple made their home at the Far West Motel and enjoyed the good weather. Among the players George helped develop in the fledgling league were Gene Alley, Donn Clendenon, and Willie Stargell, who would return the Pirates to World Series glory in 1971 and 1979.

At about the same time Sis began devoting his regular-season baseball activities exclusively to St. Louis, Branch Rickey, now eighty-two, left

33. Quoted in the *Sporting News*, November 13, 1957, 26.
34. Ibid., December 11, 1957, 8.

Pittsburgh and returned to the St. Louis Cardinals, this time in an advisory capacity. Once again reunited in Missouri, the baseball vagabonds and their wives spent many evenings together playing bridge.

In late November 1965 the paths of Branch Rickey and George Sisler crossed one last time when the pair were inducted into the Missouri Sports Hall of Fame at a dinner in Columbia following the Mizzou-Oklahoma football clash of that year. Rickey had been ill and recently hospitalized, so many thought he would not make the 125-mile trip from St. Louis. Despite a colder than normal November day, he insisted on attending not only the evening banquet but also the afternoon football game, watching as the Tigers socked the Sooners 30–0.

At the banquet later that evening, the third honoree besides Sis and Rickey was the late J. G. Taylor Spink, the scion of the *Sporting News*. According to Baseball Hall of Fame sportswriter Bob Broeg, Rickey was sick, Sisler "wasn't much of a speaker, and Spink was dead," represented at the affair by his son. When it came time for the speeches, Rickey rose and told the crowd he was there "to be with immortals, because of George and Taylor." Then as he began to speak of spiritual courage, he staggered back a step, saying, "I don't believe I can continue..." These were his last words. He lapsed into a coma and died several weeks later.[35]

The experience of seeing his guiding light extinguished in front of him was for George profoundly sad. Never one to enjoy the limelight of the banquet circuit anyway, after Rickey's death he made attendance at such affairs the exception rather than the rule. In fact, pretty much his only public appearances from that time forward were frequent visits to the new Busch Stadium, home of the Cardinals, to scout on behalf of the Pirates. For a while, he was accompanied on these outings by Kathleen. Then later, when she tired of the grind and George no longer drove his own vehicle, he was provided a limousine service with regular driver Pete Turner. On these occasions he entered by special entrance through the Cardinals' front offices, passing by a deferential staff who stood in awe while the bashful, arthritic old sports hero with the squinting eyes slowly made his way to his seat, often in the company of his devoted grandson, Peter.[36]

35. Bob Broeg, *Memories of a Hall of Fame Sportswriter: An Autobiography*, 307–10.

36. Peter Drochelman, grandson of George Sisler, telephone interview with the author, December 3, 2001.

17

Family Man

When George and Kathleen returned to St. Louis in late 1957 to again make it their home, their first Thanksgiving Day back in the city was a very special one for the Sisler clan. By now, with the addition of wives for each of three boys and a husband for Frances, plus eight grandchildren, the immediate family numbered eighteen. All were present that November day for the reunion. By then Sis and Kathleen were in an apartment on Brighton Way in the suburb of Clayton. Later they would pay thirty-two thousand dollars to purchase a comfortable three-bedroom home at 1705 Pine Hill Drive in the west St. Louis suburb of Des Peres. This new location, only a block and a half from Frances, was close enough that the grand-kids could stop by for cookies frequently on their way home from school.

Despite his love for baseball, Sis never hid the fact that his family was clearly his first priority and their education of primary importance. "He was a very unique person," eldest son George, Jr. once said. "Back then, there weren't many college-educated ball players. He met Mom at Michigan, and they never stopped emphasizing the importance of education and doing the right thing."[1]

George, Sr. did not just talk about education. His parents instilled the educational drive in him at an early age, and he sought to pass that drive

1. Quoted in *Los Angeles Times*, September 15, 2000.

on to his children. In 1923 he and his friend Roland Hoerr joined a group of parents in founding the John Burroughs School on South Price Road in West St. Louis. The private school was progressive, nonsectarian, and college preparatory. At first for males only, the school later became coeducational. Through his status in the St. Louis community, Sis was able to raise considerable funds for the school over the years. The John Burroughs School remains a fixture in the community today. Each of the four Sisler children attended. The three boys, to no one's surprise, participated extensively in athletics with much success. All of the children fulfilled their parents' wish and attended college.

From 1915 to 1932 Sis spent a good deal of each year either preparing for baseball or playing it. The profession left little time for normal parenting. But he still made every effort to raise his children in the best manner possible. Each of the children has special memories of their "Pop," and each has a fine record of accomplishment. For the Sislers, "family" was definitely a two-way street.

Born in 1917, George, Jr. had the most personal experience with his Dad's professional playing career. He recalls going to Sportsman's Park as a youngster and thrilling to the sound of thunderous applause when his father strode to the plate to hit. "That's my Dad!" he marveled, realizing when he heard the ovation, saw the name in the paper, or walked into the park for free, that his father was someone special.[2]

The winter his father managed the club in the four-team California League, George, Jr. accompanied his mother and father to the West Coast. They stayed in Laguna Beach. George, Jr., perhaps ten at the time, bought a number of local newspapers and resold them, pocketing the difference. It was a learning experience his father heartily endorsed.

The oldest son recalls his father was a strict disciplinarian. When he had something to say, he said it forcefully, but he also enjoyed a good laugh, even at his own expense. He would often impress Junior's friends by leaning back on his shoulders into almost a prone position and then flip himself forward, landing on his feet.

One time Sis was trying to teach his kids how to ski. They did not have bindings at that time, but used a loop to insert the feet into the skis. As Sis tried to put his foot through one ski to demonstrate, the ski took off down the hill by itself. They all laughed, their father most of all. Then there was the game of "catch Pop," where Junior and his siblings recklessly chased their father in, on, and around their Pershing Avenue home. Sis would

2. George Sisler, Jr., interview with author, Columbus, Ohio, November 7, 2002.

risk life, limb, and most of Kathleen's best furniture to evade capture. Often the chase would end in uproarious laughter and many a fond memory.

George, Jr. went along with the family when Sis was traded to Boston, living with his parents at the Brandon Hall Hotel. One day his "Pop" took him to Fenway Park to see the Yankees play the Red Sox. Before the game, Sis called Babe Ruth over and introduced him to his son. Ruth lifted the youth over the railing and took him down to the dugout to introduce him to the other players. It was obvious to Junior that Babe loved kids, but his father often remarked that Ruth and the other players often went their separate ways, for instance, traveling in different cabs.[3]

George, Jr. was still hanging out with his dad in 1932 when Sis was performing his last services as a player/manager at Shreveport. Sis was still going full tilt, or at least trying to, in one contest when he was called out at third trying to stretch a double into something more.

"Never mind, Pop," Junior yelled with as much optimism as he could muster. "They wouldn't've thrown you out a few years ago!" George always denied he chased Junior out of the dugout that day. "I may have sent George [Jr.] out for an ice-cream cone or something, on that occasion," is the most he will admit, "but he was in no real physical danger."[4]

Certainly some of the exposure to baseball at its highest levels had to rub off on George, Jr. and later his younger brothers. By the time Junior was in high school, he was a star pitcher for the John Burroughs varsity. Sis, however, saw few of the games. Furthermore, he did little or no coaching. When he talked of his son's baseball success, he quietly beamed with pride but took little credit. "I really never was able to play with the older ones [Junior and Dick], so the most we did was just talk, and I tried to answer questions rather than offer advice."[5]

"Frankly, I have never encouraged my sons to go in for the game," he once said. "If they've got it in them, I'll find out in time. It's silly to think you can take a boy and by practice and instruction develop him into a future big league player. . . . [I]n fairness to the boy, it is best to let him alone until he is old enough to show positive signs of his ability."[6]

Still, it was with keen interest that Sis followed Junior's progress in high school and then at Colgate, where again he starred on the mound and played the outfield. Then in the summer of 1939 a conflict in schedules really sorted out the family's priority system, leaving an everlasting

3. Ibid., September 18, 2001.
4. Quoted in Mann, "Baseball's Amazing Sislers," 87.
5. Quoted in Broeg, "Gorgeous George," 29.
6. *Sporting News*, March 15, 1934, 8.

impression on George, Jr. By unfortunate coincidence, Sis's induction to the Hall of Fame and Junior's college graduation fell on the same day. Certainly Kathleen would remain with George, Sr. to view the induction ceremony, perhaps her husband's greatest day.

"Colgate was about 100 miles away from Cooperstown and I really didn't know what would happen. But my mother chose to attend my graduation and not my father's induction. I consider that one of the very greatest things to ever happen to me, and it said a lot about what we valued."[7]

George, Jr. carried that lesson in family values through his life. It led him for a time into minor-league baseball as a player in the St. Louis Browns organization, where he played for a season with mixed results, realizing that with his poor eyesight he probably was not a big-league prospect. He soon discovered his legacy was in the administration of minor-league baseball. Branch Rickey, as a longtime family friend, was familiar with George, Jr. In 1940 Rickey hired him as the business manager for the Cardinals' Albany, Georgia, affiliate. Along the way, he went to Winston-Salem in the Carolina League, where the club broke an attendance record. While performing his administrative duties, Junior even got into a few games as perhaps baseball's only playing executive and found a lovely wife in Elizabeth. Before long, he was in the Cardinals' front office, scouting and coordinating tryouts.

Eventually, after fruitful stops in a number of minor-league baseball cities, George, Jr. landed in Rochester, New York, as the general manager of the Red Wings, his father's former outfit, which had become a Cardinals' top-level franchise in the International League. He spent approximately eleven years in Rochester in that capacity, sculpting the team into one of the minor leagues' glamour franchises. His work in Rochester earned him a place in the club's Hall of Fame and caught the eye of International League officials to the extent he became the league's president, serving an additional eleven years in that office. His last stop was in 1977 in Columbus, Ohio, where for thirteen seasons, until 1989, he served as the general manager of the highly successful Columbus Clippers, a Yankee affiliate. As a multiple recipient of minor-league baseball's Executive of the Year award, he was strongly considered for the post of general manager of the Yanks, his father's old nemesis. The slot was eventually filled by Gene Michaels.

Although George, Jr. did not play major-league baseball, other Sisler offspring did, including Junior's next youngest sibling, Dick. Born three

7. Quoted in *Los Angeles Times,* September 15, 2000.

years after Junior in 1920, Dick was an all-sport star in high school at John Burroughs, making his mark in football, basketball, track, and, of course, baseball. After graduation, Dick followed in his older brother's footsteps, accepting a scholarship to Colgate. When George, Jr. graduated from college and headed to the minors, Dick could not wait. He jumped too, probably much to his parents' chagrin, leaving Colgate and its cozy environs for a taste of the professional game.

Unlike his brother, who signed first with the Browns and later worked for the Cardinals, Dick immediately signed with the Cards. Like his brother, Dick found the early going difficult. Some of the tough sledding stemmed from his last name. As he toiled in the lower minors, Dick was taunted by teammates and opponents alike. "You've got to earn your own way in this league. Why don't you let your Dad field for you?" were typical comments.

Dick did not take kindly to the jabs. "I love my Dad," he told one writer. "I admire his baseball ability. But I got fed up with having his name thrown at me everywhere I went."[8]

Ironically, Dick pretty much made it on his own without his father's help. He and his father were always with different clubs, "and I wasn't able to take him aside for special instruction," George, Sr. said. They would see each other in the winter and talk about hitting, but according to Sis, "you must watch a man close-up for awhile, stand by his side and see that he does the right things," to really contribute much to his success.[9]

Despite the rocky start, Dick stuck it out, six years in all. After stops in Albany, Georgia, Lansing, Michigan, and Asheville, North Carolina, where he met his wife, Dorothy, and time off for three years in the Navy, he made his major-league debut with the Cardinals in 1946 as a first baseman and an outfielder. In eight major-league seasons, he hit .276 with 55 home runs and 360 runs batted in. In his first season with the Cardinals, he played for a World Champion, something his father never accomplished.

In 1947, Dick's second season with the Cardinals, the twenty-six-year-old first baseman injured his ankle. His replacement was Stan Musial, and Dick got "Wally Pipped." In the spring of 1948, Dick was traded to the Phillies for Ralph Lapointe and cash. Although he hit fairly well that year (.274), the Phils were apparently not satisfied. In late 1948 they obtained Eddie Waitkus, a good first baseman and perennial frontline performer for the Cubs. Then, tragically, Waitkus was shot by a deranged girl

8. Stan Baumgartner, "Like Sisler, Like Son," 87.
9. Quoted in the *Sporting News*, March 10, 1954, 7.

in Chicago, keeping Dick in the lineup at first base through 1949. He hit rather well at .289 and helped the team to a third-place finish. Yet in 1950 he found a place back on the bench while a recovered Waitkus started.

Frustrated with lack of playing time, Dick approached Phillies' management and reminded them he was originally an outfielder. They gave him a shot in the outfield. He responded with a career year, hitting .296 with 13 home runs and 83 runs batted in. The effort was enough to earn a slot on the National League All-Star team, something the big leagues did not have in his father's day. When he entered the midsummer classic in the late innings as a pinch hitter, Dick singled to aid a then rare National League victory.

Dick's greatest moment, however, and certainly one of Sis and Kathleen's greatest sports thrills, came on October 1, 1950, in Ebbets Field, home of the Dodgers, his father's employer at the time. The Phils, better known that year as the "Whiz Kids," held a narrow one-game lead over the Dodgers on this, the last day of the regular season. The Phillies sent their ace Robin Roberts to the mound. The Dodgers countered with the great Don Newcombe. Shortstop Pee Wee Reese tied the game in the sixth inning and lost a chance to win it when center fielder Richie Ashburn rifled a throw to nip Cal Abrams at the plate. The game went to the top of the ninth still tied, and two runners were on base when Dick Sisler, the Phils' left fielder, took his turn at the plate. Sis and Kathleen were, of course, present, but sitting in Branch Rickey's box, apart from others in the Dodger official family and "not knowing how to act." They wanted the Dodgers to win, but for Dick to play well, also. Only part of that wish was fulfilled. Beaming with pride, the couple watched as their second son hit a high Newcombe fastball into the left field bleachers for a dramatic home run and a Phillies pennant clincher. Sis recalled, "The cameras were on me to get my reactions. I sat with a straight face, with no reactions at all...an actor for the first time in my life," as he and the proud mother "celebrated with silence."[10]

The home run was the highlight of Dick's career. The Yankees swept his Phils in four to win the 1950 World Series. Dick was only able to scratch out one hit in seventeen at bats against the likes of Vic Raschi, Allie Reynolds, Eddie Lopat, and a rookie named Whitey Ford. Three years later, his playing career was over. In 1957 he resurfaced as the new manager of the Nashville Vols, a Cincinnati Reds affiliate. He was in Nashville through 1959 before returning to the majors as a coach and, in one more irony, a

10. Sisler Memoirs, 18.

hitting instructor. In spite of indications to the contrary, Dick graciously credited his dad for instilling his knowledge of hitting, telling his boss, General Manager Bill DeWitt of the Reds, he had received "a million dollars of information about hitting from the 'Old Master.'"[11] In 1964 Dick was still coaching with the Reds when Manager Fred Hutchinson took ill in midseason. Dick replaced him. This marked the first time in major-league history that a father and a son had each served as big-league managers. The Sislers held that distinction until 2002 when Joel Skinner, the son of big-league player and manager Bob Skinner, was appointed interim skipper of the Cleveland Indians.

The Reds played at a .604 clip for Dick in the fifty-three games left in 1964, and he was retained for 1965. The 1965 edition of the Reds finished in fourth place at 89–73. Dick was replaced in 1966 by Don Heffner. Despite a decent managerial record, he never managed in the big leagues again, returning to Nashville to raise a large family. In November 1998 he passed away at age seventy-eight.

George and Kathleen's daughter, Frances, was born in 1922 at the peak of her father's playing career. Although she does not recall ever seeing her father play the game, she was surrounded by baseball and the life of a professional ballplayer as she grew up. "We'd be sitting around the dinner table and he'd always be talking baseball with my brothers and I'd get so sick of it," she recalled. "But the important thing is that we'd always have dinner together—the family. His family was important to him."[12]

Perhaps this was regularly the case after Sis's retirement in 1932, but not nearly so often when he was still an active player. There were always the road trips, travel by train when Frances's dad was gone for weeks at a time. After July 4 when school was out, Frances and her mom would pack up and head for Birmingham, Michigan, near Detroit, the home of Frances's maternal grandparents. Kathleen drove the family car. They would remain in Michigan for the summer with the boys either at camp or with them. When her dad played in Detroit, he would get to see them.

When her father retired, he had time on his hands. She remembered that he did not work around the yard or build things, but he liked to read, mostly nonfiction. He had a wry sense of humor. Table manners were a priority for "Gentleman George," but not without an occasional lapse. Often at the dinner table, he would draw a laugh by quietly bringing his

11. *Sporting News,* April 26, 1950, 5.
12. *Los Angeles Times,* September 15, 2000.

finger to the side of his nose and keeping it there until one of the kids would see it and copy him, followed by the others.[13]

Like her brothers, Frances attended John Burroughs School, by then coeducational. She attended McMurray College in Jacksonville, Illinois, for a year, but dropped out during the war. In 1943 she married William Drochelman. They raised a family of three in St. Louis. Sis, who numerous times made the ninety-foot walk from home plate to first base without a care, called his walk down the aisle at the Lutheran Church at Big Bend and Forsyth in St. Louis with his "beautiful bride" daughter "the longest 'walk'" he ever took, and undoubtedly the proudest.[14]

The Sisler's youngest son, David, was born in October of 1931, shortly after Sis's first minor-league stop at Rochester. Sis quit baseball one year later and was essentially divorced from organized baseball during his youngest son's early years. David, of course, heard stories of his father's baseball prowess, but on one particular occasion he had to wonder just what was fact and what was fiction. He and his father were outside playing catch near their home on Pershing. "Pop" failed to grab a simple toss. Before he could think David blurted, "Gosh, how did you ever play baseball!" Sis, a guy who found it difficult to accept a .345 batting average, didn't hesitate. He put down his glove and walked into the house. Neither David nor his brothers ever saw him with the glove again.[15]

When David was a kid, his dad was still involved with the sporting goods business. As a result, David Sisler had the best sports equipment around. On a daily basis, Sis would ride a bus downtown to his sporting goods store. As a rule, in the evening when the bus dropped him off, his son David would meet him and they would walk home together.[16] In a small way, by this simple act of bonding, perhaps Sis made up for a good deal of the time he had missed with his children as he traveled each summer, a veritable baseball nomad.

David recalls that his father was quite frugal. Although his salary through his baseball years and the income derived from the printing and sporting goods businesses was well above the average, the Sislers of Pershing Avenue lived a middle-class lifestyle. There were no fancy vacations. "My father was the most conservative person in the world," David told one reporter. "But he was just an absolute gentleman. He was the

13. Frances Drochelman, telephone interview with the author, November 23, 2001.
14. Sisler Memoirs, 28.
15. Quoted in Salant, *Superstars, Stars, and Just Plain Heroes,* 39.
16. David M. Sisler, telephone interview with the author, November 20, 2001.

nicest person and had scruples like you wouldn't believe. All he ever tried to do was pass that on to his kids."[17]

When it came to baseball, however, Sis handled David the same as George, Jr. and Dick. He pretty much "let me develop myself."[18] And develop David most certainly did. At the John Burroughs School, he excelled on the playing field and in the classroom. While Sis and Kathleen were in Brooklyn with the Rickeys, David stayed in St. Louis with a friend to complete his high school education. Based upon his high marks, Princeton offered a scholarship, and he took it. Much like his father, David was a college pitcher who enjoyed great success. As a freshman in 1950, he won nine games, including two shutouts and a no-hitter. On the varsity his next two years, he won thirteen and lost four with a 1.23 earned run average. He also played a mean game of basketball, averaging ten points per game his junior year as Princeton won their conference title. In school he was a "high honor" student and president of his sophomore and junior classes.

Carrying the Sisler name on a six-foot, four-inch, two-hundred-pound frame, it was impossible for young David to escape the eye of big-league scouts. After all, he had pitched batting practice in summer to the likes of Jackie Robinson while visiting his parents in Brooklyn. His natural ability caught the eye of Branch Rickey. In 1951, Rickey, now with the Pirates, offered him a contract. David was flattered but at that point, like his dad, he wanted to finish college, which he could not do as a professional.

In the fall of 1952, prior to his senior year, all that changed, however. Sis and George, Jr., at the time in the Cardinals front office, learned that legislation was on the horizon that would severely restrict bonuses for young ballplayers. It made no sense to pass up a hefty bonus if offered. The Red Sox made the best offer, forty thousand dollars, and Sis's youngest child was a professional ballplayer at age twenty-one.

Publicity over the signing of young David Sisler was widespread. Much was made of the family line, much more so than with his older brothers. Through the years the sons of well-known big-league ballplayers had broken into the profession with great fanfare. To date, none, including David's brother Dick, had really made the grade in a big way. It was almost to the point where famous bloodlines were becoming a distinct drawback.

The story is told that Fresco Thompson, a Dodger vice-president who liked a good laugh, scouted David during the 1951 college tournament in

17. *Los Angeles Times*, September 15, 2000.
18. David Sisler, telephone interview.

Omaha, Nebraska. He liked what he saw of his old opponent's offspring, but was constrained to write, "The boy has a *fair* chance, if the strain of heredity is not too strong. There is a rumor that his father once had some connections with baseball."

When Sis heard Thompson's assessment, he was not so constrained. In a rare fit of pique, he shot back a response: "It's quite obvious that Fresco is still bitter over the news that his daughter, Ann, failed to make her high-school softball team."[19]

Alas, when his career is reviewed in retrospect, David Sisler was not the son who broke the chain of heirs who fell short of their father's glory. It would take another forty years until Barry Bonds and Ken Griffey, Jr., truly broke that barrier, although three generations of Boones (Ray, son Bob, and grandsons Brett and Aaron) could also stake a solid claim. In seven big-league seasons following military service in the Army, David's pitching record with the Red Sox, Tigers, Senators, and Reds was 38–44. A starter early in his career with the Red Sox, he enjoyed his best season in 1960 in Detroit, as a reliever with a 7–5 record, six saves, and a 2.48 earned run average. Following his career, David returned to St. Louis, married Janet, started a family, and embarked on a very successful career as an executive with the brokerage firm of A. G. Edwards and Sons.

When the Sisler family record is summarized, one finds three sons who made baseball either part or all of their careers. It was not a bad showing for a father who claims he "never tried in any way to influence their thinking on entering the sport as a profession." Still, the final take on baseball and the "boys" must be left to their mother, Kathleen, an extremely shy lady who was rarely photographed and seldom quoted, except when it concerned her children. As to Sis's reluctance to coax his boys into playing his sport, she told a reporter, "He didn't have to. George was such a wonderful father that each of the boys wanted to be just like him."[20]

19. Quoted in Mann, "Baseball's Amazing Sislers," 36.
20. Quoted in the *Sporting News*, December 11, 1957.

18

Historically Speaking

On March 27, 1973, sports pages around the country carried the sad news of the passing of George Sisler the previous day. He had turned eighty just two days before, after spending the eight days prior to his death as a patient at St. Mary's Hospital in the St. Louis suburb of Richmond Heights. He entered the hospital in a "generally run down condition" according to hospital officials and, in fact, was on the critical list on his birthday. He showed some improvement right before he succumbed. The immediate cause of death was kidney failure, caused by an underlying vascular disease.[1]

Several members of George's family were at his bedside when he passed, including his daughter, Frances, youngest son, David, and his beloved Kathleen, who was to outlive her husband by almost seventeen years. She died in St. Louis on February 7, 1990.

Following cremation a memorial service was held for George in St. Louis shortly after his death. At the services Carey Browne, a Christian Science practitioner, read several passages about George from *The American Diamond* by Branch Rickey, the man who knew more about the combination

1. *New York Daily News*, March 27, 1973; Death Certificate, Missouri Division of Health, Date of Death—March 26, 1973, George Harold Sisler, Retired—Professional Baseball Player and Executive.

of Sis the man and Sis the ballplayer than anyone else. That he was Rickey's favorite ballplayer was clearly established and well documented, but what about the opinions of other equally knowledgeable baseball experts?

In general, Sis's passing was noted by the sporting world as the passing of a Hall of Famer of a bygone era. As in life, George's playing ability was in the first instance compared and contrasted with that of Ruth, Cobb, and Hornsby. The *New York Times,* however, went further, recalling that Sis was "a man of compact build with extraordinary reflexes and grace" who "could do it all, long before that phrase became a cliché."[2]

A few weeks later, the *Sporting News* weighed in. Their editorial, entitled "Sisler—A Rugged Gentleman," told readers that "[n]obody hit the ball farther than Ruth, and no one hit it more consistently than Sisler." That both were initially pitchers who made their mark hitting was where the similarities ended, however. Ruth was "the carouser, crowd pleaser, instinctive athlete and product of the Baltimore waterfront; Sisler the college graduate, thinker, student of baseball and quiet gentleman." Recalling that Rickey chose Sis as his all-time favorite player because of his "high qualifications as a man," the editors asked that this superb hitter and extraordinary first baseman "be remembered above all as a model athlete and exemplary man, on the field and off it. . . . Some say baseball could use more 'colorful characters' of days gone by. Maybe so, but these days it's reassuring to know we've also had in our midst some solid citizens, of whom George Sisler was a prime example."[3]

It has now been well over a quarter of a century since George's death. Despite the passing years, statistically he still ranks quite high among the all-time leaders. His career batting average, .340, is tied with Lou Gehrig for fourteenth all-time and third for first basemen, trailing only fellow Hall of Famers Dan Brouthers, who played in the 1800s, and Bill Terry. Although he attended four years of college and missed a full season in his prime due to illness, George ranks ninetieth in at bats, ninety-ninth in runs scored, forty-first in hits, eighty-seventh in doubles, and thirtieth in triples. His career at-bats-per-strikeout mark is 25.32, ranking nineteenth all-time. He also stands seventy-fifth in runs created and eighty-first in runs produced. He is seventy-eighth in stolen bases and eighth in steals of home with twenty. In fielding, he stands fourth all-time in assists as a first baseman after leading the American League in that category in 1919, 1920, 1922, 1924, 1925, and 1927.

2. *New York Times,* March 27, 1973.
3. *Sporting News,* April 14, 1973, editorial page.

While George's lifetime stats are certainly noteworthy, some of his single-season statistics, all accumulated playing a 154-game schedule, are spectacular. His 257 safeties in 1920 remain a modern-era record (the all-time record of 275 was set by Pete Browning and Tip O'Neill in 1887) and are the main source of what little interest is still shown in his career. The last real challenger to his mark was Bill Terry, who had 254 hits in 1930. Darrin Erstad, playing the current 162-game season, made a run at the record in 2000, but fell short at 240. In fact, George's 1922 hit total of 248 remains the twelfth best single-season total. In that season he was on target for 260 hits when injured.

Much more highly publicized and seemingly untouchable records from the Sisler years, such as the Babe's home run records, Gehrig's consecutive games played streak, and a slew of others are now history, but Sis's single-season hit total remains untouched. Perhaps it deserves a higher standing in the hierarchy of baseball's "Hall of Statistics."

As of 2003 George's .420 average in 1922 remains the eleventh-highest batting average all-time and third highest of the modern era. It is the second highest American League average, bowing only to Napoleon Lajoie's .426 in 1901. Sis's .407 in 1920 is twenty-second all-time and stands seventh in modern times. That Ted Williams at .406 in 1941 is the last player to hit .400 or better should raise additional eyebrows when reviewing the record of a player who hit well above .400 twice. Only Ty Cobb, Rogers Hornsby, and Ed Delahanty (pre-1900) exceeded that mark, while Jesse Burkett (pre-1900) and Sam Thompson (pre-1900) equaled it.

There are several other single-season categories in which George's statistics still rank high. His 1920 total of forty-nine doubles is tied for sixty-fifth, while his 399 total bases that season rests in a tie for twenty-seventh. Sis's on-base percentage of .467 in 1922 ranks seventy-ninth, not a bad figure for a man who seldom walked.[4]

Naturally, since Sis was not a home run hitter, his name is missing from a number of all-time statistical categories. How much did Sis's lack of long-ball punch and his penchant for avoiding the walk hurt his overall rating? It hurt a lot, according to well-known statistician Bill James, the author of The New Bill James Historical Abstract, published in 2001. In it James calls George "[p]erhaps the most over-rated player in baseball history," pointing out that Sis's high averages and resulting admiration were accumulated at a time when there were no statisticians like himself to

4. Career and Single Season Statistical All-Time Leaders from John Shorn, Pete Palmer, and Michael Gershman, eds., Total Baseball: Seventh Edition.

point out that batting average "is less than half of a player's overall offense." In that regard, James highlights Sis's career on-base percentage, saying it is lower than more than a hundred players whose career average was under .300. Also by James's statistical model, Sis was not the great fielder others claimed. Thus, in James's opinion, Sis is only the twenty-fourth greatest first baseman of all time.[5]

James is entitled to his opinion, and his opinion is a well-regarded one at that. But isn't this the same Bill James who in *The Bill James Historical Abstract,* published in 1988, told his readers that under his system of evaluation at that time, George "is probably the only player other than [Lou] Gehrig who can reasonably be considered the greatest first baseman ever in terms of peak value"? In James's opinion, Sis was "a different type of player; he didn't have the home run pop, but he hit for a higher average, was faster and a better defensive player than Gehrig." These were all attributes that James either forgot or disregarded a decade later when he ignominiously dropped Sisler way down in his new rating system. Furthermore, in 1988 James reminded readers that "[u]nlike [Harry] Heilmann and to a lesser extent Hornsby, who became batting terrors after they began keeping fresh balls in play in 1920, Sisler was a great hitter in the dead-ball era, posting averages of .353, .341, and .352 (with a .530 slugging percentage) in the years 1917–19." Finally, James quite fairly looks at the effect George's eye problems had on his career and estimates that a healthy Sis "would have gotten over 4,000 hits and hit about .362" for his career, and yet "the peak of performance that he did reach before the illness marks him as arguably the greatest first baseman of all time."[6] It thus appears if anyone can be accused of overrating George Harold Sisler, it is Bill James himself.

So when a highly acclaimed baseball analyst is so conflicted in rating a player, where does that leave the rest of us? Perhaps the final analysis should be left to those who saw the subject play or who played against him, managed him, or wrote about him. Dr. Johnny Lavan, Sis's teammate at Michigan and later with the Browns, compared Sis to Cobb, stating he came closer to the legend than any other player, lacking "only the Georgian's fire." Fielder Jones, Sis's manager with the Browns for two seasons before walking out of the clubhouse, went several steps further, rating George the greatest ballplayer of all time.[7]

5. Bill James, *The New Bill James Historical Baseball Abstract,* 441.
6. Bill James, *The Bill James Historical Baseball Abstract,* 346–47.
7. Quoted in Grayson, *They Played the Game,* 137.

Branch Rickey's flattering comments about his favorite player are already well documented. More than one player, however, recognized that what Rickey termed the "ideal" temperament for a ballplayer also could work as a drawback. "He lacked the fiery flamboyance of Ty Cobb and the boisterous brilliance of Babe Ruth," Hall of Fame contemporary Eddie Collins once said. "George was a great first baseman, and a great hitter, but he was too quiet and clean-living to win headlines." It was the same temperament that made him so ideal that cost him the headlines and probably more than anything else made him "[t]he most under-publicized athlete ever to play," according to White Sox Hall of Fame pitcher Ted Lyons. And thus he truly was "a legendary player without a legend."[8]

But that did not mean Sisler was underappreciated by even those stars who overshadowed him. Both Cobb and Hornsby named Sis as the first baseman on their all-time all-star teams. He reciprocated in kind in his baseball manual, naming each among his all-time greats, declining to name a team position by position.[9] In addition, Sis was named an all-time all-star on countless other teams selected by various writers, players, and publications. Election to the Missouri (1965) and Summit County, Ohio (1957) sports halls of fame, as well as to the Akron Baseball Hall of Fame (1983), plus an Akron ballpark named in his honor complete the list. In 1988 the *Sporting News* named him Number 33 on its list of the 100 Greatest Players of the Twentieth Century. In connection with the turn of the century, a postage stamp was even issued in his honor by the U.S. Postal Service as a Legend of Baseball. Anonymity for George Sisler definitely did not equal being left out.

As stated earlier, to Rickey, Sisler was "the smartest hitter that ever lived." He was also, according to Hall of Famer Paul Waner, one of the greatest fielding first basemen he had ever seen. Much of George's aura as a fielder centered on his gracefulness afield. "He was," according to the fiery Frankie Frisch, who was the epitome of all-around greatness, "poetry in motion, the perfect player."[10] If that sounds familiar, Frisch's words echo those of Ty Cobb.

Sportswriter Tommy Holmes said much the same about Sis, but in harsher terms, telling readers that "Sisler was so perfect a player that it

8. Collins is quoted in Salant, *Superstars, Stars, and Just Plain Heroes*, 36. Lyons is quoted in the *Akron Beacon Journal*, December 24, 1999. The final quote is from Honig, *The Greatest First Basemen of All Time*, 21.

9. Sisler, *Sisler on Baseball*, 181, 213.

10. Rickey is quoted in Meany, *Baseball's Greatest Hitters*, 183. Frisch is quoted in "Broeg on Baseball" by Bob Broeg, *Sporting News*, April 21, 1973, 10.

was almost dull to watch him." Red Barber was kinder, labeling George "the most graceful good hitter...baseball ever saw." And closer to home, J. Roy Stockton of the *Post-Dispatch*, admitting his prejudice, wrote that after watching forty years of baseball, including twenty-nine World Series, he had "never seen a first baseman so skilled, so versatile, so stalwart on the attack and so deft defensively, as Sisler."[11]

And yet despite all these acts of commission, there is one glaring omission in George's résumé as a player. He is generally considered the greatest ballplayer never to play in a World Series. It is, to say the least, a dubious honor that he would have happily shared or even deferred to the likes of Harry Heilman, Ted Lyons, Luke Appling, Ernie Banks, or Ralph Kiner. Lack of World Series credentials for such a star player, once described as similar to a "picture without a frame," has only further served to wrap Sisler's otherwise stellar career in brown paper. As Tom Seaver once said, "There are only two places in the league. First and no place."[12] As a player, Sis never sipped the fine wine that awaits those at the summit and as such was left with a bitter aftertaste.

In capsule form, George Harold Sisler achieved a short-lived brilliance. In 1922 he was generally considered the greatest living ballplayer, but a few months later he was stricken with illness. A career .360 hitter before that illness with 1,498 hits in eight seasons, he was a .319 hitter with 1,314 hits in seven seasons thereafter. For a few years, he was the toast of St. Louis, only to be moved to the back burner by the magnificence of Rogers Hornsby and later Stan Musial. He was called baseball's best-ever first baseman, but in short order he was vastly overshadowed by Lou Gehrig. And yet through it all he never lost his spirit, battling back from a career-threatening disability to play an outstanding brand of baseball for a number of years, maintaining a friendship with Hornsby that even found the men playing together in the twilight of his career and, in a generally unknown way, even assisting the rise to prominence of his first base rival Gehrig.

It was Lou Gehrig who came forward to offer his thanks. One day while George, Jr. was a student at Colgate, he was called to the athletic director's office to give a special guest a tour of the campus. It turned out to be a command performance for a visiting Gehrig. Lou had heard that Sis's son was on campus and saw an opportunity to pay his respect. When Lou and George, Sr. played baseball, most players closely guarded their knowledge

11. Holmes is quoted in *The World Series: A 75th Anniversary*, 20. Barber, *Walk in the Spirit*, 71; Stockton, in Walsh, comp. and ed., *Baseball's Greatest Lineup*, 75.
12. Quoted in Thorn et al., *Total Baseball*, 2467.

of the game. Players seldom shared that knowledge with others. Lou wanted George, Jr. to know that his father was the only player "who helped him, gave him tips on how to play first base, and he'd never forget that."[13]

Off and on through the years, usually when some player is making a run at the single-season hit record, Sisler's star briefly glimmers. Never was this more so than in 1941 when Joe DiMaggio charged after and surpassed George's American League record of forty-one consecutive games hit in safely. George, Jr. was worried about his father's reaction during DiMaggio's chase. His worries were for naught. George told his son he was happy that a great player like DiMaggio was the one who bested his mark. He wanted the record broken by an "outstanding player, rather than some young kid on a fluke."[14]

The same holds true if someone finally breaks Sis's single season hit record. "He'd wonder what all the fuss was about," his daughter, Frances, said. "He was," according to son David, "always the last person to care about things like that."[15]

He might feel the same way about a biography. In other words, why is there all this fuss? And anyway, what about his situation as an overlooked piece of baseball history would George change if he had the chance? After all, his reserved demeanor and moral rectitude were as much a part of him as his great natural athletic ability. His old teammate Baby Doll Jacobson told him on the occasion of their last hurrah in January 1971, when Sis asked if he had any regrets, "Maybe I wish the fellows today would think a little bit more about us old guys . . . but no, I wouldn't change a thing."[16] George might well agree.

But even if Sisler would be willing to accept his slow fade into sports oblivion, should we as sports fans? At one time Sisler regularly shared bold headlines and newsprint with Babe Ruth and Ty Cobb in news journals and magazines across the country. At times he outshone each of them. In the long run, for various reasons, including four years of college ball and illness, he did not quite possess their longevity, or their greatness. It is, however, safe to assume that had he kicked up a greater fuss either on or off the field, he would be far better remembered and perhaps even more highly regarded for what he did accomplish.

Our fascination with curmudgeons and ball-playing bad boys is nothing new. As far back as 1921, Hugh Jennings accurately predicted Sisler's

13. Quoted in *Hartford Courant*, August 13, 2000.
14. Ibid.
15. Quoted in *Los Angeles Times*, September 15, 2000.
16. Quoted in Godin, *The 1922 St. Louis Browns*, 212–13.

fate when he compared him to Cobb and found George wanting in only one aspect: color. Career statistics were of no mind—Jennings needn't wait to find out, because "Cobb outclasses Sisler in his direct appeal to the public." The fact that Cobb waged war when he stepped onto the ball field thrilled the fans, leaving them breathless. Babe Ruth's tape measure clouts sent shivers down their spines. This is all the paying public saw or, for that matter, wanted. The exploits of these two men satisfied a yearning in all of us to find heroes that are bigger than ordinary life as we know it. At the same time, in order to satisfy this urge we seem willing to minimize the character flaws and misdeeds of these same heroes, often even fondly incorporating their failings into a lasting legacy. It is because of this attitude that a teammate of the Babe could say with smiling admiration, "All of the lies about him are true."[17]

A legend is defined by Webster on the one hand as a story or body of stories coming down from the past. As baseball's greatest we have the Babe and Cobb; the stuff of legends, despite substantial personal flaws, by virtue of intriguing stories passed down from one generation of fans to the next, and often amplified in the retelling. As a result, each man has become bigger than life.

A legend, nevertheless, is also defined as the person who inspires those stories. Would we not be better off if our inspirations are more often the Christy Mathewsons, Walter Johnsons, Lou Gehrigs, and George Sislers of the game, even if their exploits on the field were not quite at Ruthian/Cobbian levels? In that world good sportsmanship, clean living, and family values finds greater fan favor, becoming the stuff of legends as well. This is not to say that Mathewson, Sisler, and the like were not well thought of and idolized by the multitudes during their time, but rather that fame achieved by fine workmanlike play on the field and decent scandal-free living off it is far more often fleeting than its flashier, bawdier opposite.

In its obituary for Sisler, the *Sporting News* asked that he be remembered as a "model athlete," an "exemplary man," and a "solid citizen." It is more than a bit ironic that for being all those things, yet not more flamboyant or controversial, he is essentially a forgotten great. As one writer put it, "Perhaps if Sisler had hit homeruns instead of triples, he would be remembered as the Babe Ruth of St. Louis. Perhaps an occasional slide into third base with his spikes up would have elevated him to Cobbian status. Maybe a fight or two, and some choice language for Judge Landis, would have

---

17. Interview with Hugh Jennings, March 1921, 468; Seymour, *Baseball: The Golden Age*, 80–81; Ruth teammate Joe Dugan quoted in Benjamin G. Rader, *Baseball: A History of America's Game*, 124.

put him above Rogers Hornsby. And, if the sinusitis that ruined his career had caused his premature death, he might have outshone Gehrig."[18]

But these are all things that might have been. The reality is that in 1915 George Harold Sisler exploded onto the major-league baseball scene and affected the game in a positive manner for the next fifty-eight years. Ask anyone who really knew him or actually saw him play, and just like Baby Doll they will tell you that when it came to "The Sizzler," they would not change a thing.

18. Salant, *Superstars, Stars, and Just Plain Heroes,* 39.

Appendix

George Sisler
George Harold Sisler (Gorgeous George)

Bats Left, **Throws** Left
Height 5' 11", **Weight** 170 lb.

Debut June 28, 1915
Born March 24, 1893 in Manchester, OH
Died March 26, 1973 in Richmond Heights, MO

Inducted into the Hall of Fame in 1939.

Pitching**

Year	Ag	Tm	Lg	W	.L	G	GS	GF	CG	SHO	SV	IP	H	R	ER	HR	BB	SO	HBP	WP	BFP	ERA	*lgERA	*ERA+
1915	22	SLB	AL	4	4	15	8	3	6	0	0	70.0	62	26	22	0	38	41	4	1	293	2.83	2.87	101
1916	23	SLB	AL	1	2	3	3	0	3	1	0	27.0	18	4	3	0	6	12	1	0	98	1.00	2.74	273
1918	25	SLB	AL	0	0	2	1	1	0	0	1	8.0	10	6	4	0	4	4	1	1	41	4.50	2.74	60
1920	27	SLB	AL	0	0	1	0	1	0	0	1	1.0	0	0	0	0	0	2	0	0	4	0.00	3.90	inf
1925	32	SLB	AL	0	0	1	0	0	0	0	0	2.0	1	0	0	0	1	1	0	0	7	0.00	4.65	inf
1926	33	SLB	AL	0	0	1	0	1	0	0	1	2.0	0	0	0	0	2	3	0	0	7	0.00	4.30	inf
1928	35	BSN	NL	0	0	1	0	1	0	0	0	1.0	0	0	0	0	1	0	0	0	3	0.00	3.90	inf
7 Yr			WL% .455	5	6	24	12	8	9	1	3	111.0	91	36	29	0	52	63	6	2	453	2.35	2.91	124
162 Game Avg				9	11	45	22	15	17	1	5	209.7	171	68	54	0	98	119	11	3	855	2.35	2.91	124
Career High				4	4	15	8	3	6	1	1	70.0	62	26	22	0	38	41	4	1	293	2.83	2.87	101

* indicates the value is park adjusted
**See glossary

Statistics courtesy/**baseball-reference.com**

Pitching Glossary:

- Year - Year in which the season occurred
- Ag - Age the player was on June 30th of that year.
- Tm - Team they played for
- Lg - League they played in (AL- American League, NL- National League)
- W - Wins
- L - Losses
- G - Games pitched in
- GS - Games started
- GF - Games finished in relief (does not include complete games)
- CG - Complete Games
- SHO - Shutouts
- SV - Saves
- IP - Innings Pitched
- H - Hits
- R - Runs Allowed
- ER - Earned Runs Allowed
- HR - Home Runs
- BB - Base on Balls or Walks
- SO - Strikeouts or whiffs or K's
- ERA - Earned Run Average $9 * ER / IP$
- lgERA - Earned Run Average for a league average pitcher in that ballpark or combination of ballparks.
- ERA+ - the ratio of the league's ERA (adjusted to the pitcher's ballpark) to that of the pitcher. > 100 is above average and < 100 is below average. $lgERA / ERA$
- BFP - Batters Faced Pitching

Batting**

Year	Ag	Tm	Lg	G	AB	R	H	2B	3B	HR	RBI	SB	CS	BB	SO	BA	OBP	SLG	TB	SH	SF	IBB	HBP	GDP
1915	22	SLB	AL	81	274	28	78	10	2	3	29	10	9	7	27	.285	.307	.369	101	12			2	
1916	23	SLB	AL	151	580	83	177	21	11	4	76	34	26	40	37	.305	.355	.400	232	19			5	
1917	24	SLB	AL	135	539	60	190	30	9	2	52	37		30	19	.353	.390	.453	244	15			3	
1918	25	SLB	AL	114	452	69	154	21	9	2	41	45		40	17	.341	.400	.440	199	9			5	
1919	26	SLB	AL	132	511	96	180	31	15	10	83	28		27	20	.352	.390	.530	271	18			5	
1920	27	SLB	AL	154	631	137	257	49	18	19	122	42	17	46	19	.407	.449	.632	399	13			2	
1921	28	SLB	AL	138	582	125	216	38	18	12	104	35	11	34	27	.371	.411	.560	326	14			5	
1922	29	SLB	AL	142	586	134	246	42	18	8	105	51	19	49	14	.420	.467	.594	348	16			3	
1924	31	SLB	AL	151	636	94	194	27	10	9	74	19	17	31	29	.305	.340	.421	268	14			3	
1925	32	SLB	AL	150	649	100	224	21	15	12	105	11	12	27	24	.345	.371	.479	311	12			0	
1926	33	SLB	AL	150	613	78	178	21	12	7	71	12	8	30	30	.290	.327	.398	244	16			3	
1927	34	SLB	AL	149	614	87	201	32	8	5	97	27	7	24	15	.327	.357	.430	264	19			4	
1928	**35**	**WSH**	**AL**	**20**	**49**	**1**	**12**	**1**	**0**	**0**	**2**	**0**	**1**	**1**	**2**	**.245**	**.260**	**.265**	**13**	**1**			**0**	
		BSN	**NL**	**118**	**491**	**71**	**167**	**26**	**4**	**4**	**68**	**11**		**30**	**15**	**.340**	**.380**	**.434**	**213**	**14**			**2**	
		TOT		138	540	72	179	27	4	4	70	11	1	31	17	.331	.370	.419	226	15			2	
1929	36	BSN	NL	154	629	67	205	40	8	2	79	6		33	17	.326	.363	.424	267	20			4	
1930	37	BSN	NL	116	431	54	133	15	7	3	67	7		23	15	.309	.346	.397	171	14			2	
15 Seasons				2055	8267	1284	2812	425	164	102	1175	375	127	472	327	.340	.379	.468	3871	226	0	0	48	0
162 Game Avg			154		652	101	222	34	13	8	93	30	10	37	26	.340	.379	.468	305	18	0	0	4	0
Career High					649	137	257	49	18	19	122	51	26	49	37	.420	.467	.632	399	20	0	0	5	0

Year	Ag	Tm	Lg	G	AB	R	H	2B	3B	HR	RBI	SB	CS	BB	SO	BA	OBP	SLG	TB	SH	SF	IBB	HBP	GDP

Bold Text indicates partial season results.

Batting Glossary:

- Year - Year in which the season occurred
- Ag - Player age on July 1st of that year.
- Tm - Team they played for
- Lg - League they played in (AL- American League, NL- National League)
- G - Games played
- AB - At Bats
- R - Runs Scored
- H - Hits
- 2B - Doubles
- 3B - Triples
- HR - Home Runs
- RBI - Runs Batted in
- SB - Stolen Bases
- CS - Caught Stealing (were counted in the AL after 1919 and after 1950 in the NL)
- BB - Base on Balls or Walks
- SO - Strikeouts or whiffs or K's (are available hit and miss between 1882 and 1912, but are available for all other seasons)
- BA - Batting Average H/AB
- OBP - On-Base Percentage (H+BB+HBP)/(AB+BB+SF+HBP) (SF and HBP are assumed zero if unavailable, see SF and HBP below)
- SLG - Slugging Percentage TB/AB (see TB below)
- TB - Total Bases (Singles + 2*2B + 3*3B + 4*HR)
- SH - Sacrifice Hits or Bunts (were first counted in 1895 and includes Sac Flies until 1953)
- SF - Sacrifice Flies (were first counted in 1954, prior to that they were included in Sac Hits)
- HBP - Hit by Pitch (are available for every season after 1887)
- IBB - Intentional Base on Balls (were first counted in 1955)
- OPS - It doesn't appear here, but OPS is On-Base Percentage + Slugging Percentage. It is a pretty good estimate of offensive ability.
- Adjusted OPS+ - It doesn't appear on the player pages yet, but OPS+ is OPS (see above) normalized for both the park and the league the player played in.

Fielding ** **Bold Text** indicates partial season results. / * Indicates Innings Played rather than Games Played was used in Range Factor calculations.

Year	Ag	Tm	Lg	Pos	G	PO	A	E	DP	FP	lgFP	RnF	lgRnF	GS	Inn	LF	CF	RF
1915	22	SLB	AL	1B	36	357	18	4	20	.989	.987	10.42	10.27					
				OF	29	51	2	3	0	.946	.958	1.83	1.98			6	8	15
				P*	15	5	18	0	1	1.000	.937	2.96	3.01	8	70.0			
1916	23	SLB	AL	1B	141	1510	83	24	85	.985	.988	11.30	10.45					
				OF	3	6	1	0	2	1.000	.963	2.33	2.03			1	2	0
				P*	3	3	9	0	0	1.000	.945	4.00	2.97	3	27.0			
				3B	2	2	4	0	0	1.000	.939	3.00	3.25					
1917	24	SLB	AL	1B	133	1384	101	22	97	.985	.989	11.17	10.75					
				2B	2	2	5	2	0	.778	.959	3.50	4.95					
1918	25	SLB	AL	1B	114	1244	95	13	64	.990	.986	11.75	10.89					
				P*	2	0	2	0	1	1.000	.952	2.25	2.81	1	8.0			
1919	26	SLB	AL	1B	131	1249	120	13	62	.991	.988	10.45	10.44					
1920	27	SLB	AL	1B	154	1477	140	16	87	.990	.990	10.50	10.40					
				P*	1	0	0	0	0	.000	.000	0.00	2.70	0	1.0			
1921	28	SLB	AL	1B	138	1267	108	10	86	.993	.991	9.96	10.16					
1922	29	SLB	AL	1B	141	1293	125	17	116	.988	.991	10.06	10.55					
1924	31	SLB	AL	1B	151	1326	112	23	115	.984	.989	9.52	10.17					
1925	32	SLB	AL	1B	150	1343	131	26	120	.983	.988	9.83	9.86					
				P*	1	0	2	0	0	1.000	.960	9.00	2.70	0	2.0			
1926	33	SLB	AL	1B	149	1467	87	21	141	.987	.990	10.43	10.31					
				P*	1	0	1	0	0	1.000	.957	4.50	2.70	0	2.0			
1927	34	SLB	AL	1B	149	1374	131	24	138	.984	.988	10.10	10.28					
1928	35	WSH	AL	**1B**	**5**	**45**	**0**	**0**	**3**	**1.000**	**.990**	**9.00**	**9.90**					
				OF	**5**	**8**	**0**	**0**	**0**	**1.000**	**.973**	**1.60**	**2.22**			**5**	**0**	**0**
		BSN	NL	**1B**	**118**	**1188**	**86**	**15**	**100**	**.988**	**.989**	**10.80**	**10.17**					
				P*	**1**	**0**	**0**	**0**	**0**	**.000**	**.000**	**0.00**	**2.70**	**0**	**1.0**			
		TOT		1B	123	1233	86	15	103	.989	.989	10.72	10.16					
1929	36	BSN	NL	1B	154	1398	111	28	131	.982	.989	9.80	10.26					
1930	37	BSN	NL	1B	107	915	81	13	103	.987	.990	9.31	9.90					
Position Total				1B	1971	18837	1529	269	1468	.987	.989	10.33	10.32					
				OF	37	65	3	3	2	.958	.960	1.84	2.02			12	10	15
				P*	24	8	32	2	2	1.000	.942	3.24	2.97	12	111.0			
				2B	2	2	5	2	0	.778	.959	3.50	4.95					
				3B	2	2	4	0	0	1.000	.939	3.00	3.25					
Overall Total					2036	18914	1573	274	1472	.987	.989	10.06	10.06					

Fielding Glossary:

- Year - Year in which the season occurred
- Tm - Team they played for
- Lg - League they played in (AL- American League, NL- National League)
- G - Games played
- PO - Putouts
- A - Assists
- E - Errors
- DP - Double Plays
- FP - Fielding Percentage (A + PO) / (A + PO + E)
- lgFP - Major League Average Fielding Percentage at that position that year. (A + PO) / (A + PO + E)
- RF - Range Factor (A + PO) / G or 9 * (A + PO) / Inn
- lgRF - Major League Average Range Factor at that position that year.
- GS - Games Started (available for 2000 on)
- Inn - Innings Played (available for 2000 on)
- PB - For catchers, Passed Balls
- LF, CF, RF - Number of games played at each outfield position for years in which individual outfield stats are not available.

Managerial Record**

Year	League	Team	G	W	L	WP	Finish
1924	American Lg	St.Louis	153	74	78	.487	4
1925	American Lg	St.Louis	154	82	71	.536	3
1926	American Lg	St.Louis	155	62	92	.403	7
TOTAL			462	218	241	.475	

Managerial Glossary:

- Year - Year in which the season occurred
- Team - Team they played for
- League - League they played in (AL- American League, NL- National League)
- G - Games played
- W - Wins
- L - Losses
- WP - Winning Percentage
- Finish - End of season rank

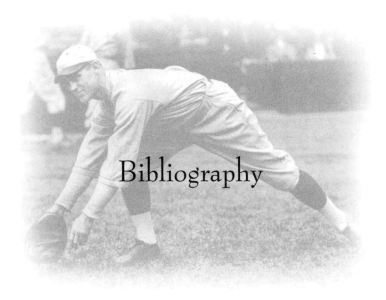

Bibliography

Manuscript Resources

Arthur Mann Papers, Library of Congress, Washington, D.C.
University of Michigan Archives, Bentley Historical Library, Ann Arbor.
Branch Rickey Papers, Library of Congress, Washington, D.C.
George H. Sisler Collection, National Baseball Library, Cooperstown, New
    York.
George H. Sisler Collection, *Sporting News* Archives, St. Louis.

Government Documents

Akron City Directory, Akron, Ohio: 1909, 1910.
Missouri Department of Health and Senior Services, Bureau of Vital Sta-
    tistics, Jefferson City, Missouri.
Tenth Census of the United States: 1880. Population, Bainbridge, Geauga,
    Ohio.
Twelfth Census of the United States: 1900. Population, Manchester Village,
    Summit County, Ohio.
Thirteenth Census of the United States: 1910. Population, Akron City,
    Summit County, Ohio.

Miscellaneous Resources

Broeg, Bob. Handwritten Notes from Speech, St. Louis, June 17, 2001.
Michiganensian Student Yearbook, University of Michigan, Ann Arbor, Michigan, 1913–1916.
Sisler, George H. Typewritten Memoirs to His Family, date unknown.
Tel-Buch Student Annual, Buchtel College, Akron, Ohio, 1911.

Internet Resources

BaseballAlmanac.com
BaseballIndex.org
BaseballLibrary.com
Baseball-Reference.com
Business-Journal.com
Ci.Ann-Arbor.mi.us
JBurroughs.org
Retrosheet.org

Personal Communications

Broeg, Bob. Telephone interview, December 6, 2001.
Drochelman, Frances E. Telephone interviews, November 23, 2001, August 12, 2002, August 28, 2002, January 13, 2003, March 5, 2003, and October 28, 2003.
Drochelman, Peter. Telephone interview, December 3, 2001. E-mail correspondence, March 31, 2003.
Fuchs, Robert S. Letter, June 11, 2002.
Katz, Steven E., M.D. Telephone interview, December 9, 2002.
Lindberg, James O. Telephone interview, May 2, 2002, and October 9, 2003.
Mott, Helen. Telephone interview, March 18, 2003.
Oehler, Jeffrey C., M.D. Telephone interview, November 14, 2002.
Sisler, Cass. Interview, July 7, 2002.
Sisler, David M. Telephone interview, November 20, 2001.
Sisler, George H., Jr. Interviews, August 14, 2001, August 17, 2001, August 21, 2001, August 28, 2001, September 6, 2001, September 18, 2001, November 15, 2001, and November 7, 2002.

Newspapers

Akron Beacon Journal, 1910–1914, 1916–1917, 1925, 1993, 1995–1996, 1999.
Akron Daily Beacon, 1885, 1902.
Barberton Herald (Ohio), 1931, 1993.
Boston Globe, 1928–1930.
Boston Post, 1928, 1931.
Detroit Free Press, 1913–1915.
Hartford Courant (Connecticut), 2000.
Los Angeles Times, 2000.
Michigan Daily Student Newspaper (Ann Arbor), 1912–1916, 1919.
New York Daily News, 1973.
New York Journal American.
New York Times, 1920, 1955–1956, 1973.
New York World-Telegram, 1931, 1952.
San Diego Sun, 1913.
Seattle Times, 1985.
Sporting Life, 1916.
Sporting News, 1916, 1919, 1921–1922, 1926, 1930, 1932, 1934, 1939, 1947–1948, 1950–1954, 1957, 1960–1961, 1963, 1968–1969, 1973, 1980.
St. Louis Globe-Democrat, 1928.
St. Louis Post-Dispatch, 1915–1928, 1973, 1993, 2000–2001.
USA Today, 2002.
Washington Post, 1927–1928, 1946.
Westerville News and Public Opinion (Ohio), 2001.

Books

Alexander, Charles C. *Breaking the Slump: Baseball in the Depression Era.* New York: Columbia University Press, 2002.
———. *John McGraw.* New York: Viking, 1988.
———. *Rogers Hornsby: A Biography.* New York: Henry Holt and Company, 1995.
———. *Ty Cobb.* New York: Oxford University Press, 1984.
Allen, Frederick Lewis. *The Big Change.* New York: Harper and Brothers, 1952.
———. *Only Yesterday: An Informal History of the 1920s.* New York: Harper and Row, 1931; reprt., New York: John Wiley and Sons, 1997.
Allen, Lee. *The American League Story.* New York: Hill and Wang, 1962.

Allen, Lee, and Thomas Meany. *Kings of the Diamond; The Immortals in Baseball's Hall of Fame.* New York: Putnam, 1965.

Allen, Maury. *Baseball's 100: A Personal Ranking of the Best Players in Baseball History.* New York: A&W Visual Library, 1981.

Appel, Martin. *Baseball's Best: The Hall of Fame Gallery.* New York: McGraw-Hill, 1980.

Barber, Red. *Walk in the Spirit.* New York: Dial Press, 1969.

Barton, Jerry. *A Treasure Chest of the Hall of Fame.* Boston: Wilson-Hill Co., 1952.

Benson, John. *Baseball's Top 100: The Best Individual Seasons of All Time.* Wilton, Conn.: Diamond Library, 1995.

Borst, Bill, and Erv Fisher. *A Jockstrap Full of Nails: A Cornucopia of St. Louis Browns History and Trivia.* St. Louis: St. Louis Browns Historical Society, 1992.

Broeg, Bob. *Baseball's Barnum: Ray "Hap" Dumont, Founder of the National Baseball Congress.* Wichita, Kans.: Wichita State University, 1989.

———. *Memories of a Hall of Fame Sportswriter: An Autobiography.* Champaign, Ill.: Sagamore Publishing, 1995.

———. *My Baseball Scrapbook.* St. Louis: River City Publishers, 1983.

———. *Superstars of Baseball: Their Lives, Their Loves, Their Laughs, Their Laments.* South Bend, Ind.: Diamond Communications, 1994.

Burkholder, Ed. *Baseball's Immortals.* Boston: Christopher Publishing House, 1955.

Burns, Ric, and James Sanders, with Lisa Ades. *New York: An Illustrated History.* New York: Knopf, 1999.

Carmichael, John P., ed. *My Greatest Day in Baseball.* New York: A. S. Barnes, 1945; reprt., Lincoln, Nebr.: Bison Books, 1996.

Chalberg, John C. *Rickey and Robinson: The Preacher, the Player, and America's Game.* Wheeling, Ill.: Harlan Davidson, Inc., 2000.

Cobb, Ty, with Al Stump. *My Life in Baseball.* New York: Doubleday, 1961; reprt., Lincoln: University of Nebraska Press, 1993.

Cox, James A. *The Lively Ball.* Alexandria, Va.: Redefinition, 1989.

Creamer, Robert W. *Babe: The Legend Comes to Life.* New York: Simon and Schuster, 1974.

Cromartie, Bill. *The Big One.* Atlanta: Gridiron Publishers, 1994.

Daniel, Clifton, ed. *Chronicle of the 20th Century: The Ultimate Record of Our Times.* New York: Dorling Kindersley, 1995.

Fireside Book of Baseball, The. 4th ed. New York: Simon and Schuster, 1987.

Ford, Barbara. *St. Louis: A Downtown America Book.* Minneapolis: Dillon Press, 1989.

Fuchs, Robert S., and Wayne Soini. *Judge Fuchs and the Boston Braves*. Jefferson, N.C.: McFarland, 1998.

Giglio, James N. *Musial: From Stash to Stan the Man*. Columbia: University of Missouri Press, 2001.

Glory of Their Times: The Story of the Early Days of Baseball Told by the Men Who Played It, The. New York: McMillan, 1966.

Godin, Roger A. *The 1922 St. Louis Browns: Best of the American League's Worst*. Jefferson, N.C.: McFarland, 1991.

Golenbock, Peter. *The Spirit of St. Louis: A History of the St. Louis Cardinals and Browns*. New York: Avon Books, Inc., 2000.

Grayson, Harry. *They Played the Game: The Story of Baseball Greats*. New York: A. S. Barnes and Company, 1944.

Gregory, Paul M. *The Baseball Player: An Economic Study*. Washington, D.C.: Public Affairs Press, 1956.

Hart, Harold H., and Ralph Tolleris. *Big-Time Baseball*. New York: Hart Publishing Company, 1950.

Hirshberg, Al. *The Greatest American Leaguers*. New York: Putnam, 1970.

Honig, Donald. *The Greatest First Basemen of All Time*. New York: Crown Publishers, 1988.

———, ed. *Baseball When the Grass Was Real: Baseball from the Twenties to the Forties Told by the Men Who Played It*. New York: Coward, McCann and Geoghegan, Inc., 1975; reprt., Lincoln: University of Nebraska Press, 1993.

James, Bill. *The Bill James Historical Baseball Abstract*. New York: Villard Books, 1988.

———. *The New Bill James Historical Baseball Abstract*. New York: Free Press, 2001.

Jennings, Peter, and Todd Brewster. *The Century*. New York: Doubleday, 1998.

Knepper, George W. *Akron: City at the Summit*. Tulsa, Okla.: Continental Heritage Press, Inc., 1981.

Lane, Samuel A. *Fifty Years and Over of Akron and Summit County*. Akron, Ohio: Beacon Job Department, 1892.

Lieb, Fred. *Baseball as I Have Known It*. Lincoln: University of Nebraska Press, 1996.

Mandelaro, Jim, and Scott Pitoniak. *Silver Seasons: The Story of the Rochester Red Wings*. Syracuse, N.Y.: Syracuse University Press, 1996.

Mann, Arthur. *Branch Rickey: American in Action*. Boston: Houghton Mifflin Company, 1957.

McBane, Richard. *Glory Days: The Akron Yankees*. Akron, Ohio: Summit County Historical Press, 1997.

McCallum, John D. *Big Ten Football since 1895.* Radnor, Pa.: Chilton Book Company, 1976.

McNulty, Elizabeth. *St. Louis Then and Now.* San Diego: Thunder Bay Press, 2000.

Meany, Thomas. *Baseball's Greatest Hitters.* New York: A. S. Barnes and Company, 1950.

Objoski, Robert. *Baseball's Strangest Moments.* New York: Sterling Publishing Company, 1988.

O'Neal, Bill. *The Texas League, 1888–1987: A Century of Baseball.* Austin, Texas: Eakin Press, 1987.

O'Toole, Andrew. *Branch Rickey in Pittsburgh: Baseball's Trailblazing General Manager for the Pirates, 1950–1955.* Jefferson, N.C.: McFarland, 2000.

Peckham, Howard H. *The Making of the University of Michigan: 1817–1992.* Ann Arbor: University of Michigan, Bentley Historical Library, 1994.

Polner, Murray. *Branch Rickey: A Biography.* New York: Atheneum, 1982.

Primm, James Neal. *Lion of the Valley: St. Louis, Missouri.* Boulder, Colo.: Pruett Publishing Company, 1990.

Rader, Benjamin G. *Baseball: A History of America's Game.* 2nd ed. Chicago: University of Illinois Press, 2002.

Rampersad, Arnold. *Jackie Robinson: A Biography.* New York: Alfred A. Knopf, 1997.

Reidenbaugh, Lowell. *Cooperstown: Where Baseball's Legends Live Forever.* St. Louis: Sporting News Publishing Company, 1983.

Rickey, Branch. *The American Diamond: A Documentary of the Game of Baseball.* New York: Simon and Schuster, 1965.

Riess, Steven A. *Touching Base: Professional Baseball and American Culture in the Progressive Era.* Rev. ed. Chicago: University of Illinois Press, 1999.

Ritter, Lawrence S. *The Glory of Their Times: The Story of the Early Days of Baseball Told by the Men Who Played It.* Rev. ed. New York: William Morrow and Company, 1984.

———. *Lost Ballparks: A Celebration of Baseball's Legendary Fields.* New York: Viking Studio Books, 1992.

———, and Donald Honig. *The 100 Greatest Baseball Players of All Time.* New York: Crown Publishers, Inc., 1981.

Salant, Nathan. *Superstars, Stars, and Just Plain Heroes.* New York: Stein and Day, 1982.

Santa Maria, Michael, and James Costello. *In the Shadows of the Diamond: Hard Times in the National Pastime.* Dubuque, Iowa: Elysian Fields Press, 1992.

Secrets of Baseball Told by Big League Players. Bedford, Mass.: Applewood Books, 1996.

Seib, Phillip. *The Player: Christy Mathewson, Baseball, and the American Century.* New York: Four Walls Eight Windows, 2003.

Seymour, Harold. *Baseball: The Golden Age.* New York: Oxford University Press, 1971.

Simon, Scott. *Jackie Robinson and the Integration of Baseball.* New York: John Wiley and Sons, 2002.

Sisler, George. *Sisler on Baseball: A Manual for Players and Coaches.* New York: David McKay Company, Inc., 1954.

Smith, Ira L. *Baseball's Famous First Basemen.* New York: A. S. Barnes and Company, 1956.

Smith, Ken. *Baseball's Hall of Fame.* New York: A. S. Barnes and Company, 1947.

Smith, Ron. *The Sporting News Selects Baseball's 100 Greatest Players: A Celebration of the 20th Century's Best.* St. Louis: Sporting News Publishing Co., 1998.

Solomon, Burt. *The Baseball Timeline.* New York: DK Publishing, 2001.

Spink, John, and George Taylor. *Judge Landis and 25 Years of Baseball.* St. Louis: Sporting News Publishing Co., 1974.

Starr, Bill. *Clearing the Bases: Baseball Then and Now.* New York: M. Kesend Publishing, 1989.

Sullivan, George. *Glovemen: Twenty-seven of the World's Greatest.* New York: Atheneum, 1996.

Taylor, Phyllis. *100 Years of Magic: The Story of Barberton, Ohio 1891–1991.* Akron, Ohio: Summit County Historical Society, 1991.

Thomas, Henry W. *Walter Johnson: Baseball's Big Train.* Washington, D.C.: Phenom Press, 1995; reprt., Lincoln: University of Nebraska Press, 1998.

Tootle, James R. *Baseball in Columbus.* Chicago: Arcadia, 2003.

Total Baseball. 7th ed. Kingston, N.Y.: Total Sports Publishing, 2001.

Tygiel, Jules. *Baseball's Great Experiment: Jackie Robinson and His Legacy.* New York: Oxford University Press, 1983.

———. *Past Time: Baseball as History.* New York: Oxford University Press, 2000.

Waggoner, Glen, and Kathleen Maloney and Hugh Howard. *Spitters, Beanballs, and the Incredible Shrinking Strike Zone.* Rev. ed. Chicago: Triumph Books, 1990.

Walsh, Christy, ed. *Baseball's Greatest Lineup.* New York: A. S. Barnes and Company, 1952.

White, G. Edward. *Creating the National Pastime: Baseball Transforms Itself, 1903–1953*. Princeton, N.J.: Princeton University Press, 1996.
Williams, Peter, ed. *The Joe Williams Baseball Reader*. Chapel Hill, N.C.: Algonquin Books, 1989.
World Series: A 75th Anniversary, The. New York: Simon and Schuster, 1978.

Pamphlets

Gardner, Richard A. *History of an Ohio Community: Manchester*. Clinton, Ohio: Self-published, 1993.
Sisler, George. *The Knack of Batting and How to Select and Care for Your Bat*. Louisville: Hillerich and Bradsby Co., 1934.

Unpublished Papers

Anderson, David. "Bonesetter Reese: Baseball's Unofficial Team Physician." Written and oral presentation, 2003 Seymour Medal Conference, Society for American Baseball Research, Cleveland, Ohio, May 2003.
Tunis, Elizabeth C. "Flaws in the Diamond: Major Leaguers Expelled from Organized Baseball, 1919–1922." Unpublished typescript, National Baseball Library, Cooperstown, N.Y., 1975.

Articles

Baumgartner, Stan. "Like Sisler, Like Son." *Sport* (October 1950): 42, 44, 86–87.
Bell, Floyd L. "George Sisler as a .400 Hitter." *Baseball Digest* (September 1920): 474, 507.
Bernstein, Sam. "George Sisler and the End of the National Commission." *The National Pastime: A Review of Baseball History* 23 (2003): 93–96.
Broeg, Bob. "The Ladies' Favorite Cardinal." *Saturday Evening Post* (April 2, 1960): 24, 110, 113–14.
Burnes, Bob. "The St. Louis Browns: Major League Club History #8." *Sport* (April 1951): 61–68.
Bush, Joe, as told to Carrol S. Slick. "On the Mound." *Saturday Evening Post* (June 8, 1929): 154.
Camp, Walter. "The Batting Eye—Singular." *Collier's* (April 26, 1924): 22.

————. "Winter Baseball." *Collier's* (October 4, 1924): 28.

Carey, Max, as told to Jack Kofoed. "The Twenty Greatest Ballplayers of All Time." *Esquire* (October 1955): 100–101, 145–46.

Creamer, Robert. "The Sad Song of Bobby." *Sports Illustrated* (May 6, 1957): 54–57.

Daley, Arthur. "Greatest in the Great American League." *New York Times Sunday Magazine* (September 2, 1951): 12–13, 16.

Demaree, Al. "Grandstand Girls." *Collier's* (June 2, 1928): 22, 36.

Evans, Billy. "Baseball's Thirteen Best Batters." *Esquire* (June 1942): 62, 106–7.

Fullerton, Hugh S. "Between Games." *American Magazine* (July 1911): 321–32.

Greene, Lee. "George Sisler 'Picture Player.'" *Sport* (March 1963): 50, 77–79.

Griswold, J. B. "Rickey Starts in the Cellar Again." *American Magazine* (May 1951): 42–43, 107–12.

Jennings, Hugh. "Will George Sisler Equal Ty Cobb?" *Baseball Magazine* (March 1921): 468, 495, 499.

Lane, F. C. "The Dazzling Record of George Sisler." *Baseball Magazine* (March 1921): 465–67.

————. "Did the American League Blunder?" *Baseball Magazine* (June 1929): 305–6.

————. "How to Tell a Good Batter When You See One." *Baseball Magazine* (April 1925): 500–504.

————. "The Last of the Great Place Hitters." *Baseball Magazine* (October 1929): 493, 518.

Libby, Bill. "The Ten Years of Johnny Podres." *Sport* (August 1963): 38–41 ff.

Lindberg, James O. "At First Base for the Boston Braves ... George Sisler." Convention publication 32, Society for American Baseball Research (2002): 27–28.

Linn, Edward. "Ballplayer vs. The Fans." *Saturday Evening Post* (August 12, 1961): 19, 53.

Losada, Luis A. "George Sisler, Manolin's Age, and Hemingway's Use of Baseball." *Hemingway Review* (Fall 1994): 79–83.

Mann, Arthur. "Baseball's Amazing Sislers." *Saturday Evening Post* (February 14, 1953): 36–37, 84, 86–87.

————. "The Dodgers' Problem Child." *Saturday Evening Post* (February 20, 1954): 27, 111–13.

Maule, Tex. "The Thinking Hitter." *Sports Illustrated* (June 5, 1961): 56, 59.

"Old St. Louis Feud of Hornsby and Sisler Is Smothered by Rajah's Boost to Hall of Fame." *Newsweek* (February 2, 1942): 50.

"Pittsburgh Never Forgave Him." *Time* (March 30, 1925): 26–28.

"Return of the Player-Manager." *Literary Digest* (August 29, 1925): 56–57.

Rice, Grantland. "The All-Star Baseball Team." *Collier's* (October 14, 1916): 14–15.

———. "Ty Cobbs of the Future Chosen by Grantland Rice." *Collier's* (October 14, 1916): 12–13.

Sisler, George. "My Best Season, So Far." *Baseball Magazine* (March 1921): 461–63.

Steinberg, Steve L. "The Spitball and the End of the Deadball Era." *The National Pastime: A Review of Baseball History* 23 (2003): 7–17.

Verducci, Tom. "Hit Parade." *Sports Illustrated* (July 31, 2000): 64–65.

Warburton, Paul. "George Sisler." *The National Pastime: A Review of Baseball History* (2001): 93–97.

Ward, John J. "The Famous Sisler Case." *Baseball Magazine* (October 1916): 33–37.

Index

Abrams, Cal, 278
Akron, Ohio, 8, 12, 40, 55, 232; growth of, 8–9; honoring George, 39, 287. *See also* Babcock and Wilcox (B & W) Boilermakers
Akron Baseball Hall of Fame, 287
Akron Champs, 12–13, 21–24, 34
Akron High School, George at, 9–14
Alcohol, George as teetotaller, 155–56, 258
Alexander, Charles C., 229
Alexander, Grover Cleveland, 67, 181, 249, 251
All-American teams: Babe Ruth's, 143, 203, 287; Hornsby's, 287; *Vanity Fair's*, 33, 39, 44
Allen, Frederick Lewis, 239
Alley, Gene, 271
All-Star Baseball School (Hot Springs, Arkansas), 249
All-star teams, 203; all-time, 254, 287; *Collier's*, 61–62; National League, 278; old-timers in, 240
Altrock, Nick, 195
Amateur standing, 20, 25, 41–42
American Diamond, The (Rickey), 18–19, 283–84

American League, 64, 95, 160, 260; all-around player nominations, 135; batting records in, 123–24, 146, 200, 221; batting vs. pitching in, 90, 203; changes in balls in, 86, 241; in competition for players, 24–25, 58; George in, 46, 234–35; Most Valuable Players in, 147, 168; pitching in, 82, 203; rumors of Red Sox conspiracy with Yankees in, 132–33; standings in, 47–48, 126, 194, 213, 224
American Softball Association, 248
Anson, Cap, 199
Anti-trust legislation, 129
Arizona Instructional League, 271
Army, George in, 73–74
Ashburn, Richie, 278
Austin, Jimmy, 70–71, 80, 121, 141, *171*; and Browns, *113*, 125, 131, 156; and George, 186–87, 197; as manager, 165–66, 168, 197

B. F. Goodrich (Akron), 8–9
Babcock and Wilcox (B & W) Boilermakers team, 14, 20–21, 26, 33, 39–42
Baer, Russ, 12, 16, 19
Baker, Sam A., 217

Ball, Phillip DeCatesby, 33, 123, 129–30, *171;* and Browns as business, 136–37, 199, 204, 219; and Browns players, 66, 68, 121, 128; feelings about Browns, 207–8, 212–13, 219–20; and George, 97, 194, 217, 221; and George as player-manager, 116, 210, 214–15; and managers, 70, 71, 162–66, 215; not signing National Agreement, 118–19; Rickey's relations with, 57, 63, 66; and Sportsman's Park, 91, 134, 208

Ballou, Win, 206

Bancroft, Dave, 229

Bankhead, Dan, 262

Barber, Red, 269, 288

Barnstorming, 67, 126, 156, 256

Bartelme, Phil, 17–18

Baseball: attendance in, 71, 83, 95, 247; batting vs. pitching in, 85–87, 90, 241; changes in balls in, 85–86, 88, 203, 286; doctored balls in, 86, 133–35; exempt from anti-trust legislation, 129; fans liking better batting, 95, 120; George giving up playing, 245–47, 280; George's love for, 243, 271; integration of, 255–58; nonplayer jobs in, 242, 247–49, 254; one hundredth birthday of, 181; in the Philippines, 34; popularity of, 7, 67, 68, 150, 255–56, 264; radio broadcasts of, 150–52; records in, 95–96; Sisler sons in, 275–79, 281–82; WWI's effects on, 64, 66, 68–73, 72–73. *See also* Major leagues; Minor leagues

Baseball Magazine, on George vs. Cobb, 117–18

Baseball players: above-average, on below-average teams, 123; conditioning, 207, 211; fans' desires from, 289–91; gambling's influence on, 93, 118–19; George as all-around player, 39, 44, 52, 55, 97, 143, 287; George tutoring, 240, 259; George's salary as, 241, 243, 245; George's savvy as, 96–97; greatest, 61, 135–36, 154; life on the road, 75–77; mortality of, 159, 188, 194; off-season income for, 97–98, 115–16, 152–53, 205–6; salaries of, 97–98, 115–17, 147, 168, 196, 216, 229; World Series receipts for, 152, 204; in WWI, 68–70, 73–74

Baseball Writers Hall of Fame, 5

Basketball, 9

Batting: Chalmers Award for, 147n18; fans coming out for, 95, 120; George on, 268–69, 269; pitching vs., 85–87, 95, 120, 188,
191, 203, 241. *See also* Home runs; specific players and teams

Batting, Browns: in 1920 season, 88, 91, 95; in 1921 season, 118, 119–20; in 1922 season, 131, 136; in 1923 season, 161; in 1924 season, 188, 192, 195; in 1926 season, 208; in 1927 season, 217, 219; managing errors with, 162–63; slumps in, 119–20, 131; weakness in, 64–65, 131, 161

Batting, George's, 14, 51, 87, *106, 109, 111;* in 1916 season, 58–59; in 1917 season, 64; in 1918 season, 69, 71; in 1919 season, 78–83; in 1920 season, 88–92; in 1921 season, 119–20, 122; in 1922 season, 127–28, 131, 133–40, 142, 148–49; in 1924 season, 189, 191, 195, 198; in 1925 season, 198–99, 201, 204; in 1926 season, 209, 212–13; in 1927 season, 216, 218, 220–21; affected by manager responsibilities, 214; for Braves, 230–32, 237, 239–41; in comeback, 187, 198; compared to Cobb's, 93–95, 117–18; compared to Hornsby's, 78; compared to Speaker's, 122–23; declining, 192, 204, 241; effects of illness and injuries on, 148, 191, 288; grand slams by, 123, 130; high school, 13; hot streaks in, 135–39; in major-league debut, 51, 56; for Michigan, 28–31, 33, 37–39, 42–44; as place hitter, 117; praise for, 49, 53; records in, 5, 73, 96; for Rochester Red Wings, 244; for Senators, 226–28; slumps in, 131, 133–34, 212–13; for Speed Boys (Boilermakers), 34

Batting averages: Browns, 201; Bush's, 197; Cobb's, 56, 59, 65–66, 152, 285; George helping to improve, 260–63, 267–68; George's, 5, 140, 152, 189, 199–200, 284–85; Hornsby's, 152, 285; Robinson's, 260; Ruth's, 168

Batting instruction: Dick Sisler, 278–79; by George, 260–63, 267–71

Batting records: Cobb's, 83, 123, 199; and dead vs. clean balls, 286; George challenging Cobb's, 73, 93–95, 133, 135, 137–41, 144, 148; George's, 140, 143, 152, 195, 213, 237–38; George's career statistics in, 284; George's hitting streak, 146, 200, 289; Hornsby's, 78, 97, 123, 204, 231–32; Williams, 152

Baumgartner, Stan, 194

Bayne, Bill, 126, 128, 144, 148

Bell, Floyd L., 114, 239

Bell, Les, 236n23

Bennett, Herschel, 209
Berger, Wally, 240
Bill James Historical Abstract, The, 286
Black, Joe, 266
Black Sox scandal, 154
Blue, Lu, 131, 222
Bonds, Barry, 282
Boone family, 282
Boston: bad teams in, 239–40; ban on
    Sunday games, 229, 231, 233
Boston Braves: 1928 season, 231–33; 1929
    season, 233, 236–38; 1930 season, 239–41;
    attendance, 228–29, 233, 236, 239–40;
    George with, *177–78*, 227–28, 233, 241–
    42; managers of, 227, 233–34, 237–38; as
    Miracle Braves, 228, 233–34; pitching
    weakness of, 229, 231–32, 236, 240;
    struggles of, 228–29
Boston Red Sox, 52, 59, 233, 281; accused of
    conspiracy with Yankees, 131–34; Fohl
    with, 168, 193; Quinn with, 162, 164
Bottomley, Jim, 203, 210
Bowman, Coach, 13
Bragan, Bobby, 270–71
Brand, Ed, 231
Braves Field (Boston), 228–29, 231, 233
Breadon, Sam, 91
Broeg, Bob, 5, 272
Bronkie, Herman, 78–79
Brooklyn Dodgers, 266; George scouting
    for, 262–63; George with, *184*, 258–63;
    integration of, 256–59; Rickey with, 253,
    256–58, 263; in World Series, 259, 263
Brouthers, Dan, 284
Brown, Joe L., 270–71
Brown, Mordecai "Three-Finger," 37
Brown, Tom, *184*
Browne, Carey, 283–84
Browning, Pete, 284
Bruce, John, 57
Buck, Jack, 271
Bulkeley, Morgan G., 251
Burgess, Smoky, 271
Burke, Jimmy, 71, 88, 98, 116
Burkett, Jesse, 285
Burns, George, 73, 134
Burrus, Dick, 230
Busch Stadium, 272
Bush, "Bullet Joe," 144–45, 196–203, 206

Caffyn, Bend, 22
California League, 97–98, 274
Camp Humphreys (Virginia), 74

Camp Kenrick (New Jersey), 74
Campanella, Roy, 260, 263
Catching, 205–7, 209. *See also* Severeid,
    Hank
Chalmers, Hugh, 147n18
Chance, Frank, 168
Chandler, Albert B. "Happy," 255
Chapman, Raymond, 92–93
Chase, Hal, 15–16, 97, 153–54
Chemical Warfare Service, 74
Chicago Cubs, 233, 238
Chicago White Sox: vs. Browns, 49–50,
    190–91; in World Series fixing scandal,
    93, 118
Chinese all-star team, 35
Christian Science Church, 162, 186, 235
Christy Walsh Syndicate, 195
Cicotte, Eddie, 93–94
Cincinnati Reds, 278–79
Clark, Earl, 236, 240
Clark, Fred, 33–34
Clemens, Roger, 251
Clemente, Roberto, 266–69, 271
Clendenon, Donn, 271
Coaching, 242, 254, 278–79
Cobb, Ty, 15, 29, 39n18, 84, 98, 115, 132, *173*,
    269; on baseball players, 75–76, 159;
    batting average of, 56, 59, 65–66, 152,
    285; batting records of, 83, 123, 199; in
    Chemical Warfare Service, 74; and death
    of Chapman, 92–93; excluded from best
    player nominations, 135, 147; on George,
    1, 5, 287; George challenging batting
    records of, 73, 93–95, 133, 135, 137–41,
    144, 148; George compared to, 33, 61–62,
    65–66, 83, 114, 153, 284, 286–87; George
    playing against, 72, 204; George's com-
    petitiveness vs., 117–18; in Hall of Fame,
    181, 251; honors for, 147, 147n18, 240;
    income of, 195, 216; personality com-
    pared to George's, 286–87, 290; as
    player-manager, 117, 135, 139, 147
Codd, Judge George B., 24–26, 40–41
Colgate University, 275–77
College, 16, 48. *See also* University of
    Michigan
Collegians (baseball team), 11–12, 14
Collins, Eddie, 15, *176, 181*, 251, 254
Collins, Pat, 125, 128, 134, 141, 147, 163,
    192–94
Collins, Rip, 141, 244
Columbus Clippers, 1, 276
Combs, Earle, 218

Comiskey, Charles, 93, 133
Competitiveness, George's, 30–31, 61, 117–18
Conlan, Jocko, 244
Contracts, 63, 281; George's dispute with Pirates over, 23–24, 40–41, 45–46, 59–60; George's extended, 116–17; minor-league, 266–67; "reserve clause" in, 23–24, 40–41; with young players, 254–55
Coveleskie, Stan, 86, 88, 95
Crawford, Sam, 15
Cuba, Dodger spring training in, 258
Cuban all-star team, vs. Speed Boys, 34–35
Cullop, Nick, 69
Cunningham, Bruce, 233

Danforth, Dave, 126, 130–31, 156, 166; demotion, 134–35; doctored balls and, 133, 164; wins by, 163, 167, 191
Dauss, Hooks, 122
Davenport, Davey, 81
Davis, Dixie, 91, *113*, 217; in 1921 season, 118; in 1922 season, 125–26, 130, 138–39, 141, 144, 148; in 1923 season, 163; in 1924 season, 194; in 1925 season, 199, 201; injuries of, 133, 161
Davis, L. C., 3, 55, 59, 122; on George vs. Hornsby, 89–90; on George's batting, 79, 93–94, 148–49; on George's comeback, 190, 197; on George's major-league debut, 49–51; on George's shoulder injury, 146–47; on George's talents, 94–95, 148; on George's trade, 222–23
Delahanty, Ed, 127, 285
Delaney, Art, 231
Delta Tau Delta, 27, 35–36
Demaree, Al, 167
Depression, 238–39, 243, 247
Derringer, Paul, 244
Detroit Tigers, Browns vs., 139–40, 162–63
DeWitt, Bill, 4, 279
DiMaggio, Joe, 146, 259, 289
Dineen, Bill, 39n18
Dixon, Leo, 209
Doby, Larry, 260
Douglas, Assistant Coach, 32–33
Dreyfuss, Barney, 23–24, 26, 41, 45–47, 59–60
Drochelman, Ann (granddaughter), *183*
Drochelman, Bo (grandson), *183*
Drochelman, Frances Eileen Sisler (daughter), 153, *179, 183*, 279–80, 283, 289
Drochelman, Peter (grandson), 272
Drochelman, William (son-in-law), *183*, 280

Dugan, Joe, 218
Dumont, Ray "Hap," 250–51
Dunn, Dr. John Randall, 186
Durocher, Leo, 259
Durst, Cedric, 160–61, 217

Earned run averages, Browns, 156, 191, 201, 208
East St. Louis, 67–68
Ebbets, Charles H., 59–60
Ebbets Field, 255–56, 258
Education: George's, 7–9, 11, 16–17; Sisler children, 274, 277, 280–81; as Sisler priority, 273–74
Ehmke, Howard, 211–12
Ellerbe, Frank, 125, 134, 148, 163; injuries, 152, 156, 162
Engineering: George studying, 16–17, 27, 44; George's lack of interest in, 242, 247
Erstad, Darrin, 284
Evans, Billy, 96, 117
Evans, Dr. Joe, 199
Evers, Johnny, 233–34, 237
Ezzell, Homer, 156, 167

Faber, Red, 86
Face, Roy, 271
Farm club system, major-leagues', 58, 253–54, 258
Farrell, Doc, 236
Federal League, 41, 45, 48, 56–58; demise of, 60, 119
Ferguson, Charles "Cy," 39, 42–43
Fielding. *See* First base; Outfield
Fielding, Browns: 1921, 118; 1922, 134, 141; 1923, 161; 1924, 188; 1925, 199; 1926, 209; 1927, 218, 219
Fielding, George's, 11, 97, *105;* for Braves, 232, 237, 241; for Browns, 83, 119, 124, 132–33; legends, 130–31; statistics in, 213, 284
Fields, W. C., 155–56
Finances, George's, 116–17, 238, 259, 280; baseball salaries, 241–43, 245; and businesses, 115, 252
First base, 55, 153, 284; Dick playing, 277–78; Gehrig at, 51, 218, 220, 289; replacements for George on, 122, 141, 147, 156–58, 160–61, 222
First base, George playing, 29, 50, *105,* 228, 245, 254; for Browns, 51, 67, 79–81, 143–44, 190, 202, 209, 214, 216; competing for position, 203, 224–26, 239–40; errors at,

52, 56, 58, 73, 195, 199, 218, 238; legacy of, 130–31, 286–88; praise for, 58, 65–66, 87, 153; and teaching, *184*, 261; and vision, 186–87

Flagstead, Ira, 139

Florida Winter League, 205–6, 224

Fohl, Lee, 12–13, 22, 168, 192; and Browns lineups, 119–20, 125–26, 134; as Browns manager, *113*, 117, 145, 164–66, 193; and Browns pitching, 88–89, 144–45; in forecasts for Browns, 118, 132; and George's illness/injuries, 140, 157; relations with Ball, 121, 162–63, 165–66

Foiles, Hank, *185*

Football, 9, 27

Ford, Whitey, 271, 278

Foster, Eddie, 125, 136, 139, 142, 156

Foster, John B., 160

Fournier, Jacques, 119

Frazee, Harry, 132, 133

Freshman Engineers team (University of Michigan), 19–20

Frick, Ford, 143

Friel, William E., 162, 165, 211

Friend, Bob, 271

Frisch, Frankie, 232, 254, 287

Fritsch, Walter, 132, 161–62, *172*, 217

Fuchs, Emil, 231; and Boston Braves, 228–29, 236; and George, 234, 241–42; managing Braves, 233–34, 237–38

Fullem, W. F., 193

Fullerton, Hugh, 76

Funeral, George's, 283–84

Furillo, Carl, 260–61

Gambling, 93, 118, 154, 259

Gaston, Milt, 197, 201, 203

Gedeon, Joe, 68–69, 80, 88, 91, 118–19, 121

Gehrig, Lou, 51, 218, 221; George compared to, 284, 286; George helping, 288–89; George overshadowed by, 220, 288

Gehringer, Charlie, 217

Gerber, Wally, 69, 71, 83, 88, *113*, 128, 144, 188; in Browns lineups, 119, 125, 199, 209, 218; injuries, 121, 210

Giard, Joe, 197, 201, 203, 208, 217

Giles, Warren, *180*, 244

Gleason, Billy, 119

Goehler, Jesse, 22–23, 25

Gowdy, Hank, 234, 237

Graney, Jack, 16

Grange, Red, *176*

Gray, Sam, 222

"Greatest all around player nominations," 135–36

Greatest First Baseman of All Time, The (Honig), 87

Greenwade, Tom, 257

Griffey, Ken, Jr., 282

Griffith, Clark, 53, 73, 224, 227

Grimes, Burleigh, 86, 240

Groat, Dick, *185*, 267–68, 271

Groom, Bob, 61, 65

Grove, Lefty, 200

Hall of Fame, 154, *181*, 251–52, 276

Haney, Fred, 265, 270

Hargrave, Bill "Pinky," 209–10

Harris, Slim, 200

Harris, Stanley Raymond "Bucky," 205–6, 215, 224–26

Haughton, Perry, 74

Hedges, Robert Lee, 31, 56–57, 77–78, 116

Heffner, Don, 279

Heilman, Harry, 97–98, 123, 132, 138, 286

Henry, Frank, 161

Hermann, August Garry, 22n12, 24–26, 40–41, 45–47, 59–60, 93

Heydler, John, 129

Hibbard, Jack, 44

Hicks, C. D., 217

Hildebrand, George, 121–22

Hoblitzell, Dick, 52

Hodges, Gil, 259–61

Hoerr, Roland, 217, 249, 274

Hoffman, Artie, 23

Hoffman, Bud, 1–2

Hogan, James "Shanty," 229

Holland, Joseph F., 157

Holmes, "Ducky," 193–94

Holmes, Tommy, 287–88

Holznagle, Frank, 36, 62

Holznagle, Kathleen Charlotte. *See* Sisler, Kathleen Charlotte Holznagle

Home runs, 161, 231, 267, 271; Cobb's, 199; Dick Sisler's, 277–78; increasing numbers of, 88, 203; in Sportsman's Park, 198, 208; Williams, 127, 129, 131–32, 134, 137–38, 152

Home runs, George's, 43; for Braves, 230, 232, 241; for Browns, 56, 58–59, 80, 82–83, 92, 122, 124, 127–28, 195, 219; effects on legacy, 285–86

Home runs, Ruth's, 218; 1921, 123; 1922, 129, 131, 133, 144; 1923, 168; records for, 81, 92, 120, 123, 127, 221

Homes, of Sisler family: in Boston, 230, 239, 275; in Brooklyn, 259; in Pittsburgh, 264; in Rochester, 244–45; in St. Louis, 62, 73, 259, 273

Hornsby, Rogers "Rajah," 56, 67, 69, 143, 168, 177, 232, 249, 286, 287; batting average of, 152, 285; batting records of, 78, 97, 123, 204, 231–32; with Chicago Cubs, 233, 238; on George, 1, 5, 287; George and, 227, 229–30; George compared to, 61, 78, 89–91, 284, 288; managing for Braves, 200, 227–28, 231, 233; as player-manager, 98, 200, 213, 215; praise for, 61–62; salary of, 216, 229; traded, 215–16, 233, 236

Horton, Willie, 251

Houk, Ralph, 251

Howley, Dan, 215–18, 220–21

Hoyt, Waite, 143, 192

Huggins, Miller, 56, 145

Hummel, Walter, 250, 252

Hunting, 249–50

Hutchinson, Fred, 279

Hyland, Dr. Robert F., 140–42, 146

I. S. Myers Clothing Store, 6, 8

Illness, George's, 270, 283; and Christian Science doctrine, 162, 200; effects on career, 286, 288; sinus, 157–60; tonsillectomy, 160–61. See also Vision

Injuries, George's, 152, 235; ankle, 202, 235; eye, 80; foot, 120–21; knee, 71, 133–34; leg, 82, 240–41; nose, 158; shoulder, 139–41, 146, 156–57; sore arm, 30–31, 34–40. See also Illness, George's; Vision, George's

International League, 242–45, 276

Jackson, "Shoeless" Joe, 16, 93, 96, 154

Jacobson, William "Baby Doll," 52–53, 78, 188, 199, 289; batting strength, 81, 83, 88, 91, 128, 136, 164; with Browns, 113, 118–19, 125, 134, 139, 209; position of, 141, 156; traded by Browns, 211–12

James, Bill, 52, 285–86

Jenkins, Tom, 211–12

Jennings, Hugh, 33, 72, 118, 289–90

Jensen, Jackie, 251

John Burroughs School (St. Louis): George in founding of, 274; Sisler children attending, 259, 274, 277, 280–81; Sisler sons in sports at, 277, 281

Johnson, Ban, 24–26, 56, 64, 88, 93, 132–33, 147n18; on Browns, 127, 190; on clean

balls, 82, 166, 188; and George's contract dispute, 46–47, 60; in Hall of Fame, 251

Johnson, Walter "Big Train," 16, 86, 147, 195, 202, 224; George pitching against, 53–55, 59; George vs., 82, 130; in Hall of Fame, 181, 251; honors for, 147n18, 254

Johnston, Willis E., 210

Jones, Fielder, 57–58, 65, 70–71, 286

Jones, Percy, 233

Jones, Sad Sam, 121, 128, 136, 163, 217–18

Judge, Joe, 130, 224–26, 235

Junior World Series, 244

Kansas City Monarchs, 257

Katz, Dr. Steven E., 161

Kauff, Benny, 61

Keeler, Willie, 97, 140, 146, 200, 251

Keener, Sid, 247

Kiner, Ralph, 265, 270

Klein, Chuck, 237

"Knack of Batting, The" (Sisler), 268–69

Kolp, Ray, 125–26, 134, 140

Koob, Ernie, 42–43, 48, 52, 64–65

Koufax, Sandy, 266

Ladies Day games, end of, 194

Lajoie, Napoleon, 15–16, 140–41, 147n18; batting average of, 152, 285; in Hall of Fame, 181, 251

LaMott, Bobby, 202

Landis, Judge Kenesaw Mountain, 60, 93, 118–19, 260

Lane, F. C., 234–36

Lauder, Harry, 115

Lavan, Johnny "Doc," 48, 51, 66, 68, 286

Lazzeri, Tony, 218

Leacock Sporting Goods Company, 248

Leary, Jack, 50–51

Lee, Dud, 119

Legett, Lou, 233

Leonard, Buck, 260

Leonard, Hub "Dutch," 58

Lopat, Eddie, 278

Lowdermilk, Grover, 52, 69

Lowe, Bobbie, 127

Lundgren, Carl L., 36–37, 39, 41–43

Luque, Dolf, 239

Lyons, Ted, 191, 209

Mack, Connie, 160, 212, 238; in Hall of Fame, 181, 251

Maguire, Freddie, 233, 236

Maier Brewing Company team, George managing, 97–98

Maisel, Fritz, 69, 71
Major leagues, 75; blacks decreed not up
    to, 260; farm club system, 253–54; father-
    son pairs in, 279, 281; George aspiring to,
    15–16; George's debut in, 49–51
Managers, 3, 154, 160, 224, 233, 243, 259;
    Austin for Browns, 165–66, 168; for
    Braves, 229, 237–38; for Browns, 162, 212;
    Burke for Browns, 71, 88, 98, 116; Dick
    Sisler, 278–79; expected to argue ump
    calls, 164; father-son pairs in, 279; Fohl
    for Browns, 121, 145, 162–63, 193; George
    as, 97–98, 205–7, 242, 245, 274; George
    mentioned for Browns, 163, 165; Hornsby
    as, 213, 227, 232–33; Howley for Browns,
    215, 220; for Pirates, 264–65, 270–71. See
    also Player-managers; Rickey, Wesley
    Branch
Manchester, Ohio, 5–8
Mann, Arthur, 57
Mann, Les, 249
Manush, Heinie, 222
Maranville, Walter James Vincent "Rabbit,"
    234, 236
Martin, Billy, 251
Martin, Pepper, 244
Mathews, Wid, 257
Mathewson, Christy, 74, 135, 228, 251
Mays, Carl, 81–82, 91–93, 129, 133
Mazeroski, Bill, 265–66, 271
McAllister, Lew, 17
McCarrick, Ed, 266
McDonaugh, James, 228
McEvoy, L. C., 245
McGraw, John J., 116, 154, 195, 203, 241, 251
McInnis, Stuffy, 156–57
McKechnie, "Deacon" Bill, 238
McManus, Marty, 217; batting strength,
    136, 139, 164; with Browns, 113, 125, 128,
    132, 188, 209; fielding by, 120, 122, 141,
    144, 161, 199; injuries of, 194, 210
McNally, Mike, 145
McNamee, Graham, 151
McPhail, Larry, 182
McQueen, Edmon, 30–31, 41–42
McSkimming, Dent, 164
Mellilo, Oscar, 207, 208, 219
Merrell's Penetrating Oil, George's
    endorsement for, 153
Meusel, Bob, 124, 126, 128, 136, 142, 218
Meyer, Billy, 264–65
Miami Shores team, 205–6
Michaels, Gene, 276

Milan, Clyde "Deer Foot," 79
Military drills, by baseball teams, 66
Miller, Edmund John "Bing," 211, 218, 222
Miller, Otto, 218
Miller, Victor, 231
Miller, Ward, 58
Minor leagues: contracts, 266–67; George
    in, 180, 241–43; Jackie Robinson in, 257–
    58; Sisler sons with, 276, 277
Minor-league system, 253–54, 264–65, 271
Missouri Sports Hall of Fame, 272, 287
Modesty, George's, 25, 32–33, 48, 114, 269
Mogridge, George, 206–7
Montreal Royals, 257–58
Moriarty, George, 164
Most Valuable Player award, 147n18;
    American League, 147; George as, 147–
    48, 192–93; National League, 267–68;
    Robinson as, 260; Ruth as, 168, 192;
    World Series, 263
Musial, Stan, 253, 277, 288
Myers, Isaac (uncle), 6, 8, 11, 101
Myers, Mel (aunt), 6

Naps (Cleveland team), 15–16
National Agreement, 118–19
National Baseball Congress, 250–51
National championship, mythical, 38–39
National Commission: end of, 93; on
    George's contract dispute, 22n12, 24–26,
    40–41, 46–47, 59–60
National Commissioner, 118–19, 255. See
    also Landis, Judge Kenesaw Mountain
National League, 48, 228, 241, 278; black
    players in, 260; competing for players,
    24–25, 58; George traded to, 234–35; and
    George's contract dispute, 59–60; Most
    Valuable Players in, 260, 267–68
National League pennants, 213, 253, 271
Negro leagues, 256, 260
Nelson, Charles, 248, 250
Neun, Johnny, 239, 240
Nevers, Ernie, 207
New Bill James Historical Abstract, The, 285–
    86
New York, popularity of baseball in, 255–56
New York Giants, 154; Hornsby with, 227,
    229; winning World Series, 150
New York Yankees, 126, 168, 195; acquiring
    players, 97, 196; Browns vs., 81–82, 90–
    91, 95, 127–30, 132, 136, 140–46, 149–50,
    190; Red Sox accused of conspiracy with,
    131–34; slumps of, 131, 201; strength of,

213, 218–19; wanting George, 97, 221–22; in World Series, 221, 232, 259, 271
Newcombe, Don, 263, 278
Ninth inning jinx, Browns', 129, 139
Northside Park (St. Louis), 248–49
Nunamaker, Les, 69

O'Connor, W. J., 55
O'Doul, Lefty, 237
Ohio-Pennsylvania League, 12, 34
O'Malley, Walter, 263
O'Neill, Tip, 284
O'Rourke, Frank, 217, 218
Orthwein, Walter, 57
Outfield: Browns, 58, 156, 205; Dick playing, 278; George in, 30–31, 34–35, 37–39, 42, 59
Outlook, 135
Overall, Orval, 37

Paige, Satchel, 251
Palmero, Emilio, 120
Pastorious, Jim, 13
Peckinpaugh, Roger, 212, 224
Personality, George's, 25, 32–33, 48, 61, 80, 115, 196, 288; compared to other stars, 114, 118, 286–87, 289–90; as a disadvantage, 118, 211; effects on managing, 208, 211; as gentleman, 147, 155–56, 279–81, 290–91; loyalty to Rickey, 258–59, 264; obituaries on, 284, 290; perfectionism, 159, 204, 215, 269; privacy/secrecy, 157–59, 214; teetotalling, 155–56, 258. *See also* Competitiveness, George's; Modesty, George's
Pettit, Bob, 271
Pfiester, Jack, 37
Philadelphia Athletics, 148–49, 238, 277
Philippines, baseball in, 34
Piercy, "Wild Bill," 126
Pipp, Wally, 51, 128, 218
Pitching, 260, 271; ball doctoring in, 82, 135, 164; Cassius Sisler's, 34; Danforth's, 134–35, 164, 166; dominance of batting over, 85–87, 120, 188, 191, 203; knuckleball, 147; left-handers, 39; screwball, 126; Sisler sons', 275, 281–82; spitballs, 82, 86, 88; stars of, 53–55, 59; use of rosin bags, 209
Pitching, Boston Braves, 229, 231–32, 236, 240
Pitching, Browns, 64–65; in 1917 season, 67; in 1919 season, 81; in 1920 season, 87, 93;

in 1921 season, 118, 120; in 1922 season, 125–26, 129, 136, 144; in 1923 season, 156, 167–68; in 1924 season, 188, 191–92; in 1927 season, 218; trading frenzy not obtaining better, 223; weakness, 133, 152, 195, 200, 205–6, 208, 211–12, 215, 219
Pitching, George's, 49, 53, 204; for B & W Boilermakers, 20–21, 26, 34, 39–40; for Braves, 232; for Browns, 49–51, 55–56, 72, 90; for Collegians, 11–12, 14; curve, 9–10; effects of, 117, 262; high school, 12–14; left-handed, 9–10; for Michigan, 19–20, 28–30, 33, 37–39, 42–43; sore arm from, 30–31, 33–34, 36, 39–40; strikeouts, 12–14, 21, 26, 28–30, 38, 40, 42–43; and vision, 186–87
Pittsburgh Pirates, 271; acquiring Clemente, 266–67; George scouting for, 263–64, 266, 271, 272; George with, *185*, 267–68, 270; George's contract dispute with, 23–26, 33–34, 40–41, 45–46, 59–60; managers, 270–71; rebuilding team, 265–67; Rickey with, 263, 270
Place hitting, 117, 269
Plank, Eddie, 69
Player-managers: Cobb as, 117, 135, 139, 147; difficulties of, 215; era of, 98, 116–17; excluded from best player nominations, 135, 147; Hornsby as, 98, 200, 213, 215–16; Speaker as, 98, 117, 135, 147, 215
Player-managers, George as, 97–98, 168, 245; for Browns, 186–88, 191, 214–15; criticized, 208, 211; pressure on, 197, 209; style as, 187, 189, 192–93; vs. umpires, 193–94
Podres, Johnny, 262–63
Polner, Murray, 270
Polo Grounds (New York), 254
Popularity, 212; Browns, 209; George's, 189–91, 217, 230, 231–32, 264; George's, vs. Judge, 225, 227, 235; Kiner's, 265, 270; Ruth's, 95
Pratt, Del, 59, 66, 68–69
Presbyterian church, Sislers', 115
Princeton, 281
Product endorsements, 61, 153
Professional baseball: contracts with young players, 23–25, 254–55; and George aspiring to, 12, 16, 45; vs. amateur, 20, 25, 41–42. *See also* Major leagues; Minor leagues; specific teams
Progressive Era, 15
Prout, Lib (aunt), 6–7

Prout, Thomas (uncle), 6–7
Pruett, Hubert "Shucks" (Hub), 126, 130, 133, 139; Fohl's managing errors with, 162–63; ineffectiveness of, 161, 194; in "little world series" against Yankees, 143–45
Pulliam, Henry, 24–25

Quinn, A. Robert "Bob," 22, 63–64, 88, 130, 162; and George's injuries/illness, 140, 157, 158; and lineup, 125, 156–57, 161; and player-managers, 116–17; trades by, 120–21, 161
Quinn, Jack, 86, 91

Rabar, Frank, 7
Race: Rickey integrating baseball, 255–58; segregation in Sportsman's Park, 78, 255; wage disparities based on, 67–68
Race riot, St. Louis, 68
Radio, 150–52, 249
Radke, Herman, 250
Raschi, Vic, 278
Reese, John D. "Bonesetter," 35–36
Reese, Pee Wee, 278
Reiser, Pete, 251
"Reserve clause," 23, 40–41
Reynolds, Allie, 251, 278
Rice, Grantland, 61–62, 151
Rice, Harry, 157–58, 208–9, 218, 222
Rice, Sam, 130, 224
Richbourg, Lance, 231, 232
Rickey, Branch, Jr., 263–64, 266
Rickey, Wesley Branch, 17–18, 182; in army, 73–74; assessment of George, 48–49, 51, 154, 267; with Brooklyn Dodgers, 253, 263; with Browns, 36, 46, 48, 52–53; with Cardinals, 63–64, 91, 168, 200, 253, 271–72; death, 272; foreword for *Sisler on Baseball*, 269; on George, 61, 283–84, 287; and George's contract dispute, 24–25; George's friendship with, 32, 258–59, 272; and George's position, 29, 50, 53, 55; hiring George, 244, 254–55, 259; integrating Dodgers, 255–58; legacy of, 32, 48, 256; meeting George, 18–19; as mentor, 245, 262; and minor-league system, 243–44, 253–54, 265, 271; and Pittsburgh Pirates, 263, 265, 270–71; relations with Ball, 57, 63, 66; and Sisler sons, 276, 281; trying to integrate baseball, 255–58; at University of Michigan, 18–19, 24–25, 27–28, 30–33

River City Press, 115
Roaring Twenties, 83–84, 239
Roberts, Robin, 278
Robertson, Charlie, 210
Robertson, Dave, 61
Robertson, Gene, 125, 130, 156, 188, 199
Robinson, Jackie, 184, 259; George working on batting with, 260, 269; as player to integrate Dodgers, 257–58
Rochester Red Wings, 180, 243–45, 276
Rogers, Will, 236
Rommel, Ed, 147
Rose, Pete, 146
Roth, Robert "Braggo," 56
Ruel, "Muddy," 227
Ruppert, Jack, 132–33
Ruth, Babe, 62, 81, 95, 126, 128, 145, 173, 195; All-American Baseball Teams named by, 143, 203, 287; in all-time all-star team, 254; batting by, 59, 88; batting records of, 73, 83, 123–24; and best player nominations, 135, 147; and George, 112, 193, 275; on George, 1, 5, 143, 160, 200; George compared to, 90, 96, 114, 154, 284; in Hall of Fame, 181, 251; home run records of, 92, 120, 123, 127; home runs by, 131, 133, 218, 221; as "Most Valuable Player," 168, 192; personality compared to George's, 287, 290; Pruett pitching against, 126, 143–44; salary of, 196, 216; Shocker vs., 128–29; in World Series, 150, 232; with Yankees, 85, 133, 218
Ryan, Jack, 249

St. Louis: baseball in, 47–48, 203–4; Cardinal fever in, 213–14, 253; cross-town series in, 55–56, 67, 124, 160, 208, 217; and East St. Louis, 67–68; fans in, 56, 121, 137, 146; George and Hornsby playing for Braves in, 231–32; George's satisfaction in, 116–17; growth of, 47; Michigan fans in, to watch George, 60–61; Sisler family in, 62, 270–71, 273, 281; Sisler-Nelson Sporting Goods Company in, 248; softball in, 248–49
St. Louis Browns, 75, 113; 1915 season, 47–48, 50, 52–56; 1916 season, 58; 1917 season, 63–65; 1918 season, 68–73; 1919 season, 78–81; 1920 season, 87–95; 1921 season, 118, 120–24; 1922 season, 127, 129, 140–50; 1923 season, 157, 160, 166–67; 1924 season, 189–96; 1925

season, 198–204; 1926 season, 207–15; 1927 season, 216–21; above-average players in, 123; attempts to bolster team, 48, 52–53, 58, 156, 196–97, 221–23; attendance at games, 124, 146, 196, 204, 213; in cross-town series, 55–56, 67, 160, 208, 217; dependence on George, 133–34, 156, 160, 198; effects of WWI draft on, 64; expectations of, 126, 186, 188–89, 197–98, 205, 208, 217; fans of, 56, 67–68, 72–73, 88, 130, 136–37, 142; finances of, 72–73, 136–37, 196, 204, 219; George, Jr., playing for, 276; George as asset to, 97, 133–34, 219–20; George honored by, 94, 193, 217; George in management for, 192–93, 214–15; George with, 4, 46, 49–51, 56; George's feelings about, 203, 235; and George's privacy about physical condition, 157–59; injuries' effects on, 133–34, 140–41, 152, 209–10; lineups of, 125–26, 163, 188, 194, 216–17; ninth-inning jinx, 129, 139; perks for stars, 76, 78; pitching weakness of, 195, 200, 208, 211–12, 215, 219; Rickey with, 31–32, 48, 52–53, 63; sale of, 57, 116, 212; Sportsman's Park as home of, 77–78; spring training, 125–26, 156–57, 186–87, 195–98, 206–8, 216; struggles of, 47, 52, 65, 70–71, 78. *See also* Batting, Browns; Managers; Pitching, Browns

St. Louis Browns Historical Society, 4

St. Louis Browns players: battling management, 66, 167–68; and George as manager, 187, 189, 209–10; relations with Fohl, 162–65; supporting Danforth, 164; wives' traveling with, 167–68

St. Louis Cardinals, 124; Browns vs., 119, 126–27, 189–90; in cross-town series, 55–56, 67, 160, 208, 217; Dick with, 277; George Jr. with, 276; Hornsby with, 123, 152, 168, 200, 215–16; minor-league affiliates of, 243–44; playing in Sportsman's Park, 91; Rickey with, 63–64, 168, 253, 271–72; segregation by, 68, 255; and Sisler statue, 4–5; in Sportsman's Park, 198, 213; vs. other St. Louis teams, 47–48; winning seasons, 203–4, 210, 213, 214, 232

St. Louis Terriers, 48, 56–58

Sandlot baseball, Collegians as, 11–12, 14

Schang, Wally, 131, 144–45, 206, 218

Schliebner, Fred "Dutch," 161

School sports: George in, 9–10; Sisler sons in, 274–75, 277

Schulte, Fred, 212, 216–19

Schultz, Howie, *184*

Scott, Deacon, 133

Scott, Death Valley Jim, 49

Scott, Everett, 145

Scouting: for black player to integrate Dodgers, 256–57; George, for Dodgers, 254–55, 258, 262–63; George, for Pirates, 263–64, 266, 271–72; George Jr.'s, 276; Rickey's, 254

Seaver, Tom, 251

Second base, 207, 260; for Browns, 118, 120; George on, 67; McManus at, 144, 161

Segregation, 68, 78, 255–56

Semi-pro baseball, 250–51, 254

Severeid, Hank, 58, 69, 73, 164; in 1921 season, 119; in 1922 season, 125, 130, 145; in 1923 season, 164; in 1924 season, 188; in 1925 season, 199

Seymour, Harold, 77, 115, 154

Shanks, Howard, 124

Shawkey, Bob, 91, 136, 141–42, 196

Shelly, Earl, 241

Sherdle, Wee Willie, 190

Shibe Park (Philadelphia), 254

Shocker, Urban, 68–69, 79, *113*, 165, 194; in 1919 season, 80; in 1921 season, 118, 123; in 1922 season, 125–26, 128, 133, 136–37, 141, 145, 147, 149; in 1923 season, 163, 167; in 1924 season, 188, 192, 195; allowed spitballs, 86; death of, 232; disputes with management, 164, 167–68, 192–93, 196; illness/injuries of, 93, 130, 152, 191; pitching against Babe Ruth, 81, 91–92, 123, 128–29; strength as pitcher, 128–29, 136–37, 149, 167, 195; against Yankees, 91, 132, 136, 145; with Yankees, 196, 201–3

Shorten, Chick, 125, 128

Shotton, Burt, 52, 66, 73

Siebold, "Socks," 233, 240

Simmons, Paul, 115, 249–50

Simmons-Sisler Printing Company, 115, 242–43, 247

Sisler, Adam (uncle), 6

Sisler, Bill (uncle), 21

Sisler, Cassius Carl (brother), 6, 8, 10–12, 34, *102*

Sisler, Cassius Clay (father), 6, 20–24, 62, *99*, *101*

Sisler, David (grandson), *183*

Sisler, David Michael (son), *183*, 252, 259, 280–81, 283, 289

Sisler, Dorothy (daughter-in-law), *183*, 277
Sisler, Efbert "Bert" J. (brother), 6, 8, 11, *102*
Sisler, Elizabeth (daughter-in-law), *183*, 276
Sisler, Frances. *See* Drochelman, Frances
   Eileen Sisler (daughter)
Sisler, George Harold, *102–12*, *171–73*, *176*;
   appearance of, 10; birth of, 6; with
   Braves, *177–78*; on cover of *Time*, *174*;
   and family, 114–15, *169*, *183*, 239, 273–82;
   at Hall of Fame induction, *181*; and
   Hornsby, *177*; as least appreciated
   player, 1–2, 5, 283–91; at Michigan, *105*;
   in minor leagues, *180*
Sisler, George Harold, Jr. (son), 65, *177*, *183*,
   273; and father, 1–2, 161, *169*, 274–75;
   and Gehrig, 288–89; and mother, *170*, *179*
Sisler, Janet (daughter-in-law), *183*, 282
Sisler, John (grandfather), 6
Sisler, Kathleen Charlotte Holznagle (wife),
   36, 73, 259, 271, 279; and children, 65,
   153, *170*, *179*, 282; death of, 283; and
   family, *183*; and George's Hall of Fame
   induction, 252, 276; marriage of, 62, 114
Sisler, Kathy (granddaughter), *183*
Sisler, Mace (uncle), 6
Sisler, Mary Whipple (mother), 6, *100*,
   115, 202
Sisler, Nancy (granddaughter), *183*
Sisler, Patti (granddaughter), *183*
Sisler, Richard Allan "Dick" (son), 97, *179*,
   183, 230, 276–79
Sisler, Shari (granddaughter), *183*
Sisler, Susan (granddaughter), *183*
Sisler Ball Field (Tarpon Springs, Florida),
   198
Sisler family, *101*, 252; education as priority
   of, 273–74; and father's biography, 1–2;
   as George's priority, 114–15, 249, 273,
   274–75, 279; return to St. Louis, 270–71
*Sisler on Baseball, a Manual for Players and
   Coaches*, 269
Sisler-Nelson Sporting Goods Company,
   248, 250, 252
Skinner, Bob, *185*, 271, 279
Slattery, Jack, 227, 229
Slaughter, Enos "Country," 253
Smith, Bob, 231
Smith, Elmer, 145
Smith, Wendell, 257
Snider, Edwin Donald "Duke," 261–62, 269
Softball, and American Softball
   Association, 248–49
Sothoron, Allen, 64, 81, 88, 91, 118, 120

Southside Park (St. Louis), 248–49
Southworth, Billy, *180*, 243
Speaker, Tris, 15, 59, 66, 89, 95, 114, 216,
   254; batting records of, 122–23, 152; in
   Hall of Fame, *181*, 251; as player-
   manager, 98, 117, 135, 147, 215
Speed, George's, 44, 48, 96–97, 142–43;
   declining, 225, 235
Spink, Al, 78
Spink, J. G. Taylor, 272
Sporting goods business, 248, 250, 252,280
Sporting Life, 30
Sporting News, 78, 143, 151, 284, 287
Sportsman's Park (St. Louis), 77–78, 91,
   175, 194, 231–32; attendance in, 141, 144;
   renovations/expansion of, 134, 198, 208
Sportswriters, player nominations by, 135,
   147
Spring training, 115; Braves, 236; Browns,
   78, 125–26, 156–57, 186–87, 195–98, 206–
   8, 216; Dodgers, 258, 260; Pirates, 265,
   271; Senators, 225
Stanky, Eddie, 260
Stargell, Willie, 271
Steals, 208; Cobb's, 56, 59, 66; Williams's,
   127, 152
Steals, George's, *107*; in 1918 season, 69, 71;
   in 1919 season, 79, 81; in 1922 season,
   131, 148; in 1924 season, 195; in 1926
   season, 210–12, 213; in 1927 season, 218;
   in 1928 season, 232; in 1929 season, 238;
   career statistics in, 284; declining, 228,
   241; at Michigan, 43, *105*; records in, 73,
   131, 221
Stevens, Ed, *184*
Stifel, Otto, 57, 70
Stock market crash, 238–39
Stockton, J. Roy, 131–32, 137–38, 200; on
   Browns, 133, 211; on George, 133, 187,
   288
Street, Gabby, 16
Sturdy, Guy, 216
Sukeforth, Clyde, 257, 264, 266

Terry, Bill, 284–85
Texas League, 245
Third base, 59
Thomas, Frank, 267
Thomas, Joe, 11
Thomas, Joe, Sr., 14
Thompson, Fresco, 237, 281–82
Thompson, Sam, 285
Thomson, William, 150

Thurston, Hollis "Sloppy," 163
Time magazine cover, *174*, 197
Tobin, John Thomas "Jack" or "Johnny,"
    68–69, 78, 81, *113*, 128, 206; in 1921
    season, 118, 119, 124; in 1922 season, 125,
    149; in 1923 season, 164; in 1925 season,
    199; aging, 188, 194; batting strength of,
    149, 164; on George, 160, 189; on
    managers, 164, 189
Transportation, for teams, 72, 76
Traynor, Pie, 264
Tunney, Gene, 216
Turner, Pete, 272
Tygiel, Jules, 150

University of Michigan, 24; fans visiting St.
    Louis, 60–61; freshman engineer team at,
    18–20; George at, 16–17; George gradu-
    ating, 44; George playing for, 27, 36–37,
    104; George's last season for, 41–44, *105;*
    George's pitching for, 28–29, 33; negoti-
    ating conference membership, 28–29, 33;
    Rickey with, 17–18, 31–33

Vangilder, Elam, *113*, 120, 137, 167, 222; in
    1922 season, 125–27, 138, 141
Virdon, Bill, *185*
Vision, George Jr.'s, 276
Vision, George's, 158–62; effects on career,
    235, 286, 288; improvement in, 162–63,
    197, 207; lasting effects of, 187–88, 190–
    91, 196; prognosis, 166–67, 186–87;
    sensitivity about, 235, 236n23

Wagner, Honus, *181*, 251, 254
Waitkus, Eddie, 277–78
Walker, Clarence "Tilly," 52, 73
Walks, George avoiding, 30, 285–86
Wallace, Bobby, 16
Walsh, Dee, 52
Walsh, Ed, 33
Wambsganss, Bill, 247
Ward, Aaron, 142, 145
Washington Senators, 195, 225; Browns'
    series against, 1922, 146–48; George

pitching against, 53–55; George with,
    221, 224; trading George, 226–27, 235
Weber, Harry, 4
Weilman, Carl, 79, 81, 118
Welsh, Jimmy, 229, 240
Williams, Ken, 68, 78, *113*, 123, 139, *171;* in
    1920 season, 91; in 1921 season, 118–19;
    in 1922 season, 125, 128–29, 138, 142, 152;
    in 1924 season, 188; in 1926 season, 209;
    batting strength of, 152, 164, 200; fielding
    by, 199; on George, 156, 189; home runs
    by, 124, 127, 131–32, 134, 137–38; sold by
    Browns, 222
Williams, Ted, 285
Wilson, Hack, 238
Winfield, Dave, 251
Wingard, Ernie, 191–92
Witt, Lawton "Whitey," 142, 145
World Series, 85; 1916, 59; 1919, 83, 93–94;
    1920, 95; 1922, 150; 1923, 168; 1924, 195;
    1926, 214; 1927, 221; 1928, 232; 1929, 238;
    1947, 259; 1950, 278; 1955, 263; 1960, 271;
    fixing of, 93–94, 118–19; George never
    playing in, 232, 288; players' profits from,
    73, 152, 204; radio broadcasts of, 150–51
World Series event, 251
World War I: armistice, 74; effects on
    baseball, 64, 68–72; George in, *110;*
    recovery from, 83–84; "work or fight"
    order in, 69, 73
World War II, 258
Wray, John E., 58, 64, 82, 121, 146, 193; on
    Browns' bad season, 209, 212; on line-
    ups, 194, 217; on Browns' profits, 136–37;
    comparing George to other stars, 90–91;
    on George, 147, 157, 212–13, 220; on Red
    Sox conspiracy with Yankees, 132–33
Wright, George, 251
Wright, Wayne "Rasty," 126, 136

Yankee Stadium, 136
Yost, Fielding, 27, 44
Young, Denton "Cy," 16, 21, 24, *181*, 251

Zachary, Tom, 192, 206, 209, 218, 221, 240